FIT TO PRINT

Books by JOSEPH C. GOULDEN

The Curtis Caper
Monopoly
Truth Is the First Casualty
The Money-Givers
The Superlawyers
Meany: A Biography
The Benchwarmers
The Best Years
Mencken's Last Campaign: H. L. Mencken on the 1948 Elections (editor)
The Million Dollar Lawyers
Korea: The Untold Story of the War
Labor's Last Angry Man: A Biography of Jerry Wurf
The Death Merchant
There Are Alligators in Our Sewers and Other American Credos
(with Paul A. Dickson)
The Dictionary of Espionage: Spookspeak into English
(as Henry S. A. Becket)

FIT TO PRINT

A.M. Rosenthal and His Times

by Joseph C. Goulden

Lyle Stuart Inc.
Secaucus, New Jersey

Library of Congress Cataloging-in-Publication Data

Goulden, Joseph C.
    Fit to print.

    Bibliography: p.
    Includes index.
    1. Rosenthal, A.M. (Abraham Michael), 1922-
2. New York times--History. 3. Journalists--United
States--Biography. 4. Editors--United States--
Biography. I. Title.
PN4874.R596G68   1988   070.4'1'0924 [B]   88-24827
ISBN 0-8184-0474-4

For ROBERT SHERRILL, whose confidence
in this book sustained me during the
longest year of my life,

And, once again,
For LESLIE CANTRELL SMITH,
the most loved woman in the entire world.

Contents

FIT TO PRINT

Prologue

For almost a year I had been interviewing people in New York who either worked for or otherwise knew A. M. Rosenthal, the then executive editor of *The New York Times*. Oddly, in all those months I caught only a fleeting glimpse of my subject, across a crowded luncheon room at an East Side cafe. His companion was a strikingly beautiful woman in her thirties, a brunette, and she seemed entranced by him, and laughed frequently. No matter. When commencing my research, I wrote Rosenthal, told him what I was doing, and expressed the hope we could talk eventually. I wished to do my homework first, I explained; otherwise both of use would be wasting our time.

Rosenthal's reply, in effect, told me not to expect any of his time; that he was a busy man and had more important things to do.

On a weekday morning in December, 1985, enroute to a theatrical district interview, I saw a Da-Vel Livery rental limousine with the license number DAVEL 32 slowly move to the curb in front of the New York Times Building at 229 West 43rd Street. DAVEL 32. Abe's usual car, I remembered from a conversation with a lawyer who went through considerable grief trying to have him served with a summons in a labor dispute. I walked a few feet into 43rd Street from Broadway and watched; perhaps I would finally get a good look at the man to whom I had devoted a year of my professional life.

The door of the limo began opening during the last few feet of the car's roll, and an arm reached out and dropped a heavy leather briefcase to the curb. Two legs emerged, slowly, one at a time, as if their owner had trouble making them work properly. Next a hand clutched the door post, and with some straining and huffing a man hoisted himself out of the car and upright.

A score of feet overhead a deep blue flag bearing the block-letters logo of the New York Times Company flapped noisily in the breeze, as did an American flag on an adjacent staff. The wind also carried along discarded coffee cups, crumpled sheets from yesterday's New York *Post*, and other grimy debris native to Times Square streets. I thought again of the oddity of the world's leading newspaper being officed in a near-slum.

The man took note neither of the flapping banners nor of the debris. Leaving the car door ajar—the driver could bother with closing it—he snatched the briefcase from the pavement and strode the few feet to the heavy metal revolving doors leading into the building lobby.

The walk was fast and pugnacious, as if daring interruption. The man's face had been locked into a deep, cheek-cleaving scowl when he climbed out of the car; now, as he entered the lobby, it deepened, as if trying to match in harshness the black horn rims of his glasses. The body, half-hidden beneath a bulky navy blue overcoat, was short, stocky, prominent-bellied. The hair, black with streaks of gray, went here and there.

By now I was a silent follower, some six feet behind Rosenthal.

The uniformed guard at the security barrier offered a slight nod, with the obvious expectation that it would not be returned, and it was not. Rosenthal's unblinking stare seemed directed at a spot on the floor perhaps six feet in front of him, and he kept it there as he walked the few feet to the elevators. He stood briefly among more than a dozen other persons waiting for the elevator—two of them I recognized as persons who worked directly under him, in the News Department—and several glanced at him as if ready to exchange a morning pleasantry. Rosenthal took no note of them; he seemed oblivious as to where he was, or where he was going, so they remained silent. An elevator arrived, and they all rode away.

Several weeks later, at 11:30 A.M. on January 17, 1986, I finally got to shake hands with Rosenthal. I had written him once again, stating that I had now done more than 200 interviews, and that I felt I had done sufficient homework to do an intelligent interview. Could we talk? He telephoned. "Come on in," he said. "I won't promise you more than an hour, at this time or any other. But at least let's talk a minute."

Rosenthal's office is on the north side of the cavernous *Times* newsroom, which runs the full block between West 43rd and 44th Streets. It is a tangle of desks and video terminals, cleaved by winding goat-trails of corridors that meander through the machinery and the 300-odd persons who work there. From the reception area you walk the longest route of all to get to Rosenthal. His office overlooks 44th Street—the Shubert Theater, Shubert Alley, the pedestrian walkway running north, and an office building with a third-floor studio filled with prancing, pretty dancers.

Rosenthal stood outside his office, deep in conversation with Seymour Topping, the *Times*'s managing editor, and Allan Siegal, the news editor, when I walked up with a secretary. As I wrote later that day in a 17-page memorandum recounting our first meeting:

> My first impression was one of surprise that the man is so small and frail, at close-hand. At a distance, he gives the impression of being a man of greater size. He was nervous; he had hoped to avoid this moment, but now he was face-to-face with someone on a mission he disliked. . . .
>
> "At last we meet," he said, smiling and shaking my hand. . . .

An hour later, almost to the minute, Stephanie Lane, Rosenthal's secretary, called to remind him of a luncheon appointment. As we moved towards the door he still had not decided what to do about my request for several hours of serious talk about his life and career. "Let me think about it over the weekend," he said. "I know what I want to do, but I don't know if that is what I will do. I have one instinct the one way, and another instinct the other." As my memo continued:

> He moved very close to me, so that his face was within a few inches of mine. "I am no reactionary, I want you to know that," he said. "I am

an immigrant, I have been poor, I have worked, I am not political. If
you call Abe Rosenthal anything, call me anti-authoritarian."

Fit to Print: A. M. Rosenthal and His Times is about the power and
insecurity of Abe Rosenthal, and how his talent and his persona com-
bined to make him one of the more successful newspaper editors in
America—and also one of the more detested. Professionally,
Rosenthal was *sui generis*, a newsman who excelled at every job he
undertook, from copy boy to foreign correspondent to editor. "The
smartest son of a bitch who ever walked into a news room," his old
friend Theodore H. White, the political writer, said of Rosenthal a
few months before his 1986 death. "Quick, quick in concept, in execution, in judgment," said another longtime chum, John Chancellor
of NBC News. "A weird bastard, but a whiz of a newspaperman," says
the non-admiring Benjamin C. Bradlee, executive editor of the competitive Washington *Post*, a man with whom Rosenthal shares a
mutual personal contempt.

Because of his special talent, Rosenthal played a dominant role in
saving *The New York Times*. In the mid-1970's the paper almost went
belly-up. This happened for a congeries of reasons, many beyond the
paper's control—changing New York demographics, the advertising
revolution wrought by television, shifting reading habits and interest
of the traditional audience, the general malaise of New York City, the
ability of strong newspaper unions to dictate production rules. During this crisis the *Times* was run by a third-generation publisher,
Arthur O. Sulzberger, Jr. ("Punch," to everyone at the paper), who
carried two liabilities. He did not particularly care about working as a
publisher; given his druthers, he would idle away his life tinkering in
his tool shed. And even his mother, Iphigene Sulzberger, considered
Punch somewhat dim.

That these two men shared the pinnacle of *The New York Times*
was an unlikely circumstance. Punch was a fourth-generation "Our
Crowd" Jew, scion of a German-Jewish family which over a century's
time earned its place in the American Establishment. Sulzberger understood wealth and privilege; that he did not care for work, even as
the boss, came largely because he never *had* to work. Rosenthal, conversely, scrambled all his life. He was of first-generation Russian-
Jewish origins, "the other Jews," the Sulzberger crowd called them
with disdain; a lame kid from a Bronx housing project who hustled for
subway nickels and ate cold boiled potatoes for dinner and pretended
to enjoy them.

But somehow the Punch-and-Abe Show succeeded, and at the *Times* they turned penury into prosperity. From the near-bankruptcy of 1975, the New York Times Company (holding company for the newspaper and other enterprises) within a decade had revenues of $1.39 billion and earnings of $116 million. Business decisions made much of the financial turnaround possible; as shall be seen, the *Times* managed to slough off restrictive union rules that contributed mightily to the return to profitability. Still, the *Times*'s main business continues to be news, and hence the importance of Abe Rosenthal as executive during the critical years.

Rosenthal's four-decade career is significant also because it coincided with the transformation of American journalism from the rowdy days of *The Front Page* newspapering, with rum-dum reporters and editors, to a computerized, videotext world of university-trained specialists. When Rosenthal joined *The New York Times* as a city reporter in 1944, that newspaper and others wrote the "official record" in relatively objective fashion. At his retirement, investigative reporting had blossomed, with newspapers going far beyond the official record; papers regularly devoted dozens of columns to stories probing the mores and morals as well as the misfeasances of society.

During these same years television surpassed newspapers as the primary source of information for most Americans. Newspapers—and especially Rosenthal's *Times*—survived and prospered by offering citizens news in a depth of detail and interpretation that cannot be crammed into the twenty-two minutes available on a network evening news broadcast.

And, finally, during the Rosenthal era the *Times* expanded its influence as America's premier newspaper to a world stage. The public perception of events, as reported in the *Times*, is now accepted as the "official version."

The New York Times, for better or for worse, has a dominant voice in setting the agenda for America. The *Times* does so because it is respected, and it takes its job of gathering news seriously. The *Times* spends more money than any other newspaper in America to collect, edit and print the news, with emphasis on reportage by its own people, not news syndicates. Although the masthead slogan "All The News That's Fit to Print" is a logistical impossibility, the *Times* maintains the largest staff of any newspaper anywhere, one thousand editors, reporters and other functionaries, who work in the Times Building at 229 West 43rd Street and in nineteen bureaus in the United States and thirty-nine abroad. This is expensive. Supporting a foreign correspondent costs the *Times* an average of $187,000 a head per year, which includes salary, housing allowance and other expenses. The news department, Rosenthal's domain, in 1986 had a budget of a shade less than $37 million.

Because of its serious-minded approach to news, the *Times* is read, and respected, in the places that count in the Boston-New York-Washington corridor, and beyond. America's elite become acquainted with the *Times* as an institution in graduate school, when they use the *Times*'s microfilm as the basic fact-stuff of their dissertations. The white-on-black image of the *Times*, courtesy University Microfilms, is sufficient affirmation that some supposed happening is certifiable historical fact. Reliance on the *Times* as a primary source of information continues when these persons go on into business and government. According to *Times* readership surveys, the weekday paper reaches one-third of all professionals and managers in the Northeast with incomes of $50,000-plus a year; the *Sunday Times*, 45 percent. Teddy White likened the *Times* to "the executive reading board for everyone of importance who lives between Boston and Washington. What is printed by the *Times* each day is read by these executives, officials and academics by eleven each morning. You assume they have all read it." Although newspapers such as the Washington *Post*, *The Wall Street Journal*, and the Boston *Globe* make periodic pretensions of importance, White's view is that "they just touch it," i.e., the *Times*, in terms of national influence.

What other media do not like to concede is that they often follow the lead of the *Times* as trustingly as do graduate students. For years the Associated Press and United Press International late each evening have transmitted to subscriber newspapers a synopsis of stories displayed on the front page of the early editions of the next day's *Times*. Spavined old geezers on the wire desks of the Dallas *Morning News* and *Los Angeles Times* and the Philadelphia *Inquirer* and elsewhere would snort disagreement—and then usually follow the lead of editors on West 43rd Street. So, too, would producers of the network television shows, especially during TV's infancy.*

Attention by the *Times* can both create and legitimize an issue as

---

*In the early 1970's, while researching a magazine article, I spent a full week watching the production of the NBC Nightly News. "How did the *Times* play this?" was the question most frequently asked, after "What kind of film do we have on that?" One producer kept a copy of that day's *Times* front page on his planning clip board. Fifteen years later, network news seems to be weaning away from such dependence.

being suitable for the national agenda. A good example was President Reagan's visit to a military cemetery in Bitburg, Germany, in 1985, which contained the bodies of American and German soldiers, including members of SS storm trooper units. The *Times*'s first story was a meager three-paragraph wire service account. Rosenthal read the item with outrage. He considered Reagan's visit an insult to the memories of the Jewish people persecuted by the SS, and he ordered what the public relations adviser for several national Jewish groups called "incessant, daily and unrelenting coverage." Other media followed the *Times*'s example, and Bitburg soon was a raging controversy. The public relations man states, "Had it not been for intense *Times* coverage, the story would have died in one or two days." (Interestingly, American public opinion did not share Rosenthal's rage. A week or so after the outcry, polls found one-third of Americans favoring the visit, one-third opposing, and one-third indifferent.)

Nor does the *Times* hesitate to throw out advertising—expensive advertising—when an exceptional story demands exceptional space. A good example is the explosion of the *Challenger* spacecraft on January 28, 1986. When the first reports came in just before noon, Rosenthal knew reflexively the story would be a big one, and editors began dispatching reporters to and fro. But Rosenthal was hesitant about what to do with the story. "I wanted to think about the story for a while before making a commitment, so I just let things go through lunch. Was this going to be a truly *major* story, or just a big one? By the time lunch was over, I knew this deserved full treatment." So he called the production department and said he wanted ten "open pages"—that is, no advertising—at the front of section one. Rosenthal notes that the *Times* could have remained with its regular format, letting stories "jump" from the first page onto interior pages with advertising; but "clearing" pages, and many of them, he says, "tells the reader the event is something special."

To Rosenthal, the episode highlighted something very important about *The New York Times*. "The point is that I didn't even pause to wonder whether I could get the space we needed. Punch Sulzberger's commitment to the news is so great that the question would not arise." Rosenthal would not even guess at what the saturation coverage of the *Challenger* disaster cost the *Times* in lost advertising space; he suggests it best that he *not* know, for a newsman works best when he does not let the balance sheet influence his immediate decisions. "The advertising we're talking about is premium rate, front of the paper," Rosenthal says. "Some of it might be re-couped, but I feel that most of it is lost forever. But that's the way the Sulzbergers want their paper run."

The *Times* exerts comparable influence in the worlds of culture and entertainment. A frowning review by a drama critic can send a play crashing off the stage. Conversely, favorable treatment can extend the life expectancy of a questionable production. Book sellers throughout America use the *Sunday New York Times Book Review* as a guide on which books to buy and promote. A front-page review can-not make a book a best-seller, but as the publicist for a major trade publisher says, "If the *Times* ignores you totally, forget the book—it's dead in the water." (There are exceptions. For years, the *Times* re-fused to review books published by Lyle Stuart; the snub did not pre-vent several Stuart titles from reaching the top of the *Times* best-seller list.)

Criticism is inherently subjective, and hence intensely susceptible to abuse. Here the *Times* was on quaky ground because of the quirks of Rosenthal and his deputy managing editor, Arthur Gelb, who had broad responsibility for coverage of cultural affairs. Gelb is a man who desperately wishes for his importance to be recognized. At Sardi's, for instance, he is careful to show a dinner companion his caricature on the wall, and to get the table directly beneath it. He hustles across the nearly-empty room (the post-theater rush was an hour away) to introduce himself to an elderly playwright dining with a young and pretty lady. That the man did not recognize Gelb, even after hearing his name, is of no import. Gelb is now busy telling a story of how he goosed Marilyn Monroe in the restaurant one night. "She was sitting at that table right there." Six hours' unbroken exposure to Artie Gelb demonstrates why many people consider him bright, engaging—and more than a little smarmy. But he has the power to decide who is important in New York culture, and he is not hesitant to exert it.

Nor, for that matter, has Rosenthal hesitated to impose his own preferences on the *Times*. That this is so resulted in ongoing confu-sion at the *Times* over almost a score of years, for Rosenthal in his initial days as executive editor seemed to lack any guiding compass other than ambition. As metropolitan editor he stressed thorough coverage of the New York city government, unleashing task forces to explore the promise-performance gap of the administration of Mayor John V. Lindsay. Then, in the mid-1970's, when *Times* management decided to present New York in a positive light and ignore the city's many blights and shortcomings, Rosenthal dutifully fell into line, and the *Times* essentially stopped covering the city. Rosenthal's *Times*, because of inattentiveness to the interlock of government and the city Democratic machine, allowed official white-collar thieves to loot the city of uncountable millions of dollars. The *Times*'s stress on upbeat borders on parody, with Rosenthal's editors seemingly able to find a bright side to any horror.

An example: In June, 1986, thugs slashed a young model's face with razors, allegedly at the instigation of a landlord with whom she was feuding. The *Times*'s headline:

WOUNDED MODEL
RETAINS HER FAITH
IN CAREER AND CITY

The seminal event of Rosenthal's first years as editor was the *Times*'s publication of the Pentagon Papers, a top-secret study of the origins and conduct of the Vietnam War. This success blooded Rosenthal's appetite for investigative reporting. That the detested Washington *Post* beat the *Times* on Watergate put Rosenthal into a jealous frenzy, and for several years he pushed journalistic ethics to their limits—and beyond—to "expose" such secrets as the inner-workings of the Central Intelligence Agency and covert portions of the war in Vietnam. During these halcyon years Rosenthal was admired by the American left. Then, abruptly, Rosenthal changed the rules, and abandoned hard investigative reporting. Several persons who had won Pulitzer Prizes for such work—notably Seymour Hersh and John Crewdson—left the *Times*, and Rosenthal did not seem to care; in fact, he now says he had "serious" qualms about the way Hersh worked. The treatment of two foreign correspondents illustrate Rosenthal's change:

In 1975 and 1976 Rosenthal permitted Sydney Schanberg to write vividly of the impact of the war on Cambodia, and of flaws in American policy there. When conservatives criticized Schanberg's rosey-lensed view of the Pol Pot faction that ultimately seized Cambodia, Rosenthal stood behind him, even after the ruthless Communist regime slaughtered hundreds of thousands of its own people. Rosenthal promoted Schanberg, and spoke of him as a possible executive editor. (They eventually broke, but that came a decade later.) In the early

1980's another young reporter, Raymond Bonner, did similar reporting from El Salvador for a brief period. When the same conservative
circles protested—specifically, Reed Irvine, of Accuracy in Media, a
press monitoring group—Rosenthal jerked Bonner out of Central
America overnight and gave him assignments that effectively drove
him from *The New York Times*.

What changed? Nothing, Rosenthal protests, publicly and privately. He is incorrect. What Rosenthal did was take the *Times* many
ideological steps towards the right. The era when *The New York
Times* was a veritable playpen of the American left ended. Instead,
Rosenthal was praised by such organs as *Policy Review*, magazine of
the Heritage Foundation, as the man responsible for the *Times*
"reaffirming its greatness by retreating from the radicalism of the last
two decades and once again taking up responsible journalism."
(Rosenthal concedes only that he had moved the *Times* to a "more
centrist" position.) He rightly notes that he developed his anti-
Communism "the hard way, watching the Commies at CCNY [City
College of New York] during the Popular Front days, and living with
Stalin's secret police in Poland during the Cold War." Such is true,
yet Rosenthal waited until very late in his career as an editor to turn
The New York Times into an active anti-Communist course. And the
turnabout was due to Punch Sulzberger, who for economic reasons
decided that *The New York Times* no longer would be an
Establishment-bashing newspaper more interested in the problems
of society than its accomplishments. Economics motivated Sulzberger
more than any other factor, for the *Times* relied for advertising dollars
upon the very institutions Rosenthal roasted during the 1970's. When
the choice came between crusading journalism and the cash register,
Sulzberger had little problem making his decision.

But something else worked on Sulzberger as well. Commencing in
the late 1970's he took serious note of criticisms of the *Times* voiced
by Reed Irvine and Murray Baron of Accuracy in Media. Sulzberger
at first dismissed these two press monitors as right-wing cranks, more
interested in their own political agenda than in press accuracy. Then
he began to listen to them, and to read their detailed critiques of
Times coverage. And, as the record will demonstrate, Irvine and
Baron slowly but perceptibly nudged Punch Sulzberger to the right—
and given Sulzberger's authority at the *Times*, Abe Rosenthal had no
choice but to go along.

The irony is that the Rosenthal who now is praised by the American conservative movement recruited the very correspondents who had so irritated the conservatives only a decade earlier.

That Rosenthal in the 1980's was suddenly anathema to the American left brought into convergence several related flows of opinion that were separate but in a sense self-supporting. First, a word about media criticism.

American newspapers seldom talk about themselves, or one another. Such is not good form. (One notable exception is David Shaw, whose periodic press pieces in *The Los Angeles Times* discuss his own newspaper as well as others.) What criticism exists comes from a narrow range of publications which set the tone for commentary elsewhere, notably the *Columbia Journalism Review*, the press sections of *Time* and *Newsweek*, and to a lesser degree the *Village Voice* and *The Nation*. *CJR*'s first major pieces on Rosenthal during the 1970's were written by Roger Morris, who served briefly on the National Security Council staff under Dr. Henry Kissinger, and resigned to protest the Cambodian incursion. *Newsweek*'s only major article on Rosenthal in the 1980's was written by Charles Kaiser, who can be accurately described as a "disgruntled former *Times* employee." Kaiser is homosexual and was Rosenthal's clerk. Rosenthal did not know his young clerk's sexual preference, and hence he spoke his uncensored mind. Kaiser kept his mouth shut, and when he joined *Newsweek* he had his revenge, in a magazine of national circulation.

For years the *Village Voice*'s "Press Clips" was written by Alexander Cockburn, whose journalistic model was his father, Claud Cockburn, the longtime British Communist newspaperman. Cockburn writes with much wit but little political sense, and he had much fun with Rosenthal during the early 1980's. Then *Voice* publisher David Schneiderman fired him (for not revealing he had taken a "grant" from an Arab group to write a book on the Middle East) and Cockburn moved his column to *The Nation*, which although of minuscule circulation is read—and heeded—by other journalists. All this is not to suggest that Rosenthal's "image problems" resulted from a leftist cabal; the existential fact, however, is that much of what was written about Rosenthal did not come from ideologically disinterested sources.

Rosenthal, for his part, contributed Rosenthal, which was unfortunate, for Rosenthal is not a very likeable human being. He is a man of strong emotions, both negative and positive. He is a weeper. The months after his separation from Ann Rosenthal, his wife of three decades, he found himself bursting into tears at unexpected moments—sitting in a restaurant, conducting a news meeting, even when walking down the street. Tragedies marked his early life, and he never forgot how to cry. He sends flowers to friends in the hospital, and he expects cards on his birthday and other occasions; persons who seek ingratiation learn to send him congratulatory notes when he writes a magazine article, or receives a plaque from a journalistic lodge. But friends also know he is hypersensitive to any criticism, however mild, either of himself or the *Times*. A person who offends Rosenthal can find himself suddenly, brutally and permanently cut out of his circle. Rosenthal can lacerate a reporter verbally for an error; more than one person has left his office choking back tears and rage. He also likes to pass along personally the good news of a promotion or a raise. Friends see in this behavior a desire to be loved; a hope that people would look beyond what he calls "my dark side" and find someone who truly cares about humans.

Rosenthal can only hope, for about the nicest adjective I heard about his conduct over two years was "abrasive," with "unfortunate" a close second. Rosenthal is a shouter, a curser, a whiner; he keeps a "shitlist" in his head and he can hold grudges for years. He is a small man physically but his rages are so violent that he intimidates persons half again his size. "Much of Abe's supposed bravery in shouting at other men lies in the fact he can say those two little words, 'You're fired,' " one of his top deputies said. "Otherwise, they'd have carried him out on a stretcher with a busted jaw back in the 1960's."

Because of his conduct, Rosenthal's coterie at *The New York Times* gradually evolved to a corps of sub-editors he has known for years, and who were willing to endure his tantrums. Stronger men said the hell with him and left. His chief deputy, Arthur Gelb, had been working at the *Times* only a few months when Rosenthal joined the paper, and their professional and personal relationship has been intimate since. Another deputy, James Greenfield, met Rosenthal when they worked as correspondents in New Delhi in the 1950's, Greenfield for *Time* Magazine, Rosenthal for the *Times*. Yet another, John Lee, encountered Rosenthal in Tokyo when he worked for United Press International.

The staff had a private name for these deputies—"Abe's Dobermans." The Doberman breed of dog is trained for nasty work. Handled properly, the Doberman is so responsive to his master's wishes that no order is needed to send him bounding for an adversary's throat. A change of the master's mood puts him into action, fangs bared.

"Abe's Dobermans" are capable of great cruelty of their own. In the early 1980's the *Times* had a deputy religious editor named Charles Austin, an ordained Lutheran minister as well as a journalist. Although not a spectacular reporter, Austin worked hard, and one colleague described him as a "straightforward delightful guy who took pride in what he did." One afternoon, when the newsroom was at its busiest, Peter Millones, a Rosenthal intimate, then serving as metropolitan editor, walked over to Austin's desk.

Ignoring perhaps ten other reporters sitting in easy listening distance, Millones said, "We have decided you will no longer cover religion for *The New York Times*. Your work has not been distinguished. You are going on general assignment, and where you are going will depend upon us, and not upon you."

Tears swelled in Austin's eyes, and the other reporters looked away in embarrassment. As one of them said, "They didn't even have the courtesy of having him come to the privacy of an office." Austin left the paper shortly afterwards.

In early 1985, when I commenced work on this book, the subject was a troubled man. The preceding December his marriage to Ann Rosenthal ended, as did his two-decade affair with a lithe actress named Katharine Balfour. In May 1987 he was to reach sixty-five years of age, the mandatory retirement age for *Times* news employees. He desperately wanted an exception so that he could continue as executive editor, for he knew no life outside *The New York Times*. He "felt a tingle" when he walked into the *Times* lobby each morning, and people who heard him believed him. As "A. M. Rosenthal of *The New York Times*" he was a commanding figure in New York and in the nation, a man sought out by hostesses. What status would he have as "Abe Rosenthal"? But publisher Punch Sulzberger told him in early 1985, No, we're going to follow the rule, but I'll take care of you.

This decision proved difficult for Rosenthal to accept, and he had friends such as Barbara Walters talk to Punch, to see if the rule might be forgotten just in this one instance. Why are you so determined to make poor Abe retire? Walters asked Sulzberger at a party.

"Because I said so," Punch Sulzberger replied.

"I Found My Own Piano to Play"

He stared into the bathroom mirror, and he made a painfully objective judgment of the unattractive spectacle reflected there. A skinny kid, barely 120 pounds on a five-seven frame. Uncombable greasy hair drooping in disorganized swirls over thick-lensed glasses with heavy black horn rims. Pocked cheeks aflame with acne welts. Out of the mirror's sight, but never out of mind, were spindly, scarred legs aching from osteomyelitis, an acute infection of the bone marrow.

He remembered with a shudder what had been said to him that morning when he rode the subway to Manhattan to try for a day's work on the receiving dock of Gimbel's, the department store. The hiring boss, a big-bellied Irishman, looked at him, and he laughed. "Hey, fuckin' four-eyes," he said, "you down here to try to make it with a manny-kin? Who the fuck let you off the subway?" Some other boys he considered friends laughed along with everyone else, and he hurried away from the receiving dock, eyes clenched against tears.

Now he looked at the image in the mirror, and he asked himself, silently, What the hell am I going to do with my life? He thought through the possibilities open to a scrawny poor Jewish kid living in the Depression Bronx.

A.M. Rosenthal decided that if he was lucky, he might qualify for a job with the post office that gave him a living wage and security.

Harry Shipiatsky came from an anti-Semite cesspool of Czarist Russia, the village of Bobrusik in Byelorussia. This is far-west Russia, adjacent to Poland, a region with a long and bloody history of Jewish-killing pogroms, with state sanction. Just before the start of the First World War Shipiatsky saved the money to go to London, by train and boat; an uncle named Rosenthal gave him passage money to continue to Canada. The uncle also suggested that Harry Shipiatsky take a new name to the new world, and he did—Rosenthal.

He was a strong man physically. He worked on a communal farm. He went into the Canadian wilderness as a fur trader and trapper. He saved. One by one he brought seven brothers out of Byelorussia. He also sent for the pretty girl he had kissed and betrothed—Sarah Riva. They married, and had five girls and then a son, Abraham Michael Rosenthal, born May 2, 1922, in Sault Ste. Marie, Ontario. He squabbled with a brother over fur trade money, and quit Canada in disgust and moved to the Bronx and found work as a housepainter. He looked for a good place for his family to live, and one of his socialist friends from Canada told him of a promising housing project.

Van Cortlandt Park is a verdant enclave stretching for more than a mile through the upper Bronx, a place of trees, walkways, a small lake and ball fields. In the 1920's the Amalgamated Clothing Workers Union, wishing to free its members from lower East Side slum tenements, built a massive housing project alongside the park that residents called "the Amalgamated," or the ACA, for the Amalgamated Cooperative Association, the formal owner. The idea was that unionists would live in president Sidney Hillman's socialist utopia of low-cost housing and cooperative stores. But the Depression wrecked the men's clothing industry, and the union opened the project to any outsider who could afford a unit.

Harry Rosenthal bought an apartment, $500 for each of four rooms, plus maintenance of about $45 monthly. Several happy years followed. To his pre-pubescent son, Harry Rosenthal was a man of dash and verve, a character from a Jack London novel who enjoyed a glass and a laugh and an occasional let's-don't-tell-Momma gamble. Above all, Harry Rosenthal was physical—a man of muscles and masculinity. He talked about Russia. He hated the Russian peasants, and how they could be incited to turn on Jewish neighbors and cause them great misery. He was not a political man, yet he recognized the innate savagery of the country he had fled. That hatred he passed to his son.

But the overriding presence in the Rosenthal home was tragedy—a series of deaths that scarred Abe Rosenthal's psyche permanently, making him subject the rest of his life to wild emotional swings and excesses. Death is Rosenthal's overriding boyhood memory. When he speaks of those years he drops his head and the level of his voice. "Some of this might be out of order, but this is what I remember," he admits. Reporters of Rosenthal's ability have the knack of remembering middle initials of obscure cabinet ministers and the exact date of an airline crash. But the family tragedies are purged from his immediate memory.

There was Pauline, whom everyone called "Bess," the "angel of the family," frail and pretty. She died on New Year's Eve when Rosenthal was eleven or twelve; he does not remember exactly, and he does not wish to relive the event by checking. Bess had pneumonia; she died at home. "There were no sulfa drugs in the 1920's; now, of course, she would have been treated, and she would have lived." Next came father Harry, his body broken beyond repair in a fall from a scaffolding as he worked. He languished three years in agony, then died. Elizabeth, the oldest, the sister to whom Rosenthal was the closest, died in the early thirties, leaving two small children.

Next was Ruth, a political activist who was an officer in the New York branch of the Young Communist League. Rosenthal had bitter arguments about Communism with Ruth and her husband, a man named George Watt. But Watt treated Rosenthal like an adult, and they respected one another despite the political disagreements. When Watt joined the Abraham Lincoln Brigade and went off to fight in the Spanish Civil War, Rosenthal became even closer to Ruth. Shortly after Watt's return, Ruth entered the hospital to have a baby; she developed an infection, and she died. Rosenthal grieved, for he felt he had never made proper peace with his sister. He identified the tragedy with her involvement with Watt, and he broke relations with his brother-in-law for years. To Rosenthal, his sister's death was yet another reason for hating Communism.

"It was like one death right after another, my father and four sisters," Rosenthal said. "I learned at an early age that death was real, that it wasn't something that just happened to other people. All this happened in a relatively short period, from the time I was eleven to eighteen.*

"This had an impact on my life I tried to deny. It was a problem I had to deal with for decades. Only recently [this was said in April, 1986] have I begun to come to grips with it." To Rosenthal, the concept of death was reality, not other people's rhetoric. Submerged feelings, he realized, are as important, and perhaps even more so, than those a person openly recognizes and accepts.

Harry Rosenthal's death meant his widow must care for her surviving children during the Depression with essentially no income beyond a small insurance policy. Just how the family survived remains a mystery to Abe Rosenthal, although the sisters who were working brought money home. He tried. The Bronx kid would ride the subway into Manhattan, hoping for a day's work as a messenger or stock room clerk; more often than not he was turned away with the derisive laugh, "Too skinny." The youth's confidence eroded. "It was not so much a sense of poverty as it was what to do with my life. I could not figure why anyone would want to hire me. I saw myself as a small, shy kid."

There was another problem. Beginning in his early teens Rosenthal's legs ached—not the growing pains of youth, but true agony. Neighborhood friends such as Richard Cohen did not realize the extent of Rosenthal's problems; they saw him as "the boy who couldn't walk just right." He willed himself to live with the pain, and he hobbled about with the help of a cane.

Because of the family's poverty, the first doctors who examined his legs were charity hospital internes, earnest but inexperienced. The eventual diagnosis was osteomyelitis, an acute infection of the bone marrow caused by germs, similar to a boil in the skin. The disease causes acute pain and high fever, and it generally strikes at the long bones of the arms and legs of children and young adults. Treatment is through penicillin and other antibiotics to clear the infection. If these do not work, surgery is required to drain off the affected area, and in severe cases the drainage lasts for years. Another technique is surgi-

---

*The fifth sister, Ann Rosenthal, died of cancer in 1963. A brother died within hours of birth in the 1910's; had he lived, he would have been Abraham Michael Rosenthal.

cal removal of infected or dead pieces of bone to permit fresh bone to regenerate.

The physicians botched Rosenthal's treatment, and horribly so. He did not receive the proper medication. At age sixteen he was operated on at the Hospital for Joint Diseases, and he was encased in a cast from his feet to his neck, horrified that he would be a cripple for life. He had to drop out of high school for a year. Sister Ann persuaded a charity to give him a railroad ticket to the Mayo Clinic in Minnesota. Rosenthal spent his last $60 for the physical examination; he could pay no more, but doctors did eighteen hours of non-stop surgery anyway. Rosenthal spent several weeks immobilized in a cast, without a single friendly visitor. (One young nurse peered at him so curiously he asked why. She explained she had never seen a Jew before.) But the operation enabled Rosenthal to put away his cane and resume a normal physical life. His gait never again was quite right, and his legs troubled him periodically the rest of his life. But he was not crippled.

But what must he now do with his life? Although his self-esteem remained low, Rosenthal realized he was smarter than most contemporaries. Although his forced absence from school hurt his grades, he read incessantly. The Rosenthal household possessed six library cards, each good for five books weekly, and Abe often read the full complement. Although his close friend Richard Cohen edited the newspaper at the all-boys DeWitt Clinton High School, Rosenthal had no interest in journalism. But as did other Clinton students, Rosenthal recognized his intellect offered him the sole chance to escape a Bronx housing project. Clinton students, Cohen said, were "upward Jewish mobile, kids from families that had high expectations of you." The goal was to earn high enough grades to win a $250 regents' scholarship to a New York State college. For those who did not win a regents', the alternative was tuition-free City College of New York, which Rosenthal described as the "place where smart Jewish kids went." His operation cost him a year of school, but he studied hard enough as a senior to achieve the 90 grade average required to enter CCNY. But when he entered the college in 1941, he still had not the slightest notion what he would do with his life.

In late December, 1941, Richard Cohen sat in the office of *The Campus*, the student newspaper at the City College of New York, worrying how the paper could continue publication. The draft had accelerated after the American entry into the war, and "guys were dropping like flies." He tensed. He saw a familiar figure coming up the walk—Abe Rosenthal, his friend from the Amalgamated enrolling in CCNY as a late freshman. Cohen yelled out the window, and Rosenthal saw him and grinned, and within a moment they were embracing, laughing, talking. "What's new with you?" Rosenthal asked.

"I'm working on *The Campus*," Cohen said, waving his hand over his shoulder towards the office. "I'm going to be sports editor next term, and then editor-in-chief." Rosenthal seemed interested, and they talked some more. "Abe, why don't you come out for *The Campus?*"

"Dick, I think I will," Rosenthal said.

"And that," Cohen says with proprietary pride, "is how Abe Rosenthal got into the newspaper business." He did not claim to have sensed any journalistic genius in Rosenthal. "Look, we needed bodies. I thought Abe could help us out."

The war dominated CCNY the years Rosenthal studied there. The pre-war enrollment of 20,000 students dropped swiftly to 15,000 by the fall of 1942, then even lower. Half the students studied engineering; 27 percent, liberal arts; 23 percent, business. The military was omnipresent, with soldier-students living in the Hebrew Orphan Asylum opposite Lewisohn Stadium, and the college offering "commando training" in the physical education department. So many soldiers attended CCNY that for a time *The Campus* devoted a page to "Army Life."

Although run by volunteers, *The Campus* was competitive, with students aspiring to staff positions sacrificing their lunch hour to courses in reporting and editing taught by the managing editor. A reporter started with one- and two-paragraph stories and gradually proved himself, remembers Anatole Shub, who attended CCNY with Rosenthal, and then worked for *The New York Times* and other publications. "The process accelerated when people went off to war."

Rosenthal soon received his first assignment; more than four decades later, he proudly recited the one-sentence story by rote: *"The Journal of Social Studies* scheduled to be published by the history department has been postponed until the spring, it was learned today." Rosenthal remained proud of the story, for "one sentence tells it all, and also leaves an aura of mystery about it."

More importantly, Rosenthal had found something he could do

well, better than other people, even from the start, and something he enjoyed.

"I was a natural. I could get a story. I could write it. God, this was *my piano!*" The special quality of being a newspaperman is something that the good ones do not need to have explained. "You have it or you don't have it. You can play the piano or you can't play the piano. It exists. A nose, an ear, an eye, an antenna, radar. It's a quick quality sometimes, quick like a snap of the fingers. Or it is slow and easy and musing like the good thoughts that come when shaving. It's knowing what the story is and where to go to get it and how to tell it, and it is the deep, deep joy of this business."

Rosenthal's name first appeared on *The Campus* masthead on April 22, 1941, as a member of the "issue staff—A. Rosenthal '45." By May 6 he had moved up to what was called the "associate news board." Abe Rosenthal's first newspaper byline appeared in *The Campus* of September 24, 1942, under a two-column headline on page four of a four-page issue:

War, Coal and Philharmonic
Kept Summer Students Busy

Most of the 3,278 students who attended Summer Session at the Main Center were too busy trying to get into the Enlisted Reserve to note what was doing on the campus, but things were happening right along. . . . Classes all summer were held to an accompaniment of hammer blows and an obligato of falling coal. The carpenters' serenade came from the boarding up of all windows as an air raid precaution. . . .

Wartime strictures meant *The Campus* received minimal official support. The normal issue, in tabloid format, was four or six pages. *The Campus* led a nomad existence, shunted from office to cubbyhole at university demand. The first "newsroom" for Rosenthal was a steel-meshed cage in the basement of Townsend Harris Hall, one of many cubicles for student activities ranging from the stamp club to *The Campus*. "These were the dungeons, all the left-over stuff in the basement," Rosenthal said. The typewriters and desks were cast-off junk, and wadded paper and dust balls littered the floors. There was no telephone. If a reporter wished to call someone about a story, "You went outside and you used your own nickel." CCNY gave *The*

Campus no financial support; its money came from a few advertisements and scattered nickels from single-copy sales. "We spent a lot of time running away from printers," Rosenthal recollected.

Frivolity went along with the work. Robert Schiffer, a Rosenthal classmate who became an official at the UN, remembers with a grimace a *Campus* game called "garlic ball," a version of ping-pong played without net or paddles. "Six to eight boys would be on each side, and the object was to blow the ping-pong ball off the other team's side of the table. The name? Well, before you played, you ate some onions and a good bite of garlic, and the more you ate the more competitive you were." *The Campus* at one point occupied a cubicle on the ground floor of Main Building barely large enough for four or five desks. "You sat where you could find an empty seat," Anatole Shub said. "Out of whatever psychological motivation you can imagine, Rosenthal chose to put his large chair on top of a desk and sit up there, holding court. Reporters were literally handing copy up to him for editing."

Once Rosenthal decided he liked journalism he marched steadily up the masthead of *The Campus.* By May, 1943, he was news editor, and also the paper's representative on the Student Council. A mystique has grown around Rosenthal's college journalism career; invariably his fellow students, many of them still friends, spoke of him as a talented and prolific writer who early displayed a knack for lively feature stories. Unfortunately, these memories are not supported by issues of *The Campus.* Only eight times during his work on the paper (issues dated September 24, 1942, through December 9, 1943) did Rosenthal's byline appear. He did show a flair for imagery. He wrote about a "commando course" (formally, Hygiene 15 and 16) to teach future soldiers "tricks which they will be able to use when face-to-face with the enemy. . . . If you'd like to know how to tear your enemy's arm off, or cripple him for life with a well-placed kick, Sam Winograd [the instructor] is your man. . . . In one corner of the gym, some boys toss a 30-pound medicine ball in a weird game—a mixture of basketball, football and murder." Yet Rosenthal was also capable of prose embarrassingly *gauche*, as in rewriting an article in a psychology journal about Frank Sinatra; "Frank Sinatra owes everything to the ego. That old Freud whipping boy is given the major part of the blame for the fantastic popularity of the crooner who parlayed a quaver into a million. . . ."

To find something he could do better than other persons thrilled

Rosenthal, and despite the academic challenges of CCNY, he found himself drawn deeper into journalism. Classmates such as George Sherry felt CCNY a "tough, excellent school" which required much homework of its students." Nonetheless, Abe thrived without as much effort as other persons. "Abe did just a little bit less," said Sherry, "and he could get an A in any course he wanted. But he didn't want it all that often." The novels of Thomas Wolfe enraptured him. He read and re-read James T. Farrell's *Studs Lonigan* trilogy; for one period his book bag always seemed to have a Faulkner novel for subway reading.

Politically the young Rosenthal was from what George Sherry called "the same liberal 'child of the New Deal' mold as the vast majority of CCNY students." He was strongly anti-Communist, and he detested the CCNY communists. He felt them more interested in disrupting student activities than in academics; he disliked their penchant for hiding their politics behind the names of supposedly patriotic front groups. Rosenthal was at CCNY for an education that could get him out of the Bronx; to him, noisy leftist demonstrations were a distractive nuisance.

To Rosenthal, the most important issue in his life was getting into professional journalism. He acquired a useful mentor, Professor Irving Rosenthal, who taught courses on reporting and editing and was faculty adviser to *The Campus*. A Jewish Mr. Chips, Rosenthal also did public relations for CCNY and had a strong voice in selecting students hired as campus correspondents for the New York newspapers. Irving Rosenthal saw talent in the young Abe, and he suggested to the New York *Herald Tribune* in the fall of 1943 that he be hired as correspondent. This was done, and for a month Rosenthal fretted and waited his turn at the top stringer job, the *Times*. The succession was formal: "Boy A would be on the *Herald Tribune*, waiting his turn until Boy B on the *Times* was drafted. Then he would move up, and he would be followed by other kids." (The *Times* offered money as well as prestige: a guaranteed $12 weekly salary, versus the *Herald Tribune*'s space rates.)

Rosenthal's turn came the first week of December 1943. He rode the subway to West 43d Street for an interview with *Times*'s city editor, David Joseph. For the first time Rosenthal walked through the lobby, and he paused to look at a bust of Adolph Ochs, the austere Tennessean who bought the paper in 1896, and whose standards of editorial and personal integrity did much to make the *Times* the nation's most respected newspaper. New York papers of the late 1800's were raucous, partisan, their news columns for sale to any commercial or political bidder. Truth was never permitted to interfere with a crusade or a profit. Ochs set a different standard, exemplified by the words carved into the stone behind his bust:

> To give the news impartially without fear or favor, regardless of any part, sect or interest involved.

The twenty-two-year-old Abe Rosenthal felt a tingle the first time he read those words, and as he was to say frequently during his decades at the paper, "I never fail to feel a tingle up and down my spine when I walk into the lobby of *The New York Times*." And no one who knew Abe Rosenthal ever expressed the slightest doubt about the sincerity of those words. The scrawny Jewish kid from a Bronx housing project, with his thick glasses and limp, was about to become A. M. Rosenthal of *The New York Times*.

TWO

"My Son Abe, the Reporter"

In late 1943 the news room of *The New York Times* was a dusty, noisy space that sprawled over most of the third floor of the Times Building at 229 West 43rd Street, between Broadway and Eighth Avenue. Cigarette butts littered the floor in such messy profusion it was barely visible; spittoons were scattered around the room, and they were used, although seldom with pinpoint accuracy. Rewritemen—the people who take a reporter's notes and fashion them into stories— kept bottles of liquor in their desks, and etiquette permitted a hasty snort in the name of creation under pressure. Bookies, some of them staff members, did a lively business on the horses. During slack periods, out came the cards—bridge during the daytime, table-stakes poker at night.

Presiding over this ménage was city editor David Joseph, an old-fashioned man who always wore spats and a vest with his severe black suits. A yellowing elk's tooth hanging from a gold watch chain bounced on his ample belly (reporters used to jest he should take the bedraggled tooth to the dentist for a crown). Although a man of some formality (even senior deputies called him Mr. Joseph) he was not oblivious to the sporting side of his newsroom. A copy boy's mother came in one day to complain that her son was squandering his salary on bookies. How could this be permitted in the dignified premises of *The New York Times?* Joseph hrrrumped and hawed and did not have the heart to tell her he, too, liked his bets.

Abe Rosenthal stood nervously alongside Joseph's desk for his interview, his thoughts literally drowned out by the jangle of telephones, the fast clicking of typewriters, and shouts of "BOY!" as editors dispatched copy around the vast room. "Irving Rosenthal thinks highly of you," Joseph said. "But what can you do for us? What's happening at CCNY that should be in *The New York Times?*"

His high-pitched voice a stammer, Rosenthal told about students purchasing $75,000 of war bonds on the promise the Treasury Department would name a pursuit plane "The Spirit of CCNY." Several months later some of the students inquired where the plane was stationed, and whether any CCNY men happened to be crew members. What plane? the government replied. Joseph agreed that the students' disappointment made a poignant story. "Write it, give me a half-column," he said. Rosenthal's first story ran in the *Times* of December 7, 1943: "Spirit of C.C.N.Y. A Sad, Sad Story."

The story appeared in *The Campus* two days later in different fashion, Rosenthal's last byline there. He had been selected as co-editor with friend George Sherry, a job he surrendered in favor of the *Times* position. Now he hustled about the campus with even more vigor, working as a *real* newspaperman. He worked through early afternoon gathering news items; he was careful about facts—whether a professor's name was spelled Schaeffer or Shaffer—for the *Times* had been known to dismiss a stringer for a single error, however inconsequential. Then he telephoned the city desk with his offerings. On good days a deputy to Joseph would say, "Give me three hundred words on that." More often, CCNY news rated a paragraph or two, for the *Times* devoted the bulk of its newsprint to war news. So Rosenthal would hurry to the subway station at 137th Street and ride down Broadway to Times Square, and then into the *Times* to find a vacant typewriter—stringers did not have their own desks—and write.

The *Times Index* contains fifty-one stories about CCNY the four months Rosenthal worked as campus correspondent, mostly short items on mundane subjects: alumni dinner plans, a Faculty Wives

Club art exhibit; a permit for a seeing-eye dog to accompany a master to class. Rosenthal wrote these as competently as can be done; such stories demand rote, and such is what the *Times* received. His major story those months concerned the chartering of the "Thomas Paine Club" as a student activity despite evidence of Communist control. The *Times* gave Rosenthal major space, and he wrote in classic *Times* style—plodding, comprehensive, and careful to give both sides of the issue, in keeping with Ochs's mandate of objectivity.

Although his work apparently pleased David Joseph, Rosenthal was not confident about getting a full staff position. In his conceived image he remained the skinny kid who had accidentally wandered into paradise, and would be shown the front gate once someone noticed him. Rosenthal's confidence did not benefit the afternoon when another campus correspondent, Kathleen Teltsch of Columbia Unversity, dropped her purse, and a reporter's press card fell out. Rosenthal, doing the same work at CCNY, had no card. His immediate anger lasted several days; the implication of the incident, the "elitist" correspondent versus the CCNY boy, rankled him for years, apparently, for he told the story on many occasions. But the slight made him even more determined to work his way on-staff.

One day in the spring of 1944 Rosenthal took especial care in combing his hair and polishing his shoes, and Sarah Rosenthal made sure his white shirt was starched and pressed. At the end of the day, as David Joseph gathered his papers in preparing to leave, Rosenthal gulped and walked to the city desk. In a rush of words he said he loved the *Times*, and what chance did he have of a job after graduation? Joseph glanced at him. "As a matter of fact," he said, "we are kind of short handed right now, what with everyone going off to the army. Come to work a week from Monday." But he admonished Rosenthal, "Complete your education."

Rosenthal left the *Times* in sheer exultation. CCNY had played its purpose, it had gotten him a real job. He ignored Joseph's parting directive. "I quit college so fast you couldn't see me leave the Bursar's Office." He also went by the *Times* Medical Department for the required physical examination.

The next day, when Rosenthal reported for work, Joseph shook his head. "You can't work here," he said coldly. The *Times* medical people had objected to Rosenthal's legs. The paper could not risk hiring an afflicted person who might be injured while covering a story and be crippled for life.

"I almost dropped dead," Rosenthal said. "This was one of the lowest moments of my life. I saw my whole world going away from me." Hot tears swelled in his eyes, and he started to walk out of the room. But a deputy city editor, Walter Fenton, motioned for him to wait a minute, and he huddled with Joseph. Rosenthal stood in the corner, ready to disappear back to the Bronx and forget journalism; he would do something for which poor Jewish kids were considered fit—stock boy at a department store, or a sales clerk. During this awful interval, which lasted only a few minutes, Rosenthal felt that something he wanted dearly was being snatched away from him. His emotional suffering hurt him in a way more visceral, more lasting, than his bad legs.

Joseph and Fenton finally ended their talk, and Joseph beckoned him over the city desk. "OK," he said, "I can't fight the medical people, they have their own rules. Let's do it this way. You can come on staff as a 'temporary employee,' and I'll work on getting you made full staff. You won't get the insurance or the other benefits, but you'll be working."

Rosenthal couldn't care less what the *Times* called him. "This was life and restoration," he said. "I was a *Times* reporter."

So now a proud Sarah Rosenthal boasted to her Bronx neighbors about "my son, Abe, the reporter for *The New York Times*," and Rosenthal's salary increased to a relatively munificent $27 weekly. He did the scout work expected of new reporters. He wrote the bulletins displayed in the moving light display on the Times Tower in Times Square. He wrote the copy for each hour's news broadcast on WQXR, the *Times* radio station. Between these chores he would rush to the city desk, eager for an assignment; the other things he considered clerk's work, and in his eagerness to obtain "real" assignments "I did eight hours work in two hours." When he did wheedle a "real" story, good friend Bernard Kalb would do the radio writing.* His confidence grew. "I knew what I could do, and I moved along."

Rosenthal also learned the realities of American journalism, and how remote the First Amendment is from the minds of persons at the working level of governmental authority. Through some act of editorial grace, Rosenthal missed permanent assignment to the police beat, one of the drearier required courses of newspaper experience.

---

*Kalb had a distinguished career with the *Times* and with NBC; in the 1980's he became the State Department's chief public affairs spokesman.

He spent only four nights of his entire career covering police news. His only experience was sour. There was a suicide at a Park Avenue hotel—"a good address," newsmen would call it—and an editor sent Rosenthal over. He marched confidently into the hotel, John Peter Zenger figuratively at his side, and rode the elevator up and knocked on the door. As Rosenthal relates the story:

> A detective twelve feet tall opened the door, and I started to walk forward, where I was introduced to his hand, about three feet wide, held up before my face.
>   "Where are you going, kid?" he asked.
>   "There's a suicide here."
>   "So?"
>   "Reporter, I want to come in and talk to you and see the body."
>   "Beat it!"
>   Beat it? I wasn't sure of the follow-through.
>   "But I am of the *Times*, a reporter. . ."
>   "So?"
>   "Don't you care if I get the story right?" I asked righteously, and indignantly.
>   "Four eyes," said the detective, amiably, "I don't care if you drop dead." Then he introduced me to the closed door.

Thus did Rosenthal learn that contrary to what he had learned at CCNY, "it was not the ordained, patriotic duty of every American to answer every reporter's question."

As his assignments bettered, Rosenthal realized he eventually must face another problem, that of his byline. Despite *Times* ownership by a Jewish family, the news operation was dominated by Protestants, apparently a decision of the Ochses and the Sulzbergers. To many persons the *Times* went out of its way to avoid "looking Jewish." This meant that "Jewish bylines" were anathema. Thus Abraham H. Raskin, the nation's leading labor reporter, had his stories signed "A. H. Raskin." (When someone offered the in-house explanation that Abraham H. Raskin was too many characters to fit into a byline, a dissenter pointed to Anne O'Hara McCormick on the editorial page— twenty-one characters and spaces to seventeen.) The irony was that Rosenthal was not religious. His father eschewed religion altogether. Rosenthal ignored religion; he was Jewish, but he had never studied Hebrew or learned any Yiddish beyond what he picked up on the street. Yet Rosenthal realized that sooner or later the *Times* would put his name on a story. He followed the Raskin example. The name tab on his message/mail box in the newsroom read, "Abraham Rosenthal." One day he changed it by inserting his middle initial M.

A day or so later Rosenthal covered the return of the battleship *New York*, a natural front-page story. It read, "The Battleship New York, sixth of her name, arrived yesterday, thirty-one months and four battles out of home port." (This was October 20, 1945.) The name above the story was "A. M. Rosenthal." And such was to remain his formal byline the remainder of his *Times* career.

Robert Schiffer, Rosenthal's CCNY classmate, had followed him to the *Times*, and they remained friendly. Before their first year on the paper had lapsed they were convinced, in the manner of reporters everywhere else in the world, that they could produce a better paper than the "old men" running the *Times*. "Each of us was better than the city editor, the managing editor, we *knew* we were." Rosenthal did his share of griping. He wanted better stories, he could have done any particular piece better than what appeared in the paper.

Rosenthal came in from assignment one day and had a heated dispute with David Joseph over how the story should be written. Although very new on the staff, Rosenthal was not modest about his talents. As Schiffer stated:

> Something touched off Abe's ire. He was furious. We walked out of the room and went into the john together. Abe went into one of the stalls and closed the door and continued his tirade against Joseph. "That no good son of a bitch . . ." The full range of abuse.
>
> As Abe was ranting away, the door opened and who should walk in but Joseph. I gulped, and I said very very loudly, "Hello, Mr. Joseph, how are you?"
>
> There was a dead silence in the john. I turned around and looked at Abe's stall. The door was still closed, and his feet had disappeared. Joseph did his business and left without saying a word.

Rosenthal's first major breakthrough as a reporter was one he fashioned himself, through quickness of wit. In 1946, Andrei Gromyko, the Soviet ambassador to the United Nations, walked out of the Security Council to prevent a vote directing the USSR to fulfill a wartime agreement to withdraw troops from northern Iran. Gromyko's walkout was the first by a Security Council member, and the fear was that the Soviet attitude could destroy the UN. Hence press attention was intense.

"Turner Catlege [the *Times* managing editor] got the idea it would
be a good thing to see what Gromyko did on his days off," Rosenthal
said. "Now the *Times* had a staff of about twenty persons covering the
UN session. Either because he liked me, or because he saw me when
he looked around the room, he pointed at me, and I came to his desk.

" 'Go over to the Soviet Consulate on 61st Street and hang around,'
he said. That was all. There was no real assignment. Well, I got to
61st Street, and about a hundred reporters were standing around,
talking to one another and looking at the buildings and acting bored.

"The big question was whether Mr. Gromyko would attend the
next meeting of the Security Council. Would he or wouldn't he? We
stood around and asked one another.

"About three o'clock Gromyko walked out of the Consulate, and
everyone gathered around and shouted, 'Are you going to the Council? Are you going to the Council?' 'Yes, I am,' he said, and he got into
his limousine. The other reporters rushed away to the telephone.
Gromyko's limousine started pulling away, and this cab came along. I
jumped in and I shouted, 'Follow that car!' That's something I'd
wanted to do all my life."

The Soviet limousine stopped briefly at the curb outside
Rockefeller Center, where the UN had temporary quarters, and a
man jumped out, and the car drove on. Gromyko obviously was going
elsewhere, so Rosenthal continued his surveillance by taxi. The limousine went south to the Battery, then back uptown to the Consulate,
Rosenthal's cab in discreet pursuit. "Obviously all the poor guy
wanted was to get some fresh air and get away from the reporters."
But of the hundreds of newsmen on the Consulate stake-out,
Rosenthal was the only person to follow Gromyko. "Everyone else
had rushed to the Security Council, thinking Gromyko would be
there." Thus Rosenthal gave confirmation to the oldest of journalistic
adages, "Never assume anything except a six percent mortgage."

Rosenthal's ingenuity produced a story that ran on the front page of
the *Times*, with an accompanying map, his most conspicuous presence yet at the *Times*. Theodore Bernstein, the assistant managing
editor who ran the "bullpen," the news desk that crafted the paper's
choice and display of stories each day, came over to congratulate the
young reporter—an honor rarely given for a local story.

But Rosenthal's most satisfying moment was yet to come. During
UN sessions Gromyko and his wife stayed at the Plaza Hotel. On an

impulse, the next morning Rosenthal rode the elevator up to his floor and knocked on the door. A surprised Mrs. Gromyko answered in her housecoat; she blinked at the sight of the unexpected visitor, but she invited Rosenthal in, and poured coffee for him, her husband and herself. When Gromyko left to walk the few blocks to the Consulate, Rosenthal strolled alongside him, not attempting questions because of the language barrier, perfectly content to be present.*

"The greatest moment of my life came when we turned the corner off Fifth Avenue into 61st Street and saw this mob of reporters waiting. 'There he is, there he is,' they began shouting. Then they began asking, 'Who is that kid with him?' "

"That kid," A. M. Rosenthal, soon was sent to the UN as a vacation replacement. "As a reward for doing well, they sent me over there for two weeks. I stayed there for nine years."

---

*An American diplomat who dealt with Gromyko several years later says the Soviet "understood spoken English, more or less," but handled even informal exchanges through an interpreter.

THREE

"Earning Less Than Clerks and Teletypists"

On one of his first days as a UN reporter Abe Rosenthal enjoyed silent laughter on the subway. He was bound for the Bronx campus of Hunter College, one of the temporary homes the UN occupied during its first years. His last trip to Hunter had been some two years before, when he had covered Board of Education meetings as a *Times* stringer.

He shook his head. The audacity of what had happened. Now he was going to Hunter to report on the organization through which the world hoped that the five great Allies of the war—the Americans, British, French, Chinese and Russians—could prevent another global conflict. From college budgets to atomic energy. Rosenthal chuckled again.

The UN's newsness made for an informality helpful to a novice reporter, for everyone mingled as a matter of course. Rosenthal was in the cafeteria line when a woman tapped his arm and asked for a pat of butter. He turned and looked face-on at Mrs. Eleanor Roosevelt, a

U.S. delegate. They chatted through the line and she invited him to eat with her at a wobbly table. For a man of Rosenthal's boundless curiosity, the UN was a constant delight. As he wrote in a 1985 *Times* article on the fortieth anniversary of the UN founding, "You had to be an ice cube not to be excited."

Rosenthal was no ice cube. He had learned to hustle for stories when the *Herald Tribune* paid him fifty cents an inch. Now veritably everywhere he looked he found a feature story. He had a haircut in the UN barber shop, and got some stories from the barber; he wrote a light article about dealing with the tonsorial demands of varied nationalities. He looked into the simultaneous translation booth and noticed that the interpreters could do needlework or read as they worked. Another story. The UN gave him an unlimited curriculum for self-education. At lunch he kept away from other Western reporters, or the staff of the U.S. Mission. Instead, he would find a Pakistani economist, or a Finnish lawyer, and turn lunch into a one-on-one seminar about their countries and their views. Rosenthal did not have to be taught the basic reportorial tool that people like best of all to talk about themselves and their ideas.

Rosenthal was the junior member of the UN bureau, which was headed by Thomas J. Hamilton, a foreign service veteran. But lack of seniority did not matter, at least in terms of stories. Eugene Rosenfeld, a press officer for the U.S. Mission (and a good friend for forty years afterwards) noted, "The *Times* was high-minded and public spirited about the United Nations which was supposed to save the world and all that. . . . There were five to seven people in the bureau, and they wrote an enormous number of words each day." Then as now, the *Times* could give importance to an event by the very fact of thorough coverage. Rosenthal's career benefitted immensely as a result.

But insecurity continued to plague Rosenthal, for he felt his work went unappreciated. Pleading with editor Catledge for a raise in March, 1947, after a year at the UN, he cited the range of stories he had covered, from disarmament through economic matters, and noted that half a dozen had been the lead article on page one, including several that were exclusive. But after three years on-staff he earned the minimum $77 weekly. "Until recently I was earning less than the clerks and teletypists and even now my salary is just about that level and a good deal less than any of the other staff members here." Catledge boosted his pay $5 weekly.

Even more irksome were constant squabbles over petty expenses. An auditor questioned $2 for phone calls from his home to UN headquarters. Rosenthal patiently replied that he made calls before going to work because "it puts me on top of the news even before I leave the house. . . ." He had to write a formal memorandum defending fifty cents in tips to a waiter and cab driver. Catledge chided him for being the only UN reporter who put in expense chits for bridge tolls.

Cost-controls are wise in any business, but the piddling amounts for which Rosenthal was taken to task seemed accusations that he was cadging pennies from the *Times*. Given Rosenthal's total devotion to his job, and his willingness to spend his days off making calls to the UN, the queries seemed to him nit-picking. He told one friend he was ready to take a job with the UN. Then, in mid-1950, the fact that he was a junior man in the bureau gave him his single most important story from the UN, and dashed for the moment any thought of his leaving the *Times*.

On Sunday, June 25, Rosenthal awoke to telephoned news that the North Korean army had swept into South Korea. Rosenthal had duty that weekend, so he hurried to Lake Success, Long Island, where the UN then had headquarters in an old defense plant. His story led the *Times* the next morning:

> LAKE SUCCESS, June 25—The United Nations Security Council found North Korea guilty today of breaking the peace, demanded that the Communist government pull back its troops at once, and called for an immediate cease-fire throughout Korea.

The three-column account was a blend of narrative and interpretation, with Rosenthal detailing how various amendments to the resolution were achieved during the day. So confident was Rosenthal of his sources—and the *Times* of Rosenthal—that he wrote a key sentence of the story on his own authority, without a hint of attribution: "The resolution carried with it the clear implication that the United Nations would move to take stronger measures if North Korea flouted the Council."

Although bureau chief Tom Hamilton took over the main Korean story, Rosenthal wrote continuously on war issues for the next three years. He saw the war also as a way of getting a foreign assignment. On July 2, he wrote to Catledge: "In the event the *Times* decides to send more reporters abroad to cover the present emergency or subsequent fighting, I should like to be considered available to go anytime." Catledge declined. Rosenthal groused: he was as good a reporter, and twice the writer, as Hamilton, and yet the *Times* kept him cooped in Lake Success. So on slow afternoons he and William Atwood of the New York *Herald Tribune* staged their own "police action," firing paper clips with rubber bands over the partitions separating their offices. "Kid stuff, we liked to horse around," Atwood said.

But the snub did not dull Rosenthal's curiosity. In August, 1952, he sat through a dull session of the Security Council. He noticed an unfamiliar man behind Jacob A. Malik, the Soviet representative. His curiosity piqued, Rosenthal casually told a Soviet acquaintance, "That guy looks like a newcomer."

"His name is Roschin," the Russian replied. Because he had done his homework, Rosenthal knew that a man named Alexai A. Roschin ran the UN division of the Soviet Foreign Ministry. Normally he stayed in Moscow. Why, then, the UN appearance?

To his surprise, the Russian he had spoken to earlier approached him in the delegates lounge. "You seem interested in our delegation," he said. "You might be interested to know that Malik is being replaced by Zorin" (referring to Valerian A. Zorin, a deputy foreign minister).

Rosenthal realized he had a scoop, but one that must be confirmed, and quietly. He did not trust his Russian source. The Russians have the nasty habit of giving unliked reporters false stories, thus hurting their credibility. Rosenthal thought of trying to find a private moment with Malik. No, this would not do; once one newspaperman approached Malik, everyone ran over. So Rosenthal shared his secret with a friend on the UN secretariat; could he obtain conformation? The man went to Malik and said casually, "I understand you are leaving." Indeed he was, Malik said, a note had just gone to the Secretary General, although the USSR had made no announcement.

Story in hand, Rosenthal fidgeted the rest of the day, hoping no other reporter would stumble onto the information. Once Malik left Lake Success, Rosenthal hurried to 43rd Street to write his story. He did not wish a shoulder-peeper at Lake Success to steal his exclusive.

The Malik story did not make a ripple in history; it would have been announced in due course. But Rosenthal's success in getting it first, and accurately, relied upon two things. He had gotten close enough to a Soviet official to receive a tip on a major UN story. And second, he had a secretariat source who could give the necessary confirmation. In his later years as an editor Rosenthal returned to these lessons time and again in tutoring young reporters: Find the people who actually *do* things, and become friendly with them, and let them know who you are. You won't need them every day, maybe not any day. But get down to the working level, and develop the sources, and you'll be doing your job.

Abe Rosenthal and women discovered each other at about the same time he went to the UN as a reporter. His status as a *Times* reporter carried a certain allure, and women of several continents shared a dinner table with him, and sometimes more. Physically, Rosenthal remained somewhat of a mess, with unkempt hair and baggy clothes. But a colleague of the era suggested, "A journalistic Woody Allen?" Something about Rosenthal's forlornness attracted women, "a puppy waiting to be mothered," the colleague said. Rosenthal had an intense affair with a woman who also reported for the *Times*, and friends expected them to marry; then, suddenly, the relationship ended.

Soon Rosenthal became the constant escort of Ann Burke, an Irish-American woman of ivory skin and blond hair, plumpish but pretty. Ann Burke came from an impoverished family, and as a small child she suffered from rickets, caused by dietary deficiency. Now she and sister Kathleen worked on the *Times* news desk at 43rd Street and at the UN on temporary assignments. Abe commenced a serious courtship of Ann Burke.

Several persons discouraged the romance; one editor who knew of Rosenthal's ambition to be a foreign correspondent told him bluntly that marriage would kill his chances for assignment out of the country. Another said, Marry her, but keep it a secret until you are sent abroad. Then make the announcement. There was also the religious question.

Gene Rosenfeld of the U.S. Mission had noticed that "Abe and Ann had become sort of a thing," so he was not surprised when Rosenthal asked him aside one day for a private talk.

"How are you and Chris making out?" Rosenthal asked, referring to Rosenfeld's wife.

The question puzzled Rosenfeld. "How do you mean? We have our own place, we like one another, we . . ."

Rosenthal waved his hand. "No, no, I mean, you're Jewish, she's Christian, how does that go?"

"Abe, are you thinking of getting married?"

"Yeah."

As it turned out, Rosenfeld discovered, Ann was "not terribly Catholic, and Abe was about as Jewish as I am, which is not much. What they were doing, they were collecting valid endorsements." In the end, for fear of offending Sarah Rosenthal, they wed almost in secrecy, on March 9, 1949, at St. Catherine of Siena on East 66th Street, with only Ann's parents and her sister present. Only then did Rosenthal tell his mother. What she said in reaction to his marriage to a *shiksa* (a gentile), is something that remains private to him. But three days later, she was present when Abe and Ann repeated their vows at a civil ceremony at the Warwick Hotel. Both Schiffer and Bernard Kalb, Abe's *Times* colleagues, served as best men, then everyone went downtown to Rosenthal's apartment in Greenwich Village, a "teeny little place," as Chris Rosenfeld described it, with perhaps thirty-five persons crammed into a room and a half.

The religious difference proved no barrier, for the Rosenthals raised their sons in ecumenical fashion, not insisting that they become either Christians or Jews. Ann continued to go to Mass on Sunday; Rosenthal seldom went to synagogue. Son Jon became attracted to Buddhism as a child in India. Andrew went through a Shinto ceremony in Japan at age four. Daniel, the youngest, was to marry a Jewish girl, but in a civil ceremony. Concisely, Judaism as a *religion* had little appeal to Rosenthal. But as a moral and political force, as exemplified by Israel, it was to be of considerable import in his later professional life.

As he proved himself at the UN, Rosenthal pushed for a foreign assignment. The *Times* foreign service was the cream of the paper. The *Times* front page of those years carried from fifteen to eighteen stories daily, more than half from abroad. The *Times* had yet to develop a national staff of any substance; hence a reporter who wished to cover anything other than New York news had to go abroad.

Several factors worked against any such assignment for Rosenthal. The *Times* had hired many men to cover the war, and they had first call on foreign assignments when peace came. Another factor—an ironic one, given Rosenthal's attitude towards religion—was that he was Jewish. The journalist Daniel Schorr received frank affirmation of the *Times* policy. Schorr had gone to the *Times* after the war and asked for employment abroad. Theodore Bernstein, the deputy managing editor, told him no, that the war left the bureaus "inflated." He suggested that Schorr pick an area of Europe, gain experience, and come back in a few years. With that bare promise Schorr moved to Holland, and from 1948 to 1953 he covered much of Europe, chiefly as a stringer for the *Christian Science Monitor*.

In 1952 Schorr returned to the *Times* for a job. Could he cover local news? he was asked. Well, that was not his desire, but he would try. During a three-day trial Schorr found a story that led the paper, the first statement by New York parks czar Robert Moses about the arts complex that eventually became Lincoln Center. Yet no offer of a job came, and Schorr returned to Europe and commenced a long career with CBS News.

Several years later Ted Bernstein and Emanuel Freedman, the *Times* foreign editor, took Schorr to dinner and with obvious embarrassment told him that they owed him an explanation. He had been derailed by a "no more Jews" policy dictated by editor Catledge and publisher Sulzberger. The staff contained so many Jewish reporters that Catledge feared criticism if the *Times* had to mobilize for coverage of renewed war in the Middle East. So the *Times* had an informal freeze on the hiring of any new Jewish reporters, or the dispatch of Jewish correspondents abroad.

Schorr did not argue with Bernstein and Freedman (both of whom were Jewish). But he thought the *Times* policy morally repugnant. The United States had just ended a war against a Nazi regime that evoked vicious anti-Semitism as state policy. And now the *Times*, with Jewish owners, used religion as a hiring test.

"This was not one of American journalism's nobler moments," Schorr said.

His Jewishness apart, something far more important worked against a foreign assignment for Rosenthal. He gravely offended a *Times* personage named Cyrus L. Sulzberger. The foreign affairs columnist for the *Times*, Cy Sulzberger seemed to know everone in Europe above the rank of deputy cabinet minister, and did not bother with anyone of lesser office. He was family, a nephew of publisher Arthur Hays Sulzberger. He had deliberately made his career on his own, chiefly through Washington reportage for United Press in the 1930's. He went to Europe, and joined the family newspaper only when the war began. He specialized in the Balkans, an area beloved by no other Western correspondent, and he won a Pulitzer Prize for articles that made sense of the hopelessly-convoluted politics there.

After the war, Sulzberger and his Greek wife Marina settled in Paris. Socially Sulzberger operated as a major figure in Parisian diplomatic society. He considered himself a part of the power structure as well as a journalist. For instance, his good friend General Alfred Guenter, the NATO commander, did not like the annual report written for him one year, so he had Sulzberger do a rewrite. Sulzberger cheerfully did so—and then praised the report in his column for wisdom and foresight. A foreign dignitary of any sense who came through Paris sought an audience with Sulzberger. In sum, Sulzberger was a man of much real as well as self-importance. And he also held veto power over the assignment of foreign correspondents.

In 1949 the United Nations General Assembly met in Paris. In those early years, the assembly was a floating road show, rotating its annual sessions between major capitals. Because he knew Paris, Sulzberger took charge of arrangements for the *Times* people, and he booked them into his favorite hotel, where the manager was a personal friend. He soon received a call from the manager, who was so outraged as to be incoherent. Never in his life had he been so insulted. He would not tolerate crudeness in his hostelry, and he wanted the *Times* party out, and immediately.

Sulzberger calmed the man and got the basics of the complaint. One Mr. Rosenthal claimed to have left traveller's checks in his room totalling about $25. When he returned and could not find them, he accused the maid of theft. The argument escalated into a loud, yelling confrontation during which Rosenthal questioned the honesty of the French in general and of the maid and manager in specific.

Earnest apologies by Sulzberger calmed the manager, who relented on his eviction threat. Sulzberger took Rosenthal aside and quietly told him that *Times* correspondents did not behave in such *gauche* fashion. Making a protest does not require one to behave like a fool. Rosenthal protested he had not been excessive; that the cash meant a lot to someone on his salary. Sulzberger sighed, for Rosenthal had not caught his point. He said nothing further to Rosenthal; he dismissed him as a young and noisy fool who was a discredit to the paper. But he sent a letter to Manny Freedman, the foreign editor, in which he said, Do not send this boorish boy Rosenthal into any area in which I must work. He has the propensity to disgrace *The New York Times*.

Not until years later did Rosenthal learn that his outburst caused a

five-year delay in his foreign assignment. He never forgave
Sulzberger, and in later years, when he rose to authority on the
Times, he found the opportunity for revenge.

Rosenthal continued to plead for assignment abroad, in letters
brimming with frustration. He wrote Catledge in September 1952:

> You know that I've been plugging away for a European assignment
> for five years now. Sometimes I get pretty discouraged about the
> chances of getting a European berth and get that helpless feeling that
> time is passing by and that the goal is as far away as ever. . . .
>
> Why all the eagerness for a European assignment? It is not dissatis-
> faction with the United Nations or anything about the job. . . . It is
> simply that a permanent assignment abroad is what I have been point-
> ing to for as long as I have been in the newspaper business. . . .

Catledge bucked Rosenthal's letter to foreign editor Freedman, who
told him in essence to forget Europe, that positions there were reserved for more senior correspondents. If Rosenthal really wished to
go abroad, he should look to Asia or Africa. What Freedman left
unstated was that these continents were backwaters where a correspondent would live in abysmal conditions and spend much of his
time on the road. Undeterred, Rosenthal on November 17 suggested
India as his first assignment. ". . . [M]y personal and professional interest have centered on India. I have a good many Indian friends now
in government service in their homeland. I have made it my business
to become as fully informed as possible on Indian politics, diplomacy
and personalities. To balance that, I have made every effort to get to
know as many Pakistanis as possible and to study Pakistani affairs.
. . ." (India and Pakistan were then girding for their second war since
the 1947 partition of India.) Again, nothing happened; Freedman
counselled Rosenthal to be patient.

And he was patient, for almost two more years, during which he
complained intermittently about the lack of merit raises (by January
1953 he earned $176 weekly) and continued to get stories on the front
page of the paper. Rosenthal began to look elsewhere. He sold several articles to *Collier's* Magazine, one of which his old journalism
professor Irving Rosenthal decided warranted the award of his long-
abandoned degree from CCNY; he did a pamphlet for the United
States Association for the United Nations; he asked journalism cronies
who wrote for periodicals whether one could make a living by free-

lance writing. One friend suggests that Rosenthal had decided that when he reached his tenth-year anniversary at the *Times*, he would leave if he did not have a foreign assignment.

His pleas finally succeeded. On October 28, 1955, Turner Catledge wrote a short note to publisher Arthur Hays Sulzberger: "I have just had a talk with Abe Rosenthal, and he is happy to go to New Delhi. He thinks he will be able to be there in three or four weeks, his family to follow later—after he gets his feet on the ground."

Rosenthal left New York via TWA at four o'clock in the afternoon on Monday, November 29, for connections via London, Amsterdam and Karachi on KLM and Air India. A cable in the *Times* archives formally announced his arrival as a foreign correspondent on December 6:

> PRESS TIMES NY
>> FREEDMAN EXTRUMBULL ROSENTHAL ARRIVED
>> MIDDLETON*

For the next nine years variations of that terse cable were to report Rosenthal's departure from or arrival in cities from Dakar to Seoul to Leopoldville. A.M. Rosenthal now had stationery printed with the words "foreign correspondent" under his name. He had moved a significant step farther from being just another lame kid at CCNY.

---

*Cablese. In translation, "To Emanuel Freedman, foreign desk, *New York Times*, from Robert Trumbull [the then-*Times* correspondent in New Delhi] Rosenthal is in town and ready for duty." "Middleton" indicated the cable went through the *Times* wire room in London, because messages so routed qualified for the so-called "Empire rate," which was a fraction of regular commercial charges. Any message routed through London bore the signature of the resident correspondent, in this case Drew Middleton.

India: "Deepest in My Heart"

Times managing editor Turner Catledge gave minimal guidance to his new foreign correspondent. But what he *had* given was valuable. Several days before Rosenthal left, Catledge took him into his back office and poured the first of countless drinks of whiskey the men were to share for the next decades, and said he was tired of the stuffiness of *Times* writing. When the *Times* hired Catledge away from the Baltimore *Sun* in the 1930's he studied the paper in advance to get an idea of the writing style. "I became very expert at eliminating periods and putting in commas and conjunctions," he said. "Oh, I could write a hundred-word sentence without any trouble at all. And then it got to the point where I could hardly write less."

Avoid this trap, Catledge told Rosenthal. "Just write me a letter about what's going on and take off the 'Dear Turner' and you'll have a pretty good story."

Rosenthal followed the advice. "I found that if I was writing for a good friend back home, I was really writing for myself, and if it was clear enough for the two of us, it would be reasonably clear for the reader."

India gripped Rosenthal's soul from the beginning, and its people and culture made it "deepest in my heart of all foreign countries." Given Rosenthal's emotionalism and tendency to equate his own interests with those of all *Times* readers, India was to receive coverage far disproportionate to its importance once he became an editor. A trivial happening in Bombay excited him more than a significant story in Brooklyn. A junior editor once complained mildly about the space given India. "You don't know what you are talking about," a deputy foreign editor growled back. "India is damned important, and if you don't believe it, check the number of stories in the *Times Index*."

The India in which Rosenthal arrived in 1956 had just won independence after a long struggle against British rule. India was unique in being a nation without any real power, other than the overwhelming mass of its population. To the West it was the "world's largest democracy," a test of whether self-government was possible amidst racial and religious strife and grinding poverty. Although Rosenthal came to recognize the "full catalogue of Indian faults, from smugness to wishfulness to self-pity," the very uniqueness of the society overwhelmed him.

With two small sons in the family, Rosenthal found a house large enough both for living and for an office, at 30, Nizamuddin East, which he rented for $210 a month. The Rosenthal's next door neighbor, Martha Keehn, wife of an official in a private U.S. advisory program, noted the arrival in a letter home: "VERY nice people and our new neighbors with dysentery troubles needing a little advice on what you eat and what you don't."

Characteristically, Rosenthal spent his first days arguing with New York auditors about his expense allotment, and the *Times*'s refusal to pay part of his house rent. He griped about prices of everything from baby cereal (sixteen cents in New York, sixty-three cents in New Delhi) to toilet tissue (twelve versus thirty cents) and pipe tobacco (fifteen versus seventy cents). Servant costs doubled from $15 for a part-time maid in New York to $30 for a full crew in New Delhi. "There is no such thing as a part-time servant and the subdivision is rigidly insisted upon," Rosenthal wrote Richard Burritt, Catledge's deputy for administration. "One will watch the children but not dust or clean. Another will sweep and wash floors but do nothing else— but nothing." He did not want servants. "But we have a charcoal stove. No American woman can use the thing. So we have a cook, about half as good as Ann." New York resisted, so Rosenthal wrote

two angry pages, now bringing up medical expenses and the necessity
for his family to leave New Delhi during the hot season for the
Kashmir hills. "Nobody forced me to take the job; I wanted it, and I
still want it." But out-of-pocket expenses "cost me a lot of money and
left me skinny in the bank." Unless more money was forthcoming
"the Indian equivalent of the sheriff may be after me. . . ." Rosenthal
eventually wheedled a bit more expense money. But once again he
felt that he was being mistreated.

Always quick of temper, Rosenthal became a terror to Indian bureaucratic underlings. He could not adapt to the *laissez faire* pace of
business. When the Indian cable office forwarded his messages by
mail, rather than phone, he created a scene that brought nervous security guards into the office. New York editors learned that he must
be treated gingerly; that he did not understand, much less enjoy,
joshing notes. A picture editor suggested that when he took photographs, subjects be positioned so that poles or trees did not appear to
be spouting from their heads. Rosenthal wrote a laborious and pained
(and unnecessary) two-page defense. In matters involving his work—
and perceived prestige—Rosenthal was humorless. And defensively
he drew tighter within himself. To Indian officials he might be "Mr.
Rosenthal of the *Times*" but to 43rd Street he was a reporter subject
to chivvying on his expenses.

But the same touchiness made him an aggressive reporter. In 1956
the Soviet leaders Nikita Khruschev and Nikolai Bulganin visited India. Because of massive crowds and police, Rosenthal and other newsmen had trouble staying within range of the visitors. So Rosenthal hid
his press credentials and decided to "encourage the world to think I
was a Russian. . . ." He told his driver to stay close to the official en-
tourage.

> Everytime a policeman stopped me or tried to bully my driver out of
> line, I would lean forward and say sternly; "*Gospidine Presidatse, ya
> vas lublu.*" Police resistance melted. The big thing was to stick to it.

The phrase means, "Mr. President, I love you," and Rosenthal said it
with such authority that no Indian dared question him. Encouraged,
Rosenthal approached a Soviet interpreter and asked about an exclusive interview with Khrushchev. The interpreter repeated the request to another man in the party.

"The man immediately began snapping insults about Americans, told me that he expected nothing good from the likes of us, and so on. I told him that I was shocked to see he had left his Geneva spirit behind and then, just to round off the conversation, called him an idiot."

The interpreter "turned white," and the next day Rosenthal learned the man he called an idiot was Ivan Serov, head of the Soviet KGB. "Serov immediately pointed me out to his boys," Rosenthal related. "After that, all over India and Afghanistan . . . whenever I was near the center of attention, I never lacked for attentive, muscular company."

By happenstance, the Rosenthals' good friends from their UN days, Chris and Gene Rosenfeld, were assigned to the U.S. Embassy in New Delhi months after their own arrival. As embassy press officer, Rosenfeld felt Rosenthal's strength was that "he was interviewing persons that other reporters and our political officers [in the embassy] weren't touching. He was out in what the Indians called the *mofussil*, the country out away from the cities and the suburbs, where you saw the bullocks and the sacred cows, the real India."

The *Times* bureau was organized to permit travel. Rosenthal inherited an office factotum, T. V. Rajagopalan, who had worked for the paper since 1947, and who did leg work and routine reporting. Such a deputy is essential to a foreign correspondent; he knows the local languages and he has sources a newcomer would spend years developing. He pays bills, deals with bureaucrats, and directs stringers in the bureau's territory. These persons—every *Times* bureau has them—are the skeleton of the foreign service.

So Rosenthal travelled constantly. In a *Times Talk* article he joshed about riding a horse to a remote village, and walking three miles behind the bier of the King of Nepal. His personal complaint against socialism was that it "eliminated the first-class coach," meaning a train trip forced him to sit on a bench with no drinking water or dinner. He joked that he spent half his time in DC-3s, the workhorse plane that got over steep Indian mountains. He contrived an excuse to go deep into Pakistan so he could file a story datelined The Khyber Pass.

He also made wide circles in peripheral countries included in his beat. Colombo. Kabul. Kuala Lumpur. Katmandu. New Guinea. ("Mud. Pygmies and mud. Dutchmen and mud. Missionaries and mud. Me and mud. Mud. Mud," he wrote in *Times Talk*). He spent a short assignment in Vietnam when the regular man vacationed. ". . . [T]he government fought a rebel gangster army that has been swaggering arrogantly in the city. It was a time of local terror, when the rebels lobbed their mortar shells from across a canal into the city." The "rebel gangster army" turned out to be the Viet Cong, a force of more importance than Rosenthal's dismissive description implied.

By going into the field Rosenthal avoided a trap that snares many foreign correspondents—reliance upon the American Embassy as a primary source of information. He did not shun the embassy altogether. Rosenthal was aggressive in demanding access to persons within the embassy when he wanted information; such was his right as a newsman. He liked Rosenfeld as a friend, yet he made plain his first loyalty was to the *Times*. He told Rosenfeld early, "Look, I love you, but if you get in my way on a story, I'll run right over you."

Ann Rosenthal meanwhile stayed in the stifling heat and discomfort of New Delhi, caring for two small sons. Chris Rosenfeld remembered an exception to Abe's rule of not purchasing anything from the embassy commissary, a privilege routinely granted to American newsmen. Rosenthal pointedly told many persons he would not use the privilege. Ann dissented. She asked Chris Rosenfeld to buy her baby food, which otherwise had to be imported at enormous expense, or bought locally as an inferior brand. "Ann had no qualms about stuff for her children," Chris Rosenfeld said.

Abe's travels also denied Ann regular access to the parties that made New Delhi bearable for Western wives. When not travelling, Rosenthal wrote articles, for the *Times* Magazine, for *Times Talk*, for *Collier's*. He did much work from home. "Ann guarded him when he was at work like he was the Crown Jewels of London. She was the total security guard. . . . His work was numero uno," Chris Rosenfeld said. Ann would go to the occasional party alone, and try to socialize. She could be happy on her own. But she kept away from any organized activities, such as the American Women's Club of Delhi.

Ann Rosenthal had other problems. In December, 1955, late into her third pregnancy, she encountered "serious difficulties." As Rosenthal wrote Manny Freedman, "It turns out that she is an Rh negative [blood type]. We did not know this, since our doctor at home had never bothered to inform us of the fact, a terrible piece of negligence." In the U.S. the problem "would not be terribly serious. But here, there are no decent facilities for blood examination or transfusion." He rushed home from Afghanistan before Christmas to arrange to have a plane fly her and the baby, expected in February, to Bombay if necessary. Catledge had the *Times* medical expert, Dr.

Howard Rush, inquire about an American military medical flight and he authorized Rosenthal to charter a plane at *Times* expense. The episode ended happily. On February 25, 1956, the *Times* wire carried a message:

CATLEDGE FREEDMAN EX ROSENTHAL ANDREW ROSENTHAL
ARRIVED TWENTY FIFTH STOP
MOTHER SON WELL FATHER TOO.*

But Rosenthal's travels meant that Ann Rosenthal spent much of the Indian years alone with her small sons. New Delhi was not pleasant for a woman. Rosenthal jested in one letter, "Every restaurant in this town should have a large sign outside: dysentery served within." Reality deserved no jests. Periodic floods drove water into homes and did horrible things to the primitive sewerage system. Martha Keehn, the Rosenthal's neighbor on Nizamuddin, wrote her parents about six inches of mud in her living room, and an encephalitis epidemic. She, too, was pregnant, and she feared viral damage; she wrote of the wife of a Western correspondent who had one child born retarded, and another without a palate. Ann Rosenthal was to tell a New York friend years later that her years in New Delhi were "the worst time of my life." She feared for the survival of her small sons. She knew Abe's job dictated travel, but she felt lonely and isolated. It was in India that she came to realize the relative priorities her husband assigned to *The New York Times* and to his family.

But there were more pleasant times, the summer months, when the Western community in New Delhi moved en masse north to the mountains of Kashmir. The Rosenthals and Rosenfelds took adjacent houseboats on Nagin Lake, near Srinagar. The wives and children would stay the summer—both women nursed babies one season—while the husbands came up from Delhi on weekends, via a four-hour DC-3 flight through Bonnyhall Pass, 10,000 feet high.

The Rosenthals' preferred boat was the *New Eagle*, accompanied by a cookboat and a smaller boat, a *shikara*, the Indian equivalent of a gondola. The *New Eagle* had a bedroom, dining room, and a verandah, all "properly furnished in Kashmiri-Victorian massiveness," Rosenthal wrote. Rosenthal liked to take the *shikara* ashore, and rent

*Andrew Rosenthal followed his father into journalism, working in Moscow as an Associated Press correspondent. After Abe's retirement, he joined the *Times* in the Washington bureau.

a pony and ride into the mountains, for the joy of looking down into the meadows. He liked most to swim in the cool lake, and to forget about the heat, and the complex politics of New Delhi.

In New York, Rosenthal had realized the importance of *The New York Times* in his own country. In India he recognized the increasing international stature of the *Times*. Chris Rosenfeld, who monitored Indian official and public opinion from the embassy, says, "*The New York Times* was beginning to supplement *The Times* of London as the world's most important newspaper in the minds of Indians. The man from *The Times* of London historically had been more than a reporter; he was a representative of the British Empire. So was the BBC [British Broadcasting Corporation] man. But given India's increasing economic dependence on Washington, *The New York Times* now became the most important outlet and source of news." Hence Indian officials spoke freely with Rosenthal, for they recognized his newspaper as a conduit to Washington.

Copy editors on the *Times* foreign desk had ambivalent views about Rosenthal. Most, if not all, admired his feature articles on Indian life. Others wished he would report more hard news, or at least attempt analyses of what was really happening in the Nehru government.

Rosenthal, however, wished to depict India as an upbeat country, one in which the United Nations and such private groups as the Ford Foundation could foster democracy. He believed in India. In one of the last conversations Rosenthal had with Gene Rosenfeld before leaving the country, he said, "I wouldn't invest $5 of my own money in India, but I would invest $5 million of my government's." But he had disdain for journalists who overlooked the flaws of the subcontinent. After one trip to Afghanistan he wrote Manny Freedman, "The country is run by a ferocious dictatorship and naturally I mentioned that important fact several times. I see Jim Michener wrote a piece about the place for *Reader's Digest*, all about cute tea shops and beautiful children, without mentioning such ugly things as beatings and jailings. That's like going into Moscow and concentrating on those subways of theirs." Because he wrote of the dictatorship Rosenthal had "no idea whether the Afghans will let me in again." He did not care; he would write the truth, and not worry about visas.

In May, 1957, Rosenthal came to New York on home leave and talked about his future with Catledge and deputy Robert E. Garst. For family and health reasons he wished to leave India; too, the country was no longer fresh. They discussed numerous possibilities for future assignments, including Rome, Vienna and Athens. Garst reported on these talks in a memo to Catledge in May, 1957:

> . . . [M]y feeling is that his chief interest is in the Mideast and that, if the attitude toward Jewish reporters should change in that area, he would welcome Cairo or any other Mideast job. . . . [H]e liked a roving assignment and if . . . he were sent to Athens, he would like freedom to cover adjacent countries.
>
> His ultimate aim . . . is to return after say ten years abroad to the U.N. Bureau, preferably as the chief of that bureau.

In later letters to Manny Freedman, the foreign editor, Rosenthal listed priorities as Tokyo, Rome and Bonn, or as second-man in London. Freedman replied that correspondents in the first two cities seemed set; if Bonn did open, "some men senior to you would have to be considered first." As an alternative, Freedman offered Poland, replacing Sydney Gruson. Freedman described the post:

> Poland, as I am sure you know, is *the* critical country in the ideological struggle now going on in Eastern Europe. There is more information available in Warsaw than anywhere else behind the Iron Curtain, and the flow of news is steady and interesting. . . . If you should settle in Warsaw, you would not be confined to coverage of Poland alone. You would be expected to participate in the coverage of the whole satellite area . . . with the Vienna and Belgrade correspondents.

Rosenthal accepted the offer but only after two and one-half pages of various complaints. Warsaw would be "rather difficult living." That he could overcome, for given his choice between hardship and a good story and a comfortable city and no story, Rosenthal chose the former. ". . . [E]ven the most enjoyable city would pall quickly without a good story. I've never thought of Scandinavia, for instance, because I know smorgasbord would hold me just so long and then I would get awfully itchy for something to write about. . . . A good story . . . makes up for the city. . . . A marginal story in a marginal city I think might make for a rather grumpy Rosenthal." Then Rosenthal seized upon a line in Freedman's letter, about "men senior to you" having priority for such assignments as Bonn and vented his continuing insecurity about his status:

I had comforted myself all this time with the thought that I was at least senior enough to be considered for almost any reportorial job. If seniority is based on the time a man serves abroad, of course this is not true. But the fact is that I have been a reporter on the *Times* for fourteen years and that twelve of them have been spent under the foreign desk service covering diplomatic or foreign news. That's a heftily respectable chunk of time and experience, I think. . . .

This is terribly important to me. . . . I would like to stay a reporter abroad for the indefinite future. But, still, every man wants to think that there is a certain amount of upward and onward in his own field. In my case, that consists entirely of having the feeling of security that I would be considered for some of the larger-bureau jobs when they come open and even perhaps that the *Times* had some such thoughts in mind for me. I would hate to think this was a day-dream.

So once again the Rosenthals began packing their household goods for a move halfway around the world. Rosenthal's work in India had been oustanding; persons in the newsroom who cared not a whit about the country had come to look for the sparkling reportage beneath his byline. Yet Rosenthal could not shake the nagging feeling that *The New York Times* did not appreciate him or his work.

FIVE

Poland: "Probed Too Deeply"

Poland in 1958 was a grim, shabby country, its people suppressed beneath an omnipresent Soviet yoke. The 1956 uprising gave the Poles a brief taste of post-Stalin liberalization, quickly betrayed by Wladyslaw Gomulka, the party boss and chief of state. Himself a former inmate of a Stalin prison, Gomulka took office with broad popular support. But within two years he willingly returned Poland to Soviet domination. The Red Army's demonstrated readiness to crush dissidence left Poles resigned to misery.

Abe Rosenthal found no affection for Poland. He had fleeting empathy for the nationalistic fervor of some of the people, even for local Communists who ran their country under Moscow's *de facto* overlordship. But as he wrote years later, "There was a stone in my heart that prevented me from becoming a sentimentalist, which was to the good, and which created the sense of separatedness from an abused people, which I always had wished I did not feel. That stone was the realization that there was a miasma of anti-Semitism in Polish history." Poland's savagery towards its own Jews, a hatred far pre-dating Naziism, sickened Rosenthal.

He, Ann and the three boys settled into a small house on Chodkiewicze Street, modest by the standards they had enjoyed in India. Rosenthal had an office there and in the dowdy old Hotel Orbis Bristol, where Western correspondents lived or worked, for lack of any choice.

The on-going story in Poland involved the attempt of reformists to keep alive the impetus for change they had stirred in 1956. The veteran diplomat Jacob D. Beam, the American ambassador in Warsaw, says these reformists formed a "mutually profitable" alliance with foreign correspondents. "In studied disregard of party discipline, they told key foreign correspondents about what was going on within the local cells. These reports, which were played back to Poland by radio from abroad, helped disseminate the reformers' views, their aims, and the nature of their opposition." The American embassy encouraged such reporting because it provided material for Radio Free Europe. As Beam states, "If the CIA had done no more to further this cause than providing the facilities of Radio Free Europe (which it then secretly financed) it would have justified its existence."

Abe replaced Sydney Gruson, a dour-faced Irishman in his early forties who had joined the *Times* during the war in London, a rising star of the *Times* foreign service. Now in his second tour in Poland, Gruson knew the country and its people well. "The Poles knew me as a trustworthy journalist who never did them dirt. They turned to me rather than the Embassy when they wished to speak. The Poles wanted an opening to the West if the Russians marched." The reformists arranged regular off-the-record briefings for Western correspondents. "They in effect used us, in the best sense of the word."

Given Gruson's long stay in Poland, he and his then-wife Flora Lewis, the columnist, felt the country could come out of the post-Stalinist period liberalized. It was into this milieu that Rosenthal arrived as Gruson's replacement. As Gruson said, "This was Rosenthal's first look at a Communist country, and he was pop-eyed. But he is a quick learner." So quick, in fact, that Rosenthal delivered a correcting lecture to Gruson veritably within hours of his arrival.

Daniel Schorr, who was reporting from West Berlin for CBS News, happened to be in Warsaw when the Rosenthals arrived, and he attended a party the Grusons gave them at the Orbis Bristol. "Sydney began expounding about the liberal atmosphere in Poland, and how 'this is really becoming a liberal society, with freedom of speech.'

"Abe cut him short. 'Sydney, they don't have freedom of *speech*—they have freedom of *talking*, that's all. They give you an illusion. They talk to one another, but if they start sounding off publicly about the regime, they get arrested, just as they would in Russia.' Well, he stopped Sydney, and that proved to be a very perceptive line."

Schorr was surprised that a newly-arrived correspondent would "lecture" an experienced predecessor, especially in front of other persons. (Gruson did not remember the incident cited by Schorr, but he added, "I covered Poland—he covered Poland, and we had different ways of writing about the country. He could humanize better than anyone I've ever known in the business.")

Gruson made the rounds of sources with Rosenthal, then they went to Poznan to cover a demonstration at a factory. Back at the hotel, Gruson stretched out on the bed and began reading.

"Aren't you going to write?" Rosenthal asked.

"No, you are the correspondent, *you* write," Gruson said. He felt it important that he get out of the newcomer's way as swiftly as possible.

So Rosenthal began working his new beat, and he did well. Ambassador Beam soon became most impressed with the correspondent. Rosenthal "got right to the point in his writing. In fact, at times he seemed to have better insight on Gomulka than we did. Gomulka was caught between his own people and the Russians, and he was such an obsessed man that he was going absolutely crazy. The Russians could not do business with him." But as in India, Rosenthal remained aloof from the "official" American community. For reasons Beam never understood, "he was one of the most dour men I've ever met. He went around with a constant frown on his face, as if he was unhappy about something."

Rosenthal quickly put together a string of Polish contacts, however. Several months after Rosenthal arrived in Warsaw, his old friend William Atwood, now writing for *Look* Magazine, came into Poland with his wife. "We didn't know a soul in the city except for the Rosenthals, so we called them up, and stayed with them for a day or so. 'You want to meet some people?' Rosenthal asked. 'Sure,' I said." Abe busied himself on the phone. "He rounded up the top journalists and party people and politicians, and we had a fine time, talking. I did much work in a short time because of what Abe did for me." Atwood thought Rosenthal's quick immersion all the more remarkable be-

cause he knew only a few words of German and Yiddish, which luck-
ily enabled him to converse, more or less, with the Poles. "He spoke
'waiter Polish,' that's about all."

Western correspondents worked in Eastern Europe those years on
borrowed time; going beyond surface events for hard analytical reporting meant summary expulsion. So reporters had to choose.
Avoiding controversial stories meant they could work in the country,
and no medium wished to be *persona non grata* in the event of a major news story. Hence, some men "wrote for their visas"—often, it
must be stressed, at the express direction of their employer. Schorr
says, "This means pulling their punches to be sure they'd be welcomed back. But this can also mean your byline appears on something
not the truth, and you mislead the public. It's not an easy call." Most
correspondents settled on a course of what Schorr called "oscillation,
where you move from one category to another. You start by being
very conscious about the truth, that you are not going to blight your
career by writing untruths, but that you are not going to risk being
kicked out, either."

The Polish government pressured Rosenthal immediately. The
Foreign Office summoned him to complain about a story he considered innocuous. The implication was clear that "I might not be a welcome guest in Poland if I continued writing stories that embarrassed
the Government of the People's Republic." Rosenthal sensed the
Foreign Office was testing him, so he made light of the warning. He
told the functionary he was reminded of an episode in the current
musical comedy *Call Me Mister*. A sergeant harangued a private at
length, and the private finally said, "So go ahead. What can you do—
bust me to civilian?" The official laughed.

As the months passed, Rosenthal came to detest Poland and the
failure of the Communist system. As he was to write years later, "The
Poles led a dreary, tiring existence of want and deprivation, when life
was to line up and buy this and line up to buy that . . . when everything was shabby, fifth-rate, crowded and unpleasant and you had to
shove and use your elbows to get along, when faces were drawn with
working two jobs, when bribing and cheating and cutting corners
were considered almost moral necessities, for how else could you live
when life was a daily insult." The police state apparatus was stifling.
Even the privacy of the Rosenthal home was invaded by microphones
of the UB, the Polish intelligence service. The line, "Remember,

you're in the police station," became a family joke; anything said was overheard by Gomulka's cops.

To the surprise of his superiors, after only nine months in Warsaw Rosenthal asked to be relieved. In a letter to Manny Freedman on March 21, 1959, he questioned whether the *Times* should even have a full-time correspondent in Poland. He had benefitted from reporting from a Soviet bloc country. "But . . . I feel that the time is approaching when I will have received all there is to receive out of the Polish experience," Rosenthal wrote.

> If that were all that were to it, I would not be writing this, trust me, because I am not all that self-centered. But I do feel that the time is approaching when the paper might put me to better use . . . This is not a matter of lusting after the front page—I have been around long enough to know there is more than one page in the *Times*—but of being interested in having an expandable mind. Put less fancifully, I think that after a reporter has fairly well exploited a marginal story it may be best for him, if possible, to move on.

Rosenthal then proceeded to lecture his foreign editor on how Eastern Europe should be covered. He was being wasted as a full-time Warsaw resident correspondent. ". . . I would not be honest if I did not say that I feel a little like a chief petty officer, assigned to the command of a rowboat. I am not looking for the battleship, but I do feel uncomfortable sitting too long in a rowboat." Rosenthal closed with a direct reminder that he was not wed to the *Times*. For eighteen months "I have been regularly turning down offers of fancy magazine jobs that would have put me anywhere I wanted including Hong Kong or Rome or Tokyo and turning them down without a twinge."

Rosenthal's request caused consternation and anger on 43rd Street. Moving a correspondent and his family is expensive. That Rosenthal wished to abandon an assignment so soon seemed selfish; that he would lecture *Times* management on how to run the foreign service was presumptuous beyond belief. By one second-hand account, Catledge said, in effect, Tell him to take one of those magazine jobs, because I don't want anything else to do with him. Freedman wrote Rosenthal a stern letter denying the request, and telling Rosenthal his job was not to sit in Poland, but to obtain visas for other Soviet bloc countries. No, Rosenthal could not have Rome or Tokyo, and why did he even ask? "If Poland and Eastern Europe are 'marginal,' by what standard do you consider Rome to be in the mainstream of the news? As for Hong Kong and Southeast Asia, if you found India physically too trying what makes you think that the Southeast Asia beat, with its constant travel over long distances and under unsatisfactory conditions, would be less of a hardship?" Then, in indirect but clear sentences, Freedman suggested that Rosenthal in fact *might* be happier working somewhere else:

> All this is to say that if we accept your own standards I do not see how any of the pastures that you have indicated would be greener for very long. This is not to say that professionally I would not be delighted to see you in any one of these jobs but as a practical matter I just wonder how long you would regard any one of these assignments as satisfactory.

Rosenthal apparently realized he had offended 43rd Street. His reply to Freedman was contrite. He professed to be "a little upset at first, because of the realization that for the first time in sixteen years The Authorities seemed mad at me." He admitted he was "premature in raising the question" of leaving Poland.

To suggest that Rosenthal's ill-advised request for transfer endangered his career is perhaps an overstatement. But the tone of Freedman's rebuttal was by *Times* standards a ringing rebuke, and one that told Rosenthal that he best not risk any further breaches of protocol. Further, it added to his growing reputation as a difficult person, whether he worked in New York, New Delhi, or in Warsaw.

The cable exchanges carry another irony. A correspondent who behaved similarly two decades later, when Rosenthal was executive editor, would have had his career ended with the swiftness of a Telex message. That Turner Catledge tolerated Rosenthal's petulance is explicable only for two reasons: that crankiness aside, Rosenthal was already being eyed as a future editor; and that his brilliance as a reporter and writer made it possible for superiors to overlook periodic tantrums.

In the end, Rosenthal's premature departure was determined not by editors on 43rd Street but by strongman Gomulka. The tone of Rosenthal's reportage hardened after the Freedman cables, and the Poles finally slapped back at him in August, 1959, when Vice President Richard M. Nixon stopped in Warsaw enroute home from the USSR. Although the government discouraged a crowd, by forcing Nixon's plane to land at an obscure military airport outside the capital, Poles turned out by the scores of thousands to greet him. Rosenthal wrote of the warm reception as an expression of pro-American sentiment: "It was as clear as anything tangible can ever be that Warsaw was greeting not so much the man as his country." He contrasted the spontaneous crowd with the indifference of the organized reception for Premier Khrushchev the previous month.

The next day Rosenthal wrote movingly of Nixon's visits: first, to a Roman Catholic cathedral; next, to "that wrenchingly desolate area . . . where the city's Jews were exterminated behind the ghetto walls they built at Nazi gunpoint." Based on Rosenthal's dispatches, the *Times* commented editorially, the reception "destroyed the propaganda campaign which had sought so hard to prove that Communist totalitarianism had won over the people of Eastern Europe so there could be no more talk of captive nations."

That evening Rosenthal was standing around at an official party for Nixon sipping a drink when Jan Cywiak, a foreign ministry press functionary, plucked him out of the crowd and delivered a formal warning. The government made the "utmost strong objection" to the editorial; if "this sort of thing continued," Rosenthal faced the "unpleasant consequence" of expulsion. Rosenthal demanded that Cywiak repeat the "plain threat" to James Reston, chief of the Washington bureau, travelling in the Nixon party. Cywiak did so. Rosenthal replied that although he did not write editorials, "I was quite willing for the Polish government to consider me as responsible for NYT in any way it saw fit."*

To Reston, Cywiak argued that the *Times* and its "representative" were obliged to follow "laws and usage" of the host government.

Well, Reston replied, "there was another way to make government's view clear, namely that whole situation including warning could be reported in tomorrows [sic] NYT, which Cywiak thought was not repeat not a great idea."

Rosenthal felt it significant that the Poles issued the warning at an official government function; he filed a lengthy memorandum via cable but said New York editors must make the decision about pub-

---

*These quotations are taken from a cable Rosenthal sent to 43rd Street that night reporting on the episode, hence the cableese syntax.

lishing a story. Editors concluded publication surely would cause Rosenthal's immediate expulsion, hence no story appeared. And although several reporters travelling with Nixon heard the exchange, they chose not to write about it.

By late autumn circumstances suggested strongly to Rosenthal that his days in Poland were numbered. Police surveillance of his house and office intensified; the noise on his phone grew so loud he realized wiretappers no longer bothered to conceal their snooping. Rosenthal decided that if he must be expelled, let it be for respectable journalistic reason. In a week's time in November, 1959, he wrote four dispatches which told of deepening problems within Poland; two of them also reflected badly on Gomulka's relations with his Soviet protectors. The first article appeared November 6 under an inconspicuous one-column headline on page six:

GOMULKA IS TESTY,
POLES ARE UNEASY
They Wonder What Is Next
in His Drive for Discipline
—Few Get Near Him

Rosenthal drew a portrait of a man isolated from his own people, ready to deny Poles even such trivial pleasures as rock 'n' roll music. "Always moody and irascible," Rosenthal wrote, "Mr. Gomulka is more withdrawn these days and seems hotter-tempered than ever. He is said to have a feeling of having been let down—by intellectuals and economists he never had any sympathy for anyway, by workers he accuses of squeezing overtime out of normal day's work, by suspicious peasants who turn their backs on the Government's plans, orders and pleas."

The next day, Rosenthal wrote that Poland's writers, "squeezed economically and politically," were considering a boycott of their own national organization to protest governmental policies. The article avoided mentioning any names (to reveal sources meant prison terms for the speakers). It told of their disillusionment with the passing of liberalism in Poland, and of the censorship of films, books, even poetry.

On November 8, Rosenthal revealed the increased Soviet role in a crackdown on Polish dissidents. He obviously had good sources, for he gave a detailed account of an off-the-record meeting of the Soviet ambassador with Polish journalists. He reported that the "embittered opinions" of Gomulka "on the state of Polish culture are not far from Moscow's." Rosenthal continued, "It is reported, however, that Mr. Gomulka was displeased over the Ambassador's comments. The party chief is reported to have snapped that what the Ambassador said in the way of criticism might have been right but that it was not his job to say it." That the Ambassador did so anyway highlighted Gomulka's subservience.

Rosenthal's final dispatch was necessarily incomplete. Weeks earlier he received word of the defection to the U.S. of Colonel Pawel Monat, who coordinated Polish military attachés worldwide. Given the closeness of the Polish UB and the KGB, Monat's defection was a disaster for Moscow, and gave the Soviets an excuse to install a controlled agent to direct Polish intelligence. The position, as Rosenthal wrote, went to Lieutenant General Kazimierz Witawzewski, who had opposed Gomulka during the 1956 uprising and fallen from favor. Rosenthal saw the appointment as a return of Stalinist influences and "an indication that some of the men against whom the [1956] . . . revolution was fought are being brought back to power. . . ."

What Rosenthal omitted in the story was any mention of the Monat defection. "To have written it in Poland would have meant immediate expulsion and possibly arrest," he said later.

> There is also the possibility, which has to be considered by Western newsmen working in a Communist country, that a secret already known to the West was dropped into a correspondent's ear by a Communist contact as a provocation—to find out whether he knew about it or to entice him into using it while within the territory of the Communist state and subject to reprisals for "espionage."

The day the truncated Witaszewski article appeared, Rosenthal was summoned to the Foreign Ministry and told he must leave the country for "exposing too deeply the internal situation in Poland." The ministry spokesman, coldly formal, told Rosenthal he had "probed too deeply in his reporting of current economic and political problems and matters concerning the Communist leadership."

Rosenthal asked whether he was accused of reporting false information. The response was an obviously unintended backhand tribute to his skill as a correspondent:

> The question of falseness or otherwise does not enter into the question. You have written very deeply and in detail about the internal situation, party matters and leadership matters, and the Polish government cannot tolerate such probing reporting.

Pressed for specifics, the spokesman would refer only to Rosenthal's dispatch concerning Gomulka's withdrawn mood, and the barriers between him and the people. Rosenthal argued, futilely, that the article was true, and that the situation was "known to most of Warsaw's politically informed." Correctness was not at issue, the functionary repeated, "but simply the fact that it had been reported."

Rosenthal asked for a week to prepare his household for departure. This was arranged. (The next spring, in an advertisement hailing Rosenthal's Pulitzer Prize, his photograph ran over a bold-face caption: ". . . One Week to Get Out of Town.")

The expulsion caused the Rosenthals grave logistical problems. Ann and seven-year-old Jonathan were in Vienna for dental treatment. The Poles permitted Ann to return to help Abe assemble their household goods for shipment. Ann did the work. She fought with packers, with shipping bureaucrats, with various Polish officials, and she was swift to invoke Gomulka's name when she ran into barriers: "He [Gomulka] wants us to get out and if you don't want him angry at you, you better give us the shipping documents, because I am not leaving without them."

Abe, "angered beyond words," sat in morose silence. His friend Daniel Schorr, who had been in Warsaw for his arrival, by happenstance was there for the departure as well. Schorr did what he could. "You are so overwhelmed with the logistics that you are numb. 'Was everything packed? Can we make the train on time? Dan, will you make this call for me?' " Schorr, who had endured his own expulsion from the USSR, did what he could to help.

Rosenthal's Polish friends and news sources kept a discreet distance. Rosenthal cabled Freedman, "Surveillance by car and foot part of situation but more amusing than bothersome. Please keep this aspect confidential since publicity on surveillance might stir them to greater efforts." Rosenthal made farewell calls on Western friends and newsmen. As he talked to a Western correspondent he noticed the man's Polish assistant was weeping. This surprised Rosenthal, for he did not know the man well.

"Stefan, what is the matter?" Rosenthal asked.

"Oh, Abe, Abe," the man said, "you are the lucky one."

Rosenthal knew what the man meant. With his United States passport he could leave the country. The Pole could not. Abe felt less sorry for himself after leaving the office.

Ambassador Jake Beam and Dan Schorr escorted Ann and the boys to the train; dour Abe watched them depart for Vienna. He followed by car later in the day, and he was happy to be out of a land he had grown to detest.

Back in the United States, James Reston and assistant managing editor Clifton Daniel talked with various Polish diplomats in Washington and the UN about reversing the expulsion. The answer was the decision had been Gomulka's, and was unlikely to be changed. Reporting these failures, Daniel suggested that Turner Catledge ask Charles Merz, editor of the editorial page, to go easy on the Poles. ". . . [T]hey are in a very difficult and delicate situation. . . . We could have a more-in-sorrow-than-in-anger editorial that would say everything we wanted to say . . . in a tolerant tone."

Rosenthal was not in the mood for rapprochement. From Vienna he began writing stories he had planned for months. He told of the defection of the intelligence officer Pawel Monat. He wrote about differences between Mao Tse-Tung of Communist China and USSR Premier Khrushchev about a forthcoming summit conference in Paris. This article resulted in the Poles denying a visa to Rosenthal's intended replacement in Warsaw, M. S. Handler. Jerzy Michalowski, chief of the Polish delegation to the UN, told Clifton Daniel on November 27 that Rosenthal, by attributing the story to a Polish source, "had printed it as a kind of 'vengeance.' " As Daniel reported, "He said the article might get one man in Warsaw into trouble and harm Poland quite a bit."

But Rosenthal's major effort the first days of December was a series in which he denounced Gomulka's Poland as an utter failure. The bits of information he had obtained the past eighteen months, the in-confidence leads and insights from Polish officials and laymen, the

personal observations he made in his travels around the country—
these Rosenthal melded into taut, vivid reportage. The *Times* gave
the five articles major space, and promoted them heavily. What
Rosenthal wrote about Poland was his capstone as a foreign
correspondent—multi-sourced articles supported by his own impressions. And in May, 1960, Rosenthal of the *Times* won the Pulitzer
Prize for distinguished foreign reporting. The reporter who a year
earlier had been in the Catledge-Freedman dog house for trying to
leave Poland prematurely was now featured in *Times* promotional advertisements as the very best the *Times* foreign service had to offer.

By happy coincidence, the formal announcement of the Pulitzer
came on Rosenthal's birthday. His friend Dan Schorr had invited
Rosenthal to a birthday lunch at *Le Globe*, one of Geneva's simpler
but nicest restaurants. "Abe was quite elated, and he got to talking as
he does, changing from one subject to another very rapidly. Then he
suddenly leaned forward and pointed to a tourist family sitting
nearby, a man and his wife and two children. 'Any minute that guy is
coming over to congratulate me,' Abe said. 'They are looking at me
and talking about me.'

"Sure enough, the man did walk over, and he said to me, 'Mr.
Schorr, we watch you on television all the time, and I just want to say
what an honor it is to see you in person.'

"I was happy to see a real live fan, but this was Abe's day, so I said,
'I'd like to introduce Mr. A.M. Rosenthal of *The New York Times*.
You surely read about him in the [Paris] *Herald Tribune* this morning, for winning the Pulitzer Prize.' The tourist glanced at Abe and
said, 'Oh, that's nice,' and he continued talking about watching me on
television.

"When the tourist left, Abe shook his head. 'Schorr, this is the last
time I have lunch with a television man on the day I win a Pulitzer
Prize.' Then he brightened and grinned. 'Hey, has anybody ever won
it two years in succession?' That's pure Abe—he has the endearing
quality of flaunting some of his faults by making fun of them before
you do. *He* made the joke about it, of winning two of them back to
back."

So what would Rosenthal do now? The premature departure from
Poland left the foreign service without a spot for him. But as Catledge
wrote publisher Arthur Hays Sulzberger, Rosenthal's "talents are too
good to let lie fallow." The "best solution," Catledge decided, "would

be to send him to Geneva as sort of a free-wheeling correspondent.
. . . [and] send him out anywhere in Europe when necessity should
arise." Catledge had grander things in mind for Rosenthal. "As you
know, he is one of our best and we want to use him to the fullest.
Furthermore, we think he is entitled to a comfortable spot for his
family for a while because they have really 'had it' for the last several
years."

So for several months Rosenthal was the fireman of the Geneva bu-
reau. Geneva was a "comfortable spot" for Ann and the sons, but
Rosenthal sought assignments anywhere. For instance, he cabled
Freedman January 29, 1960: FLYING PARIS TODAY STOP IF YOU
HAVE NEED OF ANOTHER EMERGENCY HAND IN ALGERIA OR ANY-
WHERE AFRICA EYEM EAGER TO GO AND HAVE TROPICAL
CLOTHES IN SUITCASE ROSENTHAL.

Although the foreign desk did not accept this particular offer,
Rosenthal spent several months in 1960 in Africa—first to report on
the civil war in the Congo, then from Mali and the Sudan. But the
nomadic roaming proved tiring, and it caused constant separation
from Ann and the boys. He began to plead for a permanent post.
Somehow he had the idea (which Catledge, Daniel and Freedman did
not credit) that he had been promised Tokyo, and in late 1960 he began insisting upon it as a matter of right. Correspondence in
Catledge's papers leaves unclear just how the misunderstanding
arose. Daniel finally wrote Catledge (who was travelling in Europe)
that if "Abe Rosenthal is so insistent, we should give him the Tokyo
assignment, although we think his best interests, and ours, might
best be served by keeping him in Western Europe." Daniel explained:

> The difficulty is that this has gotten to be almost a point of honor with
> him. He apparently has convinced himself that this is the only place
> that will really satisfy him and that we are somehow thwarting him if
> we refuse. . . . None of this, of course, is true. But I personally feel it
> is worth our while to sustain Abe's morale for the long run. . . . My
> own feeling is that he is taking a retrograde step by returning to the
> Far East. . . .

In a sense, Daniel's prediction about a "retrograde step" proved
correct, for from Tokyo Rosenthal did much the same sort of work he
had performed earlier in New Delhi. The preponderance of his file

consisted of "soft" features about Japan and the countries which he visited. He roamed almost incessantly—to the Phillipines, to Taiwan, to New Guinea, to Okinawa, to South Korea. He spent a month back in New Delhi, substituting for the vacationing correspondent Paul Grimes. "The Philippines today, Korea tomorrow, India the day after—what an interesting life away from the cares of home!" Manny Freedman wrote him in 1962. Rosenthal developed a love for Japanese culture close to his affection for India. He jested about such customs as sitting on mats on the floor. "It changes your whole perspective and I am keeping notes for a piece on what the world looks like from on the floor," he wrote Catledge. "For one thing, I find it is harder to carry on an argument when you are sprawled on a floor mat than when you are sitting in a chair."

And it was in Japan that Rosenthal truly came to appreciate the advice Catledge gave him when he first went abroad—to write stories as if he were composing a letter to a friend. As he wrote Catledge in September 1960:

> It works two ways. There is the fact that it makes for better reading. I think also that it makes for better reporting when it is done because it forces the reporter to arrange his thoughts more neatly and avoid taking the easy way out—jargon. In the end, I think, he gets a more sharply focused picture himself of what he is covering, simply because he has to stand away a bit and look at the subject and ask himself what it all really means or should mean to the reader.

Rosenthal found the letter technique useful when dealing with an unfamiliar subject. In conventional news writing the reporter often slips into jargon, or terms the exact meaning of which he is unsure. Writing a story as a letter permits him to do his own thinking, in natural language. As an example, Rosenthal cited his reporting on the 100,000-odd American military men and women stationed in South Korea. Rosenthal did not posture as a military expert; he knew the silliness of pretending to be another Hanson Baldwin, the *Times*'s longtime military writer. So he wrote about the military's daily life— the thoughts of a jet pilot as he watches other planes land on the *Coral Sea*, how special forces troops learn foreign languages, the political demands on an admiral.

Some persons who worked on the *Times* foreign desk during Rosenthal's years in Japan faulted him then and later for concentrating on features; one insists that his over-eager attempts to "prove the importance of Japanese intellectuals" caused him to miss the importance of the Japanese technological revolution and what it portended for American industry.

This person did not comprehend what Catledge wished from Rosenthal and other correspondents—stories that did more than recite the proceedings of the national parliament, or what politicians or ministries said in formal statements. This Rosenthal did better than any other writer the *Times* had, Catledge concluded, and in 1962 he decided to ask him to bring his special talents back to 43rd Street.

SIX

"Wanted for Breeding Stock"

During the years that Abe Rosenthal and other correspondents chased news around the world for the *Times,* managing editor Turner Catledge daily travelled a shorter but far more destructive route—the several hundred yards separating the newsroom from the bar at Sardi's, the restaurant-saloon at Eighth Avenue and West 44th Street. *Times* drinking is hierarchial. Reporters, junior editors, pressmen, ad salesmen and the like congregate at a ramshackle bar called Gough's, out the front door of the Times building and a few feet up 43rd Street towards Broadway. Gough's is not for the fastidious. When a patron complained that the resident cat had lapped at his glass of Heineken's, the barkeep shook his head and said, "That's odd, he usually drinks only Budweiser."

The upper ranks prefer Sardi's, and they have their private route: down a gray-painted stairwell that stretches from an unmarked door off the third-floor newsroom, out onto a loading dock, and then a few strides to the west. The bar is to the right inside the door. Sardi's is a *Times* clubhouse, a place for socialization but where an uplifted hand signals that this particular lunch is private, and please keep away. Times people hear of promotions in the Sardi's dining room, and they look up at the pencilled caricatures on the walls and long for such recognition. Times custom is that Sardi's is *never* used to announce a firing or a demotion; such is done at other West Side restaurants. Sardi's is the place for serious drinking, however.

Turner Catledge sat at the Sardi's bar often during the late 1950's and early 1960's, drinking far too much bourbon and talking about his life. He was a man of talent. A Mississippian, he worked for newspapers around the south, and in the 1930's Arthur Krock hired him away from the Baltimore *Sun* to join the *Times*'s Washington bureau. Preparing for the new job, Catledge bought the *Times* daily, and he studied the laborious writing style, and decided it must be followed. But Catledge "knew deep inside of me it was wrong. I could make a lot of fun of it, but a newspaper story is a communication. Unless it's received on the other end and understood, it isn't worth a damn; you might just as well keep it on a spike and save all the trouble and expense and the hair-pulling. . . ."

When Catledge became managing editor he tried to reform *Times* writing, but several things got in his way. Correspondents, especially those working abroad, had learned one system; they did not intend to try another. Catledge's marriage fell apart, and he got into serious whiskey-drinking at Sardi's. Many nights ended with the managing editor of *The New York Times* being carried out, unconscious, and put into a cab.

In 1961 Catledge met and married a gracious woman named Abby Ray, who nudged him back into sensible drinking and other habits. As if emerging from a stupor, Catledge took a serious look at the newspaper he managed, and how he could improve it. Catledge won minor skirmishes. Since the late 1800's the lead story each day was topped with a one-column headline the *Times* called the "A-head." As Catledge said, "My god, our A-heads used to fill up half a column. . . . By the time you'd read the headline, you didn't have to read the paper." Catledge managed to shrink the A-heads considerably.

Substantive changes would come harder. As deputy managing editor Catledge suggested that foreign correspondents tighten their writing, that their audience was the American public, not foreign ministries. The response, in effect, was that he should mind his business.

So Catledge took a different tack. He had learned much about politics during the years he had covered Washington, when his fellow Southerners dominated Congress. Although Catledge could sip fine whiskey at Sardi's, he did politics in cold-eyed white lightning style. Lesson One: Go for the weakness; work on a part of the *Times* controlled directly from 43rd Street, and forget about the baronies (Krock's Washington bureau; the foreign service, under C.L. Sulzberger; the Sunday sections, under Lester Markel). The city desk, a few feet distant from Catledge's office, was the logical proving ground. Lesson Two: Use as a cutting edge someone who comes from the *Times*, but who is not wed to the existing system, and who has been away long enough to forget old loyalties. Lesson Three: This "cutting edge" must be someone willing to do dirty work.

In 1962 the city editor of the *Times* was Frank Adams, who had been in the city room, as reporter, rewriteman and editor, since 1925. He was a portly fellow who came to work in a midnight-blue homberg, did his work, and tried to be out of the office by sundown, leaving details to others. Adams edited the city report pretty much as it had been done for half a century. In keeping with the *Times's* insistence on being "the paper of record," for instance, Adams insisted that the *Times* City Hall bureau write in decimal point detail about each year's budget. Adams was a gentleman, an editor who did not shout but who could hurry people along when a deadline threatened. No one remembered him ever criticizing a person within earshot of a colleague. Such was not the style of either Adams or *The New York Times*.

Beyond Adams's city desk, the tone of the paper was set by a unique *Times* institution called the "bullpen," in effect a master desk responsible for the content of the entire daily newspaper. (*The Sunday Times*, under the editorship of Lester Markel, was a separate operation.) Under the bullpen, individual departments had little direct control over their product. The various desks—city, national and foreign—would assign stories, and editors would go over articles to see that they covered all salient points. But the stories then passed to the bullpen.

Under the bullpen system, the *Times* was an editor's newspaper. A copy editor, not the writer, determined the final form of a story—a process guaranteed to bleach the life from reportage. Cumbersome, all-inclusive leads written in obedience to a formula the goal of which seemed to be to pile as many words as possible into a single heap. A horror of adjectives and adverbs, and of any direct quotations that suggested citizens spoke in other than sentences with a high grammatical shine. A reverence for the subject, be it the latest planned works of the Sanitation Department or a rabbinical conference or the derailment of a subway train. Mild witticisms found their way into print only with specific bullpen dispensation.

In 1962 Theodore Bernstein was the second ranking editor in the bullpen, behind the news editor Louis Nichols, and as a person who loved the English language he flinched almost every day as he saw it abused in the columns of his newspaper. Bernstein was a man obsessively fascinated with words and their usage. The author of *The Times Style Book,* he was the paper's ultimate authority on writing. He wanted a better paper, in the literary sense, and in 1961 and 1962 he and Turner Catledge had long conversations on how this could be brought about. Bernstein's suggestion was that change should begin on the city desk, where geography permitted close interplay between reporter and editor. Changing *Times* reportage could not be done via cables to Bonn or Cairo; what was needed was a hands-on editor who would transform one department of the *Times*, and create the example by which the rest of the paper should be judged. Bernstein and Catledge agreed that Rosenthal's approach to the news was what the paper needed. Given his relatively long absence from New York, he was not involved in city desk politics, hence he could make objective decisions about coverage.

The unseating of Frank Adams commenced with an innocent lunch on April 11, 1962, of Adams and Clifton Daniel, Catledge's deputy. The ostensible subject was a replacement for Adams's retiring deputy, Joseph Herzberg. Adams was sixty years of age, and he said that the deputy should be the person who would be his successor. He mentioned Sheldon Binn, then an assistant editor; Walter Sullivan, the science writer; Richard Witkin, a city reporter; and Max Frankel, a former city reporter then working in the Caribbean. Daniel wrote in a memo that day, "Ted Bernstein proposed that we should move fairly promptly to replace Frank Adams, and his nomination is Abe Rosenthal." Robert Garst, an assistant managing editor, "thought that such an appointment would be highly injurious to the morale in the existing setup [sic] . . ."

Bernstein, however, went directly to Catledge. Go for Rosenthal, he advised, here is the chance we've been waiting for. Catledge agreed. In July 1962 he and his wife went to Tokyo, and he put the question to Rosenthal. "He asked me to be metropolitan editor, just like that. I looked at him in astonishment. I thought for a moment he must be thinking about someone else."

City news had absolutely no interest to Rosenthal; he had put New York out of his mind when he went to the UN. In his then-opinion, city reporting was something done by novices, didn't-make-its, and older people looking for comfortable jobs. "I thought of myself as the ultimate foreign correspondent. I could see myself puffing my pipe around the Council on Foreign Relations, something like that. I told Turner I didn't want it, that I wanted either one of two things, to write a column, or to get the London bureau." Rosenthal had worked everywhere—India, Poland, Geneva, Southeast Asia and Japan—and the other places he could go were limited. He spoke no French. London was the prestigious—and comfortable—post in the *Times* foreign service. "I told him that, politely, but Turner is one of those men who gives the appearance of hearing only what he wants to hear. I would say, 'I don't want the job,' and he would reply, 'September would be a good time for you to start, could you be back in New York by then?' " When Rosenthal replied he preferred to write a column, Catledge replied, "Columns are out of my jurisdiction," and he continued talking about the city job.

Rosenthal was not totally candid with Catledge. He was already in correspondence with John Oakes, the editor of the editorial page, who asked him to write editorials. Oakes wanted his overture confidential. (By long and wise policy, the *Times* keeps a sharp division between the news department and the editorial page, for fear of cross-contamination of news and opinion.) As Rosenthal apologetically told Catledge later, "A person who violates one man's confidence can violate another's; I know you would not want me to be that kind of person."

Catledge made his first offer when he and his wife were with the Rosenthals in Tokyo, and the conversation continued as they toured Japan. The Catledges flew on to New Delhi, and they met again in the Imperial Hotel. Catledge had a new issue of *Times Talk*, the paper's house organ. Rosenthal skimmed through it, reading about old colleagues.

He stopped short. Oakes had announced that Russell Baker of the Washington bureau would be writing a column for the editorial page. The news stunned Rosenthal, for he knew the page did not have space for two new columnists. Catledge noticed Rosenthal's reaction, how his "usually cheerful face was deflated like a balloon pricked by a pin. He fell into a terrible state of depression." Not until he returned to New York did he realize what so upset Rosenthal. Rosenthal confessed that he had been negotiating with Oakes by mail. "You may have seen my jaw drop open slackly when I read . . . about Baker," Rosenthal wrote. "This was because the realization had suddenly come to me that I should hitch up my little knickerbockers and put in a suggestion for a column." Rosenthal apparently sensed he was getting into potentially dangerous *Times* politics by playing Oakes against Catledge. "I realize quite well that the *Times* is not a smorgasboard table for me to examine, picking what I think is the choicest morsel. The chances are good that the *Times* longs for a column by Rosenthal like you long for a dish of raw fish." He confessed, that through his manipulations he might "have dropped the ball on my toe." He concluded:

> Would I rather be a foreign affairs columnist for the *Times* than anything else? Yes. Do I think the suggestion you made [to become city editor] is the most attractive if I cannot be a pundit? Yes.

Oakes resolved the question by writing Rosenthal that the page could not take two columnists; if he wished to write editorials, fine, a column might open later. Rosenthal told Catledge that if the city job remained his for the asking, he would take it. In late 1962 Catledge told him to prepare to come home, but to say nothing for the time being, for Frank Adams had to be nudged out of his job "in a humane manner." Although Adams was promised a new job as editorial writer, he protested about being displaced only four years shy of retirement; he told Catledge he would prefer to work with Rosenthal a "year or two or three before he passes on the baton to you," as Catledge wrote to Tokyo. But in the end Adams yielded gracefully, and the way was cleared for Rosenthal to return.

Catledge made plain to Rosenthal that he expected him to be something other than the conventional city editor—that he wanted to redefine the *Times*'s approach to city coverage, with the longterm aim of rejuvenating the entire paper. "Turner used some sort of horseracing term, that he wanted me for 'breeding stock.' I asked

him, 'What the hell do you intend to do—put me out to stud?' "
Catledge wrote him in April, 1963, that editors in New York were
already planning the reshaping of city desk operations.

> I still have a few of those pencils around my desk inscribed, 'Make no
> small plans,' and we are not making any small plans for the city staff.
> . . .
>
>   The city staff is the foundation of our entire news operation. It is a
> reservoir from which all of our talents are drawn. It is the training
> ground for our young people. It is the reserve on which we call when-
> ever there is an emergency in town, out of town or on the other side of
> the world.
>   Moreover, the function and scope of the city staff has [sic] changed
> enormously. . . . It used to be very self-centered and inward-looking,
> but now its domain stretches from Albany in the north . . . to Wash-
> ington in the south, and, incidentally, to any air disaster anywhere in
> the world. [This was because the *Times* aviation writer worked under
> the city desk.] The people who cover science and the people who cover
> space all work in the city room, although their assignments from time
> to time may be in the hands of other departments.

Since the title "city editor" no longer accurately described the jurisdiction that Rosenthal would control, the position would be
renamed "metropolitan editor."

Rosenthal's private feeling was that he would stay in New York no
more than three years. "I figured that I would do my best, and that at
the end of three years I would persuade Turner to send me either to
London or the Middle East. I felt that either the Arabs would permit
Jews to come to their countries as correspondents, or that maybe
Tony Lewis [the London bureau chief] would break a leg."

But late one night, as he talked with Ann about their return, he
asked, Would accepting Catledge's offer put him on a career track he
did not really want? He told Ann, "Here I'm a major. If I go back, I'll
be a colonel or a brigadier. You get one star, you want two—or you
even want to be a field marshal."

SEVEN

"I'm the Best City Editor Ever"

Returning to New York to direct city coverage of the *Times* left Rosenthal "a bit panicky," as he was to acknowledge years later. The job "was one which was about the last I had ever considered holding on *The New York Times.* . . . I was panicky about it because for eighteen years, although I had been a New Yorker, I had been out of touch with reality in New York. Nine of those years I spent in the glass box covering the UN and then we [the Rosenthal family] went abroad. So there I was, facing the problem of leading a large and openly skeptical staff in the coverage of a city with which I had been out of touch for almost twenty years."

The "openly skeptical" staff indeed was just that—more than one hundred men and women shaken by the announcement that an outsider from the foreign staff would now be their boss. That Rosenthal had performed brilliantly as a foreign correspondent was beyond dispute. "A.M. Rosenthal was one of the bylines you looked for, and which you read, even if you didn't give a half damn about Poland or

Japan," said a man who was then a journeyman *Times* reporter, and who now runs a key foreign bureau. "He was that good." But the talk around Gough's, the bar across 43rd Street from the *Times*, came back to experience, and fairness. Rosenthal knew *nothing* about New York; how the hell could this foreign correspondent come into the city and keep from falling on his ass? And was it *right*? Others had worked on the city desk for years, decades, waiting for promotion. Now Catledge's whiz-bang kid is run in over their heads. Bah. Rosenthal had his defenders among the old guard. John Hess, a night rewriteman, told colleagues, "Hey, guys, give him a chance." Hess felt that former copy boys and clerks had taken over the *Times* city desk because "the reporters had been off either fighting the war, or reporting it." To Hess, "Here we have a bona fide reporter as a boss—let's give him a chance." (Hess later would become one of Rosenthal's most vociferous critics.)

Frank Adams apparently sensed the latent hostility towards Rosenthal as a newcomer, so a few days after he began work he sat quietly alongside his desk and offered to do what he could for him. He gave Rosenthal some forewarning. After about a year, he said, you are going to feel like a nail driven into the ground. "This was true," Rosenthal told me. The metropolitan editor deals with reporters and deputy editors face-to-face, all day, every day; he does not have the luxury of the national or foreign editor who works by cable or telephone, rather than across a desk or in a corner of the newsroom.

In a symbolic gesture of openness, Rosenthal turned around Adams's old desk so that he worked facing his reporters, but Rosenthal did not follow the gesture by initiating any significant dialogue with the staff. He had returned to New York as the outsider; such was how he felt, and such was how he acted. So Rosenthal began building defenses against his own people.

Rosenthal did not intend to bog himself in details of administration or management, two subjects about which he knew nothing. On his foreign assignments he had basically worked alone. "In Japan, I had this nice card printed up—'A.M. Rosenthal, Tokyo Bureau Chief, *The New York Times*.' I would go into Sony or some other business and hand over my card—the Japanese are big on business cards, you know—and this guy would look at it and say, 'Ah, yes, Mr. Rosenthal, bureau chief.' Sometimes they would ask, 'And just how many persons are in your bureau of *The New York Times*, Mr. Rosenthal?' I would shrug and say, 'Oh, it's a very small bureau, very small.'

"Once or twice the guy would pin me down, and I would have to grin and say, 'Me, I'm the bureau.' I actually had an office factotum and a chauffeur who didn't even work for *The New York times*. It was the same in Poland, India, a secretary and a driver and a translator."

So Rosenthal did little administrative work. "I wasn't hired to approve overtime slips," as he puts it. Thus one of his first decisions was to retain Frank Adams's deputy, Marshall F. Newton, to be in charge of "staff operations and administration." An even more important selection, however, was that of deputy metropolitan editor for assignments. As Rosenthal well knew, the choice of which stories to cover, and by what reporters, was vital to a local news operation. Rosenthal wanted three qualities in this deputy: a person with an intimate (and current) knowledge of New York City; who was also skilled in internal office politics; and who would be totally loyal to A.M. Rosenthal. Rosenthal's choice was an old friend named Arthur Gelb, with whom he had worked as a reporter on the city desk in the 1940's. The selection was to have long-range significance, for "Abe and Artie," as the pair came to be known, over the next years would oversee the restructuring of *The New York Times*. In sentimental moments, enhanced by a few glasses of Scotch, Rosenthal could call Gelb "the brother I never had, the most important man in my life." On other occasions, again with Scotch in hand, Rosenthal could lash out at Gelb in terms almost obscene in their viciousness. But in the autumn of 1963, Rosenthal needed Gelb.

Gelb was born in 1922 in Harlem, where his parents, both Czech immigrants, lived in a small apartment behind his mother's children's dress shop. The father had been a cigar maker upon coming to the United States, but during a strike the manufacturers retaliated by moving the entire industry to Tampa, Florida. So the father began working in the dress shop as well. He read, and he encouraged young Arthur to do the same. Gelb spent much of his youth in libraries or in fifty-cent seats watching Broadway plays, and in 1944, while still a student at City College of New York, he talked himself into a job as a copy boy at the *Times*.

Gelb loved it from the start, although he was scared witless when he walked into the newsroom to start work Memorial Day 1944. "To

see the dozens of typewriters, the wire machines, the suspended
lights hanging down from the high ceilings . . . what a glamorous
world!" Gelb was not hesitant about self-promotion, and a few weeks
after joining the staff he approached managing editor Edwin L. James
with pounding heart.

"Mr. James, can I ask you something?"

James stared at him. "Who are you?" he asked in a gruff voice.
Gelb's heart pounded faster.

"I'm a copy boy," Gelb began; his voice choked with nervousness,
he could not continue.

"Go on, what is it? What is it?" James did not like to stand around
the newsroom chatting with anyone, much less a copy boy.

Gelb managed to stammer that he had noticed the *Times* had no
house organ, and that he and several other copy boys wished to publish one. "Would you give us a chance?" James thought a few minutes. "Go ahead, mimeograph it—but let me see it first."

Gelb and friends put together their first issue, which included an
interview with Ted Bernstein and an article on the life of a foreign
correspondent. James liked it. "Forget the mimeograph," he said,
"have the composing room print it for you." Gelb was to edit *Times
Week* for two years while working as a copy boy and news assistant.
The publication continues as *Times Talk*, with a full-time staff.

Gelb went on to become a city reporter and a rewriteman, and he
did well at both jobs. He also fell wildly in love with a *Times* secretary
named Barbara Gordon, who had come to the *Times* after dropping
out of Swarthmore College at age seventeen. When he discovered
that she not only loved theater, but was the stepdaughter of the playwright S. N. Behrman, he had to marry her, and he did, in June,
1946.

Gelb's first sustained contacts with Abe Rosenthal came at about
the same time as the wedding, when he worked temporarily at the
United Nations bureau. The two men discovered a shared love for
good writing, and during evenings with their wives they would dis-
sect the current issue of *The New Yorker*, and wish they could use the
style of the "Talk of the Town" column in their *Times* writing. He and
Rosenthal had a special love for the short stories of J. D. Salinger, and
one evening after much Scotch they discussed "Day of the Banana
Fish." "What do you think it means?" Gelb asked. He did not like
Rosenthal's answer, and they began arguing, first in a friendly manner, then more heatedly.

"Goddamn it!" Gelb finally snapped. "Why the hell am I arguing with you about this?" He arose and grabbed the much-shorter Rosenthal and pushed him to the floor and held him there, knee firmly planted on his chest.

"Let me up, let me up, what the hell are you doing?" Rosenthal protested, squirming and trying to free himself.

"No, you're not getting up until you agree I am right," Gelb said, increasing the pressure of his knee.

"No," Rosenthal shouted.

"OK, then you are staying there," Gelb said. Both wives were shouting for peace by now, and Rosenthal finally reluctantly accepted Gelb's interpretation of the story. The argument over the story continued for years, but in much friendlier fashion.

When Rosenthal went overseas, Gelb shifted to the theater department as an assistant to the critic Brooks Atkinson, and in time he became chief cultural reporter. In the 1950's he loved to visit small clubs in Greenwich Village after attending off-Broadway shows. "Hey, catch this kid at the Bitter End," someone told him. "He's funny as hell." Gelb went to the coffee house. "I see this wisp of a man. He looked browbeaten, and he was all hunched over. And he was hilarious." Gelb did a short review, the first press mention given Woody Allen. Chet Huntley and David Brinkley read the review over their NBC radio show, chuckling at Allen's one-liners, and suddenly the comedian was a hot attraction at the Blue Angel and the Village Vanguard.* Gelb also found a new singer, "a little girl with an incredible voice," and he wrote the first major review of Barbra Streisand.

But Gelb's first love remained the theater, and especially Eugene O'Neill. Barbara Gelb shared the passion; indeed her first gift to him was the three-volume Random House edition of his plays. Barbara had left the *Times* soon after the marriage to raise a family, but she and Arthur wrote together, first articles, then a book on Bellevue Hospital. (Gelb dismisses it as a "potboiler" but a profitable one, with

---

*Whether Woody Allen recognizes Arthur Gelb's role in his "discovery" is problematic. In 1984 Gelb was pleased—and a bit dismayed—to find himself sitting at adjacent tables with Allen at lunch. According to Gelb's luncheon partner, "He wondered whether 'Woody recognizes me? Does he know who I am?' He is really insecure about it." Gelb obviously felt that Allen should recognize the "cultural czar" of the *Times.* In the end, Allen and Gelb exchanged what the luncheon partner described as "weak waves," with Allen giving no sign he recognized Gelb.

a serialization in *The Saturday Evening Post* and respectable sales.)
With these earnings as a nest egg, and a $5,000 advance, they com-
menced work on an O'Neill biography, labor that stretched over six
more or less non-stop working years. They scraped for money; many
years they planned vacations so they could do research in sites important to O'Neill's life. At one point they were so broke Barbara could
not afford a tube of lipstick. Gelb would come home from work at the
Times, write until three A.M., sleep until six, then write some more
before returning to the *Times*. Eventually they were $40,000 in debt,
and the tedium and long hours caused permanent damage to Gelb's
eyes. As Gelb says, "We were in trouble. I used to pray to God, 'Help
us.' "

The book was published in 1962 and it was an immediate commercial and critical success, the first book ever priced over $10 to make
the *Times* best seller list. The publisher, Harper & Row, was so
pleased it offered what Gelb called "an enormous advance" to do a
biography of publisher Henry Luce. And about this time his old
friend Abe Rosenthal returned from Japan to become metropolitan
editor, and asked him to become his deputy.

Gelb shook his head. "Abe, you're crazy. I have the best job in the
world. I don't want to work on the city desk." Rosenthal persisted,
and soon Gelb was standing before Turner Catledge.

"Look, I'm not going to beg you," Catledge said. "I want you, Abe
wants you, and Abe really needs you. If it's important enough for us
to bring Abe back home, you should accept that it is important to the
paper. We're giving Abe a mandate to change the paper. Don't you
want to be part of it?"

Gelb could not refuse. He and Rosenthal commenced a series of
meetings that would last far into the night. Gelb sat with a yellow pad
on his knee, jotting down ideas by the dozen. Rosenthal's fears about
being able to direct city coverage lessened the more they talked, and
he finally hit upon an obvious solution to his problem of knowing little
about New York:

> I dediced to try to handle this as if I were a foreign correspondent ar-
> riving in a new post. . . . I reasoned that as a foreign correspondent,
> the first thing I would do . . . would be to learn who ran it, who con-
> trolled the levers of governmental power, who were the people who
> were the creative thrusts in the town or in the country, who were the
> business people, who were the artists, who could tell me what I
> needed to know about New York in a relatively short period of time—

before the reporters found out that their suspicions about me were entirely correct: that I really didn't know what was going on. So I set out to meet the mayor, the business people, the artists and all those others who make this city what it is.

Rosenthal found that these meetings disturbed many reporters. "It shocked some of them for editor Abe to be lunching with the mayor or the police commissioner. This was something editors didn't do, and lots of reporters got nervous." Several political reporters felt that Rosenthal lunching with the mayor might "influence" *Times* coverage of City Hall. "All this talk was buzzing around, so I got together with the political reporters." By Rosenthal's reconstruction, the talk went as follows:

Rosenthal: You see this guy [the mayor] every day?
Reporters: Yes.
Rosenthal: You have lunch with him?
Reporters: Yes.
Rosenthal: Are you influenced by him, in the negative sense of the word?
Reporters: No, no, oh no.
Rosenthal: Then why am I worse than you for having lunch with the mayor and finding out what's on the guy's mind?

The reporters had no answer. "As far as I am concerned, that ended it," Rosenthal said; he continued his lunches.

In March, 1964, a lunch resulted in a landmark story for the *Times*. On March 14 the *Times* ran a routine four-paragraph item about the fatal stabbing of Catherine Genovese after three o'clock in the morning as she walked from a parking lot in her home in Queens. Rosenthal did not notice the item. Nor did he pay attention when police arrested a man named Moseley and said he confessed to the Genovese killing and of two other Queens women named Johnson and Kralik. But he did take notice when the *Daily News* reported that police were holding another man who also confessed to the Kralik murder.

By happenstance, Rosenthal lunched with Police Commissioner Michael J. Murphy at Emil's, a City Hall hangout, and he asked about the double-confession. Murphy said he knew nothing, then he talked about "the Queens story," and how thirty-eight persons had watched or heard a woman being killed, with no one calling for help.

Rosenthal felt the inner tingle that told him here was a story. Back at 43rd Street, Rosenthal summoned reporter Martin Gansberg, just transferred from the copy desk, and told him to check out the story. On March 27 the *Times* published Gansberg's story under a four-column single headline at the bottom of page one. It began:

> For more than half an hour thirty-eight respectable, law-abiding citizens in Queens watched a killer stalk and stab a woman in three separate attacks in Kew Gardens.
> Twice the sound of their voices and the sudden glow of their bedroom lights interrupted him and frightened him off. Each time he returned, sought her out and stabbed her again. Not one person telephoned the police during the assault; one witness called after the woman was dead.

Gansberg quoted the silent witnesses as saying, variously, they "didn't want to get involved," were frightened, or thought they were hearing a lovers' quarrel.

The story horrified the country, a testament to New Yorkers' indifference to fellow humans. Editorialists, churchmen and pop psychologists undertook a noisy "re-examination of the American soul" and talked at pious length about collective guilt which they unilaterally assigned to the populace in general. (Much of this "national debate" was generated by the *Times*, whose correspondents canvassed assorted savants for their opinions. Few professors or other persons interested in publicity deny themselves the opportunity to be quoted as authorities by the *Times*.)

In journalism, the story grew to mythic proportion as an example of Rosenthal's sagacity in finding stories overlooked by conventional newsmen at the *Times*. Although Rosenthal's role was editor, not reporter, the Genovese killing was indelibly "Abe's story." Genovese also demonstrated several flaws of the 1964 *Times*—including one that continues in 1986. As Rosenthal put it, *"The New York Times,* which has full-time staff correspondents in Karachi and Stockholm and Leopoldville and Algiers, has no full-time reporter in Queens," although the borough was the fastest-growing in the city, and home to 1,800,000 persons. Writing in 1964, Rosenthal confessed, "It can be shown statistically, I believe, that in the past few years *Times* reporters have spent more time in Antarctica than in Queens. It is one of those places about which editors keep telling themselves that they really should get around to covering. . . ." *Had* a *Times* reporter been covering Queens, he conceivably would have discovered the story before Rosenthal stumbled over it by pure chance. (When Rosenthal left the luncheon with Commissioner Murphy, he thought the silent witnesses were to *another* of the three Queens murders; reporter Gansberg made false starts as a result.) Oddly, even when Rosenthal became managing editor, he never got around to assigning a full-time reporter to Queens. He dismissed the borough—which has one-third of New York's population—as a "place of shopping centers and baby carriages and sewer troubles and . . . paralyzing ordinariness."

One fringe benefit Rosenthal received from the Genovese story was the chance to write his first "book." Rosenthal's devotion to the *Times* was so intense when he worked abroad that he did not write a book about the countries in which he was based, as did many of his colleagues. Immediately after the Gansberg article and the follow-up stories appeared, Rosenthal wrote about the affair for the *Times* magazine. An editor there suggested he expand his article into a book, and gave galleys to McGraw-Hill on a Thursday. Friday noon McGraw-Hill asked Rosenthal to proceed. He spent the weekend assembling material, and Gansberg wrote him a memorandum on his reporting of the story. On Monday Clifton Daniel, the managing editor, strolled by the metropolitan desk and asked Artie Gelb where Abe was.

"He's taking the day off," Gelb replied. "He's writing a book."

Thirty-Eight Witnesses was published June 8, eighty-six pages, chiefly a reprint of Gansberg's first article, a rewrite of the reaction stories, and strong emotionalism by Rosenthal, who called the witnesses' silence a "symptom of a terrible reality in the human condition—that only under certain situations and only in response to certain reflexes or certain beliefs will a man step out of his shell towards his brother."

The *Times*'s critic, Orville Prescott, in an eight-paragraph review, twice used the words "little book" in describing *Thirty-Eight Witnesses*, a tacit dismissal that irked Rosenthal. But the Genovese story made the desired impact on New York—and the *Times*—and established Rosenthal as an editor who could adapt to the city the talent he had demonstrated abroad.

Concurrently the Rosenthals became another New York family. No longer did they list as home Nizamuddin in Delhi, or Chodkiewicze Street in Warsaw. The family settled into an apartment on East End Avenue, the boys started public schools, and Abe found the focus of his life shifting to a "great city I thought I no longer knew, but which I found more a part of myself and my half-hidden memories than I had ever realized." One immediate loss was the amenities that go with the job of foreign correspondent: the chauffeur-driven automobile, the lack of formal office hours, the freedom of working thousands of miles from an editor. (But there were offsetting perks. For instance, after his periodic luncheons with police officials, Rosenthal would be driven back to West 43rd Street in a police car.) Rosenthal adapted to the new environment. "I found myself missing the liberty I had abroad, but so enveloped by the pace and excitement of New York and fascinated by the always elusive goal of trying to figure out a way of pinning down the city in newsprint that past freedoms lost some of their poignancy," he wrote less than a year after his return.

Rosenthal's curiosity was boundless, about subjects both important and trivial. Waiting for the elevator one evening he noticed the pristine white sand in the ash trays in the lobby. Where does this sand come from? he asked another man. How does clean white sand get to the city? And who brings it around and puts it into ash trays all over New York? Several days later the *Times* had a feature article answering the questions Rosenthal raised. Rosenthal noticed the sharp increase in public visibility of New York's gay community. Where did all these . . . *these queers* come from? he asked at a news meeting. Several men there did not know what Rosenthal was talking about; they, too, had witnessed the increase, but it was so gradual as to seem insignificant. Rosenthal had another just-returned foreign correspondent, Paul Hoffman, do a major takeout on the New York gay community, one of the first such articles to appear in a main-stream American newspaper. (His curiosity satisfied, Rosenthal let the subject lie for years, until gay protests about *Times* homophobia forced the paper into renewed coverage of the community.) During a sixteen-block cab ride, a friend later said, "Abe pointed out no less than seven things that he thought would be news stories, all the way from how Con Ed [the New York power company] gets permits to block streets to why the diamond industry is concentrated in a single block.

But Rosenthal met continuing resistance from old-line reporters, the men who had been around the *Times* city room for years. Rosenthal wanted fresh talent, writers not blighted by that most deadly of journalistic rules, *"But they always did it this way."* Any number of bright young men* were scattered through the enormous

Times bureaucracy laboring their ways through a "training program" idiotic in conception and application. The *Times* theory was that even a college graduate trained in journalism should spend three, four, even five years in the equivalent of a clerkship before being entrusted with a reporter's credentials. The appeal of the *Times* was such that many sensible persons entered the program. These persons clamored around the new city editor, begging for a chance to demonstrate their talent. Caption writers in the sports department, compilers of the stock tables in business-finance, dictationists who typed out the telephoned dispatches of correspondents working outside New York. Rosenthal realized that these young persons were an uncontaminated pool of talent; if he chose carefully, he could craft a staff of his own design. The immediate beneficiary would be *The New York Times*, for eager young journalists, in New York and elsewhere, *knew* that Rosenthal's city desk would be a reporter's desk, where style and substance would not be mutilated by sour old farts in green eyeshades, the copy editors. Rosenthal had endured agony with "the pencils," the men determined to slash the life from his copy. Now he intended to return the *Times* to its reporters; he would hire men he trusted, and what they wrote would go into the paper.

Such was the positive Rosenthal, the new editor with a broad if unspecified mandate to pep up a portion of the *Times*. Unavoidably, to make room for this newly-hired talent, he displaced a considerable portion of the existing *Times* staff. To persons supportive of Rosenthal, the process was clear: "Abe cut down enough dead wood in the city room to start a forest fire, the guys who took up desk space and wrote their little stories and waited for retirement." There was another opinion, and a strong one. Many persons had done exactly what they felt Adams required of them; not told anything to the contrary, they continued at their jobs. Now, in their mid-fifties, they were not acceptable to a whizbang city editor whose determination to *change* the paper paid no heed to human sensitivities.

Because of American Newspaper Guild contract strictures, Rosenthal could not outright fire people. But as he recognized, much of newspapering is pride, and in the early 1960's a byline was a valued supplement to the paycheck. Rosenthal disposed of the unwanted by reassigning them. A rewriteman who had worked a day shift for a de-

---

*Use of the male gender reflects early 1960's realities at the *Times*.

cade would be dispatched to the police shack for night duty in a distant borough. A copy editor who had handled City Hall would deal
with mundane items from Connecticut. Other people were given
seats in the rear of the city room and told to wait. Oh, they would get
"assignments" from time to time—to rewrite a release from a charity
about a ball or an award ("hold it to a graph") or to see if a local angle
could be found on an announcement from Washington that federal
grants for libraries would increase ("Make some calls"). The degrad-
ing feature of such "assignments" is that both the editor and the reporter know they involve make-shift work that will never reach the
paper. Pride is a bitter lump. This Rosenthal knew, and thus he rid
the *Times* of the reporters, rewritemen and editors he did not want.

In a memorandum to Catledge in January, 1965, two years after he
became metropolitan editor, Rosenthal listed eight persons who had
joined the metropolitan staff since December, 1963, either as new
hires or promotions. (Of these eight, two left within a year.) He also
listed twenty reporters who left in the same period. Rosenthal made
clear that he had rid the *Times* of persons he did not want.

From two decades distance, judging the talents of each person
nudged out of the *Times* by Rosenthal in the mid-1960's is impossible.
Even persons now unfriendly to Rosenthal state that he rid the paper
of persons who no longer should have worked there. But even in
these instances Rosenthal behaved with a personal brutality
uncharacteristic of *The New York Times*. The persons who worked at
43rd Street witnessed first-hand an ugliness of behavior that would
cause turmoil at the paper for two decades.

Exactly what Rosenthal disliked about some of the staff members
he inherited was not always easy to understand. Douglas Robinson
provides a good example. A Californian, Robinson joined the *Times* in
1955 as a news assistant in the Hollywood bureau, a half-clerk, half-
reporter who spent his mornings gathering and writing news and his
afternoons working in the office. He wrote bylined stories for the
Sunday paper; he filled in for the movie and televisions columnists
when they vacationed. He did so well he was brought to New York
and after a couple of years on police in the boroughs, "learning to talk
cop," he was made a night rewriteman.

Night rewrite, although an anonymous job, is important, for even
such a large newspaper as the *Times* keeps few reporters around in
the evening. Both big stories and odds-and-ends fall to the

rewriteman, who uses the telephone to find a politician at his summer home, or to cajole information on a murder from an upstate policeman, and write publishable copy at speed. As Doug Robinson puts it, "After seven o'clock at night, you [the night rewriteman] were THE *New York Times*." Because of his hours, Robinson had minimal contact with Rosenthal during the new editor's first months in New York. Robinson did observe Rosenthal as being "brusque, short with people," and not given to small talk. Thus Robinson's first personal encounter with Rosenthal came as a surprise.

Robinson was at a cocktail party at reporter Homer Bigart's place, sipping Scotch and exchanging war stories with other *Times* people, when he felt a tug at his arm. It was Rosenthal. "Can you come over here in the corner a minute? I'd like to talk with you."

Once they found privacy, Rosenthal stared at Robinson intensely. "You sit out there in the news room glowering at me," he said. "You do that all the time. I see you. You don't like me."

Robinson shook his head in disbelief. If he *did* glower at Rosenthal (he did not think he did), what difference could it make?

"I'm the best city editor who ever came down the pike," Rosenthal said. "But unless you learn to love me, you're not going anywhere."

Robinson had heard enough. He could not decide whether the man was drunk or truly offended by some unwitting slight. "Well, you're right," he told Rosenthal. "I *don't* like you."

"I warned you," Rosenthal said, and he strode away.

The episode disturbed Robinson. However far-fetched and zany Rosenthal's accusation might be, Rosenthal was his boss, and in a position to do him professional harm. Robinson had friends in the newsroom, and his own rise had been steady; further, the *Times* news operation was large enough that he could work elsewhere than under Rosenthal. But what of the future, if Rosenthal in fact was the "editor of the future," as gossip forecast? "This was the first time I ever heard an editor talk like that," Robinson said. "I decided I didn't care for the guy. And I decided also I had better watch out for Doug Robinson. I became a shop steward [for the American Newspaper Guild] as fast as I could."

Persons other than Robinson came to treat Rosenthal with wariness, and a recognition that the mercurial editor should be dealt with at arm's length. Richard Severo came to the *Times* in 1968 after work at the Poughkeepsie *Record*, the Associated Press, CBS News (he wrote much of the continuity the first days of the Kennedy assassination) and the Washington *Post*, where he was an urban affairs columnist. Initially he liked the way Rosenthal and Gelb ran the metropolitan desk. Severo's first major stories concerned the New York City Human Resources Administration. Working with reporters Richard Reeves, Barnard Collier and Richard Phalon, Severo produced "an interminable series of articles" on wrongdoing in HRA. Rosenthal nominated the articles for a Pulitzer Prize. The circumstances gave Severo the chance to hear Rosenthal evaluate the metropolitan staff.

"Scotty Reston [then the executive editor] called us back into his office with Rosenthal and Gelb for a congratulatory drink," Severo recollected. "Rosenthal has a problem—alcohol goes to his head very quickly. A minuscule amount makes him tipsy." This evening a single drink sufficed to start Rosenthal into a tirade against the *Times* metropolitan staff. Many of the persons he "inherited" were "punks and twerps." Oh, but Rosenthal had tried to get along with these persons, to show that he was an open man, and to attempt to improve the "poor morale" under Frank Adams. He talked about turning his desk around so that he faced the city room. "I wanted to face them," he said, "to let them know they could come to me at any time. But why do they hate me so? Look what's happened. These people sit in the back of the room and complain all the time. And they grumble and complain because they are not as good as we thought they were."

Arthur Gelb, who was also drinking, chimed agreement. "That's right, Abe, that's right."

Rosenthal warmed to the subject. "We've got to start building a bigger and better staff here, and you are going to be a part of it," he told Severo. Rosenthal turned again to the subject of bad staff morale, with Gelb offering calming and reassuring remarks. Gelb asked Severo how he liked the paper.

"Fine," Severo replied.

"See, Abe," Gelb explained excitedly, "it's not so bad. Dick, he's been here six months, he likes it. He's a happy man."

Gelb's cajoling had no effect. The tipsy Rosenthal continued what Severo called "his ranting about the paper." Later that evening, when the cocktail session ended, Severo felt troubled. "Here I was, a relative newcomer to the newspaper, and the top two editors spoke in such devastating terms about men who were senior to me. Right there, I saw trouble. For him to call these men—reporters in their fifties and sixties—punks and twerps was a sad commentary on him, not on them."

Journalism being an inherently gossipy profession, the "Abe stories" made their way around New York and elsewhere. Rosenthal's friends had long realized his mercurial nature; now they were alarmed that the nasty side of his personality was becoming so dominant. The labor reporter Stan Levey, for instance, had become one of Rosenthal's first friends when he joined the *Times*. The men were so close that when Levey's son Robert, now the Washington *Post* columnist, was circumcised in 1946, Rosenthal was one of eight men Levey persuaded to go to the hospital in a driving rainstorm for the ceremony. When Rosenthal returned to New York, Levey had left the *Times*, first to report for CBS News, then for the Scripps-Howard newspapers. Rosenthal and Levey had their first reunion in Washington in 1964. Levey had remarried, to Nan Robertson, a charming lady who joined the *Times* in 1955, and who covered the women's side of the Johnson White House.

The trio met at Le Bistro, and over drinks the men laughed about past times. "This is the guy," Rosenthal told Nan Robertson, "who taught me two important things for a man to know—how to tie one of those damned bow ties, and how to mix a decent martini." Then the talk turned to the current *Times*.

"Abe," Levey said, "I'm your friend, and I think I can talk straight to you. OK?" Rosenthal shrugged, as if to say, "Go ahead, try me."

"I don't like some of the things I'm hearing out of New York," Levey continued. "You are being damned ruthless towards people. I know Turner wants you to turn some things around. But do you have to be so damned mean to people when you are doing it?"

Rosenthal's face darkened as Levey continued, and he took off his glasses and squirmed in his seat. Then in Robertson's words, he "blew his stack." Cursing vilely, his voice shrill and garbled, he retorted that indeed he had a job to do. "These assholes, these fuckers, some of these people are coasting on their reputations, they're contributing nothing to the paper," he said. He listed names of some persons Levey knew as competent news professionals, men with whom he had worked.

Rosenthal's tirade lasted for some minutes, and other diners looked over to see what was causing the disturbance. Robertson's hushing motions finally quieted him.

Levey stared levelly across the table. "Abe, whatever your reasons, you are being a ruthless shit. Stop it." An awkward silence followed. When Levey spoke again, it was on another subject, but the dinner never regained any semblance of gaiety.

The episode preyed on Robertson, for it showed clearly how Rosenthal reacted when challenged. Rosenthal made his own mental marker as well. In January, 1975, Robertson, who had been working in Paris, came into 43rd Street on home leave and Rosenthal greeted her warmly and took her to his rear office for a drink.

"We had our Scotch, and commenced what was to be a 'love feast' talk about the good old times," Robertson said. But Rosenthal wanted to talk about something else.

"Nan," he said, "you've only been disloyal to me once, in all these years."

Robertson, puzzled, asked, "What do you mean, 'disloyal,' Abe? I thought we'd always been friends."

Rosenthal smiled. "That night back in Washington, when Stan got all over me about ruthlessness. You didn't stand up for me, Nan, you didn't stand up for the *Times*." He let the episode pass and turned the talk to another subject.

Robertson recollected, "I found it amusing at the time. I thought, 'This guy never forgets anything.' " Robertson had hit upon a major truth about Abe Rosenthal.

That the city room was in unhappy turmoil did not go unnoted by Catledge and other executives. In 1966 *Times* management brought in the consulting firm of Yankelovich, Skelly & White to do an "attitude survey" of employees, including those in the news department. A summary of the findings contained tart comments on the *Times* newsroom.

> It is reported that there is favoritism toward outsiders and an undervaluation of the *Times*'s own people—"They bring in new young men at high salaries who don't work out well."
>
> Feeling of being manipulated and made to compete with each other is expressed. Many respondents claimed that the competitive feeling has become excessive.

There is a feeling that society, fads, etc., get space that should go to important stories. . . . Some claim that the desire to turn in "exciting" story is so intense now it fosters distortions in reporting—look for "angle" they think the editor will like. . . . New rules are claimed . . . to be arbitrary and unreasonable; e.g., must travel economy, no pinochle in news room, no beer with lunches sent in; "petty" economies. . . .

There are complaints about cliques. Respondents say they can't go to Rosenthal with problems about Gelb because they are close buddies. . . .

There is concern expressed that desire to please Rosenthal and other news editors has led to tampering with story so that less important or reliable information gets played up in the lead paragraph because it's unusual and the story gets the wrong slant to make it more readable. Gelb is cited most frequently as being guilty of this in his editing of stories. . .

Rosenthal did not like either the idea of a survey or the report that resulted. He wrote an angry memorandum to Clifton Daniel, a deputy to Catledge, stating that the study "might be taken by the staff as a kind of confession by management that it did not know how to deal with its own staff members, a strange and unpleasant thing for a company that prides itself on a kind of special intimacy and family feeling and had to go outside for help." He felt the study "would make for poorer morale, rather than better."

Rosenthal noted that management wanted a better news report, which meant imposing "new and often tougher techniques of editing and assessment." Inevitably this meant unhappiness, for which he did not apologize. If management wanted "harmony and staff happiness this could be done by lowering our quality objectives. . . ." Exactly what did management want—a good newspaper or a cheerful staff? Rosenthal intended to do his job as he saw fit; the dissension he dismissed as newsroom gossip.

Rosenthal's reaction to the report displayed characteristics that were hallmarks of his career as an editor—outrage about being criticized by anyone outside the *Times* family; a tendency to regard any comment on his performance as a personal affront; and an inability to take seriously any suggestion that he could perhaps do his job differently. My way or else; if you put curbs on me or try to change me, the paper will suffer. Such was the direct threat he posed to Catledge and

Daniel. Significantly, they chose not to challenge him. Although the
Yankelovich study apparently recommended substantive changes in
the way the news department was managed, neither of Rosenthal's
superiors applied them to the metropolitan desk.

Rosenthal recognizes now (or so he said in 1986) that he made serious management mistakes as metropolitan editor—chiefly because of
different perceptions held by him and his staff. He starts with the
premise that he was "very popular the first few weeks. I was one of
them, another reporter working in the newsroom." He was comfortable with his own understanding of how Catledge wished him to
change and improve city coverage. Rosenthal wanted to behave like
an enthusiastic reporter, to do things the "right way," the reporter's
way, as he and friends had talked about in incessant newsroom sessions in the 1940's. His perception was that when he said, "Let's do it
this way," reporters "would be delighted." What he felt he was doing
was accomplishing the reporter's dream—that of making the *Times* a
reporter's newspaper, where the writer had more control over the
shape and substance of his story than did an unfeeling copy editor.

What he did not realize, he now concedes, was that persons to
whom he suggested change were hearing him saying, "The way
you've done it is no longer good enough." And in many instances, indeed, this was true; many reporters did not meet Rosenthal's measure of excellence. As Rosenthal said, "Not everybody could accept
that; there were varying degrees of acceptance from different people."

The Yankelovich study, in a sense, marked a watershed for
Rosenthal as metropolitan editor. He gave Catledge a choice, a happy
staff or a quality city report, and Catledge opted for the latter. Hence
Rosenthal now accepted what he considered to be a tacit mandate to
run the city room as he wished.

Rosenthal perceived himself as a swift and accurate judge of talent,
and he divided the city staff into three broad categories. The *Times*
had some "very talented people" who were not being used to their
capacity. Other persons "could be encouraged to do better." Finally,
there were "other people who could not perform, regardless." So
Rosenthal did the journalistic equivalent of battlefield triage. If a reporter was so flawed that no amount of training would transform him
into a *Times*-quality professional, Rosenthal shoved him aside. He
preferred to use his energies on someone who could be bettered. But
each discarded reporter meant a bruised ego—complaints, and bitter

ones, from persons who had settled comfortably into a routine of life, and who now worked for an editor who demanded something entirely different.

But for persons who performed to his liking, Rosenthal offered not only display space in the paper but also increased salaries. Here he broke with Frank Adams's practice. As Clifton Daniel noted about Adams, he was a "conservative, old-fashioned fellow and his thinking about salaries hasn't changed since the day when $10 a week was considered quite a substantial raise. Frank . . . tends to spread his raises thin. He would rather give a small raise to each of ten people than a substantial raise to two." To Daniel's thinking (a concept endorsed by Rosenthal) the *Times* "should definitely adopt a policy of considerable disparity in wage rates . . . consciously and carefully planned to favor and encourage excellence." Rosenthal's first round of pay raises, only two months after he became metropolitan editor, reflected this philosophy. Gay Talese went from $208.25 to $280; Homer Bigart from $368.50 to $410, and Charles Grutzner from $265 to $315. *Times* policy at the time was to limit merit increases to ten percent; both Grutzner and Talese went far past this "limit." The raises were Rosenthal's way of rewarding talent, and encouraging it to stay with the *Times*.

Another priority was bringing respect to the city staff. During the years he worked in New York, Rosenthal learned acutely the difference in prestige afforded national, foreign and city reporters. "I wanted to demonstrate that the metropolitan staff was as good as the foreign staff, and had the same rank. I wanted to show people that they could go to the metropolitan staff and . . . be treated with dignity. Now this was a terribly important thing. This also involved getting metropolitan reporters into thinking they were as good and as important as anyone on the paper."

So Rosenthal fought for a byline policy that rewarded his people for good work. The national and foreign desks almost reflexively put a reporter's name on any story of half a column or more. When the national desk "borrowed" one of Rosenthal's reporters for an assignment, say, in Kansas, he received a byline; not so for comparable work in New York. Rosenthal argued heatedly with the news desk, which had the power to give bylines, and he often won. "The bylines were very important in establishing that the city staff was as good as any other staff on the paper."

Gaining prestige also prompted Rosenthal to carry out what he called "the building of a land empire, an expansion, empire building, whatever." Under Frank Adams the city desk had been responsible for the five boroughs of New York City, Westchester County, New York; Fairfield County, Connecticut; parts of New Jersey; and the state government in Albany. But if a New York reporter went to Buffalo, he reported to the national desk. Even when in hot pursuit of a story, a reporter had to "clear it with national" before going outside city desk territory. To Rosenthal this division was rank nonsense. "We didn't want any of that crap," he said, "so we started a war with the national staff." This was Rosenthal's first major exercise in *Times* office politics, and Harrison Salisbury, then the national editor, and a man who aspired to replace Catledge, soon realized his flanks were endangered by the newcomer. Rosenthal overheard him giving a pep talk to his reporters and editors one day. "You guys better pull your socks up," Salisbury warned.

With vivid displays of anguish, Rosenthal protested his cause all over the newsroom. Boundaries, he said, are artificial lines on a map, and in the name of efficiency his staff should be given jurisdiction over the broadest conceivable definition of the "metropolitan" area. (By putting the word "metropolitan" rather than "city" in Rosenthal's title, Catledge gave him justification for the attempted territorial grab.) As Rosenthal recollected with relish, he put Salisbury into the position where the national desk "was the black flag group," whereas his staff worked "under the flag of virtue." More importantly, Catledge and his deputy managing editor, Clifton Daniel, backed Rosenthal, and the "city" expanded to encompass all of New York State, plus Connecticut and New Jersey.

At an editorial meeting soon after these changes, someone asked about the current definition of metropolitan coverage.

"All the way to the Canadian border," someone said. Rosenthal had won his first power struggle within the *Times*—quickly and smoothly, and with important backers.

So what was Rosenthal's goal? He wanted reporters who could see beyond conventional news coverage, who could write without blind obedience to the who-what-when-where-why-and-how formula so long sacred to American newspapers and the journalism trade schools which supplied their manpower. In later years Rosenthal would argue that the "fifth w," the "why," should be dropped from the formula; for a reporter to pretend to know a person's motivation for an action was usually guessing or editorializing, neither of which belonged in a news story. Rosenthal's idea was a reporter who could think in terms of concepts, who could recognize significant trends in an area, and then describe them in vivid prose that let the reader share the experience.

In screening new reporters, Rosenthal talked about how he had reported from abroad. When he wrote about peasants in India, he wanted *Times* readers to feel the mud squish between their toes; when he described a street market in Poland, he wished to convey the degradation of daily life there. He demanded the same performance of his reporters who were writing about New York.

Myron Farber was a reporter who felt Rosenthal's sting—then, his friendship. When Farber came to the *Times* in early 1966, after three years with the Hartford *Courant*, he thought Rosenthal an "intense man who, whether seated at his desk or prowling the newsroom, seemed always to be smoldering." One of Farber's early assignments was to cover the occupation of the Board of Education's conference room by activists protesting the quality of the city's schools. After a few days the police arrested the "rump school board" and its leader, a preacher named Milton Galamison. "I soon received a call from Rosenthal," Farber related. "He didn't like the beginning of my story. He wanted to be able to 'feel' and 'see' the hand of the policeman on Reverend Galamison's shoulder, and the expression on the minister's face. And if I couldn't achieve that, he said, maybe a rewriteman at the *Times* could." Farber could not, and Rosenthal took his byline off the story, the only time he ever did so. "But he had made his point."

Rosenthal also made his point with bullpen editors, who for years had imposed their own concepts of style upon the paper's writing. These men, few of whom had worked as reporters, seemed determined to leach color and flash from stories. Rosenthal changed this system, and noisily. Once a story left the metropolitan desk, he demanded, the bullpen should not touch it save for spelling, grammar, or an obvious factual error, and only then after consulting with the original editor. A former bullpen editor said, "Abe was profane, wild, when he argued with the bullpen. 'You are the dumbest cock-sucking son of a bitch in the newspaper business, you should be out selling insurance policies, if the bastards would be dumb enough to hire an ignorant asshole like you.' I wrote that one down one night in 1965, because I thought the guy he cussed was going to stand up and kill him, and I wanted to have the exact language for my statement to the police."

Rosenthal's face would become so twisted that his features were unrecognizable, he would stand at the bullpen and pound his hands on the desk, spewing invective. "I am the goddamned metropolitan editor of this goddamned newspaper, and when I approve a god-damned story for goddamned publication, I goddamned well mean it. Now if you are too goddamned dumb to goddamn realize that, you keep your hands off my goddamned stories." Ted Bernstein, who ran the bullpen, would come over and try to soothe the raging Rosenthal. But carefully. He once stood behind Rosenthal during a particularly nasty scene and tugged at his arm. Rosenthal was so caught in his anger that he turned and almost hit Bernstein before he recognized him.

A man who reported for the city desk at the time at first thought these eruptions were for effect, to let the bullpen know that injudicious editing would result in a stormy scene, and that they would stop bothering copy simply to avoid arousing Rosenthal. Such was not the case. "Abe could not control himself. When someone changed a story he or his deputies had edited, he took it as a personal affront." Catledge had told him to improve the paper's writing, and he was not going to be sabotaged by some gray-faced old man who had never covered a story in his life.

The inevitable showdown came late in a day when Rosenthal and Artie Gelb nursed a Gay Talese story through a long process of writing and editing. Telling the story properly required almost a column of space. Ted Bernstein ordered it cut by a half, so it would fit the space allotted on the metropolitan page.

Rosenthal made the usual arguments, and of course he lost. And this time his reaction was totally different. He turned and walked away from Bernstein's desk, and he put on his overcoat and he strode out of the news room with the determination of a man who just might not return.

"Where's Abe going?" someone asked Gelb.

The better question, Gelb suggested, might be, "Is Abe coming back?"

He did, but he had made his point. Several days later Catledge passed along word that no more cuts in city stories would be made without Rosenthal's consent.

Rosenthal's special talent was for what the news business calls "take-outs," lengthy stories of 5,000 to 7,000 words that permit a reporter to explore, in depth and detail, an important issue. When Martin Tolchin was assigned to cover the city's hospital, his byline vanished from the paper for six months. His articles, when they finally appeared, were explosive, and cut to the causes of the failure of the system, an analysis far superior to the "snake-pit" approach usually found in daily newspapers. J. Anthony Lukas spent weeks researching the troubled life of Linda Fitzpatrick, a young woman who in a less turbulent era might have been a debutante; she chose terrorism and was blown to bits making a bomb.

Arthur Gelb worked closely with Rosenthal on such stories, so much so that *Times* people referred to them almost as a single person, "Abe-and-Artie." Gelb, a tall and gaunt man, would stalk around the city desk, flinging his arms into the air and then clutching them to his body, as if trying physically to pull something into him. "Give me stories, *give me stories*," he would demand of the city reporters. "A fountain of ideas." "A genius, the best newspaperman of his generation." "The creator of the really good stuff the *Times* did in the 1960's and the 1970's." Such are the things that people who worked for Gelb said about him. David Burnham, who worked directly under Gelb for several years, came to appreciate his strengths, and also to recognize his flaws.

After working for United Press International, *Newsweek*, and CBS News, Burnham served briefly in the late 1960's as press man for the President's Commission on Law Enforcement and the Administration of Justice, chaired by Nicholas Katzenbach. The deputy director, the Washington lawyer Henry Ruth, wanted to get newspapers into the habit of investigating workings of the criminal justice system to spur better performance. At Ruth's request, Burnham wrote Gelb a letter suggesting "a lot of things you could be covering," such as the actual workings of jails and the courts. Ruth's idea was that "if we can get *The New York Times* to start covering this kind of thing, the rest of the papers will follow." Burnham met with Gelb; to his surprise he got a call a month later. "Would you like to cover police for *The New York Times*?"

Burnham hesitated, for the thought of going to the *Times* "scared me to death. I had just read Gay Talese's book on what kind of place it was." But the fact that Gelb had not gotten defensive when an outsider suggested stories encouraged him. "He was hungry for stories, and he saw these ideas as a means of getting them."

His first six months Burnham was an absolute flop, and even Gelb began to act like both sides had made a mistake. Burnham had not signed on to do stabbings and shootings, "but on the workings of the New York Police Department." But how could he cope with a department that had 30,000 officers spread over five boroughs? Then one day a source told him about "cooping," police jargon for officers who sleep on the job. The source said that many—perhaps even a majority—of New York policemen who worked at night slept at least part of the time, so they could hold other jobs during the day.

The notion sounded far-fetched, but Burnham decided to check. A sub-editor told him to forget it, "that's not a story." Curious, Burnham pursued cooping on his own. Several mornings he arose so he could prowl the streets at two o'clock. He found a news clerk at the *Times* who worked the late shift and had a camera and tripod for the time exposure needed for pictures in near-darkness. They found cops sleeping almost every place they looked—in parks, behind buildings, on the dock. One photo showed three squad cars parked together—the entire patrol element of a precinct. Figures slumped in the front seats were sleeping policemen.

Gelb was so pleased with the story he ran around the news room flapping his arms with excitement. "Terrific! Terrific!" he cried. The cooping story attracted national attention, and as Burnham says, "My career was made with that story." He was to do many other stories, notably on a policeman named Frank Serpico who informed on crooked colleagues, and was nearly shot to death as a result. The theme of the Serpico and other stories was that the entire criminal justice system was collapsing; at Gelb's insistence, Burnham and other reporters explored *why* this was happening.

But even Gelb had his limits. One of Burnham's primary sources was Harry Subin, of the New York University Law School and the Vera Institute of Justice. They talked one day after the cooping story. "It's easy to kick around cops," Subin said. "Why not go after the judges?"

How? "Go look at the number of cases handled on Monday and Friday, and compare them with Tuesday through Thursday. Go down and clock them, watch when they're working and when they're goofing off." Burnham did, and he also obtained a transcript of a meeting of the judges themselves at which complaints were voiced about some jurists not working. One judge said, "You all know the story—everybody is flying the coop," that is, leaving court on Friday to start the weekend early.

Burnham built his story carefully. The first five paragraphs he told his own observations, and how the shortened work week hurt the courts. The next paragraph he used the "flying the coop" quotation, having laid the background for it. "Arthur was very excited when he read the story. 'Good story, good story,' he said. Then he went off about half an hour—I guess to Abe, because that's who he reported to. He came back shaking his head. 'This story is much too abrasive,' he said. 'Who are *we* to say this about judges?'

"Well, we fought and fought. One thing I'll say about Artie. You could fight with Artie, and he wouldn't get mad with you." They finally reached what Burnham thought was an agreement; he did minor tinkering with the first version, and left for a weekend in Vermont. As he walked out of the office he noticed something unusual—Rosenthal sitting in his glassed-in office, busily at work on a typewriter. "It was very weird, for Abe didn't write often in those days."

As it happened, that weekend a blizzard hit the Northeast, and Burnham was incommunicado. When he returned he read the courts story, and he flinched. The "flying the coop" quotation now was in the lead paragraph and his own observations were shoved well down into the story. "They deballed it, totally." Burnham made inquiries. One editor told him Rosenthal personally rewrote the story. Burnham feels this a common failing of the *Times*, to use an outsider's statement over the observations of its own reporter. In a sense, this continued the "paper of record" syndrome, the preference for the "official source," even something as casual as a transcript of a judges' conference. Here also a dichotomy. The *Times* trusted Burnham's personal account when he wrote about lower-middle-class policemen sleeping in their squad cars. Yet the *Times*—that is, Rosenthal— hesitated to go after judges on its own initiative.

Gelb's conduct vividly illustrated the realities of the relationship between him and Rosenthal. Although people said "Abe-and-Artie" in one breath, Rosenthal definitely dominated. Gelb could be shameless in changes of attitude towards a story. If he liked something, and Rosenthal later criticized it, Gelb immediately changed his mind,

without explanation or apology. Few persons who worked under Gelb
questioned his skills as an editor. But the recurring epithet was
"Abe's toady." One man still at the *Times* offered a defense, of sorts.
Had Arthur Gelb ever given Abe Rosenthal a serious argument, he
would no longer work for *The New York Times*. Gelb was to trail along
after Rosenthal the next two decades as both men rose through *The
New York Times*.

Rosenthal's knapsack of favorite stories includes an account of how
he came to distrust all politicians and government officials. He asked
an Indian diplomat at the United Nations whether such-and-so was
true, and the man gave an answer that events soon proved to be an
outright lie. Enraged, Rosenthal asked the Indian why he chose to lie
when he could simply have said, "No comment." The Indian wagged
his finger at Rosenthal. "Aha, had I said no comment, you would have
known what you asked was true." The moral of this story, Rosenthal
would say, is that newspapermen should never trust politicians to tell
the truth about *anything*.

Unfortunately, during his first years as metropolitan editor,
Rosenthal did not follow his own adage in dealing with New York City
politics. Although Rosenthal knew nothing about it, one of his first
acts was to shove aside the three men who had covered the beat for
the *Times*: Douglas Dales, Paul Crowell and Lehman Y. Robison,
who collectively had more than half a century of experience.
Rosenthal put them in make-work jobs, and all left the paper. As the
chief political writer, Rosenthal selected Richard Witkin, a good
friend from his local reporting days, but a man who had never covered local politics. Several persons noted a juxtaposition of Witkin's
appointment with Rosenthal's and Gelb's interest in the mayoralty
candidacy of Congressman John Lindsay.

Lindsay was a major media political star of the 1960's, the patrician
WASP, lean and intelligent, who promised to restore good government to New York City. Rosenthal and Gelb lunched with him several times before he announced his candidacy; shrewdly, he asked
what *they* felt he could do to help the city. Lindsay could recognize
an ego across a crowded room, and a few strokes sufficed to transform
Rosenthal and Gelb into true and important believers. He and campaign manager Robert Price became social friends of Rosenthal and
Gelb. To the rage of several *Times* reporters, during the campaign

Price had carte blanche to come into the newsroom and sit on the edge of reporters' desks and talk politics. As one of these men stated, Price "had the run of the office, he was in the office all the time."

Reporter Douglas Robinson had an annoying experience that satisfied him that Rosenthal and Gelb had gotten too close to Lindsay for their own good—and that of the *Times.* As a general assignment reporter, Robinson covered Lindsay one day when the candidate decided to have a luncheon for the press. "Bob Price said everything was off the record, which was fine," Robinson said. "This meant we could shoot the breeze with Lindsay and see what makes him tick." But midcourse in the luncheon Robinson noticed that the reporter for the New York *Journal-American* was taking notes.

Hey, wait a minute, Robinson said, I thought this was all off-the-record, and here this guy is, writing things down.

The *Journal-American* man explained that he was taking notes for future use, not for the next day's paper.

Whereupon Price stated, "You guys can write stories if you wish; just don't hurt the candidate."

Just don't hurt the candidate. Geez, Robinson said to himself, is this guy Price some sort of idiot? The words rankled. His job was not to protect a politician, but to write "what made the best story." He went through his notes and wrote a story quoting Lindsay's prediction that he would win the mayoralty by several hundred thousand votes. Since Lindsay's campaign strategy relied heavily upon his posture as an underdog, his boastful prediction could cause him tactical problems.

Robinson recollected, "That night, around 9:30 or ten o'clock, I got a call at home from a friend on the copy desk. He asked if I was aware that Bob Price had spoken to Richard Witkin, and that they were changing my story. No, I hadn't, and I immediately called Witkin. He told me Price had argued with the story, and that, yes, he had changed it.

" 'What the hell are you doing?' I asked Witkin.

" 'Bob Price says this isn't so,' Witkin told me.

" 'How the hell do you know? You weren't even there.' "

Robinson's original story was restored, but Gelb assigned him to no more John Lindsay stories. On election night Robinson stood in the newsroom with Martin Arnold, another city reporter (deputy editor of *The New York Times Magazine* in later years) and watched an odd spectacle. "Abe, Gelb and Witkin were dancing up and down as the returns came in, showing a victory for Lindsay. 'We won! We won!' they were shouting. We [Robinson and Arnold] were both appalled.

"This kind of cemented my feelings about Abe Rosenthal. Abe is on the take—not for money, but for recognition, and for 'being somebody.' Helping Lindsay be elected mayor made him feel like he was somebody. For a newspaperman this is the worst sort of dishonesty, because the reader and the public get hurt."

Rosenthal's romance with Lindsay and his administration soured before the 1960's ended, and he and Gelb loosened reporters who did damaging stories about virtually every city agency. In talks with reporters Rosenthal groused about "promise and delivery," and how newspapers should be "vigilant" in reporting on government and what it actually did. This proved to be another instance where Rosenthal did not listen to himself. In the late 1970's and early 1980's, as shall be seen, *The New York Times* essentially stopped any serious journalistic oversight of New York City government. Because such supposed watchdogs as the *Times* had not done their jobs, politicians put New York into its worst corruption scandal in a century.

But in the 1960's the talk in New York journalism was about the exciting atmosphere at the *Times*. One such person who felt the lure of Abe-and-Artie was Sidney Zion, whose antecedents are equally Damon Runyon and Yale Law School, a Broadway hipster in a Brooks Brothers pinstripe suit. Zion learned formal law at Yale; he learned street law prosecuting federal mob cases in North Jersey. Writing about the people he prosecuted—creatures of a milieu with its own values and morality—seemed infinitely more interesting than putting them in jail. So Zion hired on at the lively but corrupt New York *Post*, where advertiser and other pressures killed his best stories. At newspaper bars around town—Zion likes a Scotch or two—all the talk was of Abe-and-Artie. So in late 1964 Zion talked to Rosenthal, commencing a love-hate relationship that finally evolved into mutual respect.

Zion found Rosenthal to be a man "in his early forties, a pudgy, chain-smoking energy plant with an owlish face that displayed an oddly sweet smile." The rapport was instant, for Zion grasped immediately the sort of reporting Rosenthal wanted. Talking together, they developed a job they would call "metropolitan legal correspondent," responsible for broad trends in the law—the impact of Warren Court decisions at the local level, say—rather than daily coverage of trials. (Harrison Salisbury, then an assistant managing editor, almost black-balled Zion because he submitted stolen *Post* morgue clips, rather than copies, with his application. Salisbury, himself no stranger to pilfered documents, considered Zion dishonest. But executive editor Turner Catledge approved his hiring with the jaunty advice, "Now go back downstairs and make sure the boys don't screw you too much on money.")

Zion was to work for the *Times* for five glorious years, before distant sirens lured him to other ventures (first the radical magazine *Scanlan's Monthly*, then Broadway Joe's Restaurant and other affairs), and while it lasted he "whistled my way to the paper every morning. . . . I was a kid on a carousel." And the carnival masters were Abe Rosenthal and Art Gelb. As Zion has written:

Abe and Arthur, hungry and on the make—what a commotion it was. Like great coaches, they molded a team out of veterans, rookies, a free agent here, a sleeper there. Abe was Vince Lombardi to Arthur's John Madden. Together they drove, cajoled, drank with you, lunched with you, *lived* with you. They were there when you weren't there.

So omnipresent were the two editors, indeed, that a lady finally tired of hearing their names at dinner one night and scrawled on a napkin:

Let's fly away,
  Let's find a land that's warm and tropic
  Where Abe and Arthur ain't the topic
All the live long day.

Such were the glory days of Abe-and-Artie.

For the first of these years, Abe Rosenthal lived with a secret, one that for months he would not share even with such friends as Arthur Gelb. Rosenthal fell in love with another woman, and he commenced an extramarital affair that was to span almost two decades. This was not Rosenthal's first adultery. While based in Tokyo he had gone through a brief but torrid affair with the wife of another correspondent. During his Asian travels he learned of the good and most trustworthy brothels in each country, and he patronized them regularly. But the new affair was serious.

In 1965 Katharine Balfour was a slim, Titian-haired beauty in her early thirties, an actress who made her film debut in 1946 in *Music for Millions* in a cast that included Margaret O'Brien, Jimmy Durante, June Allyson and Jose Iturbi. She married, to a psychotherapist; she had a daughter, Mary; she divorced in the early 1960's, and resumed her career. She did theater in New York and in stock companies; she was nominated for an Emmy for a public television show; she hosted a radio interview show on a labor-owned station in New York. Balfour was by no means a star, but she was considered a woman with the potential to become one. At a dinner party one night she enjoyed a chat with a Pakistani diplomat who looked at her high cheek bones and decided she must be Iranian. No, Balfour laughed, she was not, but her parents were of Russian Odessa stock, which was close enough.

Several days later the Pakistani diplomat rang her, late in the afternoon. He was apologetic. He had a problem, he knew she was single and perhaps available. He was hosting a very important dinner party that evening to welcome a new diplomat to New York, and one of the other guests had telephoned to say his wife was ill, and could not attend, and could he come anyway? The Pakistani asked if Balfour would be so kind as to be his dinner partner? The man's name, the Pakistani continued, was "Aybee Rosenthal," who worked at *The New York Times*.

Balfour thought the pronunciation strange; she knew some people at the *Times* through her career, but the name Rosenthal meant nothing to her. The man, of course, turned out to be Abe Rosenthal, who arrived from the *Times* at a trot, once the metropolitan page was secure—a man with unruly hair, a suit that seemed designed for someone with shoulders of a different dimension, and a paunch with a slight bounce. As a newly-single woman Balfour shrugged; she had seen worse, but not voluntarily. She remembered nothing of consequence being said during dinner.

"Afterwards, Abe sort of plopped down on the couch beside me, and we started talking. I liked him. He was bright, intellectual, he knew something about almost any subject. He asked if he could take me home." He did, and he said goodnight at the lobby.

Rosenthal told Balfour the first evening that he was married. He phoned, they had dinner. Within two months or so they were lovers. Rosenthal never told Balfour directly that his sexual relationship with wife Ann had ended, but he so hinted, and in increasingly specific terms. "Nothing happens between Ann and me, that's all over," he said several times. Ann was ill with rheumatoid arthritis and grossly overweight. As the years passed, Ann's obesity and arthritis became so acute she was at times confined to a wheelchair.

From their first intimacy Rosenthal told Balfour he loved her, that he would like to marry her, and spend the rest of his life with her. Ann, he said, she was a problem. Their sons must be considered. He would not leave a marriage, however flawed, so long as any of the sons lived at home. But could she bear with him for the time being?

Yes, Balfour decided, she would; she trusted Rosenthal when he said they would eventually wed. So Rosenthal became a frequent but discreet visitor to Balfour's apartment off Lexington Avenue in the East Eighties. He would come directly there from the *Times*, two to three nights a week. He would drop his briefcase on the living room floor, and slip off his shoes and lie on her bed. He loved to have her rub creams into his face (he suffered a recurring problem with his complexion) and then he would arise and go out to the couch. Balfour would bring him a tray with a Scotch and water and snacks. Her daughter Mary, then in her teens, would snuggle next to Rosenthal, and she called him "Daddy" when he stroked her hair.

As the months and years passed Balfour neglected her own career to devote herself to pleasing Abe Rosenthal. She worked on his physical reformation. When they first met Abe was a "horrible dresser," so she insisted on taking him to shops where he could buy clothes that fit his distinctive frame. She would watch as he tried on different coats, and she would say, Yes, Abe, or, No, Abe, please, not that one. He followed her advice. She worked on Rosenthal's hair. Photographs from the early 1960's show Rosenthal with his hair either totally unruly, as if he did not acknowledge it, or else plastered to the side of his head. Balfour convinced him to let it have a more natural look, to throw away the hair oils, and to shampoo daily.

To Rosenthal the sexual part of their relationship seemed secondary; several times he experienced what Balfour called a "potency problem." Nevertheless he liked to feature himself as a Lothario, and he told her freely of some of his other affairs.

By another account Rosenthal enjoyed the ego gratification available to a free-spender in a brothel, even in the absence of direct sexual contact. A tour of the Southwestern United States in the late 1970's took Rosenthal to Laredo, Texas, and his "eyes lit up" when a local editor referred to "Boys' Town," the famed whorehouse complex just across the Rio Grande in Mexico. Once luncheon ended, Rosenthal insisted that he be taken there. According to a most reliable bystander:

> We found it, picked one of the cantinas at random and went in. It was about three in the afternoon and there was nobody there but us and about 20 young women, dressed in the most outlandish costumes— corsets, garter belts, you name it. We sat down and ordered beers.
>
> Inevitably, a few of the young women descended on us. Jones and Crewdson and Stevens looked quite uncomfortable (nobody spoke any Spanish and they didn't speak much English except for a few graphic terms).
>
> Abe, however, was enjoying himself hugely, buying them all drinks. Here was a man in his element—surrounded by attentive women. No one, of course, took the women up on their offers.
>
> But the women obviously thought Abe was cute, and I remember thinking, "This is really what he likes best, to be surrounded by attentive people who treat him like royalty."
>
> The talk turned to other world-famous whorehouses. Abe mentioned one in Taiwan that I think was called the "Literary Inn." I asked him how it compared to Boys' Town. After a pregnant pause, he said, "I've only heard about it." Then he gets the Cheshire cat smile on his face. "Yes," he said, "I've heard about it." Very coy.
>
> As we left the cantina Abe turned to Crewdson and Stevens and Jones and me. "If anybody ever finds out about this, it's the Brooklyn police shack for all of you."

To Balfour, her relationship with Rosenthal transcended sex. When he had a leg operation, she carefully checked to insure that Ann Rosenthal would not be around, and she brought him flowers and a hug. Balfour helped Rosenthal stop smoking; she gave him sympathy after a hemorrhoid operation; she kept a bottle of Scotch ready for whenever he could visit.

She also abandoned her career. She had offers; if they interfered with her relationship with Rosenthal—the man she expected to marry—she rejected them. She took several roles. In *Love Story*, she played the upper-crust mother of Ryan O'Neil, opposite Ray Milland. The same year she was in *The Adventurers*, with Candice Bergen, Ernest Borgnine and Olivia de Havilland. These appearances were in 1970. Both required her to work in Los Angeles. She declined later movie work. She chose to remain in New York, to be near Rosenthal.

In time Rosenthal dared to make the affair quasi-public, first among such close friends as Artie and Barbara Gelb, then on his travels around the United States and elsewhere. On a trip to Los Angeles he was invited to the home of television producer Norman Lear, along with Aljean Harmatz, the *Times* entertainment correspondent there, and her husband. Would it be proper to bring along Katharine? Abe asked. After all, we're not married. Don't be silly, Abe, Harmatz told him, you're in *California*. They sailed off the Italian coast, they spent a week in a Long Island cottage. These trips Rosenthal took independently of his wife, and he offered no explanation to Balfour, other than that he packed his bags and told Ann he was going on vacation.

Rosenthal's drinking the first years alarmed Balfour, for she saw the nastiness of his moods once he was into Scotch. By forcing him to eat sensible foods—he said he usually ate "hot dogs and pickles at home"—she rid him of much of his paunch. But for years his drinking was something he did not care to discuss with her, and when he thought she was nagging him on the subject, he reacted violently. The worst of these episodes came one night at Elaine's, on Third Avenue, just a few blocks below Balfour's apartment.

Because he charged off much of his dining and drinking to a *Times* expense account, Rosenthal paid little attention to prices when he ordered wines. He liked a white wine that Elaine's sold for $12 to $14 a bottle. Once he ordered something else, and he did not blink when the waiter informed him this particular wine sold for $100 a bottle.

The night of the quarrel, the Gelbs were at the table, and Rosenthal did most of the drinking as the party went through two bottles of wine. At around 11:30 P.M. the Gelbs began making signs they were ready to leave. Rosenthal beckoned the waiter and ordered a third bottle of wine.

Balfour reached out and touched his arm. "Honey, don't get another one—we're all ready to go." She wanted no more wine, and neither of the Gelbs were drinking much. Balfour's thought was that she did not want the new bottle to go to waste, for Abe to drink a sip or so and leave the rest for the waiter.

Rosenthal became indignant, and he insisted that the waiter bring the new bottle (as Balfour expected, he drank very little of it). Rosenthal was still mad when they walked outside, but he held his tongue while the Gelbs got a taxi. As he and Balfour walked towards her apartment, he abused her loudly. Using profanities liberally he told her he could not stand to be around a woman who criticized his drinking; that he would drink what he wished, in whatever amount he wished, and this was none of her blinking business; further, if she didn't keep her blinking mouth shut, she could just stay the blink away from him and out of his blinking life.

Rosenthal did not go upstairs with her that night. He called the next day, still in a rage, so mad he would not even let her say a word. Then for about three weeks he did not call at all, and Balfour feared she had lost him. But he returned, without a word of contrition, and they resumed their relationship, and in time, on his own initiative, he did begin to cut back on Scotch.

When they were apart Rosenthal showered Balfour with cards and letters. She went to Cornell University to research an article for *Family Weekly*, the *Times*-owned magazine for which she had started writing. She arrived to find her hotel room adorned with a huge floral display. When Abe went to China he sent three, four postcards daily. My darling, I love you, I wish to be with you forever. My darling, you are the most beautiful woman in the world. I want you for my wife. I shall cherish you always.

When Mary finished school Rosenthal helped her to get a job as a graphic designer at the *Times*, and she performed well. Rosenthal would come around for a talk and a hug, and his strong feelings for her were obvious to anyone who saw them together. Artie Gelb was also friendly with Mary, and when they encountered one another in a cafe near the *Times* he, too, would greet her with a warm embrace. And when Mary was hospitalized, Rosenthal visited her daily, and sat by her bed for hours, offering her cheer.

Many times Rosenthal talked of his wife Ann, and her poor health. However, when Balfour would ask why he did not leave her he would become evasive. More than once she told Rosenthal, "Give her everything you have, come live on me, I'll take care of you." He would change the subject. Then he would call in the morning, the sound of desperation in his voice, and say, "We had another white night," his way of saying he and Ann had had a bad quarrel.

So Balfour settled into an unsteady relationship. She told herself she was a fool to make such a commitment to a married man, over such a prolonged period. Her explanation, of course, is simple. "I loved Abe Rosenthal, and I wanted to be with him."

Coincidental with Abe Rosenthal's start of a new career as editor, another person was learning an unexpected role at *The New York Times*. Arthur Ochs Sulzberger, son of Arthur Hays Sulzberger, was suddenly thrust into the position of publisher in May, 1963, years ahead of schedule and expectation—and, in the view of most persons around the paper, light years ahead of his ability to hold the most important job at the paper.

EIGHT

"Take Something of a Gamble"

Arthur Ochs Sulzberger, the only son of Arthur Hays Sulzberger, was a man-child never taken seriously even by his own family, much less executives and editors of the *Times*. Sulzberger grew up in the protective cocoon provided by great wealth and three doting older sisters. No one ever posed him any particular challenges, intellectual or otherwise, and he certainly sought none of his own. Trust funds created by the family fortune insured him a comfortable living regardless of whether he chose to work, and for a significant part of his life he chose *not* to work, at school or elsewhere. As a lad Sulzberger went through a succession of private schools. In a perhaps unwittingly biting profile written for *Times Talk*, the paper's house organ, on his appointment as publisher, sister Ruth Sulzberger Golden commented of Punch:

> Nearly every school in the vicinity of New York was graced by Punch's presence at one time or another. They were all delighted to

have him, but wanted him as something other than a spectator. One after another confessed that though they found him charming, they were not "getting through" to him. One school kept him rather longer than the others. It turned out that the Headmaster's wife was a sculptress and thought Punch had such a beautiful head that she was using him for a model.

Since he did not afford anyone the opportunity to judge what was inside his head, it was gratifying that the outside at least was admired.*

Sister Ruth did not exaggerate; young Punch by age seventeen had attended no less than six private schools—Browning, Lawrence, Smith, Morningside, St. Bernard's and Loomis. Sulzberger was one of the few Americans happy about the Japanese attack on Pearl Harbor. "This gave me the excuse to finally quit school, otherwise I might still be up there in Loomis, trying to graduate." He entered the Marine Corps at age seventeen and, despite a couple of piddling illnesses—measles at boot camp and jaundice in the Pacific—he drove a car in General Douglas MacArthur's headquarters briefly.

But his two years in service seemed to have the proper settling influence, and Sulzberger finished both high school and Columbia University, with a bachelor of arts degree. As Sulzberger put it, "I settled down in a hurry." His family ties dictated that Sulzberger would go into the newspaper business, although no evidence exists that the profession interested him in the least. Turner Catledge remembered meeting Punch at age ten, when his mother brought him and the three sisters to the 1936 Democratic National Convention. Catledge, ever the gracious host, showed the Sulzbergers around. "Punch spent some time examining the news ticker. He was far more interested in the mechanics of the thing than in the words coming out of it. This was typical of Punch, for he has always been mechanically inclined."

Sulzberger proved a bust during his half-hearted attempts as a working reporter. An early assignment was to attend a banquet and write a few paragraphs about the main speaker. During the introductions Sulzberger wandered off to the men's room and the telephone;

*Sulzberger acquired his nickname from an illustrated book Arthur Hays Sulzberger produced to commemorate his birth. Writing in the style of Howard Pyle's *Story of King Arthur and His Knights*, the grandfather remarked that the baby had "come to play the Punch to Judy's endless show." Executives and others on a first-name basis with the publisher call him Punch rather than Arthur or any of its variations. Sulzberger is not the sort of personality one would refer to as "Artie."

when he returned, someone was speaking, and so he wrote the several hundred desired words. What he missed was an announcement that the scheduled speaker could not appear, and hence there was a substitute. The *Times* ran a correction. Had Punch's surname been other than Sulzberger, he would have been fired.

War again gave him a respite. Sulzberger joined the Marine Corps reserves while at Columbia, and he was called to active duty in 1951 and sent to Korea as a public information officer with the First Marine Division. About all he remembered about the war was the time his daddy came out to "view the troops." Arthur Hays Sulzberger was given a helicopter tour of positions behind the lines, and Punch rode along as an escort officer. After Punch's discharge the elder Sulzberger apparently decided that his restless son might do better in a non-familial job. Through the publishers' old boy network he arranged to send Punch to the Milwaukee *Journal* for a year; the boy's work did not improve, so he gave him yet another chance, this time in the *Time*'s Paris bureau.

One episode alone is graphic demonstration that Sulzberger should have chosen a line of work other than reporting. On June 11, 1955, Sulzberger and a gala party of friends went to LeMans for the Grand Prix auto race. A French driver, Pierre Levegh, ran into another car while pitting, became airborne, and crashed into a crowd. Levegh and 82 spectators died, and scores more were injured. To actually witness a tragedy is rare in journalism; reportage usually consists of reconstructing a scene from the words of bystanders, often hours after the fact. The LeMans disaster occurred literally in front of Sulzberger, and common sense would have suggested to the rawest cub reporter that a news story was warranted. Not only did Sulzberger pass up the chance to write a story of his own, he did not even have the wit to call the Paris bureau and tell what had happened. The race continued (LeMans officials did not want exiting crowds to hamper rescue work) and Sulzberger and friends remained in their spectators' box, swigging champagne and cheering.

The elder Sulzberger perhaps by now realized he had a son on his hands who should be tucked away where he could do no harm to the family business—and not be the laughing stock of the entire news department. One man who worked for the *Times* in 1955 said the consensus opinion among "real reporters" was that "the old man ought to put Punch in a sack with a heavy rock and drop him in the river." Other problems existed. While still at Columbia in 1948, Punch married a woman named Barbara Grant, who lived near the Sulzberger family estate in suburban Hillandale, New York, and who worked briefly in the *Times* executive offices. They had two children, Arthur Ochs Sulzberger, Jr. ("Pinch" to family and friends) and Karen Alden. Turner Catledge called her an "attractive, vivacious woman," but in Paris Punch's eye began to roam, and Barbara returned to New York with the children. The elder Sulzberger was so outraged that he refused Punch's request to return to 43rd Street, telling him there "seemed to be no clear-cut opening on the paper." Sulzberger was sent to Rome to work for a year under Arnaldo Cortesi, who had the deserved reputation of an autocrat. Cortesi in essence told Sulzberger to make himself comfortable and keep the hell out of the way, an edict he competently obeyed. The elder Sulzberger relented after some months and permitted Punch to return to 43rd Street with the title of "assistant treasurer."

In later years Sulzberger was the first to acknowledge that his talents did not include reporting. "I knew I was not that great a reporter," he said with much understatement. "I was not in the class with guys I was competing with who had gotten there, shall we say, by different means." Indeed.

The new job seemed amorphous, as if the family had fashioned make-shift work for a loved son who needed something to do. Sulzberger spent much time roaming the building, measuring an office here, suggesting a change in a paint scheme there. He and Barbara Grant divorced, and he drifted through a series of sexual liaisons. One woman, a *Times* reporter, claimed that Punch fathered her son. He denied paternity, but she pursued her claim through the courts for years, to Punch's embarrassment. One phase of the case remained alive almost two decades later, after Rupert Murdoch purchased the New York *Post*, and several Page Six gossip items stung Sulzberger with mention of the long-ago affair. Oral historians at the *Times* remember when the child in question, then a teenager, came to the newsroom with a chum to meet his mother. Sulzberger happened to be walking across the room. "'Hey, that's him, that's my dad," the kid shouted to his friend. Sulzberger walked on, a bit faster. Although Sulzberger never conceded paternity, the woman continued working at the *Times* until a terminal illness forced her retirement.

His first years in New York Punch spent much time with Turner Catledge, managing editor. Like Sulzberger, Catledge was between marriages, and they became fast carousing pals. At the close of work

Sulzberger would go to Catledge's private hideaway on the third floor, to a group that contained Irvin Taubkin, the promotion manager, Nat Goldstein, the circulation manager, and others. Each was a good man with a glass, and the fun often carried over to Sardi's or another bar. Catledge came to feel that people underrated Punch, that "he had far more ability than he was given credit for." Given the age difference (Catledge was a quarter-century older), Sulzberger looked upon the editor as an uncle as well as a friend, a "dry shoulder when he needed one," in Catledge's words. The bond was tightened when both men remarried at about the same time, and their wives became close.

The friendship with Catledge—and through him, the other working-level executives—was important, because it gave Sulzberger the chance to know the key people who actually ran *The New York Times*. When they talked, he listened, and over the years he acquired a good deal of practical knowledge about the paper. In turn, they recognized him as a man who had the sense to ask intelligent questions—and, even better, to listen. Finally, an alliance with the wily office politician Catledge never harmed anyone at the *Times*. So Sulzberger bided his time, getting his life in order, and showing no visible concern as to what the future might hold for him.

Sulzberger must have realized his immediate future promised little excitement, much less room for advancement. The heir-designee as publisher was his brother-in-law Orvil Dryfoos, a darkly handsome stockbroker who married Punch's sister Marian Sulzberger in 1941. Although Dryfoos was well on his way to becoming a millionaire on his own, he followed his father-in-law's suggestion that he join the family business, as an executive vice-president. Dryfoos had the Sulzberger style: an "Our Crowd" Jew whose social graces and quiet confidence meshed smoothly into the extended family. The clear implication was that if Dryfoos did well, he could expect to be publisher someday. (Dryfoos hedged: not until eight years after his marriage did he sell his stock exchange seat. By that time, his success at the *Times*—and as a Sulzberger—was assured.)

Dryfoos liked to quip of his success, "I got there by marrying the boss's daughter," the sort of self-effacing humor the Sulzbergers liked. Such, however, was not the case, for his business ability supplemented personal warmth. As Iphigene Sulzberger said of her son-in-law, "he was not the driving executive type, but he had an easy and affable personality that made him very popular with the staff, from executives and reporters to office boys and mail clerks." In the summer of 1961, citing declining health, Arthur Hays Sulzberger stepped aside as publisher in favor of Dryfoos.

Conceivably, as eldest son, Punch Sulzberger would have felt justified in claiming the position as his birthright. Indeed, some persons at the *Times* at the time suggested that Dryfoos's selection "made Punch sore as hell," in the words of one man. Sulzberger insisted such was not the case. "Just the opposite," he said. He cited the difference in their ages (thirteen years); when Dryfoos married Marian, he noted, "I barely came up to Orv's shoulders." Further, the relationship between the men was personally intense. Dryfoos was the person with whom Sulzberger could discuss subjects he would not raise with his father; during the months preceding his divorce, "he was my good friend, my confidant."

Nonetheless, Dryfoos did not take advantage of his own appointment to give Sulzberger more responsibility. His chief lieutenant remained an aloof, self-assured lawyer named Amory Bradford, who had joined the paper in 1947 as an assistant to Arthur Hays Sulzberger. Before the *Times*, Bradford was a minor official at the State Department, then with the New York superfirm of Davis, Polk. Bradford quickly became a power at the *Times*: a board member, business manager, then general manager. But he was not popular. Bradford's arrogant self-confidence more than balanced Dryfoos's modesty. He knew more about the *Times* than the people who ran individual departments, and he did not hesitate to say so. Gay Talese wrote of Catledge going to Bradford with an editor to appeal for a modest $25,000 increase in a news budget. Bradford rejected the appeal out of hand, humiliating Catledge. This was one of uncountable such incidents. Suffice to say that Bradford had few friends at the working level of the *Times*. But his efficiency as a manager satisfied the Sulzbergers and Orvil Dryfoos, the other person to whom he answered, and the paper operated at a profit. Amory Bradford treated Punch Sulzberger horribly. As Turner Catledge said, "His attitude towards Punch was 'Go away, boy, you bother me.' . . . I several times told Dryfoos this was a degrading way to treat a future owner of the paper, but Dryfoos would throw up his hands and say he didn't know what to do with Punch."

Given Bradford's aloof personality, it was unfortunate that circumstances thrust him into a role in 1962 for which he was temperamentally unsuited. After four months of fruitless negotiations, the printers union on December 8 struck four New York newspapers—the *Times*, the *Daily News*, the *Journal-American* and the *World-Telegram and Sun*. The *Post*, the *Mirror* and two Long Island dailies shut down on their own to demonstrate publisher solidarity. Coming at the start of the Christmas advertising season, the strike cut the newspapers to the economic quick, hence a fast settlement was imperative. The publishers joint bargaining group chose Bradford as their chief negotiator in the thought that he could match the union's Bertram Powers.

The antipathy was instant, and deep. Bradford's imperial I'm-smarter-than-you attitude grated on the plebeian Powers, and the real issues in the strike (automation, job guarantees, and the like) soon submerged in a nasty clash of personalities. Heckling politicians, including even President Kennedy, sided with the publishers, succeeding only in stiffening Powers's resolve. The strike dragged for 114 awful days before settlement, the first of a series of such work disruptions that eventually killed all save three of New York's daily newspapers. A year after the strike, collective newspaper circulation remained a million copies daily less than the pre-strike level. Readers learned they could rely upon television for news, particularly in the evening. Many advertisers left newspapers for TV and other media, never to return. Shock waves from the 114-day stoppage were felt in American communications for years.

On a direct level, an immediate victim was Amory Bradford, who ironically learned of his fall from grace from a story in his own newspaper. During negotiations Orvil Dryfoos lost confidence in Bradford; he felt he needlessly offended Bertram Powers, and that his arrogance prolonged the dispute. There were several ugly scenes when Bradford refused to discuss the negotiations with Dryfoos in the presence of Punch Sulzberger and Catledge. But circumstances put Bradford squarely in Catledge's gunsights, in a classic example of how good journalism can also coincide with good office politics. The scenario developed as follows:

Since the 1930's, A. H., "Abe" Raskin had been the nation's premier labor reporter. In 1959 he moved to the *Times* editorial board as a deputy to editor John Oakes. Although no longer a Guild member, he declined to cross the picket line. Ted Bernstein, the deputy managing editor, and Frank Adams, the city editor, called and asked for a meeting at a "neutral" site, which of course was Sardi's.

Bernstein asked Raskin to write a take-out on the strike, rather than the usual modest "settlement" story. Fine, Raksin said, but you'd best know in advance there might be problems. "One of the things you'll discover is personal conflict between Bertram Powers and Amory Bradford."

"Abe," Bernstein said, "the only instruction we'll give you is not to pull your punches."

Raskin went to work, and he wrote seventeen columns. A copy found its way to Bradford's desk, and he stormed into Orvil Dryfoos's office and demanded that the story be killed; old news, he said, and besides, it's inaccurate. Dryfoos refused to intercede; if you have problems about the news department, take them to Turner Catledge.

In his memoir, Catledge does not permit himself the glimmer of a gloat at his adversary's pleading that a story be killed. He gave Bradford a polite reception; if errors exist, point them out, and I'll check with Raskin.

The story ran on April 1, 1963, the first day the *Times* published after the strike, and it filled two full pages. In retrospect, the criticisms of Bradford are relatively mild, but the circumstances gave them the rumble of serious thunder insofar as Bradford's career was concerned. As Raskin wrote, "One top-level mediator said Mr. Bradford brought an attitude of such icy disdain into the conference room that the mediator often felt he ought to ask the hotel to send up more heat."

The day the story appeared Raskin was on the elevator when Punch Sulzberger stepped into the car. Raskin had a head-nodding relationship with Sulzberger. He considered him a "playboy who would go nowhere." Raskin was pleasantly surprised when Sulzberger spoke up.

"Gee, Abe, a terrific story," he said.

"Punch," Raskin replied, "the really great thing was that the *Times* wanted it, and used it."

Without a second's hesitation Sulzberger stated, "That's what the *Times* is all about."

Flash! Raskin thought, *this guy is something!* He left the elevator with a new-found respect for Punch Sulzberger—more so, as it turned out, than that of the Sulzberger family.,

The strike exhausted Orvil Dryfoos, and a few days after it ended, he and wife Marian flew to Puerto Rico. Dryfoos had known since a military physical in 1941 that he had a bad heart, and he had cut back on strenuous activities such as tennis. He enjoyed his first hours of vacation, then keeled over, writhing with pain, victim of a severe heart attack. Flown back to New York, he died in Columbia Presbyterian Hospital on May 25. He was but fifty years old. The Sulzberger family now had to choose a new publisher for *The New York Times*.

Under the established rules of regency, Arthur Ochs Sulzberger was the logical choice for the position. But for three agonizingly embarrassing weeks his parents explored other options. Dryfoos's premature death upset family plans. The expectation had been that Dryfoos would serve until the mandatory retirement age of sixty-five. As Iphigene Sulzberger said, "Arthur and I *hoped* [emphasis added] that by that time, Punch . . . would have accumulated enough experience to take over." But was Punch ready, fifteen years ahead of time? The Sulzbergers apparently felt not, because they gave serious consideration to other persons. The other son-in-law could be dismissed. Ben Hale Golden, husband of second daughter Ruth, was in the newspaper business, as publisher of the Sulzberger-owned Chattanooga *Times*, but their marriage was a mess, and would soon end in divorce. Richard N. Cohen, the second of Judy Sulzberger's several husbands, was making a fortune in insurance and cared little about newspapers beyond reading them. Ruth Golden herself apparently received fleeting consideration, for she had executive responsibilities on the Chattanooga *Times*; 1960's chauvinism barred her, however. Cousin John Oakes, the editorial page editor, was accepted as Punch's intellectual superior; however, he had no executive experience, and the Sulzbergers knew the *Times* needed a businessman to get it through the trying years ahead. One person rejected out of hand was Amory Bradford. Although he was "capable of handling the job," as Iphigene Sulzberger said, "he had shown himself during the strike to be an arrogant man who didn't get along with people. Many staff members made no secret of their view that Amory's unapproachable and superior airs made candid discussion difficult."

Iphigene Sulzberger made no secret of her choice. She wanted James Reston, the Washington bureau chief, upon whom she had lavished affection and admiration over the years, to the extent that her own son, Punch, felt excluded and more than a little jealous. Reston-watching for decades was a serious pastime at the *Times*. His public persona was of the gifted reporter who through wit, guile and good hard work obtained exclusives on many of the major diplomatic stories of his era, and then graduated into the role of middle-aged statesman of American journalism, as chief of the *Times* Washington bureau and columnist. Reston commanded the confidence of presidents and most everyone else of substance. He had another side as well. He was keenly ambitious, a hustler if you would, and he considered his charm just another tool when he wished something. And charm he certainly expended on Iphigene Sulzberger, to the extent that she told her husband he was the man she wished as publisher.

Arthur Hays Sulzberger, listened, thought, and then resisted. He, too, recognized Reston's talents, but he could also see shortcomings. For starters, Reston was foreign born, a Scotsman. Sulzberger remembered the trying days of the First World War, when the *Times* was unjustly accused of being an American outlet for the British Foreign Office. He had suffered personally the slight of being a cultural outsider, a Jew, in New York, even into the 1960's. And besides, the *Times* was a business, not just a newspaper, and Reston knew little about running a business.

The overriding factor, finally, was the desire to keep *Times* management within the family. Through elimination, Punch Sulzberger was the only survivor. Years later, Iphigene Sulzberger spoke of the choice in something less than a ringing maternal endorsement: "After much deliberation, we decided to *take something of a gamble* [emphasis added] and name our son as the new publisher." Punch was only thirty-seven years old, and, as his mother said, he was "still learning the newspaper business." But "we believed he had definite potentialities as publisher and would grow quickly with the job in the face of new responsibilities."

Arthur Hays Sulzberger, however, continued reluctant to give total control of the family business to young Punch. His notion was that Amory Bradford would continue as a regent, a brains-behind-the-throne. Punch would have none of this. Turner Catledge happened to be with him the day Iphigene Sulzberger came into his office and said, "Darling, I'm sorry, but that's the way your father wants it." The young Sulzberger dashed out of his office, saying, "I won't take it then." Five minutes later he returned with a smile. His father had relented. Amory Bradford resigned from the *Times* the day Punch's appointment as publisher was announced.

In his statement of the appointment, the elder Sulzberger stressed the family nature of the business:

> For over 65 years a member of the family of Adolph S. Ochs has been the publisher of *The New York Times*. . . . It is our intention to

maintain this family operation and insure continuance of the newspaper that the *Times* has come to be under those who by sentiment and training are particularly tied to its principles and traditions.

After several months as publisher, Punch Sulzberger realized that *The New York Times* was in serious trouble, possibly terminal trouble. The 114-day strike, "long and debilitating," left morale shaken throughout the paper. "You could sense the frustration of people, the lack of confidence, the idea that 'nobody knows what was going on.' " For the first time in its history, in 1963 the *Times* lost money on its newspaper operations, $527,084. The Times Company as a whole stayed in the black only because of the profits of its partially-owned paper subsidiary, Spruce Falls Power and Paper Company. The newspaper loss, of course, was directly attributable to the lost strike revenues. But bad omens were obvious. Even in 1962 the paper had earned only $599,350 on operating revenues of $117,409,925, or about one half of one percent.

As Sulzberger said years later, "The problem was not editorial, for the quality of the product, the newspaper we sold every day, was reasonably good. The problem, and it was a real one, was on the business side." From the business viewpoint, the *Times* was haphazardly run. Incredibly, Sulzberger found, "There was no budget, *nothing*. What numbers existed were made available only to a select number of people." The analogy Sulzberger used to describe the 1963 management system has been repeated so often by him and other *Times* officers that it virtually became an executive suite joke. He likened the *Times* to a "tall stand of reeds, each a fine specimen, and each running high into the sky. While their roots were in the same soil, when they reached up there was often little to join them together." No less than fifteen separate departments reported directly to the Fourteenth Floor, the *Times* executive offices.

Orvil Dryfoos during his brief months as publisher had begun to tighten management, but very slowly. Both he and Bradford knew enough not to try to push the elder Sulzberger. And although partially crippled by strokes, and confined to a wheelchair, Sulzberger kept a keen eye on *his* newspaper, and Dryfoos had the good sense to realize that any significant changes must await the old man's death. But now both Dryfoos and Bradford were gone, and any move towards changing *Times* procedures must come from the untested Punch Sulzberger.

Those first months Sulzberger fretted; he recognized his limitations as an executive, yet almost daily he came across things that did not make sense. He drew on his instincts, the tinkerer determined to find how things work. He relied even more heavily upon what he had learned about the *Times* during Turner Catledge's "happy hours" of past years. Here was one of Sulzberger's strengths. The persons with whom he drank Scotch in Catledge's offices were subordinates but also friends, men who could speak frankly with him, with no imposition of rank. Conviviality does not always equate with good management. Communication generally does. Catledge's coterie gave Sulzberger access to the ideas of the people who actually ran the paper. As Sulzberger himself says, two decades later, the paternity of specific changes in the *Times* is difficult to establish. But Turner Catledge had immeasurable influence on the young publisher—even if Sulzberger did not so realize at the time. The Catledge imprint is distinct on two disparate issues, the creation of a budget for the paper, and the consolidation of the daily and Sunday papers under a single editor.

Sulzberger made the budget his first priority, for this was the mechanism through which the various departments would have to justify their expenditures, and by doing so study them closely. To Sulzberger, a compulsive housekeeper—the sort who won't let a filled ashtray go unattended—the order possible through numbers was a good starting point. He did so through some political craft. "I decided to work on Turner first. I figured that if I could persuade the news department to go along with the idea of a budget, the business side would go along, too. So I went to Turner, and I made a passionate plea, and he went along with me." The other departments, as expected, fell into line. This took months, but after a year, Sulzberger had the *Times* under a budget. (Catledge liked the idea in theory better than in application. "The first time Turner breached his budget," Sulzberger said, "Turner simply announced that he was 'withdrawing the news department from the budget,' I had to convince him all over again that, "no, Turner, we can't have a real budget unless it includes your department' ").

In his swift maturation Sulzberger showed no signs of lack of confidence in his ability; he behaved, as one executive put it, "like the proprietor, not a trustee." He had been denied any role in decision-making before Dryfoos's death, and persons who should have known better treated him shabbily. Now he made these persons explain to him what they were doing, and why. And in the eyes of the news department, Sulzberger truly came into his own in the late summer of 1964 when he finally did something about what was called "The Markel Problem."

Lester Markel for four decades had run the Sunday edition of the *Times* as a personal fiefdom, treating the daily newspaper as a stepchild that must be tolerated, but not taken seriously. Markel's domain covered the entire Sunday paper—from the news sections to the magazine, the book review, and the cultural sections. "We had two newspapers," Sulzberger said of the situation. Markel didn't even bother to follow the *Times Style Book*, the Torah of the copy desk. He edited the News of the Week in Review Section with the seeming assumption that no one read the daily paper. He generally behaved as if he were angry about something or someone. Eliot Fremont-Smith, who reviewed books for the *Times* in the 1960's, felt that Markel "had a big sadistic streak." Markel had on-going feuds with such key subordinates as Francis Brown, the book editor. Fremont-Smith stated, "Markel was addicted to memos. Brownie once showed me two that came the same morning. The first was dated 10:31 A.M. 'Please come in here. I want to talk to you.' The second was 11:10 A.M. 'Why haven't you come in?' These men sat not more than fifty feet apart, you must understand."

Administratively, the two-paper operation caused problems. Daily editors could not count on seven-day continuity in news coverage. A daily reporter working on a major story often found himself undercut by a Sunday article, in the magazine or the News in Review.

All that Markel had in his favor was the fact he was a newsman of brilliance found nowhere else on the *Times*. He created the magazine and the cultural sections. From 1939 to 1945 his News in Review contained the most comprehensive account of the Second World War of any publication, instant current history each Sunday morning. Although artists, composers and playwrights argued with Markel's *Times*, they respected it. In the magazine Markel preferred an article *by* a Secretary of State to an article *about* a Secretary of State. Markel wanted the man's thoughts in his own words, not through the critical filter of an outside writer.

No one argued about the quality of Markel's Sunday editions; the sticking point was what Catledge called "diffuse organization." Despite much talk about a forced merger of daily and Sunday, no one dared suggest that Markel yield his autonomy. Markel seemed to enjoy the discomfort of mice arguing about belling a cat. Orvil Dryfoos once remarked at an executive meeting he would not impose a single editor over the entire paper until Markel either died or retired.

˜"That's OK," Markel said.˜"I intend to edit the Sunday paper posthumously."

To the surprise of almost everyone, Sulzberger summoned Markel to his office in late summer 1964 and told him that henceforth the *Times* would be run by a single editor, and that Markel would no longer be the Sunday editor. Sulzberger stated his decision as an announcement, rather than an invitation for discussion. That he did so bluntly, and with no advance notice, shocked the old man into anger, then into silence. Markel was more astonished with Sulzberger's methods than his decision; after all, he had come to the *Times* under Punch's *grandfather*, and preemptory dismissal was the last thing he expected. He could have asked that he be permitted to "resign" the Sunday editorship but this would have been a false representation. Markel, the newsman, had too much respect for the truth for any such sham. The directness of Sulzberger's action surprised even Turner Catledge. "I can't say I was wholly pleased with the way he handled it. But he was a young man, and young men can be cruel, sometimes without even knowing it."

What Catledge did not realize, for Sulzberger never told him, was that the move against Markel took just about every bit of nerve the young publisher could muster. "It took me a couple of years* to build up my courage to talk with Mr. Markel," he said. As a consolation, Sulzberger let Markel continue working for five years or so past retirement, on an amorphous project on the "future" of the paper.

To Sulzberger's disappointment, the merger did not work as intended. Catledge never brought the two departments together in the true sense. The new Sunday editor, Daniel Schwartz, a Markel protégé, continued working much as had his predecessor. "Turner made peace between the two departments, but he never restructured the way they operated," Sulzberger said. The true merger was several years distant, when A. M. Rosenthal became executive editor. "Not until Abe came in did we take the various pieces apart and reassemble them," Sulzberger said.

Nonetheless, the deposing of Markel indicated that Punch

---

*Actually, about fifteen months, the time between his appointment as publisher and his dismissal of Markel.

Sulzberger should be taken seriously. Jokes persisted about him being the "accidental publisher," who got his job only through an untimely death. But Sulzberger had achieved something no one else
had attempted: the consolidation of the *Times* under a single executive editor.

Sulzberger's sacking of Markel carried implications beyond the unseating of a single editor. The supposedly-benign "boy publisher" had
a bite. He possessed arbitrary power, and he would use it. So
Rosenthal and other persons at the Times spent much time in ensuing
years trying to predict what Sulzberger wanted, and do it.

But Punch's attempted meddling in other news department affairs
was not as welcome. Although he had failed miserably as a reporter,
Sulzberger's new exalted rank gave him the confidence to send
suggested-story memoranda to Catledge. These notes read as if
Sulzberger was writing deliberate parodies—a not-so-bright publisher giving idiotic ideas to an important editor. Alas, such was not
the case. What Sulzberger wrote to Catledge reflected his ideas on
what *The New York Times* should be covering.

April 10, 1964

As you will notice from the attached letter . . . Coca-Cola Bottling
Co. . . . is having a rather large meeting here in New York on September 17-18.

This is really a fascinating organization that sells the syrup to practically the entire east coast of the country, excluding New England. Every gallon of syrup brings two cents into the organization.

I think this will be quite a meeting, and thought it would be an excellent time to do a really comprehensive story on the Coca-Cola
enterprise—how it works, who gets the money and where it goes.

What do you think of this idea?

October 26, 1964

Last Sunday I went to Radio City with the children and saw an absolutely fabulous movie, "Mary Poppins." I forget how old the theater is,
but it certainly is a fantastic institution which seems to continue year
after year with little change, except as I get older, the Rockettes look
younger.

I wonder if there is an anniversary of some type coming around
where we might take a look at Radio City Music Hall and perhaps let
our music expert say a critical word about the orchestra and our dance
expert, the ballet. As you will remember, when we have a movie opening, they are just barely mentioned.

I realize in saying this that [Harold] Schonberg [the *Times* music critic] will take the orchestra apart, as probably will our dance friend. Obviously, this is not the intention of this note. But, to my untrained ears, this is a symphony orchestra of a very special Americanized type, and a critical review having this in mind might be interesting. I guess the same probably goes for the corps of ballet and the Rockettes.

Having this in mind might let us have some fun.

October 27, 1964

My mother-in-law told me that a small art gallery with a Greek name at _____ Madison Avenue has a show of incredibly near-pornographic material relating to the campaign.

It might be worth a look. . . .

April 9, 1965

If we really don't have any trouble, I am thinking of celebrating by replacing my Chrysler station wagon. What was the name of the Chrysler man I met in the club one night who said he would be happy to be helpful?

For the time being Sulzberger was powerless to address the overriding problem threatening the *Times* and other New York newspapers: the ability of the printing and other unions to wrest handsome contract increases each time they negotiated. The *Times* was doubly-captive. Since the newspaper was the major source of its revenue, the company did not have the financial strength for a confrontation with the unions. Contract negotiations siphoned money that could have made the *Times* a diversified company. "We had to find a way to get out of a terrible cycle," Sulzberger stated. "Every three years, when the contracts came up, the costs of labor increased drastically, and the restraints the unions put on us were unbelievable."

Sulzberger's gloomiest moment came when an executive displayed a chart predicting the *Times* could be out of business unless things changed. The exact date, and the specific figures, are items Sulzberger let slip into the crevices of a merciful memory. Yet the import of the message remains as vivid as if the figures were branded on his forehead. He could be the generation that let the *Times* slip out of Ochs-Sulzberger control. Sulzberger shivered when the New York *Herald Tribune* closed in 1966, for he could see the same fate for his own paper. Even the gain of former *Herald Tribune* readers was expensive, for the *Times* lost seven cents on each new daily reader and seventy cents on each Sunday reader because advertising rates could not be raised fast enough to cover increased printing costs.

Yet each new contract seemed increasingly costly—11 to 15 percent in salary and benefits per year. Much of this Sulzberger now blames on two other publishers, Richard Berlin of the Hearst Corporation, publisher of the New York *Journal American*, and Jack Howard of Scripps Howard, owner of the *World Telegram & Sun*. Because of their revenues elsewhere, and their desire to keep flagship papers in New York, the bargaining tactics of Berlin and Howard dismayed Sulzberger. They liked evening sessions, so they "would come to the bargaining table tipsy after dinner, and start negotiations." Sulzberger at the time liked his Scotch as well as anyone, but he was not about to face Bertram Powers of the printers union without full command of his faculties. During one particularly memorable session, the publishers' committee suggested contract language on automation to Powers which he accepted. "We all went out to dinner, and then we came back and rejected our own language," Sulzberger stated. Powers, angered, insisted on a complete halt to automation.

Sulzberger had made a credible start towards revitalizing *The New York Times* financially; however, he was shrewd enough a businessman by the late 1960's to know he eventually must confront the unions directly. In the meantime, the ambitious A. M. Rosenthal was ready for another boost up on the ladder by his patron Turner Catledge.

NINE

"Not Only an Anachronism but a Defect"

In mid-1966 Turner Catledge began planning for his retirement in 1970, and he thought both about his replacement as executive editor and bringing a new generation of editors into place for the following succession. Good management required no less. Catledge loved the *Times*, and he wished to do what he could to leave it in trusted hands.

For the immediate job of executive editor, the *Times* was blessed with an abundance of mid-career news executives, all in their fifties, each seasoned with experience not only on West 43rd Street but in foreign bureaus as well. The first "working list" Catledge jotted on a small *Times* memorandum pad contained three names: Clifton Daniel, managing editor since 1964; Harrison Salisbury, the veteran foreign correspondent now directing national news coverage; and Sydney Gruson, the foreign editor. But when Catledge looked to the next generation, he gave only one name serious consideration for high office—A. M. Rosenthal.

To most persons at the *Times*, Catledge's logical successor was Clifton Daniel, a handsome gray-haired Carolinian who started with the *Times* in the London bureau during the war, and then held a plethora of important jobs elsewhere. In an era when few media figures enjoyed "stardom," Daniel was known to the general public as the husband of Margaret Truman, daughter of the former president. But Catledge had doubts about Daniel's suitability for the executive editorship. In an appraisal memorandum written at Punch Sulzberger's request in the summer of 1966, Catledge displayed *Times* office politics at their best, which is to say, their most savage. The technique could be called praising with faint damns. Catledge noted "certain rough spots in his [Daniel's] operation" and said he "had some way yet to go to establish the lines of loyalty and authority through which he can best exercise his functions." More serious liabilities were Daniel's temper and health. "He has a degree of impatience, exhibited at times in flares of temper, which are somewhat disturbing." Although logically ten years more work could be expected of Daniel, "we have to realize he has had previous flare-ups with ulcers and in his position ulcers are an occupational hazard." Catledge felt it "incumbent upon us to develop a successor as soon as possible."

Daniel's own choice as the next managing editor was the veteran Salisbury. Catledge, however, already had his doubts about Salisbury, which were soon to be amplified. Rather than promote Salisbury, already in his mid-fifties, Catledge "would much rather go for the long haul." He had two nominees—Abe Rosenthal and Thomas Mullaney, the latter the *Times* business-financial editor. Catledge's first choice was Rosenthal. "He has imagination and drive, and at forty-three is one of our most promising young executives."

In its totality, the memorandum was a two-level boost for Rosenthal. Catledge essentially dismissed Daniel as not being worthy of further promotion. In the next breath, he disposed of Salisbury by suggesting the *Times* should look beyond his generation to the next— and that the person he gave high marks was Abe Rosenthal. His casual pairing of Rosenthal and Tom Mullaney was a sophisticated insider's thrust, for Sulzberger knew that Mullaney, while a sound man, was not a brilliant editor. Sulzberger would recognize that the man being recommended was Abe Rosenthal.

At Catledge's urging, Rosenthal wrote a memorandum outlining what he felt were the inherent weaknesses in the managing editor's office. His main concern was the "anachronism" of the bullpen, the news desk responsible for the physical production of the daily paper, in terms of allocating space to various departments, designing pages, doing the final editing on stories and writing headlines, and directing the flow of copy from the newsroom to the mechanical department. Rosenthal wrote:

> It has always struck me as strange that the Managing Editor's office does not exercise direct leadership or supervision or intimate liaison—I am not choosing words carefully—with and over the bullpen.
>
> Every other part of the news department takes pains to keep the Managing Editor's office informed of its important plans. And yet when the time comes to put these plans into production, to decide how they should be played and where, there is no such connection.
>
> Perhaps the single most important thing the *Times* does every night is to plan the front page; this has worldwide impact. But, almost always, the ME's office does not have a part in this and is not asked for its opinions or suggestions or whatever. I doubt that there are many papers where this happens. . . .
>
> It is not only an anachronism but a defect. . . . [A]ll during the day, editors work to get ideas, stimulate reporters, perfect copy, and develop concepts of the news of the day. This is then turned over for final decision to a group of men who, however talented, have by the nature of their jobs and by the hours they work, no connection with the job of shaping the product.

Based on his own experience as metropolitan editor, Rosenthal felt control should be retained by responsible editors, rather than by copy readers in the bullpen. Further, the managing editor *"or his chief assistant"* should assume control of the front page. "Preferably, it should be dummied right in his office." The managing editor should designate one assistant to be liaison between his office and the bullpen; this would not be a "matter of commanding or overriding," but of "understood relationship rather than command." Rosenthal wrote that the process could be improved "not entirely without pain, but perhaps with less upheaval than one might fear."

The audacity of Rosenthal's memorandum was that it called for a fundamental revolution in the *Times* newsroom—and that the call came from an editor of only three years' direct experience in the process. The memorandum was not widely distributed, but persons who read it recognized it for what it was: a description of the job Abe Rosenthal wanted next for himself. But a formidable personage stood between him and advancement to the next rung of the ladder—Harrison Salisbury.

Harrison Salisbury was someone Rosenthal deeply detested, personally and professionally, for he seemed to personify the worst feature of the *Times* foreign service—the inclination of certain correspondents to adopt revolutionary political causes as their very own, and push suspect characters without question. To Rosenthal, Salisbury stood as the inheritor of the soiled reportorial cape of Herbert L. Matthews, who had covered the Spanish Civil War from the Communist side, and then wrote extensively about Fidel Castro's revolution in Cuba without paying undue attention to evidence of its Communist underpinnings. A gaunt, brooding man with talents—and political connections—extending far beyond 43rd Street, Salisbury's career was marked with equal portions of acclaim and controversy. He bears a startling resemblance to a stork, and he walks with hands clasped behind his back, lean frame tilted forward, as if anxious to arrive faster than he is moving. Salisbury invites respect but not affection, and his true friends in the *Times* newsroom were few.*

A Minnesotan, Salisbury worked for United Press for two decades, from Chicago through Washington and Europe, where he reported from Moscow from 1944 on. In the late 1940's, back in New York, Salisbury decided he wanted to work for the *Times*, and he went to Edwin L. James, then the managing editor. James said the *Times* had nothing. James mentioned, though, the Soviet government had just closed the *Times*'s Moscow bureau to protest the reporting of Brooks Atkinson. If Salisbury could obtain a visa to reopen the bureau, he could have a job. James never expected to see or hear of Salisbury again. He was wrong. Within weeks Salisbury appeared with the visa, and in 1949 he went to Moscow to report the last years of the Stalin dictatorship. He won a Pulitzer Prize, and he came away with an empathy for the Soviet people that permeated much of his later writing. (Moscow took a personal toll: Living behind the Iron Curtain during the Cold War put so much strain on Salisbury that he spent weeks in the Payne-Whitney Hospital psychiatric unit after returning to the United States.)

*Salisbury was one of five judges who in 1965 selected me for an Alicia Patterson Fund fellowship for a year of study in Mexico and Guatemala on divergent forms of Latin nationalism.

Salisbury's value to the *Times* lay in his value to write on any subject, at any length, from a concise five-paragraph article explaining a Politboro decision to a multi-page spread on the death of Sir Winston Churchill. Salisbury's aloofness did not make him popular. His first days in the city room after Moscow, some editor suggested—perhaps facetiously, to humble a correspondent who had never worked at 43rd Street—that he write about the New York "garbage crisis." This is an assignment easily ignored or sloughed off. Not with Salisbury. His series won national prizes. As national editor he roamed the South reporting on the civil rights rebellion. A Salisbury article on police brutality in Alabama brought about the landmark libel decision by the U. S. Supreme Court, *Times v. Sullivan.* The court held that for a public figure to win a libel judgment, he must prove that an inaccurate statement resulted either from malice or reckless disregard for the truth. The fact that an article was factually wrong did not automatically entitle a public figure to collect damages. *Times v. Sullivan* became the broad license for much of the media's investigative reporting since the 1960's, for it meant a lesser burden of proof in writing stories about controversial figures in public office or otherwise in the limelight. Finally, Salisbury played a dominant role in directing *Times* coverage of the first stirrings of the anti-war movement beginning in the 1960's.

In the newsroom Salisbury's politics made him both a god-figure and a lightning rod of controversy. A hard-headed iconoclast, by the 1960's Salisbury was finding many of his better friends and news sources on the far left or outright Communist end of the spectrum. Anti-Communists long had badgered him for the tone of his Moscow reportage (the *Times* unwisely having not noted that his dispatches were filed through censorship.) And Salisbury's Moscow articles abounded with howlers. For instance, immediately after Stalin's death in 1953; Georgi Malenkov and the secret police chief, Laventri Beria, took power. Salisbury wrote: "Mr. Malenkov's words were those of a man who sounded as if he were prepared to negotiate frankly and honorably with other nations in the interests of peace. . . . Good to Soviet ears were Malenkov's words and Mr. Beria's pledge of security and constitutional rights." During the preceding fifteen years Beria had directed the murder or imprisonment of millions of Soviet citizens—facts known in the West because of the eye-witness accounts of uncountable refugees and defectors. In one of his books, *Russia on the Way*, Salisbury scoffed at notions that the

NKVD (predecessor to the current KGB) terrorized the Soviet people. "Most people think of the NKVD as a sinister secret police which
carts off Russians in the dead of the night and sends them packing to
Siberia," Salisbury wrote. "Well, there is something in that impression, of course. The NKVD does things like that, occasionally. . . ."
With the body count and *gulag* population in the millions, the word
"occasionally" seems oddly out of place.

For Rosenthal, such blindness to the realities of Communism and
the Soviet state was appalling, and he frequently said so, first in letters to friends when he worked abroad, and vocally when he returned
to New York. As he told one colleague, "The slop-over from the Russian secret police that I saw first hand in Poland was so vicious that
what it must have been in the Soviet Union was unimaginable. How
the hell Salisbury could live in a police state and be so oblivious to
reality is beyond me." Rosenthal seemed irritated that young reporters idolized Salisbury. He took particular offense at the friendship between Salisbury and David Halberstam, who had won great public
celebrity for his coverage of the Vietnam War. His own Pulitzer
brought Rosenthal only fleeting attention in the small world of the
professional media. *Times* house advertisements boasted of Abe's
prize, but Poland was a European backwater where people had been
kicked around for centuries. Rosenthal's chronicling of the Soviet-
inspired brutishness impressed a Pulitzer jury, but the story quickly
slipped from public attention.

Halberstam's Vietnam reportage, by contrast, made him arguably
the most famous media figure in the United States during the first half
of the 1960's. Halberstam came to the war early, and claimed it for his
very own, and his reportage formed the bedrock upon which opposition to American involvement in Southeast Asia was based.
(Halberstam today finds it odd that no one remembers that his first
stories "bitched about the United States not making a *stronger* effort
militarily." That changed.) Historians shall quibble over Halberstam's
work for decades; none can deny, however, that it made him a lion-
ized figure, on campus and in the intellectual salons of the Boston-
Manhattan-Washington circuit, a handsome and articulate man with
the glamour of a Richard Harding Davis and the youthful earnestness
of a graduate student. In short, the adulation denied Rosenthal.
When reassignment brought both Rosenthal and Halberstam to New
York, "it was clear that Abe liked me a lot," Halberstam said.

Superficially, perhaps, but the circumstances of Halberstam's rapid rise grated on Rosenthal.

Halberstam came to the *Times* with experience in rural Mississippi and at the Nashville *Tennessean*; after only six months on the paper he was off to the Congo, and then to Vietnam, and the Pulitzer. Rosenthal had fretted at the United Nations for nine years before *he* went abroad. And, besides, Rosenthal worried about "the wonder boy's" closeness to Salisbury. Rosenthal would see the two men talking in the corner of the newsroom and he would glower; tipsy once at Sardi's, he referred to them as the "VC"—the initials used for the Viet Cong, the Communist faction in Vietnam. Rosenthal fretted when James Reston, at Halberstam's urging, began hiring reporters with whom he had worked in Vietnam, men such as Neil Sheehan of United Press International, and Charlie Mohr and Malcolm Browne of Associated Press. Rosenthal joked to Halberstam, "You are going to come in here some day and stage a *coup d'etat*." As Halberstam says, "It was clear to me he did not like what we had done in Vietnam; we were not anti-Communist enough."

To Halberstam's chagrin and irritation, Rosenthal would lead him into a discussion of Vietnam, and then say pointedly, "Someday we'll have to find out what *really* happened out there." To a reporter such a comment is about as close as one can come to a personal insult without provoking a punch in the nose. Halberstam went on to report from Poland (as was Rosenthal, he was expelled for "slanderous" writing) and then from Paris. Back in New York in 1967 he did not receive the sort of assignments that satisfied him, so at age thirty-three he quit to join *Harper's Magazine* under the brilliant, if short-lived and erratic, editorship of Willie Morris. "Abe was nicer than most people when I left," he remarked years later. Such should not be surprising, for Halberstam's departure stripped the "Salisbury crowd" of one of its better reporters.

Ironically, Salisbury spoiled whatever chances he had for either the managing or executive editorship through reportage that was both acclaimed and marred, but which the *Times* nonetheless pushed for a Pulitzer Prize. Salisbury in 1966 was principal assistant to managing editor Clifton Daniel, with broad responsibilities for direction of *Times* news coverage, and also a license to travel to find stories. Salisbury desperately wished to go to North Vietnam to report on the war from behind Communist lines and to evaluate the massive U. S.

bombing raids. Hanoi was accusing the United States of "barbaric attacks" and "indiscriminate bombing" that killed civilians and destroyed non-military targets. Among the persons to whom Salisbury
turned for help in getting a North Vietnamese visa were Victor Louis,
a KGB agent used by the USSR for liaison with Western journalists;
and Winston Burchette, an Australian-born reporter who covered the
Korean and Vietnam wars from the Communist viewpoint, and who
was blindly obedient to whatever line Moscow pushed at any given
time.* Salisbury also applied to North Vietnamese diplomats in Paris
for a visa, and it was through that channel that he says he ultimately
obtained the document.

Salisbury began filing articles from Hanoi on December 27, 1966,
and he was remarkably precise in his statistics. "The cathedral tower
of Namdinh (fifty miles southeast of Hanoi) looks out on block after
block of utter desolation; the city's population of 90,000 has been reduced to less than 20,000 because of evacuation; thirteen percent of
the city's housing, including homes of 12,464 people, have been destroyed; eighty-nine people have been killed and 405 wounded."

Salisbury flatly accused the United States of bombing civilian targets: "It is apparent, on personal inspection, that block after block of
ordinary housing, particularly surrounding a textile plant, has been
smashed to rubble by repeated attacks by Seventh Fleet planes. . . .
Whatever the explanation, one can see the United States planes are
dropping an enormous weight of explosives on purely civilian targets.
Whatever else there may be or not have been in Namdinh, it is civilians who have taken the punishment." The theme of indiscriminate
bombing ran throughout Salisbury's articles.

To anyone familiar with the *Times* policy, a striking omission in the
first four articles was any cited source for the specific damage figures.
The *Times* has a fetish about attribution; a city room joke for years was
that even when a thunderstorm deluges the city, the weather bureau
must be named as the authority for the announcement that it rained.
Robert Phelps, who had been Salisbury's deputy as national news editor, noticed the omission immediately. "When I picked up the paper
I sucked in my breath," Phelps said. "He reported flatly Americans
had bombed civilian areas. He accepted what the North Vietnamese

---

*Salisbury wrote a glowing preface to Burchett's memoir, published by Times Books
in 1983. Neither the preface nor the book mentioned Burchett's odious role in preparing "germ warfare confessions" for captured American servicemen in Korea, the
major Communist propaganda effort of the conflict.

said, and reported it as his own. Someone should have edited the attribution into the articles. The whole fuss easily could have been stopped." Phelps felt Salisbury might have been "set up" within the *Times* for embarrassment. Salisbury had accumulated many enemies over the years, and any number of editors had the chance to insert an attribution; none chose to do so. "Somebody didn't like it [the trip] and said, 'Let that son of a bitch have it,' " Phelps said. Not until near the end of his fifth article did Salisbury write, "It should be noted, incidentally, that all casualty estimates and statistics are those of North Vietnamese officials." This line was inserted at the cabled urging of editors on 43rd Street.

Salisbury was late, far too late, for a firestorm of rebuttal fatally scorched his career. As *Aviation Week* pointed out, in one "correction" among scores, the North Vietnamese had 100 anti-aircraft batteries around Namdinh, which contained a thermal power plant, a rail marshaling yard, and petroleum storage facilities. Namdinh also happened to be the impact area for North Vietnamese anti-aircraft rockets fired from defenses ringing Hanoi. As the Pentagon suggested, much of the destruction Salisbury witnessed could have come from the Communists' own fire. *Time* Magazine spent two full pages picking holes in Salisbury's articles, concluding that he was "getting little more than a guided—or misguided—tour."

That Salisbury's articles were both a coup and a career-ender was made plain in a memorandum Clifton Daniel wrote to the travelling Turner Catledge on January 4, 1967:

> The Publisher [Punch Sulzberger] is perturbed about Harrison Salisbury's pieces. He will undoubtedly want to talk to you about them very soon after you get back. I will be glad to give you fill-in detail. Meanwhile, my summary conclusions are as follows:
>
> Getting into Hanoi was a journalistic coup. Harrison, as might be expected, very promptly dug up some interesting facts that weren't known before. He disclosed that there was considerably more damage to civilian areas than Washington had ever intimated. Washington was quick to acknowledge that this was so.
>
> At the same time, he obviously gave comfort to North Vietnam by affording an outlet for its propaganda and point of view, and comfort to those who are opposed to the bombing and opposed to the war. Our mail to date shows more letters in favor of Harrison than against him.
>
> While Washington has sought to counteract the more damaging allegations in Harrison's reporting, there has been, as far as I know, no

general denunciation of him or of the *Times* from high quarters or any attempt to bring pressure on the paper. . . .

As you know, Harrison has complicated matters by failing in his first dispatches to attribute casualty statistics and other controversial information to those from whom he received it. I asked him in a telegram to do this, and he has complied.

The desk was instructed not to print anything without attribution, or, if the attribution was obvious, as it was in most cases, they should simply put it in. For example, "147 were *said* to have been killed," or "This correspondent was told . . ."

There have also been some expressions in the stories that readers might interpret to be editorial or emotional. I asked from the beginning that these be eliminated by the desk. Most of them were, but now and then one crept through. Consequently, I have now been reading all the copy myself.

Harrison, in general, betrayed the tendency of so many correspondents—of seeming to identify himself with the place from which he was writing and the sources from which he was deriving his information. . . .

Daniel's concluding paragraph was the most damning that can be written about a reporter. Prompted either by emotion or by politics, Salisbury had allowed himself to be caught up in a news story to the extent that—by the judgment of his own editor, Daniel—he had lost objectivity. Such is a cardinal sin by a reporter of any rank. Although *Times* editors and executives defended Salisbury in public statements, what appeared in the paper was more resounding than their words. Hanson Baldwin, the *Times*'s military correspondent, and a man with whom Salisbury shared a mutual detestation, wrote a 2,000 word article beginning on the front page that said in effect that Salisbury did not know what he was talking about, that "You can't fight an immaculate war." Editor John Oakes, who opposed the war, wrote an editorial that was close to a total *Times* disavowal of Salisbury: ". . . [W]e reject the sweeping deductions and false conclusions many Americans seem to have drawn from the statistics of civilian deaths and the pictures of destruction reported from Hanoi last week by this newspaper's correspondent, Harrison Salisbury."

The *Times* would nominate Salisbury's articles for the Pulitzer Prize, and in one of the less convincing passages of his memoir Turner Catledge told of having to hold back tears when they did not win. His more telling, and accurate, judgment occurred the very day

Salisbury returned to 43d Street from Hanoi. Catledge posted a newsroom announcement that Rosenthal would be assistant managing editor for news, and that Salisbury henceforth would be working on "special projects." Although he would hold other titles his last years at the paper, chiefly as the compromise choice as editor of the op-ed opinion page when it began in 1970, Salisbury's reportage from Hanoi effectively ended any chance for further advance in the news department.

Abe Rosenthal did not weep. He saw Salisbury's collapse as a reaffirming signal that Catledge and Sulzberger wished to purge the *Times*'s columns of reporting tinged by ideology. Rosenthal would now proceed to pursue what he considered lapses of objectivity elsewhere in the *Times*. But in terms of career advancement, the demise of Sulzberger meant that one less person stood between A. M. Rosenthal and the managing editor's office.

One other person remained in contention for the position of managing editor—Sydney Gruson, a onetime foreign correspondent (Rosenthal had succeeded him in Poland) and then foreign editor. Gruson is a man of deceptive mildness who always seems to prove he is a bit smarter than he appears on the surface, insofar as *Times* politics are concerned.

Many persons at the *Times* joked over the years about Gruson's opportunism; Gruson smiled along with them, and continued advancing. He is a squat Irishman who puts a self-conscious emphasis on his ability to appear suave and continental; he loves to roll French phrases off his tongue, and to refer to remote European hotels as if they are but a pace or two from West 43rd Street, and surely known to anyone of sense.

One of his many sometime lady friends recalls asking Gruson once what he would *really* like to do in life.

"To be the perfect weekend guest," he replied.

A native of Ireland, Gruson was raised in Canada; he came to London during the Second World War for a Canadian press service, and through his friend Clifton Daniel he joined the *Times* bureau in 1944. Gruson did it all for the *Times*. He reported from bases in Warsaw (twice), The Hague, Israel and Mexico. The latter assignment ended in embarrassment. Catledge came to Mexico City for a visit and Gruson gave him a choice: "Do you want me to go around and do some work with you following me, or do you want me to do what I usually do?" Catledge chose the latter, and Gruson promptly took him to the local racetrack, where one of his stable of horses was competing that day. Catledge said nothing; immediately on return to New York he recalled Gruson and gave him a desk job on 43rd Street. But Gruson survived, and he went on to become foreign editor. His wife, Flora Lewis, became a foreign affairs columnist first with the Washington *Post* syndicate, and later (after they divorced) for the *Times* itself.

In 1966 Punch Sulzberger offered Gruson an important job, to go to Paris to oversee the *Times*'s international edition as editor and publisher. Although Gruson had no business background, he felt capable for the job. "I had some aptitude for it—business decisions are mostly common sense decisions." Even from New York Gruson could tell that the *Times* and the *International Herald Tribune* "were cutting up the same market, and that both would continue to lose even more money." Gruson expected to be in Paris no more than six months. Artful in office politics, he elicited from Sulzberger an agreement that he would receive a worthwhile job when he returned. Scrambling was already underway to see who would replace Daniel and Catledge, and Gruson did not wish to get too far from the center of things.

In Paris, Gruson's original hunch proved correct: the market could not support two English-language dailies. He called Sulzberger. "I suggested we go over and talk with Walter Thayer," the owner of the *Herald Tribune*. Within two weeks a merger deal was struck, with the Washington *Post* coming in as a one-third owner. The final details were worked out at a Paris meeting involving Gruson, Sulzberger, Thayer, and Fritz Beebee of the Washington *Post*. When the question of naming a publisher arose, Sulzberger asked that Gruson step outside a moment. Later, as they walked back to the *Times* bureau, Sulzberger asked, "Did you hear what we were talking about?"

"No, I don't listen at keyholes," Gruson said.

"Well," Sulzberger said, "the agreement is that you will be publisher after one year." He explained that the current publisher of the *International Herald Tribune*, Robert McDonald, needed to stay in Europe another year for tax purposes. After a year lapsed, he would return to America, and Gruson would become publisher.

"Sulzberger told me, 'Take a sabbatical and hang around the country for a year.' " Gruson and his family moved into a splendid French country house and he played golf and for the first months he relaxed.

Then uneasiness began to nag at him. He had left a good position at the *Times*, and although he enjoyed the inactivity, being on the sidelines disturbed him. Worst of all, he began to hear hints that in fact he might not become publisher.

Katharine Graham of the Washington Post Company, the third partner in the merged paper, happened to come to Paris, and at Gruson's request they met for tea at the American Embassy, where she was staying as a guest of her old friend Ambassador Charles Bohlen. "Kay said to me at the start, 'It is a pity, that after what you did, there is nothing for you at the newspaper.' "

Gruson relates this statement as if reliving a very bad experience. "To put it mildly, I was stunned." He explained to Mrs. Graham the deal that had been made by Thayer, Sulzberger, and Beebee. Mrs. Graham shook her head. "No, I would know about it if there were an agreement." The tea finished in a strained silence; Gruson realized that somewhere, somehow, he had been double-crossed.

"After Katharine breaks that little bit of news to me I go back to the Paris bureau and telephone Punch and tell him, 'We don't have an agreement.' Sulzberger seemed surprised. 'What do you mean?' he asked." Gruson told him of the conversation with Mrs. Graham. "I'll check it out," Sulzberger said.

The next day he telephoned Gruson with bad news: "They're going back on their agreement."

Reconstructing the incident almost two decades later, Gruson surmised that Mrs. Graham did not wish such a prominent *Times* person as publisher of a paper in which her *Post* had an interest. And since she was close to the Thayer crowd, the other one-third owner, "they went along with her." All Gruson could do was to write an angry letter to Thayer in which he flatly accused him of a "double-cross" and asked, "How could you do this?" He continues to see Kay Graham as the "guiding light" in the switch; he notes that she remains adamant against sharing the publishership of the paper with the *Times* even on a rotating basis. Philip Foise, a former *Post* foreign editor, in 1986 was the publisher. Gruson said the *Times* frequently suggests a change, but Mrs. Graham resists, saying, "This is not the way we do things."*

The experience left Gruson most unhappy. "I am in left field, sit-

---

*In the 1987 staff reshuffling following Rosenthal's retirement as executive editor, John Vinocur, a former *Times* foreign correspondent and metropolitan editor, became editor of the *International Herald Tribune*.

ting in Paris without a job." He continued on the *Times* payroll. "I've got salary coming out of my ears, I have a car and a driver, but I have no work to do." Sulzberger told him, "Don't worry." Gruson did anyway. "I am a very active guy. I was fifty-nine years old. I wanted a meaningful job." Returning to his old position as foreign editor was out of the question, for Seymour Topping, another veteran foreign correspondent, had moved into that slot. At Sulzberger's suggestion, Gruson flew to New York to discuss his future. Sulzberger told him, "Turner Catledge says he will look after you. Why don't you go down and see Turner?"

Now came the real shock, the snub that made Gruson wonder whether Sulzberger or someone else in the *Times* was trying to elbow him out of the paper. By Gruson's account, Catledge expansively told him, "You've never really worked in the United States. Why not take a desk in the general newsroom and let's see what happens."

To Gruson such an offer was an insult—a suggestion that he sit in the corner while Catledge decided what use, if any, to make of his talents. Such was the technique the *Times* used to discard worn-out reporters, knowing that the embarrassment of a non-work "assignment" would force them into resignation. Yet Gruson was a senior person at the paper. "This struck me as an odd reward for having saved the situation in Paris, and for having served abroad and as foreign editor. I walked out of Catledge's office as mad as I've even been."

What Gruson did not recognize at the time was that Catledge was taking full advantage of an opportunity to derail an Abe Rosenthal competitor. Catledge had reason to believe Gruson's vanity would not permit him to continue at the *Times* in a lesser position, and he was right. Gruson telephoned Harry Guggenheim, the minerals mogul whose wife, Alicia Patterson, had started the newspaper *Newsday* in a Long Island garage in 1940 and built it into a journalistic powerhouse. Alicia Patterson was now dead, and "Captain Harry" had just hired Bill Moyers, President Johnson's press secretary and intimate, as publisher. Gruson sensed an opportunity. He had visited Guggenheim's chateau on Sands Point, and he called and said he wished to talk. Over dinner on a Monday, Gruson told him, "Harry, I'm going to leave The New York Times. Is there anything at *Newsday*?"

"Yes, Moyers needs help," Guggenheim said. "Go out and see him."

Gruson went to the *Newsday* offices at Garden City the next day, and he and Moyers liked one another. Moyers promised an answer by the end of the week, so Gruson flew back to Paris and wrote Sulzberger a letter of resignation. "I did not call him." The *Times* had treated him so shabbily, he felt, that Sulzberger did not deserve that courtesy. Within several days Moyers offered Gruson the job of associate publisher, and Gruson accepted.

"Sulzberger received my letter, and he called and screamed at me. How could I do this to him, to the *Times*? Wouldn't I reconsider? Something good would be found for me. No, I was angry. Also, I had given my word to Guggenheim, and I wasn't going to break it." Gruson did fly to Florida with his wife for two days of talks with the Sulzbergers; at the end, he said, "I stand with it."

Sulzberger wrote Guggenheim, "Dear Harry: I've been unable to talk him out of going, but I want you to know I'm going to get him back."

Gruson was to survive at *Newsday* only nine months. He and Moyers got along famously, but Gruson's problems with owner Guggenheim were immediate, and severe. "Harry was beginning to lose his mental capacity. A sad sight, but a real one," Gruson said. During one of Moyers's absences from Garden City, Guggenheim appeared in Gruson's office and demanded that he fire Clayton Fritchie and Flora Lewis, the paper's featured columnists.

"Why, Harry?" Gruson asked.

"They're left-wingers, they're communists," Guggenheim said.

"No, Harry, they are not. Flora, you must know, is my wife, and she's no more a communist than you are. Nor is Fritchie. I'm not going to do it."

Guggenheim continued talking in the same vein. He warned Gruson, "Be careful of that city room—it's *full* of communists." Gruson tried to ignore these remarks as the utterances of a man rapidly sinking into senility.

On election night 1968 Gruson was in the group in Guggenheim's office listening to the returns. Once Richard Nixon's victory seemed assured, Guggenheim said, "Well, now that he's been elected, I hope we can get behind him. He's *our* president."

A voice from the crowd said, "Well, he's not *mine*."

Guggenheim turned in anger. He could not single out who spoke, but he made his displeasure known.

Gruson wished no more. He realized that although the drive from

Garden City to Manhattan took an hour and a half, he frequently went to the city for lunch, often with old *Times* friends. "I was drawn strongly to this place, and to my friendship with Punch. It was almost impossible for me to break the psychological cord." So he telephoned Sulzberger, and he asked, "Can I come home?"

So Gruson became a special assistant to Sulzberger, still entertaining ambitions for high responsibility in the news department. Several years later, when Rosenthal was named managing editor, he told Sulzberger, How about making me executive editor? He was senior to Rosenthal, and he felt he could give good overall supervision of the paper without getting in Rosenthal's way. Sulzberger, perhaps naively, asked Rosenthal what he thought of the idea, and the response caused him to back away in a hurry. (Rosenthal's opposition almost ended an already-cool relationship with Gruson, and for several years the men scarcely spoke to one another.) As a consolation prize Sulzberger walked over to a junk shop on Eighth Avenue and bought a large plaster cast of a hand with the classic upraised finger and gave it to Gruson. This is Sulzberger's brand of humor, and Gruson accepted it as such; the finger remains in his office.

The other consolation prize was much more valuable. In time Gruson became the third-ranking corporate officer of the New York Times Company, behind Sulzberger and president Walter Mattson. Moving into the corporate side of the paper meant abandoning any residual hope of becoming a high news executive. But Gruson by this time did not care; leave that to Catledge and Rosenthal and Daniel and Reston and Wicker and the other men wanting power in the newsroom. Gruson was content to settle into an easy relationship with Punch Sulzberger, and to work on acquisition programs, and do myriad detail work. Some afternoons he would ride the elevator down to the third floor and find a seat in the back of the executive editor's conference room and listen to the front page planning conference. He would fold his arms, and cup his hands behind his head, and rock back to the limit of his chair's swivel, and listen as editors talked about the next day's *New York Times*.

Whatever wounds Gruson had about being cut out of the news department were soothed by the sweetest of corporate salves, money. Gruson's salary in 1986 (his last year at the *Times*) was $290,000. He received another $226,940 under the *Times*'s "executive incentive compensation plan," and yet another $149,983 as a "long-term performance award," a total of $666,923.

Although Rosenthal was but one of four persons holding the title of assistant managing editor as of January, 1967, circumstances soon identified him as first-among-supposed-equals. A congeries of factors worked for Rosenthal, foremost his continued strong support by Catledge. The scope of his promotion was described in a memorandum circulated to key editors on December 30, 1966, labelled "not for general distribution."

> Mr. Rosenthal will be responsible for news development. He will take over some of the duties formerly performed by Harrison Salisbury, such as passing on out-of-town assignments. In [Clifton Daniel's absence] Mr. Rosenthal will preside over the news conference, and will be in charge of the managing editor's office.
>
> Also, Mr. Rosenthal will act as a bridge between those who are making assignments and developing the news report and those responsible for presenting the news report to our readers. For this purpose, duplicates of the news summaries should be supplied to him, and he will sit with the bullpen editors as they lay out the paper whenever it seems useful.

As he advanced, Rosenthal carefully constructed his own supporting power base. He insured that his sycophant Arthur Gelb became metropolitan editor, thus guaranteeing his continued strong influence over city coverage. Gelb, in turn, brought along as *his* school of deputies, persons who were loyal to Rosenthal.

None of the other three assistant managing editors had any chance of keeping pace with Rosenthal. For reasons discussed, Salisbury was finished. This left Emanual Freedman and Theodore Bernstein.

Freedman, the longtime foreign editor, was serving out his time doing clerk's work. Only Punch Sulzberger and Turner Catledge and perhaps two *Times* lawyers knew that bad investments in Canadian stocks had Freedman on the brink of bankruptcy. The transactions involved poor judgment, not his work at the *Times*, but a near-$100,000 debt, and lawyers clamoring for payment, meant Freedman had to be shoved aside. One claimant suggested that the *Times* pay off Freedman's liabilities to avoid embarrassment; Sulzberger refused. So Freedman spent his final years doing personnel and administrative work for Daniel. The *Times* encourages communications in writing, with multiple copies; the thinking is, "writing it once saves saying it five times, and you don't garble in the retelling." A good management theory, perhaps, but someone must pilot the massive paper flow. Such was Freedman's last job.

Ted Bernstein's situation was considerably more complex. More than any other person in the *Times* hierarchy he had championed Rosenthal as a future editor, and he was the man who pointedly brought the young correspondent to Catledge's attention. To credit Bernstein for Rosenthal's success at the *Times* would be an overstatement; nonetheless, he had given his career a significant first boost by engineering his appointment as metropolitan editor.

Bernstein had his own ambitions. Although in his late fifties, in 1966 he harbored hopes he could cap his career as a desk man by becoming managing editor for a couple of years. Because he never wrote for the paper, his name, via a byline, was unknown to *Times* readers, and Bernstein craved public recognition. His perception of himself was as an editor who had done the actual *work* of putting out the paper all those years when Catledge politicked and manipulated people, and drank. Although Bernstein approved of much of what Catledge did, he griped from time to time about his superior's "wonderful capacity at wearing either of two faces, depending on which would be the most useful." But he toiled as the faithful servant, awaiting the pat on the head acknowledging his loyalty to Catledge and *The New York Times*.

Such was not to be. Unfortunately for Ted Bernstein, his own aspirations lay directly athwart the career march of Abe Rosenthal. Bernstein was of no further value to Rosenthal, hence he could be shoved aside, ignored. Bernstein recognized the turn of events the first afternoon Rosenthal walked into the bullpen just as he and subordinates began making up the paper.

"Don't mind me," Rosenthal said, "I'm just a spectator."

Several men present gave Bernstein veiled glances. Rosenthal clearly was intruding into a process that was none of his business. The bullpen was restricted to the editors assigned there, and the iron-clad rule in the newsroom was that outsiders did not meddle.

Bernstein, however, was painfully aware of the new realities in the newsroom. He sat and seethed. As he told one colleague later, the invasion was as gross, as unwelcome, as if Rosenthal appeared in his bedroom just as he and his wife commenced *coitus* and stated, "Don't mind me. I'm just here . . ." Bernstein did not argue. He knew too well Rosenthal's nasty temper when challenged, and he did not wish to spark an ugly scene. So he said simply, "Sure, Abe, make yourself comfortable." Then he resumed the meeting.

Rosenthal sat quietly, his owlish eyes darting around the little circle of editors as they planned the next day's paper. But Bernstein was not deceived. Rosenthal had just taken a most important step towards exerting his authority over the entire paper. After the meeting Bernstein did make a *pro forma* protest to Turner Catledge. If he was to be responsible for the paper, he did not want Abe Rosenthal, or anyone else, coming to the planning meeting and second-guessing him.

Catledge smiled and brushed Bernstein aside with a so-so shrug and suggested that he make a closer reading of Rosenthal's new job description. Under the new system, Rosenthal would have a direct input into the work of the bullpen, and, as Bernstein feared, he soon was the dominant figure.

Bernstein's chief loss was damage to his pride. He had not cared about titles; his personal reward was being known to others in his profession as "the man who produces *The New York Times*." That he had been shunted aside in favor of a man he considered a protégé made the loss of power all the more galling. Bernstein turned bitter towards Rosenthal (although he had the good political sense not to challenge him) and newsroom friends recall him complaining of "nasty elbows," in obvious pain.

Rosenthal's advance taught several things to persons at the *Times*. He could sense a power vacuum, a job that needed to be done. He would move for it, confident of Catledge's support. And if the person he shoved aside happened to be a friend or a mentor—well, too bad; personal feelings were not nearly so important as the well-being of *The New York Times*.

Bernstein learned something else. He could forget his quiet dream of someday becoming managing editor of *The New York Times*. And he was to carry with him to the grave the conviction that A. M. Rosenthal, whatever his professional abilities, was something less than a perfect human being.

The summer before his promotion, Rosenthal wrote a seven-page single-spaced memo detailing for Clifton Daniel his perceived shortcomings of the *Times* news product. He felt reporting and editing were "becoming more knowledgeable and tighter and generally rather more sophisticated." Most of the lapses were due to editors failing "to carry through an execution, rather than failure of editors to understand the direction in which the paper is moving, namely in the direction of more knowledgeable reporting follow-through, sharp story ideas and more lucid copy." He had specific criticisms for all departments. Writing on his own metropolitan desk, he said it "sometimes still is soggy," and he had not found good replacements for reporters he lost to the foreign staff. The foreign staff had reporters who could not get at the sense of a country. His sharpest words were for the national desk. "We seem to be huffing and puffing after magazines and other papers more in the case of national reporting than in almost any other part of the paper," he wrote. Claude Sitton, the distinguished southern correspondent who had been national editor for two years, "has the hard police reporter . . . approach to news," but lacked intellectual awareness. Rosenthal learned more about America from other publications than he did from the *Times*.

Soon afterwards Sitton returned to North Carolina to become editor of a newspaper there, and as his replacement Rosenthal picked Gene Roberts, who had been covering national news in the south. Roberts and Rosenthal never meshed. Roberts was a low-key man who could sit silently for many minutes while thinking about what next to say in a conference or even a casual social conversation. Reporters working for him in the field often thought he had hung up on them, the telephone silences lasted so long. But Roberts was a man of immense talent and popularity, and he put together the backbone of the national staff that continued to serve the *Times* in 1986. Roberts handled Rosenthal's temper tantrums the way he handled any problem; he simply sat and listened, and then made his decision and did what he thought right. He knew he could never advance to the top of the *Times*, so when the Philadelphia *Inquirer* offered him the job of executive editor in 1972, he left.

As an assistant managing editor Rosenthal now had a mandate to pursue flaws anywhere in the paper, and he did not hesitate to do so, either in sharp personal talks with reporters and editors or in biting memos. Rosenthal stressed always that a newspaper must be written for its readers, not for other reporters or for the insiders involved in a story. A special peeve was "the recurrent tendency of some reporters, particularly those covering legislative bodies, to wrap themselves and the readers up in intricate procedural detail before telling us what the issue is all about." One such memorandum criticized an article by Robert Semple of the Washington bureau in May, 1967, concerning a rent subsidies bill. Semple had "great detail on the political maneuvering" but "only . . . almost as an afterthought told us what the . . . bill was all about. And he told us little or nothing about what the model cities program was all about." Rosenthal wrote:

> . . . [T]his is not simply a matter of nitpicking or journalese. It has to do with the whole philosophy of news coverage. We believe that the significance of a legislative action or almost any important action lies in its impact upon people. The political infighting and maneuvering is interesting but it is ephemeral. Tomorrow nobody will give a damn about the intricacies of a vote but tomorrow and the day after that a lot of people will care about how the rent supplement program cutback affected them or affected other people.

Rosenthal also demanded more reportorial effort, that staff members should not be content to let part of a story slide after a perfunctory telephone call. In a May, 1967, memo to Seymour Topping, the foreign editor, Rosenthal complained of how John Finney of the Washington bureau handled a story about the defection of a Hungarian diplomat:

> There was an embarrassing line in Finney's story on the defector today: "He was believed to be in his residence at _____ Arizona Avenue, N.W., Washington, D.C. The telephone there was not being answered." It is obvious what I am getting at—that it is almost shameful to tell our readers that in an important story like this that we did no more to try to reach the subject than to pick up the telephone. Obviously somebody should have been sent over by the Washington bureau to that house.
>
> I have discussed it with [Robert] Phelps [news editor in the Washington bureau]. If Finney was not able to go, then somebody else should have been sent over. On Washington's part, this was a news editing failure. On the part of the copy editor or whoever was on duty at the desk last night, it was a failure to insist on normal journalistic practice. If the bureau was short on men, it simply should have foregone another story. I know we will all understand that if Washington is to do this kind of follow-up on important stories, there will be times when they cannot fulfill lesser requests; this is simply a matter of day-to-day judgment. . . .

I would also like to stress what I said to Phelps—that it is no good for editors just to say this back and forth to each other. It must be discussed with the reporter carefully so that he understands and agrees.*

In scores of similar memos Rosenthal critiqued the performance of the entire newspaper; countless other times he did so in person, to the responsible editor. Persons who felt the sting of Rosenthal's tongue often would give the grudging admission that he was right, that a story had been mishandled. Yet the abrasiveness that marked his years on the metropolitan desk now spread throughout the newsroom. His omnipresent scowl seemed even deeper and more menacing. One of his friends from those years (this man no longer sees Rosenthal socially, by choice) says, "The tragedy of Abe Rosenthal is that he could be absolutely right on a subject and make his case in such a nasty fashion that he would offend people, rather than convince them. I used to wonder where Abe found the energy to stay so actively mad so often and so long." Says another man who never cared for Rosenthal: "To put it unkindly, Abe got the reputation around the paper as being some kind of nut."

Rage of another nature burned within Rosenthal those years—rage at the protests against the Vietnam War that escalated into attacks on a broad range of American institutions, from the government to the corporations, the universities, the church and even the press. Rosenthal did not consider governments infallible, yet he had not the slightest patience with revolutionaries who would sweep them away to be replaced by a society of their own indefinite design. Almost from the day he became assistant managing editor Rosenthal kept a skeptic's eye on protests and the people running them. He recognized many such incidents as emotional episodes staged to attract media attention. He was equally skeptical of ringing campus manifestoes. He told one friend during the late 1960's that the press, not "the mob," was the proper monitor of America.

But Rosenthal had problems enforcing his standards of objectivity. Many *Times* reporters were of the same generation or a few years dis-

---

*Rosenthal's memo belies his ignorance of Washington. A bloc country diplomat who had just announced his defection would not be sitting around the house awaiting interviews with reporters; American security services would have hustled him away for safety and debriefings, a fact surely known to reporter Finney and others in the Washington bureau. Rosenthal's point is valid in that reporters too often rely on the telephone rather than attempts at in-person interviews.

tant from the campus demonstrators whose rallies they covered. Regardless of intent, many sympathized with what they witnessed in the streets. Thus Rosenthal found himself in the fireman's role, stamping out ideological blazes whenever he thought he saw one in the *Times*'s news columns.

Rosenthal had especial problems with the *Times*'s coverage of student protests at Columbia University commencing the spring of 1968, ostensibly to halt demolition of housing in Riverside Heights to permit construction of a new gymnasium. Students eventually seized several campus buildings, including the office of the Columbia president, Dr. Grayson Kirk. After several tumultuous days Columbia officials asked that New York police run the students from the buildings. Rosenthal heard from his friend, Police Commissioner Howard Leary, of the intended raid; his reflexive request was that the police move before the *Times*'s final deadline, so that the paper had the story the next day. Leary refused, fearing the confrontation might slop over into racially-tense Harlem. He would wait until well after midnight to move.

Rosenthal went to Columbia to witness the denouement of the struggle, and against the advice of such persons as Clifton Daniel he wrote a highly-emotional eyewitness account that ran on the *Times*'s front-page on May 1 under a three-column headline, "Combat and Compassion at Columbia." His article was a moving descriptive narrative; through Rosenthal's words one could sense the agony the confrontation brought to the campus; his vignettes of students seeing their university smashed were vivid word portraits. Yet the overall thrust of the piece did exactly what Rosenthal had forbidden for the *Times* staff. His article had a viewpoint, and a hero. He supported the Columbia administration for calling in the police, and he cast as the victim Dr. Grayson Kirk. Rosenthal walked with Kirk as the university president entered his office.

> He wandered about the room. It was almost empty of furniture. The desks and chairs had been smashed, broken and shoved into adjoining rooms by the occupying students, who had just been led down the stairs, manacled and whistling, "We Shall Overcome."
> Dr. Kirk picked his way slowly through the dirty blankets, half-eaten sandwiches, comic books and tin cans on his spattered green rugs. . . . A policeman picked up a book on the floor and said, "The whole world is in these books; how could they do this to these books?"

To Rosenthal, "a place of learning became a place of destruction."

Rosenthal's story brought yelps of outrage from the students and their supporters, and from many reporters on his own staff. Rosenthal had exempted himself from the standards of "objectivity" he had imposed on coverage of demonstrations. If the *Times*'s assistant managing editor could write of a confrontation as a political event—as Rosenthal did—why should not the same license be permitted others on the paper? These persons argued that a "revolution"—and they insisted such was in progress in America—could not be described accurately by conventional journalism. The day after the Rosenthal article appeared, hundreds of Columbia students picketed Punch Sulzberger's apartment, charging that since he was a university trustee, the *Times* had not given the strike fair coverage.

No particular insight into Rosenthal is required to understand his rage. The major struggle of his boyhood was to get into college, and to make enough money to stay there, and to use education as a springboard out of a Bronx housing project. For that privilege, he ate catsup sandwiches and skimped so he would have subway fare. To Rosenthal, books were the precious first things to be purchased should he have a spare dollar after meeting other expenses. At Columbia in 1968, he saw affluent louts deliberately destroying a university, and crushing books into the floor along with cigarette butts and beer cans. On the fourth or fifth reading of the article the eye catches Rosenthal's most telling epithet about the persons who occupied Kirk's office; their debris included not only half-eaten sandwiches and tin cans but also "comic books."

The Columbia article brought Rosenthal his first sustained outside criticism, in the *Village Voice* and elsewhere. Critics such as Jack Newfield and Nat Hentoff savaged him in the *Voice*; neither bothered to talk with him before writing. Such is not required of persons who write editorial opinion; they base articles on the existing public record. Rosenthal saw no such distinction; by his standards, any person criticized deserved the right of explanation, or reply. Columbia marked the beginning of a permanent estrangement of Rosenthal from what he called the "left-wing know-nothing press." In the multiple criticisms Rosenthal saw more than a reaction to a single story. Three weeks after the Columbia story he wrote a long memorandum to Clifton Daniel.

As you know, I have felt that there is a deliberate left-activist campaign to damage *The New York Times* and to try to destroy its credibility. . . . [I]t is not necessary to believe that all of this is centrally directed or minutely organized. Some of it is, perhaps, some of it may not be.

A few nights ago, a couple of political scientists I know at Columbia visited me at home to tell me that they thought that this was taking place and that we should be prepared for it. They did not proceed particularly on the basis of any documents or courtroom evidence, but on the basis of their own long study and acquaintance with left-wing activist movements. Essentially, they were describing the kind of political logic which they believe the left-activists had adopted in relation to *The New York Times.*

Their theory is that the left-activists' objective is to try to damage or destroy as many establishment centers as possible, in the hope that there would be a contagious effect. They believe that that is the reason that Columbia was selected. These people also say that it is only logical to assume that the left-activists will direct as much of their attention as possible to the main opinion molding and news gathering organization in the United States, which is *The New York Times.* They believe that the effort will concentrate on the *Times* because it is through the *Times* that news of their own activities is spread, particularly among college youth. Therefore, their political logic goes, they will attempt to influence the *Times* coverage by pressuring tactics, *and by infiltration* [emphasis added] and simultaneously to try to discredit the *Times.*

Some of this, of course, has already taken place—the attacks in the *Village Voice,* the rumor mongering at Columbia about ties between Columbia and personnel of the *Times,* the picketing at Punch's house.

As I say, it is not necessary to believe that every attack is centrally directed or that the *Village Voice*'s attacks stemmed from any kind of written directive. I think that two things are taking place—a planned attack . . . and a simply carrying out of attacks on the *Times* by left-activist individuals because they see the *Times* as a primary target, with or without directive.

Of course, the *Times* has been subject to organized attacks in the past, particularly by the right wing activists. But what makes this current attack more important is that whereas the right wing attacks were directed primarily toward right wing sympathizers, the left wing attack is aimed at influencing students, liberals and others who are not part of the left wing.

I think we should be aware of this and discuss it and see if there are any measures we can take to counteract it. It may be that there are no measures and that we simply will have to rely on the integrity of our own reporting to defeat these attacks.

Other than what he was told by the Columbia political scientists, Rosenthal's only concrete evidence was a two-page memorandum entitled "Spring Offensive Proposal: Deobfuscate *The New York Times.*" Jack Gould, the *Times* television critic, obtained the memo from a friend who "thinks a student at Rutgers may have given it to him." Gould, in turn, gave the paper to Arthur Gelb, who passed it to Rosenthal. The memo's thought-line seems to track an argument that dates at least to Students for a Democratic Society, and that has been heard from other leftists for almost two decades. Leftist cant is not easily summarized. But the thrust of this particular memo was that "one of the cherished liberal myths . . . objective news coverage by established progressive media" has quickly dissolved. The *Times*, for political reasons, denied "the legitimacy of the radical, anti-imperialist potential of the peace movement, since the *Times* politically desires change only within the structure of American corporate capitalism and will legitimate news that falls within this perspective." The *Times* was a "megacorporation" with "interlocking connections with other large corporations" whose owners "are some of the key figures of the ruling class." The "action" part of the memo consisted essentially of distributing leaflets attacking the *Times* as "part of our anti-imperialist education . . . [on] how information and media are controlled. . . ." By the standards of 1960's leftism the memo was low-caliber, and no physical demonstrations of note ever ensued.

Rosenthal, however, considered himself a marked enemy of the left, and he came to hear criticisms of any sort with this defensiveness in mind.

At West 43rd Street Rosenthal's physical presence and dominant personality gradually reshaped the news report to his liking. But to his continuing distress one important part of the paper remained beyond his reach—the Washington bureau. This Rosenthal could not tolerate.

Washington was important because it produced a high percentage of the front page stories in the *Times*, and because government and political news enabled the paper to shape public perceptions of the country and the men running it. But Rosenthal's dream of putting the bureau under the control of West 43rd Street ran counter to tradition. Under bureau chiefs Arthur Krock and James Reston, Washington for three decades had operated as an independent branch of the paper. Washington decided which stories would be covered, and how, and even the feared bullpen did not tinker with copy once it left the bureau.

Krock and Reston convinced the Sulzbergers that their knowledge of Washington was superior (they were perhaps right) and that as the *Times*'s ambassadors in the capital, their judgment should not be questioned. They also performed. Reston, the bureau chief in the 1960's, had come to Washington in the mid-1940's, and the underlings with whom he then shared backyard cookouts and cocktail parties now were at the top of government. Reston was a whiz of a reporter; he plucked off scoops with the seeming ease of a gardener wandering through an orchard, gathering fruit. Reston was a good politician. He cultivated with especial attention Iphigene Sulzberger, wife of former publisher Arthur Hays Sulzberger, and mother of Punch. Iphigene Sulzberger gushed over Scotty Reston, taking him by the hand when he came to visit and making sure he sat next to her on the couch, behaving as if she wished she had been blessed with such a gifted son. Reston's abilities included a sense of timing; he of all *Times* people knew when to step up a pace and let a younger generation move forward.

In 1964 Reston had two very bright young men in Washington. The most conspicuous, in the public sense, was a round-faced Carolinian named Tom Wicker, who had a most non-*Times* background. Son of a railroad trainman, Wicker had edited a country weekly, done public relations for a Carolina chamber of commerce, and written editorials for the Nashville *Tennessean*. When Wicker first applied for a job at the *Times*, after a Nieman Fellowship at Harvard, Clifton Daniel sniffed at his beard and told him to go away. Reston hired a now clean-shaven Wicker in 1961 and put him at the White House, and in November, 1963, Wicker did one of the better on-the-spot news stories of the century in describing the murder of President John F. Kennedy.

In 1964 the networks were waving money before Wicker in denominations seldom seen in the newspaper bureau or city room, and Reston knew he had to either promote Wicker or risk losing him.

The other Washington bureau star, Max Frankel, had travelled a more conventional route, through the *Times* city room (as a rewriteman he did the main story on the sinking of the Italian liner *Andrea Doria*) and then on to Cuba and the Caribbean. A squat, stoutish man with an omnipresent pipe in his mouth, Frankel loved being a Washington insider, and his admiration—and emulation—of Reston was seemingly boundless. Frankel loved deep diplomatic stories involving material whispered by diplomats at parties, and the *ex officio* status he carried as a *Times* correspondent. New York thought him valuable; in a memo in April, 1963, Catledge told of plans to give Frankel the title of diplomatic correspondent. "What we have in mind is the kind of reporting that Mr. Reston did before he became a columnist, and through which *The New York Times* developed quite a reputation for reporting and explaining diplomatic moves." Another motive for the promotion, Catledge noted, was that the New York *Herald Tribune* syndicate had just offered Frankel "a rather lucrative position." So with the new title went an increase in salary from $14,326 annually to $20,000, a raise of almost one-third.

Max Frankel's world crumbled beneath his feet in the early fall of 1964 when Reston announced he was stepping down as bureau chief, and that Wicker would be the new chief. Although Frankel has never criticized Wicker publicly, he told two close friends at the time that he felt Reston erred greatly; that Wicker's bumpkin qualities, while temporarily an asset in Lyndon Johnson's Washington, in the long run would hurt the *Times*'s image. On September 3, Frankel wrote a "Dear Punch" letter resigning from the *Times*. He denied any connection between his decision and the "recent reorganization." He wished to write without the tyranny of a daily deadline and without the annoying inhibition of avoiding ideological or philosophical commitment. In sum, he wished to be a journalist in the European sense. To pay the rent, he intended to become national correspondent of *The Reporter* Magazine, based in Washington.

Catledge sent Frankel a warm but polite note on September 8 thanking him for his service, and adding, "As much as I regret it, I cannot quarrel with your decision."

Reston intervened to salvage Frankel's career at the *Times*. He took the younger man into the privacy of his office and looked at him reflectively across the desk. Reston shook his head, slowly and sadly, and he talked about the importance of *The New York Times*. "I know you are unhappy," he told Frankel, "for there are times in life when you seem to be treated unfairly. But *The New York Times* is a large institution, and also the most influential newspaper in the Western world. When you write for the *Times*, Max, you write with a *voice*, for an *audience*. You certainly would do wonderful work for Max Ascoli [the publisher-editor of *The Reporter*]."

Then Reston delivered the clincher: "Max, who would be reading you, and how many of them? Max, *The New York Times* is too damned important for you to leave. I want you to stay."

Reston's mix of plain-talk and cajolery worked as intended upon Frankel, who was already having deep second-thoughts about the insecurities of writing for a respected but financially-troubled magazine. He told Reston he might be too late, that Catledge had already accepted his resignation, a statement which Reston dismissed with a wave of his hand. "No worry," he said, "I'll square it with Punch." He did, and Frankel continued to write from the Washington bureau—careful to say nothing indicating jealousy of Wicker.

But that Frankel had actually resigned in a snit of temper did not sit well with Punch Sulzberger, who felt the act immature and disloyal. To Sulzberger the *Times* was a family which no one left lightly. Frankel was to spend many years regaining Sulzberger's total trust.

Good reporter and writer as he was, Wicker found running the bureau beyond his capabilities. He felt overwhelmed by becoming bureau chief only four years after joining the paper—and, in fact, he *was* overwhelmed. Wicker had no flair for management or for directing a staff. He admits now that, "I should have stayed with the typewriter, all of us would have been better off." Forty-third Street began picking at Wicker almost immediately, knowing that, because he was not performing as had Krock and Reston, he was vulnerable to pressures to bring Washington directly under New York's control. The only inhibiting factor was Reston, who continued to write his column from the bureau, and whose power (and friendship with Iphigene Sulzberger) was not challenged casually.

So New York moved obliquely. In 1965 Clifton Daniel sent Robert Phelps, a deputy national news editor, to Washington. Daniel did not tell Phelps the real reason for the assignment; he mentioned only that the paper was having trouble with Ferdinand Yerxa, Wicker's deputy. Wicker right away suspected an ulterior motive, and he told Daniel he resented Phelps "as a spy for New York." Phelps says his role was unwitting. "At no time did Salisbury, Catledge or Daniel say, 'Go down there and tell us what's going on and straighten these guys out.' I was told to do a right job of editing, that Wicker was a poor manager; that I should manage for him and straighten the bureau out."

By Phelps's account, Catledge was so disillusioned with Wicker's performance that he wished to remove him as bureau chief after only five months.

"What are we going to do with Wicker?" Catledge asked Phelps, as if Wicker's shift was a decided fact.

"Why don't you give him a decent chance to do something?" Phelps replied. "Everyone is riding him."

Phelps himself began to have problems with Rosenthal soon thereafter. Rosenthal probed, as if to see how far his authority as an assistant managing editor ran. Rosenthal had no real power over Washington, and both he and Phelps knew it; nonetheless, Rosenthal pushed. "Abe would call and suggest a story," Phelps said, but "he could not order it. . . . It must have been maddening." One of Rosenthal's calls came at a time when Phelps had a tight personnel problem in the bureau. He desired a certain feature article, and Phelps carefully replied, "I'll see what I can do." As Phelps relates, "Abe read that as 'I'll do it.' "

But as Phelps knew, only two reporters were available. One was recuperating from severe personal problems, and Phelps knew he would fail the assignment. The other, science writer Harold Schmeck, was gifted in his own field, but the story Rosenthal wanted was beyond his range. So Phelps did nothing.

An angry Rosenthal telephoned. "I thought you promised me you would do that story." No, Phelps said, I did no such thing. He explained why he had not made the assignment. Rosenthal would not listen. His voice a screech, he said, "When I ask for a story, I want it!" He banged down the phone. Almost two decades later, Phelps recounted the incident—one of many such brushes with Rosenthal—and he said, "I still think I'm right."

What Rosenthal ultimately wished for the *Times* he made clear one night at dinner with six or so Washington bureau men at the Federal City Club. Phelps was there with reporter John Finney, Wicker and others. The conversation ranged over many news questions, and finally reached the relationship between editors and reporters. Finney, a gifted beat reporter at the Pentagon and the Atomic Energy Commission, had spent years building the tedious, long-term sources essential to the working reporter. Because of his longevity, Finney often knew more about the subject he covered than the relevant bureaucrats. In essence, Finney said, in reply to Rosenthal's question, those of us who cover beats know what is important, and you editors think you know. We think the reporters' view should prevail. What do you think? he asked Rosenthal.

With neither hesitation nor a smile, Rosenthal replied, "I'm greedy—I want it all!"

Another factor, and a large one, was the way the *Times* Washington bureau covered the domestic debate over Vietnam policy. Reporters writing about the war from Washington realized from at least mid-1967 on that administration officials of all levels—including President Johnson—were misrepresenting what was happening in the war, if not outright lying about it. For Hedrick Smith of the Washington bureau, the disillusionment came one Sunday afternoon when Nicholas Katzenbach, the under secretary of state, invited a group of diplomatic correspondents to his Georgetown home for a briefing. The U.S. had just begun bombing Hanoi, the North Vietnamese capital, and the official talk was of "surgical air strikes" against railroad bridges and military installations. Katzenbach talked about bombs falling "one kilometer, two kilometers, even five kilometers" from Hanoi. The previous implication had been that any stray bombs fell in the open countryside. Smith suddenly realized, and confirmed through a question to Katzenbach, that when he spoke of a bomb falling one kilometer off target, he actually meant *from the center of Hanoi.* Rick Smith was (and is) a man who would prefer to believe what his government told him. Years later he shook his head in disgust at the memory of what he heard from Katzenbach. "On a Sunday afternoon, you discover what they had been telling you was baloney." Smith's experience was not isolated. E. W. Kenworthy covered the Senate Foreign Relations Committee hearings on Vietnam, during which Senator J. W. Fulbright, a former college president, conducted what was tantamount to a national "teach-in" on the war. Ned Kenworthy, a small and intense man, carried annotated copies of past hearings, and when he saw a discrepancy between 1968 testimony and what some official had said five years earlier, he was quick to give other reporters chapter-and-verse on "the damned lie." Given the administration's inconsistency, Kenworthy had much material to peddle.

What Rosenthal thought about Washington coverage of the war was colored in large part by the views of an old friend, James Greenfield, whom he brought to the *Times* in 1967. As did Rosenthal, Greenfield came from a hard-scrabble background. Son of a job printer in Cleveland, he was on his own financially from age fourteen, when he took an office job on the Cleveland *Press* and slept wherever he could find a bed. His scholastic ability won Greenfield a scholarship to Harvard, and he then worked for the Voice of America in New York, and the Far East. (CIA supported the Voice of America in those years; as of late 1986 several persons in the *Times* newsroom cling to the silly notion that Greenfield has been a CIA agent since 1949.) During the Korean War Greenfield moved to Time-Life, and in New Delhi in 1956 he became a close friend of the newly-arrived Rosenthal. He found that Rosenthal kept a competitive distance. "I got plenty of Abe Rosenthal rockets," meaning cables from *Time* editors demanding to know why he did not have a story that Rosenthal had published in the *Times* that day. "Abe's attitude was that they could buy what he wrote for twenty cents the next day, so he would not tell me anything." Greenfield went on to London, then in 1961 he joined the State Department as an assistant secretary for public affairs, aglow at the opportunity to be part of the Kennedy Administration. After government he worked a year or so with Continental Airlines, which Kennedy press aide Pierre Salinger headed briefly after the White House.

After a year or so Greenfield decided to return to the media, and Rosenthal hired him, at a lesser salary ($25,000 annually) and a lesser position (deputy metropolitan editor) than he could have commanded elsewhere. But Rosenthal's luring carrot was that he wanted to send Greenfield to Washington to run the bureau.

Although Washington was far beyond his responsibility, Greenfield began meddling there very early, apparently at Rosenthal's instigation. He remained close to Robert McClosky, the State Department spokesman who had been his colleague in government, and he spoke by telephone with him almost daily, to discuss the *Times*'s coverage of war policy issues. What McClosky told Greenfield, he relayed to Rosenthal as the "real story about what is happening." And Rosenthal often accepted the Greenfield-McClosky version over the accounts filed by his own reporters. Washington reporters such as Rick Smith soon realized what was happening; they resented Greenfield's intrusion and his acceptance of a government press officer's interpretations of news over their own.

Rosenthal, meanwhile, lobbied strenuously for Greenfield's appointment to Washington. Wicker's bureau, he argued, was out of control. Wicker spent most of his working time writing his column; if he wanted the title of bureau chief, he should do the job; otherwise, he should step aside. (Wicker said in 1986, "Abe had a point.") Rosenthal eventually convinced Punch Sulzberger, who gave what Rosenthal considered to be final approval. What Rosenthal overlooked was Sulzberger's ability to smile pleasantly and mumble meaningless nonsense when he is thinking through a problem. And what Rosenthal also overlooked was the considerable influence of James Reston.

News of the pending Greenfield appointment appalled Reston. Putting a former government press officer at the helm of the *Times* Washington bureau literally would destroy an institution he and Arthur Krock had spent four decades building. Reston had no special dislike for Greenfield as a person; but as a bureau chief—well, as Reston told a colleague at the time, the only parallel example that came to mind was the Emperor Caligula's appointment of his horse as proconsul of Rome. And everyone knew what happened to Rome. Reston got on the Eastern Air Line shuttle to New York, and he spent a busy day lobbying, first with the elder Sulzbergers, and then with son Punch. What Reston said to these persons, and what they replied, has never been revealed. But apparently he said the Greenfield appointment would be costly, that it could cost *The New York Times* not only his services, but also those of Wicker, Max Frankel, and Anthony Lewis, a Pulitzer Prize winner then running the London bureau. If these persons left the paper, Reston implied, a mass exodus from the Washington bureau would follow. Catledge in his memoir told what happened next.

During the afternoon news conference Catledge received a call that Sulzberger was in his office and wished to see him immediately. "When I got there I found Punch pacing the floor and puffing hard on his pipe. 'Professor,' he said, 'I can't go through with it.' " Catledge knew that Sulzberger was under great stress, that he had made up his mind, that further argument was futile.

"Aren't you taking some people for granted?" Catledge asked.

"You're absolutely right," Sulzberger replied, "I *am* taking you for granted."

Catledge walked back to the news conference and when it ended he motioned for Daniel and Rosenthal to remain. "Gentlemen," he said, "I have bad news for you. The publisher has reversed his deci-

sion on the Washington bureau." Rosenthal tried to telephone
Sulzberger immediately (over Catledge's protest) and could not reach
him. He strode out into the newsroom and collared Greenfield and
took him into a private interview room. A few minutes later
Greenfield, his face grim, went to his desk and scooped up his personal belongings and left.

That night Reston and Tom Wicker went to Abe Rosenthal's apart-
ment. They realized the publisher's turn-around had caused
Rosenthal great humiliation, both in the office and in the eyes of the
public. (Newspaper gossip being what it is, talk about the Greenfield-
Wicker shift was rife among journalists; indeed, one of the last phone
calls Greenfield received before his horrible moment was from a
Newsweek writer asking about the appointment.) Wicker felt
Rosenthal needed collegial solace.

"We found a cornered animal who was not intimidated in any manner by being cornered," Wicker said years later. "This was one of the
most excruciating hours I ever spent in my life. It was Abe Rosenthal
defending his views, and what he was trying to do. He was defiant,
and unintimidated, and unapologetic." Wicker could take the tension
only for an hour; he left Reston alone with Rosenthal. As he stood on
the street and hailed a cab, he realized that whatever defeat
Rosenthal suffered was temporary.

Several days later Rosenthal got an audience with Sulzberger, and
told him in effect that he was angry, that he felt Punch had led him
into an embarrassing situation. Nonetheless, he said, you own the paper, you make the decisions. Rosenthal is mad, but I'll get over it.
They shook hands, and that weekend for the first time, Abe and Ann
Rosenthal were guests at the Sulzbergers' second home in Connecticut.

Tom Wicker, who built his career on good political analysis, feels
that Rosenthal's fatal error was that he overreacted. "Reston took this
as a move against him, which at that time was an unwise move to
make." The essential conflict was between what Wicker called the
"public personalities and private powers" at the *Times*. "The latter
inevitably felt the public personalities get too much attention." For
this very reason a quiet conflict had simmered for years between
Catledge, invisible outside the professional world of journalism, and
Reston, whose byline gave him celebrity status. Losing Reston over
essentially a personnel matter was something Sulzberger would not
risk.

The Washington battle had secondary casualties. Wicker knew he was through as bureau chief. During the turmoil he gave Reston an undated letter of resignation. "Use it when it is to your advantage," he said. Coolness developed between Catledge and Sulzberger. Within months, Sulzberger unexpectedly asked Catledge to step aside two years early and accept a position on the board of directors, and a vice presidency. Reston would become executive editor. "I was visibly shaken by the suddenness of the move, and by the manner in which it was announced to me," Catledge wrote in his memoir. "Perhaps by then I should have been accustomed to Punch's abrupt actions."

Clifton Daniel also was shoved aside. He had wished to be executive editor, now Sulzberger told him, No, the job was going to Reston. So Daniel took the vague title of "associate editor," with a medley of make-work responsibilities including directing the *Times* radio station WQXR. Wicker was told his undated resignation was "accepted," and that Max Frankel would now run the Washington bureau. Since he was going through a sad divorce, and wanted out of Washington, Wicker was happy to take a new job as a columnist, based in New York.

The last part of the shift involved Rosenthal, who was named managing editor—and this only six years after his return from Tokyo. He successfully resisted attempts by Reston to impose Anthony Lewis as his deputy; when Sulzberger backed him, he realized he had won a final victory over "the Reston crowd," that he would now be running the *Times*, in fact if not in title.

Through those six years he had benefitted greatly from the protective embrace and patronage of Turner Catledge. But the competitive environment of the *Times* permits a patron to carry a protégé only so far; talent ultimately is the critical fact. Mentor Catledge nourished Rosenthal; he gave him the job that allowed a display of his abilities; he did the political hatchet work that cleaved away such potential competitors as Harrison Salisbury and Ted Bernstein. In the end, though, Rosenthal went to the top of the *Times* because he was the best newspaperman in New York, and because he wanted the job more than anyone else. And he got it.

TEN

"Abe Slipping on His Brass Knuckles"

Losing the fight over the Washington bureau chastened Rosenthal, for previous to it he boasted an unbroken skein of bureaucratic victories in his rise towards the top of the paper. But now he nursed a new fear, that James Reston would use his new position as executive editor to groom one of his own favorites for the top position on the paper. Many of "Scotty's boys" thirsted for the job. There was Wicker, whose rise had rivalled in speed that of Rosenthal's. There was Anthony Lewis, the gifted Supreme Court reporter and London bureau chief, one of the paper's more deft writers. Max Frankel seemed to be over his pique about being denied the Washington bureau in favor of Wicker, and he had made peace with Punch Sulzberger over his abortive resignation.

But none of these men were ideologically capable of producing the sort of paper Rosenthal felt the *Times* should be. (Of the three, Rosenthal considered Lewis the most dangerous; when drunk, on at least two reported occasions, he called the now-columnist "a fucking lefty, or even worse, because he doesn't have the balls to admit it.")

So Rosenthal set for himself a complicated agenda. As managing editor he wished to produce a daily news report so striking that Punch Sulzberger would have no choice but to ultimately make him the top editor once Reston was gone. As office politician he must fend off any power gains by "Scotty's boys." And, lastly, he must change the thrust of *Times* reporting, and ward off what he considered to be a dangerous trend in American journalism.

The trend was "new journalism," the novelistic form of reporting encouraged by editor Clay Felker of the newly-formed *New York Magazine*. *His* reporters, Rosenthal announced, could do their work without resort to what he considered trickery and literary flim-flam. If a reporter could not describe a political event without injecting his own opinions, he should find another line of work.

During the tumultuous 1968 Democratic National Convention in Chicago, Rosenthal's battles with Harrison Salisbury, who directed *Times* coverage on the scene, at times seemed as noisy as the clashes between the protestors and the Chicago police. Time and again Rosenthal would demand that editors change copy to "take out the goddamned editorializing." When Salisbury protested, "You are cutting the guts out of our stories," Rosenthal snapped, "No I'm not, I'm trying to make them honest."

The dispute was to continue the next year, at the trial of the so-called Chicago Seven, the radicals accused of fomenting riots at the convention. The *Times's* reporter, J. Anthony Lukas, a star of the staff, a Pulitzer winner in his mid-thirties, fumed that he could not cover the trial as did Nicholas von Hoffman of the Washington *Post*. In those days the *Post* considered von Hoffman more of a commentator than reporter, and ran his stories on a new "Style" page which did not pay even lip service to objectivity. Hence von Hoffman wrote as if he were attending a political circus rather than a criminal trial, a "shoddy parody of jurisprudence." Judge Julius Hoffman was an "aged hobbit who never stops talking . . . with the voice of a man reading horror stories to small children." Defendant Jerry Rubin was a "free-lance wild man."

Lukas, by contrast, was held to conventional reporting, and he did not like it. As he complained to Edwin Diamond of *New York* Magazine, von Hoffman caught the trial's "tone and flavor in a way that has been almost impossible for those of us operating under tighter editing restrictions." The demands for "objectivity" imposed by *Times* editors (i.e., Rosenthal) made it "very difficult to give a true picture of what is happening in the courtroom." Lukas was so upset that he spoke publicly about his tribulations at a seminar at the Columbia University Graduate School of Journalism, a talk that mightily displeased Rosenthal. Lukas was to leave the *Times* soon thereafter to become an initial editor of *[MORE]*, a journalism review that devoted much space to criticizing *The New York Times* and A. M. Rosenthal.

Other *Times* people had their own problems, especially the critics. Rosenthal felt that critics should not go beyond artistic judgments, that their political views had no place in reviews. Otherwise, "we'd have a dozen columnists running around all over the paper, out of control." He told one person, "I don't think a guy reviewing a Cuban restaurant has to get on a horse about the Bay of Pigs." One noisy clash was with theater critic Clive Barnes, who insisted in a review of the play *Inquest* that Julius and Ethel Rosenberg were innocent victims of McCarthyism. At Rosenthal's insistence, the sentence was deleted, causing Barnes to write an angry memorandum about censorship. (Oddly, although Rosenthal intervened to edit out a questionable judgment, the review did not mention a central fact about the celebrated case, that the Rosenbergs were convicted of selling atomic secrets to the Soviets.)

In the winter of 1969-70 complaints against Rosenthal's mode of editing went a significant step beyond the conventional gripe session. One Sunday about a dozen persons came to the apartment of William E. Farrell of the metropolitan staff to discuss what they felt was going wrong with the *Times*. Someone jokingly called the gathering "The Cabal," which implies more unity and organization than existed. As one of the participants told Edwin Diamond of *New York* Magazine, "The *Times* has been recruiting a different kind of staff over the last five or ten years. It has attracted bright, articulate young people who tend to have more radical views. And the paper has gotten considerably less tight about style. . . . Now the fear is that the paper is moving, not necessarily to the right, but to a quieter position. The concern is not about the editorial page, or the Sunday Department, or the columns like Tom Wicker's—there's no trouble there—but in the news sections." The Sunday meeting evolved into a series of gripes about specific career problems; eventually someone suggested it might be fruitful if Abe Rosenthal listened to complaints. The group was careful to make no threats or demands. As someone said at the time, "I don't remember anyone being ready to throw himself on a sword just because an editor changed one of Tony Lukas's leads."

So one of the "Cabalists," reporter Joe Lelyveld, was delegated to report on the meeting to Peter Millones, then Rosenthal's assistant for personnel matters.* Millones agreed to hold a small dinner party at his West Side apartment, to permit a free exchange between Rosenthal and the Cabalists.

Rosenthal was not comfortable with the idea, which smelled of revolution. When he arrived he confided to one man he was so nervous he brought a magazine to read during the short taxi ride, that "I could not let my mind run at will unoccupied." For the first hour all attending shared Rosenthal's nervousness, so the only talk was of journalistic war stories—Richard Reeves on John Lindsay, or someone about covering Bob Kennedy. Millones deliberately reached outside the Cabal for the guest list; one person present estimated that of the twenty people there, half a dozen "had no interest whatsoever in any movement against *Times* management."

Reporter Paul Montgomery finally broke the ice. "Abe, how do you think the paper is going?"

"I'm glad you asked," Rosenthal replied. He intended to "keep the *Times* straight," he would entertain no challenges to his editorial judgment. Montgomery suggested that reporters should have a say in the editing of the paper; he mentioned that the staff of *Le Monde*, the Parisian daily, recently got the authority to elect its own editors.

"At this point Abe got vituperative," an attendant said. "It was the verbal equivalent of an alley fight, with Abe slipping on his brass knuckles." He demanded of Montgomery, "OK, so we elect an editor. Who the hell would you vote for?" Montgomery stammered, then said, "I guess we'll all elect you, Abe."

Rosenthal proceeded to address his critics, one by one. Tom

---

*Millones began his career at the *Times* as a City Hall reporter, and, by his own account, he was not a very good one. Rosenthal first noticed him when he married Deidre Carmody, who had endeared herself to Rosenthal when she worked as his secretary; Carmody eventually became a reporter herself, and a good one. Millones joked that "Abe admired my taste in marrying Deidre, and that's when my career really began." He eventually became metropolitan editor and then an assistant managing editor.

Johnson, one of the few black *Times* reporters, had just returned from Vietnam, and he did not like how the editors handled his stories. Rosenthal thrust a fist at him, jabbing, voice rising. "You were nominated for a Pulitzer Prize. You would never have been nominated if Jerry Gold [a foreign copy editor] hadn't worked on your stories." Johnson was so shocked at the vehemence of Rosenthal's attack "he sort of levitated out of his chair."

Rosenthal next turned to Montgomery, correctly recognizing him as a prime mover in the Cabal. "You were a failure when we sent you to Brazil," he said. "The paper carried you, and saved you, and here you are, bitching about editors."

In a few terse moments Rosenthal changed the rules of combat. Instead of listening to gripes about editors, he took the war to his adversaries, letting them know there was an important *other* side to their complaints. "Rosenthal prefaced some of his rebuttals, 'I'm not saying this to hurt you,' then—WHAM!—very basic, and very true," a man present said.

Someone finally broke the tension (several memories pointed to Joe Lelyveld) by saying, "Isn't it funny that the two people most intensely involved [in the discussion] are people who care the most about the paper—Abe and Paul?" This had the effect of being the magic words that ended the meeting on a positive, if inconclusive, note.

Several persons left the meeting not exactly sure why it had been held. Robert Lipsyte, then a sports writer, asked another man in the elevator, "You ever heard so much shit in your life?" The other man thought his remark a "fair summation." Another reporter present, Richard Severo, a man not interested in office politics, was so puzzled that the next day he sought out Deidre Carmody and asked, "Deidre, will you kindly tell me what the hell went on?"

"We didn't know who was in the Cabal," Severo quotes her as replying. "Peter decided to cast out and find out who was happy and who was unhappy so he could improve morale." Severo likened Millones' tactic to the "Let a Thousand Flowers Bloom" campaign of the late Chinese Communist ruler Mao Tse-tung, who encouraged freedom of speech to lure dissidents out of anonymity, and then systematically destroyed them. Many of the unhappy persons indeed soon left the *Times*; Paul Montgomery, for instance, went to *The Wall Street Journal*, and then left journalism altogether. But the overwhelming majority stayed on the paper, and in Rosenthal's good graces. Whatever the strength of the Cabal, within months it was forgotten by everyone at the paper. Everyone, that is, save perhaps A. M. Rosenthal. That the Cabal proved impotent did not encourage Rosenthal; his thinking was that once again someone had dared challenge not only him but what he considered to be the integrity of the *Times*. Rosenthal was comfortable with his own perception of what the paper should be; persons should either accept it (he was after all the boss) or leave. Rosenthal spelled out his definition of the *Times* in a three-and-one-half page memorandum which praised how the paper had changed in a decade.

> Our business is facts. We have learned to search deeper for facts, to dig for the meaning of facts, to relate facts to each other, to analyze them and put them into perspective.
>
> We've learned too that a social movement, a change in life styles, a trend in music or art, an emotion spreading among people, can be as real a fact as a speech or a parade.
>
> Newspapers were always quite good at reporting what people said, and then what people did. Now we are also reporting that people think—theology, scientific thought, the meaning of the law—because what people think influences what they say and do.
>
> I think the *Times* has shown that it is capable of giving room to a variety of forms of self-expression and intellectual endeavor on the part of its reporters.

Such was Rosenthal's depiction of what he considered the positive growth of *The New York Times*. Much of the remainder of the memorandum was tantamount to a Rosenthal credo on preserving what he considered to be the character of the *Times*:

> The belief that although total objectivity may be impossible because every story is written by a human being, the duty of every reporter and editor is to strive for as much objectivity as humanly possible.
>
> The belief that no matter how engaged the reporter is emotionally he tries as best he can to disengage himself when he sits down at the typewriter.
>
> The belief that expression of personal opinion should be excluded from the news columns.
>
> The belief that our pejorative phrases should be excluded, and so

should anonymous charges against people or institutions.

The belief that every accused man or institution should have the immediate right of reply.

The belief that we should not use a typewriter to stick our fingers in people's eyes just because we have the power to do so.

The belief that presenting both sides of the issue is not hedging but the essence of responsible journalism.

Rosenthal felt adherence to these principles especially important during the turmoil of the late 1960's, for "there are fewer and fewer journals in the country and particularly in New York that a reader can turn to confident that he is getting the utmost possible in fairness and objectivity and is being allowed to make up his own mind. The turmoil in the country is so widespread, voices and passions are at such a pitch that a newspaper that keeps cool and fair makes a positive, fundamental contribution without which the country would be infinitely poorer. The goal of objectivity is made more difficult—and becomes even more important—as the stories we go after and the issues we cover become more and more complex." Rosenthal continued:

> I am bringing all this up, not as a warning nor as a cry of alarm, because neither is needed, but simply as a reaffirmation of the determination to maintain the character of the *Times* as we grow and develop.
>
> An across-the-board commitment is needed, a continuing commitment by reporters and editors to the character of the paper, to its belief in objectivity, to its principle of eliminating editorializing from the news columns. I am not talking about cold, dry reporting—just fair reporting. . . .
>
> Editors and reporters must share the responsibility. Editors play an obviously important role in their decision as to what stories to cover, their assignment, the handling of the copy and the display. Every decision they make in some way or other touches on the nature of the paper.

Then Rosenthal addressed his restive staff directly, telling them he did not wish any subtle attempt to evade his goal of objectivity:

> As for the stories themselves, the essence of the paper, the basic responsibility lies with the reporter. Desks can change copy but the desk should not be cast in the role of a policeman, always on edge to catch a loaded phrase that a reporter might put in to see if he can get it by. For reporters to cast editors in the role of policemen is to denigrate the

function and responsibility of the reporter, of himself, and to his paper. Achieving the highest possible degree of objectivity and impartiality may no longer be as easy as it used to be—I know that. But for that very reason it becomes increasingly important that we reach for the goal and that the reporter believes it, does it willingly and takes his full responsibility to the paper.

During the next years, as shall be seen, Rosenthal frequently would abandon his own guidelines, for he permitted, even encouraged, stories that treated humans and institutions unfairly. More than one person was to complain that the *Times* in fact did "use a typewriter to stick our fingers in people's eyes." The Cabal was significant—but only relatively so—because it marked the last quasi-organized attempt within the *Times* for line reporters to question the growing omnipotence of Abe Rosenthal.

James Reston's tenure as executive editor was short, by decision both of him and Punch Sulzberger. The ugly squabble over the Washington bureau, and the rescinding of Jim Greenfield's appointment as its chief, brought the *Times* unwelcome media attention. So one thing Sulzberger told Reston when he gave him the job was, "Keep us out of the papers." By Reston's interpretation, this meant keeping the *Times* on an even keel, and not to make any decisions unpopular enough to cause unhappy staff members to gossip to the rest of the press.

Such suited Reston fine. He did not care for the administrative details involved in running the intricate bureaucracy of the *Times*. After a few days he did not even attend the daily meeting of editors at which the next day's paper was discussed. He took an office down the hall from the main newsroom, designed so that visitors could come to him privately, and he spent most of his time there. He continued writing his column, which meant he occupied himself with long phone conversations with old friends and sources in Washington.

Which is not to say that Reston ignored the news department entirely. One idea of which he was particularly proud, and which he spent months crafting, was of creating a new corps of "special correspondents," writers who would be based in New York, or Washington, and be available for assignment anywhere in the world. These would be persons of special talent who liked newspapering, but not the constraints of working on humdrum daily stories. They would be paid more than other reporters, and they would be expected to perform better as well.

Reston had seen such talented persons as Gay Talese, David Halberstam and Richard Reeves and others leave the paper because the *Times* had no satisfactory place for them. Keep such men on the payroll, Reston reasoned; give them sabbaticals if they wish to write books. But when a special story arises, the *Times* should have a special person to cover it, and in detailed and knowledgeable depth. Creating such an elite staff would also make the *Times* more attractive to bright young graduates of Harvard and Radcliffe and other universities, persons wanting a challenge more intellectual than writing daily news stories. Reston is a thinker, a man who sees events in the broadest of terms. America and the world were becoming more complex places, and he wanted to create a staff that would analyze and explain them. In a sense Reston wished to replicate the special majesty of his Washington bureau, but on a grander scale. Further, the group would work independently of the news bureaucracy, directly under the executive editor.

Reston knew that Rosenthal was dissatisfied with the overall course of the newspaper; both men felt that the *Times* had yet to find a way to give adequate coverage to a changing world, or to persuade talented young men to stay with the paper. There was circulating in New York at the time a memorandum carrying angry marginal scrawls by David Halberstam that told the story well. While in Warsaw a few years earlier Halberstam received a note from the foreign desk stating that, when in doubt, a correspondent should file stories exactly 600 words in length. Some events might warrant more, some less—but 600 words should be the goal. The directive angered Halberstam; setting such an arbitrary limit seemed micro-editing of the worst sort. He sent a copy of the memo to his good friend Tony Lukas, then reporting in India, and he jotted in the margin: "Lukas—There are only two kinds of stories in the world: those about which I do not care to write as many as 600 words, and those about which I would like to write many more than 600 words. But there is nothing about which I would like to write exactly 600 words."

To Reston, Halberstam's anger summarized tartly why the younger reporters were leaving the *Times*. And hence Reston was most surprised at Rosenthal's instant reaction when he outlined his scheme for a "super staff."

Although time has since smoothed some of the details, Rosenthal's outburst remains vivid in Reston's memory as one of the most volatile he witnessed in more than half a century of journalism. Screaming, cursing, his arms flailing the air, Rosenthal said no—as long as the New York Times hired *him* to run the news department, *he* would decide where and how reporters worked, and that if Reston was inclined to impose a bunch of blank-blank-blank elitists over him, why, that was all very well and good, but A. M. Rosenthal was not going to stand around and watch. In fact, A. M. Rosenthal was of a mind to go clean out his desk *right now* and get his coat and leave.

Reston sat helplessly, unable to cope with such a torrent of emotion. As Rosenthal's superior—he *did* have the title of executive editor—he could have imposed the new staff by fiat. But: Punch Sulzberger had supported him in the too-recent controversy over Jimmy Greenfield's appointment to the Washington bureau. Would Sulzberger go along with him in yet a new internal argument, one that well might result in Rosenthal's resignation? (Reston sensed that Rosenthal was bluffing, not unlike an angry child bent upon getting his way on the playground; he, for one, could not envision Rosenthal leaving his beloved *Times*. But uncertainty nagged; perhaps Rosenthal *was* serious.) The second factor was Sulzberger's clear mandate that he did not want the *Times* "in the papers again" with a personnel fight, for he had not liked the publicity over the Greenfield imbroglio. Win or lose, Rosenthal could cause a nasty fuss. So in essence the mere fact of Rosenthal's objection left Reston's grand plan dead in the water.

After listening to Rosenthal rant for perhaps half an hour Scotty Reston quieted him with a casual wave of his pipe, and he said, OK, Abe, if you feel that strongly about it, let's let the whole thing slide. They ended the meeting with a casual handshake but Reston knew it meant nothing. He had covered diplomatic conferences for years, and he knew when one side or the other lost in bargaining, and Rosenthal clearly had come out the winner. As Reston was to remark years later, "On the issue, Rosenthal was willing to throw his body into the path of a subway train if necessary to win. Well, I wasn't. I thought it was a good idea, certainly, but not enough to risk disruption of the paper and my life. Rosenthal wanted something more than I did, and he got it. That's pretty much the story of Rosenthal's professional life, isn't it?"

So after a year Scotty Reston gracefully withdrew from New York and returned to the comfort of the Washington bureau, to write his column and hobnob with the people who run America. He was seen less and less in the bureau. He lived in a comfortable house in Kalorama Place Northwest, and he did his writing from there, and the bureau would send over a messenger to pick up his twice-weekly column. He would go to the Metropolitan Club for lunch and talk with the men he had known for years in the Capital, and over soup and sandwiches in the second-floor dining room he could learn more about Washington and the world in an hour than most other reporters could in a month. He had done what he could for the *Times,* and now clearly Punch Sulzberger wanted a different sort of editor running the paper. Reston essentially withdrew from involvement in the daily paper. He felt himself not a victim of Rosenthal outright, but of an ongoing process that was inexorably changing the *Times.* No, he was not totally happy with the progress of matters, for he did not trust Rosenthal's manner of doing things, the way he brutalized other people, especially those subject to him. Nor did he consider Rosenthal a particularly deep thinker. Like the professional diplomat and bureaucrat, Reston puts much store in the process, the proper way to do things, the way history and current happenings interact. His basic objection to Rosenthal—a deep one—was that Rosenthal reacted emotionally to situations, rather than rationally; a smart man, to be sure, but one whose knowledge of the world was visceral, not intellectual.

In a sense, Reston came to feel, Rosenthal was not all that different from Ronald Reagan, who many years later became president: One good anecdote that proves the point you wish to make is good in the immediate sense of winning a debate—but do you really want to run a country (or a newspaper) on such a flimsy intellectual basis?

So once again there were changes in the Washington bureau, although Reston this time was a sidelines player. Clifton Daniel, his hopes for the top editorship dashed, had gone to Washington as an interim bureau chief, a graceful way for his career to end. Soon after Reston returned, in 1970, Daniel retired, and Max Frankel, only six years after his angry (but retracted) resignation, replaced him. According to John Finney, who worked in the bureau for three decades, from 1956 to 1986, lastly as news editor, Rosenthal's assertion of authority over Washington was an evolutionary process that began in earnest during Daniel's brief tenure. "Clifton was a caretaker and he knew it, and therefore was not an assertive bureau chief." Nonetheless, the continued presence of Frankel and other Reston loyalists meant that Rosenthal must bide his time. In retrospect, two events, one a success for the *Times*, the other a failure, gave strength to the argument that the bureau should work directly under 43d Street.

The oft-told story of the Pentagon Papers may be summarized briefly. Reporter Neil Sheehan since his days in Vietnam for United Press International had maintained close contacts with persons actively opposing war policy, especially working-level officials both in and out of government. One of these persons, Daniel Ellsberg, a onetime analyst for the Rand Corporation, cached in his office safe in California a multi-volume history of the evolution of the war, compiled and written within the Pentagon at the direction of Robert S. McNamara, the former defense secretary. Through intricate negotiations Sheehan obtained copies of most of the papers, and the *Times* set up a secret task force to cull through the papers and write a comprehensive series.*

Abe Rosenthal knew immediately when he read a sampling of the papers that they must be published. The government had clearly lied to the American people—at best, concealed the truth from them—for almost thirty years. This Rosenthal could not tolerate, although he knew the papers would give solace to the very anti-war forces he detested. Rosenthal told Salisbury he realized publication would "hurt my views and hurt the views of my friends. I don't want to see it published but it must be published." His chief concern was authenticity. Were the documents real, or forgeries contrived by "some radical kids in a basement"? Sheehan knew the origins, authors and source; don't worry, he told Rosenthal, they are genuine.

Rosenthal's next decision, also an important one, was that the *Times* in writing the articles would use the government's own words. For once the paper would not insist on comment from the multitude of persons named in the papers. A mini-staff of sixteen editors, writers and aides holed up in the New York Hilton Hotel to put a mass of material into publishable form. And as they worked a fierce battle raged over whether the *Times* could risk publishing top secret documents. Absolutely not, maintained longtime counsel Louis Loeb; when he realized he was outnumbered, he withdrew representation

---

*The best book-length account is *The Papers and the Papers*, by Sanford Ungar. Much of Harrison Salisbury's *Without Fear or Favor* is devoted to mechanics of how the *Times* obtained and decided to publish the Pentagon Papers.

on the matter. The great imponderable was Punch Sulzberger, who apparently never read more than a smattering of the documents. Sulzberger waffled. As the *Times*'s chief corporate officer he worried about responsibility to shareholders should the paper be prosecuted criminally. He complained about the space Rosenthal wanted, twelve full pages daily for a week. (They compromised on six pages.) He suggested writing stories without printing the documents. But finally he approved, and on Saturday afternoon, June 12, 1971, Rosenthal stood in his office and stared down at a proof of the front page of the next day's *Times*. The headline, spread over four columns at the top of the page in twenty-four point type, read:

VIETNAM ARCHIVE: PENTAGON STUDY TRACES
THREE DECADES OF GROWING U. S. INVOLVEMENT

As Rosenthal was to say later, the realization that the story was to be published overwhelmed him emotionally. "Seeing all those documents from government files! You can't imagine the feeling it gave you. It was strange. I just walked around looking at them. I could hardly believe it. This hadn't been done before. The *Times* was publishing secret documents."

Two days later the Washington *Post* began publishing its own articles based on the papers, and attorneys for the Nixon Administration, charging that revealing secret diplomatic dispatches endangered relations with allies, asked a federal court to enjoin further publication. Both the *Times* and the *Post* voluntarily suspended publication; ultimately the courts held the government could not impose prior restraint on a newspaper; that if a law was violated, prosecution must await actual publication.

Rosenthal's nervousness about his personal liability for the publication continued for weeks, for the Nixon Administration debated bringing criminal charges against persons beyond Daniel Ellsberg. (It finally chose not to do so.) Speaking at the University of Arizona in late 1971, Rosenthal said that for the first time he realized the true implications of the lawyer's phrase "chilling of rights." He said:

It means that as I stand here, I know that every word I say will be examined by the government, not because they are particularly fascinated by Rosenthal and his words of wisdom, but because they are looking to see if I will say something that will somehow help them in one or another of the incredible series of investigations and grand jury hearings now taking place. . . . I used to believe that the government found a crime and then looked for a criminal. Now, apparently, they have decided that they have a criminal—Neil Sheehan, or the *Times*, or both, or whatever—and are now looking through the fine print for a crime to hang on them.

To Harrison Salisbury, Rosenthal recounted a nightmare: that Nixon would put the living former presidents, Truman, Eisenhower and Johnson, on national television to denounce the *Times*.

In the Tucson speech Rosenthal made a strong case for publication of the Pentagon Papers. Depriving the American people "of information rightly belonging to them," he said, would have been a "contribution to the miasma of doubt and suspicion and emotion that has surrounded the Vietnam war and everything that flowed from it." Not publishing would have made mockery of freedom of the press.

We send people out at great personal risk to themselves to places like Vietnam. . . . We and they accept the risk because we believe we are doing something not only worthwhile but essential to the functioning of American democracy, and that is to provide the people of the country with as much meaningful information as possible on which to base their own judgments. I have lived in authoritarian societies and it strikes me that this is the essence of democracy and one of the basic differences between a democratic process and an authoritarian process.

. . . [H]ere came the biggest and most important storehouse of information quite possibly in journalistic history. Could we have said no, we will not take the risk to ourselves, we will withhold information from the public that we ourselves consider of utmost importance and, in the deepest meaning of the phrase, a contribution to the national interest; we will buckle to government pressure?

No, it was impossible; we could not have done that. . . .

Another positive consequence, Rosenthal said, was that "a lot of young people who, for reasons with which I do not agree, have been losing faith in the press, found that newspapermen were indeed contributing in important ways to American democracy. I think that some of them were rather surprised to find that middle-aged establishmentarian types like the people who run newspapers had a set of ethics of their own and were willing to stand up for them."

The Pentagon Papers, by Rosenthal's estimate, was *The New York Times* at its best—a concerted effort by reporters, editors—and the publisher—to spend the energy and the money necessary to put an important story before the public. The Pentagon Papers episode, to Rosenthal, also offered further argument for bringing the Washington bureau under 43rd Street's control. The papers began as a Washington story; ultimately the decisions that had to be made, and the physical labor involved, meant its transferral to New York. Rosenthal felt his active lobbying for the story weighed heavily in Sulzberger's difficult decision to publish. Had the story been handled from Washington, the outcome well might have been different.

A year later another story did not turn out nearly so well for *The New York Times*, providing a further argument for 43rd Street control of Washington. The story was Watergate.

In a prescient memo to Turner Catledge in 1966 Tom Wicker of the Washington bureau warned of a determination by a rejuvenated Washington *Post* to "become a major competitor" of the *Times*. Katharine Graham became publisher of her family-owned paper in 1963 upon the suicide of husband Philip, and her shrewd first move was to offer the job of editor to Ben Bradlee, who ran *Newsweek's* Washington office. A knife-lean New Englander who could pass as a Corsican hood, Bradlee sighed and said, "Oh, Kay, I'd give my left one for that." An old *Post* joke had been that the paper would cover any story around—so long as it wasn't more than one taxi zone distant from the office. Graham gave Bradlee the money to build a staff, and as Wicker warned, "In the view of everyone who has watched what is going on, [Bradlee] has been commissioned to put the *Post* 'on the map' and he is regarded here as a very bright, very capable, very energetic man."

But neither Rosenthal nor anyone else took the *Post* seriously until June 1972, when fledgling reporters Bob Woodward and Carl Bernstein seized Watergate, and held it for their very own for months. The *Times* bureau, Reston's pride, thirty-five reporters and editors, was skunked by two rookies, one of whom (Bernstein) Bradlee had been about to fire for general sloppiness. Why? Max

Frankel, the bureau chief, unwittingly gave the most plausible answer two years later when he talked with Philip Nobile of *Esquire* Magazine. Frankel considered Henry Kissinger a friend; he and the Secretary of State shared lunch, and Henry would return his phone calls. When Watergate got out of hand Frankel consulted what he considered the ultimate Washington source. Kissinger shook his head, oh so slowly, and he assured Frankel that Watergate had nothing to do with the White House. Bernstein and Woodward, meanwhile, continued grubbing around with secretaries and middle-echelon political operatives in the Nixon campaign, and they exposed Watergate as part of an extensive White House operation that went far beyond a third-rate burglary.

In post-mortems the *Times* offered many excuses—but no good reasons—for its Watergate failure. Frankel had already been selected to become Sunday editor, and he was spending time at 43rd Street. He took that summer to accompany President Nixon on the historic trip to the People's Republic of China. The deputy bureau chief, Robert Phelps, vacationed in Alaska for six weeks. The national editor, Gene Roberts, had given notice he was leaving to become executive editor of the Philadelphia *Inquirer*. Much of the bureau scattered to cover the political conventions and the campaign. Rosenthal had yet to give major attention to Washington. Through these massive chinks fell the most important political story of the half-century, and America learned of it chiefly from the Washington *Post*.*

As Frankel lamented, "Perhaps the lack of dirty-mindedness was the essential." This is a *Times* euphemism that means gentlemen do not lie to one another. James Reston in his era could do his reporting on the assumption that people might say "No comment" or tell him something off the record and explain why it should not be reported. But lie? Never. Washington changed in the 1960's, when Vietnam made lying a national policy. That the rules of conduct now were different seemed to slip past Frankel (and other people at the *Times*), the lessons of the Pentagon Papers notwithstanding. By the time Frankel realized his friend Henry Kissinger and others in the Nixon

---

Times people, past and present, protest that they indeed obtained some exclusive Watergate stories. Granted. But the overall scandal was etched into the public consciousness by Bernstein and Woodward—not because (for instance) Times reporter John Crewdson conned a copy of the infamous "Houston Plan" out of its author. Some individual *Times* people did good Watergate work; overall, the Frankel bureau got its ass kicked.

White House were not gentlemen (that is, people who do not lie to friends) the Washington *Post* had its Pulitzer Prize, and Ben Bradlee proudly crowed, "Eat your heart out, Abe Rosenthal, eat your heart out!" Watergate made the Washington *Post* a national newspaper.

The Pulitzer season that year was not one of Abe Rosenthal's happier times. He considered the Washington bureau a mess; yet the omnipresent Reston meant he could not take control. The *Times* would reestablish itself in Washington not with the dignified reporting of "Reston's boys," but with hard-nose scrambling of a new generation of reporters personified by Seymour Hersh.

Appropriately, the first time Sy Hersh spoke with Abe Rosenthal on the telephone, he said, "Go fuck yourself," and some other things and then slammed down the receiver and grinned. He waited, and the phone rang, and Hersh heard Rosenthal demand, "Do you know who I am?"

"I sure do, you motherfucker," Hersh said, and he slammed the phone down again.

Hersh's approach is not the way one gets on *The New York Times* payroll. But Hersh has done things his own way, so long and so well, that he is *sui generis* in contemporary American journalism. Few of his generation, or any other, can touch Hersh in his ability to get a story. A Chicagoan who ran the family dry-cleaning store from age sixteen, Hersh for years was a journalistic knock-about who did well wherever he worked, in Chicago, in South Dakota, in Washington, mainly for the Associated Press. As a Pentagon reporter he became interested in chemical warfare; when the AP messed up a long investigative article he did on the subject, he quit, wrote a book, worked briefly for Senator Gene McCarthy's presidential campaign in 1968, quit again, and began free-lancing. In 1969 he received a tip about a supposed massacre of civilians by U. S. troops in a Vietnamese village named My Lai, and within a very few weeks the name "Sy Hersh" was an important one in American journalism.[4]

The *Times*, which seldom prints non-staff news stories, wished to

*Hersh's derring-do in obtaining the My Lai story is a novella in itself, best told in two interviews with Joe Eszterhaus in *Rolling Stone*, April 10 and 24, 1975. Through guile, bluff and charm Hersh not only found My Lai principal Lt. William Calley in an Army hideaway at Fort Benning, he also persuaded him to talk, even though the officer faced capital murder charges.

do an article about one of Hersh's followup pieces concerning the Army's investigation of My Lai. Hersh was in New York, where he had arranged for CBS News to interview several soldiers who had been at My Lai. Rosenthal telephoned him at CBS. He praised the stories. "Look, terrific story, kid," he said, "we're going to run it tomorrow." He wanted to know where to find one of the persons, a Brooklyn man, mentioned by Hersh. Why? Hersh asked. "You've bought rights to use my material any way you wish. . . ."

"We're *The New York Times*," Rosenthal said. "We can't run other people's quotes. We have to verify them."

Rosenthal's statement outraged Hersh, who has a low boiling point when he senses a challenge to his work. "Christ," he said, "Rosenthal must have thought I was just off the boat." He said something nasty and hung up. He was no more pleasant when Rosenthal called back and said, with a snarl of his own, "Nobody treats *The New York Times* like that!" Rosenthal's second effort netted him a second shouted obscenity, and another banged-down telephone. (The *Times* had no recourse but to get the desired quotations from the CBS News telecast.)

Within months, Rosenthal and Hersh made their peace, and they talked seriously about the young reporter's joining the paper. Hersh was ambivalent. He had become a contract writer for *The New Yorker*, and the spinoff of My Lai-related material earned him a comfortable living. Yet, as did most journalists of his day, he considered the *Times* a goal, the premier newspaper in the world; if the chance arose to work there, he would take it.

In the spring of 1972 Hersh received a visa to travel to North Vietnam, and Rosenthal suggested he talk to James Greenfield, the foreign editor, about filing stories for the *Times* while there. Unlike the unfortunate Harrison Salisbury, who had blighted his Times career in Hanoi earlier, Hersh had the good sense to report only what he saw, not what he was told by his propaganda-minded hosts. In the first stories the *Times* identified him as a "free-lance writer"; then bylines carried the tag, "Special to *The New York Times*," Rosenthal's way of welcoming him to the staff. Hersh's rise thereafter was meteoric. The peace talks on ending the war began in Paris; since Hersh knew some of the North Vietnamese, Rosenthal rushed him to France, and he led the paper with several stories. Then to Washington, as the producer of the sort of heavy stories Rosenthal wanted to offset the competitive edge the *Post* had taken through Watergate.

For the next three years Hersh was the most prominent byline in

American journalism. He wrote about the secret bombings of Cambodia, about which Secretary of State Kissinger and other Nixon people flatly lied. (Hersh developed a churning dislike for Kissinger; he still has trouble saying the name without his face twisting into a grimace.) A congeries of scandals revolving around the CIA, including the extensive spying on domestic opponents of the war ordered by Presidents Johnson and Nixon. (That Hersh's figures on the number of Americans subjected to snooping were off by a factor of several hundred never caught up to the public consciousness. Nor did the fact that CIA acted at White House direction. The never-resolved oddity of the story was why William Colby, then the director of central intelligence, chose to give Hersh the off-the-record confirmation that enabled him to get into print.) In late 1973 Hersh even got a grip on Watergate, with a string of front-page stories about the Nixon people's attempts to buy the silence of the conspirators.

Rosenthal knew that Hersh enjoyed playing tough guy, and that he pushed journalistic ethics to their limits—or beyond—in going after stories. Indeed, one person who complained personally to Rosenthal about claimed victimization was one of his oldest professional friends, Edward Korry, whom he had met in 1946 when both covered the United Nations as newsmen. Korry went on to become chief European correspondent for United Press International, and as he wrote me in 1986, the relationship with Rosenthal was very close during two decades. "I alone among his chums encouraged him to marry the woman he has long since shed; he and Annie shared my final weekend in France before I departed for years into communist Europe in 1948; he provided invaluable help and hospitality to my wife and me during three months spent in India in 1958 and without which I would surely not have won the Page One Award of the Newspaper Guild; I persuaded him, as he would later ruefully remind, to accept the assignment in Poland which may have been a factor in his later eminence." Korry left journalism in 1963 to become United States ambassador to Ethiopia; in 1967 he went to Chile as ambassador, serving there until 1971.

In 1973, two years after Korry left Chile, a Senate subcommittee on multinational corporations chaired by Senator Frank Church, the Idaho Democrat, held hearings on supposed CIA plots to prevent the inauguration of leftist politician Salvador Allende Gossens as president of Chile. Korry testified that the United States did not attempt to pressure any Chilean congressmen against Allende "at any time in the entire four years of my stay. No hard line toward Chile was carried out at any time." In September, 1974, Hersh commenced a series of articles on the CIA and ITT scheming against Allende by stating that "high officials in the State Department and White House repeatedly and deliberately misled the public about the extent of United States involvement" in anti-Allende activities. The next paragraph quoted Korry's previous denial of any such activities. Next came the committee counsel, Jerome Levinson, Hersh's source, stating that the subcommittee was "deliberately deceived."

Hersh did not call Korry before implicitly accusing him of perjury; the implication in his story was that he was still ambassador during the anti-Allende plotting. This story appeared on September 10. A week later Hersh wrote that the "subcommittee staff"—that is, his source, attorney Levinson—was recommending that Korry, Richard Helms, the former director of central intelligence, and other Nixon Administration officials be indicted for perjury. Korry immediately cried foul play to Hersh; he had left Chile in mid-October 1971, and the "plots" charged by the subcommittee (and on the front page of the *Times*) started later.

Hersh played tough. OK, he said, you might be right, but tell me about Henry Kissinger. What was his role? Korry turned him aside. He had not come into government to become a kiss-and-tell informant; all he wanted was that Hersh set the record straight. That Hersh did, but in such backhanded fashion that not even a close reader of the *Times* would have noticed an "exoneration." He wrote on September 24 that the Nixon Administration's "change of . . . clandestine policies" against Allende began in mid-October 1971. His "retraction" consisted of a single sentence: "A change of ambassadors took place on Oct. 12, 1971, with Edward M. Korry, a Kennedy Administration appointee, being replaced by Nathaniel M. Davis. . . ."

Korry appealed to his old friend Rosenthal. Surely Abe would be willing to clear his name, in intelligible fashion. Rosenthal refused. He wished to hear no more from Korry. The *Times's* story about possible perjury indictments had relied upon credible sources; if Korry had any complaint, it was with the Senate, not *The New York Times*. Korry found his attitude unbelievable. In a letter to Rosenthal he recollected Kitty Genovese, the young Kew Gardens housewife beaten to death on the street while thirty-eight witnesses listened or watched in silence. You, Abe, you are doing the same thing to me, your friend—and this after twenty years of friendship.

Korry did not give up. He appealed to a number of mutual friends he and Rosenthal had shared over the years, including Elie Abel, the dean of the Columbia University Graduate School of Journalism. Abel telephoned Rosenthal, and as a result James Greenfield, the foreign editor, met Korry at the Century Club for lunch and a discussion. "During that lunch," Korry said, "Mr. Greenfield told me and others who passed by his table and paid him homage that I had been the victim of an assault on my civil rights and that the *Times* intended to do a story about it."

Greenfield arranged for Korry to spend several days talking with John Burns, a reporter who had recently joined the *Times* after working five years in China for a Canadian newspaper. Having been absent from the Western Hemisphere during the Chilean disclosures, Burns listened to Korry with a mind untarnished by preconceptions of the scandals. According to Korry, Burns said he intended to write stories "not only about the lesser civil rights complaint" (i.e., his mistreatment by the *Times* and the Senate) but also about the full Chilean situation. Korry quoted Burns as saying that "I had been badly mistreated and that he wished me to know of his sympathy." Burns wrote an eight-column article. The story never appeared in the *Times*.

As Korry bitterly commented, "the *Times* had been corrupted into actions not at all dissimilar from those taken by the White House during the Nixon incumbency." He so told his former friend Rosenthal in a letter. Another person at the *Times* later reported to Korry that Rosenthal shouted at a group of editors, "I never want to see Korry's name in the paper again!"

To Korry, clearing his name of the taint of alleged perjury became an obsession. He circulated thick packages of documents to newsmen and officials who had know him in the past. He heard reports that people were saying, "Korry had gone overboard, keep away from him." Most did. In all of American journalism, only one reporter sat down and studied the documents—Joe Trento, of the Wilmington *News-Journal*, who saw the same evidence Korry had produced for Hersh, Rosenthal and others at the *Times*, and who concluded Korry had been victimized. Trento's story appeared in the Wilmington paper in December, 1976, far too late, and in far too obscure a newspaper, to salvage Korry. The former ambassador found himself unemployable. He took part-time teaching jobs at Connecticut College and at a Harvard graduate program.

Hersh suddenly appeared in his life again in late 1980, this time as supplicant, by Korry's account. Hersh was writing a book on Henry Kissinger; he needed Korry's help. He had uncovered "new material" that convinced him that Korry in fact *had not* been involved in the Allende plots. That's exactly what I told you eight years ago, Korry stormed; why didn't you give me a fair shake then? To Korry, Hersh's implication was that if he would help on the Kissinger book, his name would be cleared.

"Put it in writing," Korry said. Give me assurance from Abe Rosenthal that you will set the record straight, and I will talk to you. Hersh did, and on Monday, February 9, 1981, the *Times* ran a three-column headline at the bottom of the front page: "New Evidence Backs Ex-Envoy on his Role in Chile." In some 2,300 words the article gave Korry a clean bill of health and noted his "particular bitterness towards *The New York Times*" for what he said was unfair reporting." Only one journalistic culprit was named in the story, Jack Anderson, the columnist, for writing in 1974 that ITT documents linked Korry to joint CIA-ITT operations against Allende's election. Significantly missing was any admission by Hersh that he wrote the articles about which Korry had "expressed particular bitterness."

Hersh flatly denied that he made any "deal" with Korry to clear his name in return for cooperation on the Kissinger book. "Look," he said, "it's like this. When I started researching the fucking book, I got inside the fucking CIA station in Santiago. I got the actual fucking cables. Once I had these, I knew Korry was not involved. But I did not know this in 1974; I did not know this until I got along pretty far on Kissinger. Sure, I told him the *Times* would run a story. That's being only fair, to set the record straight. But as a *quid pro quo* for him helping me on Kissinger—no fucking way, it just didn't happen."

Five years later Korry wished the entire episode put behind him. He still accused the *Times* and an unprincipled Senate staff for ruining his life and his career. The entire Chilean situation was interpreted through a fatally-flawed perspective, one that kept the truth from emerging. Powerful Senate Democrats did not wish to explore covert meddling by the Kennedy Administration in Latin politics; the Nixon Administration wished to protect undercover CIA operations. Hence Chile was presented in hopelessly muddled fashion, and Korry happened to be a victim.

Korry could take unfairness no longer. He sold his home and moved to Switzerland "because it has become too tormenting and painful to live in a country where I no longer believe in the integrity of the Congress . . . and the press." He wrote in a long, bitter letter from his new home that "I suppose Abe Rosenthal is as responsible as anyone, other than myself, for my departure as well as drastically altering the past dozen years of my life. . . . Hersh said to me in 1975 that 'the American press is shitty,' and he operated on that principle."

Rosenthal now concedes that he had serious second thoughts about some of Hersh's reporting, even during the glory days of the 1970's when his stories featured prominently on the *Times*'s front page. Some of the stories (he would not specify which ones) would not be publishable under the standards he demanded of *Times* reporters a few years later. As if citing a mitigating factor, Rosenthal said, "We were all learning how to do certain things." Rosenthal shook his head in remembering watching Hersh at work during those years. He was once in the room when Hersh telephoned someone for information on a story. "He was practically blackmailing this guy. He was saying, 'Either you tell me what I want to know or I'll. . .' I put my hands over my ears and ran out of the room. I didn't want to hear this sort of thing, I didn't want any part of it. Let him get the story, but leave me out of it, how he got it."

Rosenthal could clamp his hands over his ears, but this did not absolve him of responsibility for Hersh—the stories he obtained for years went into the paper with minimal editorial challenge. In Hersh Rosenthal clearly had a star who could make the public (and other American newspapers) forget about the Woodward-Bernstein team. On the personal level the relationship was never particularly smooth, and the men said nasty things to and about one another. (The first time I spoke to Hersh about Rosenthal, over the telephone, "motherfucker" was one of the nicer things he called his former editor. Hersh then went on to praise Rosenthal as a man of "absolute brilliance, the smartest cocksucker who ever walked into a newsroom.") Rosenthal, for his part, constantly irritated Hersh by patting him affectionately on the shoulder and saying, "Well, well, how's my little commie today?"

Hence the relationship was symbiotic. Hersh gave Rosenthal the whiz-bang stories he wanted for the *Times* through the mid-1970's. Rosenthal gave Hersh the premier showcase of the American media, the front page of the *Times*. Only the direct intervention of an offended Punch Sulzberger would give Rosenthal the mistakable nudge that meant the time had come to curb Hersh, and eventually create circumstances that made him impossible to work for the *Times*. But Punch's frown at Hersh was not to come for several more years.

Yet, the evidence is that Rosenthal had second thoughts even at the time about the way some *Times* correspondents operated in the field. Hersh was a special case. Hersh, Rosenthal once said, "is like a puppy that isn't quite house broken, but as long as he's pissing on Ben Bradlee's carpet, let him go." (By "Ben Bradlee's carpet" Rosenthal meant that Hersh was snatching stories off the turf of the rival Washington *Post* and that, therefore, occasional excesses could be excused.)

During the same period Rosenthal was having serious reservations about Gloria Emerson, a woman alternately melancholic and dramatic ("a sloe-eyed iron maiden who had equal concerns for her tough image and her hair curlers," in the words of a former colleague) who went to the *Times*'s Saigon bureau in 1970. Emerson decided in advance that the war was awful, just awful, and such is what she wrote: that when people shoot at one another, people are killed, and such is a pity, what with all the blood. So *ghastly*. Emerson took a unique approach to war coverage. She would write through what is called "transactional journalism," in which the reporter shares the experience of the persons about whom she is writing.

Gloria Emersons's first venture into transactional journalism was to follow four Vietnamese "students" on a mission in Saigon where they intended to fire bomb an American vehicle, with the aim of burning to death the American soldiers inside. Emerson accompanied the students, who rode on motorcycles, to a busy Saigon intersection where American jeep traffic was heavy. The ambush called for one "student" to dash into the roadway and wave his arms until the vehicle stopped. Another "student" would toss a plastic bag of gasoline inside the jeep, while the third "student" tossed in a lit match. As Emerson claimed in her Vietnam memoir, *Winners and Losers*, "I remember praying that no one would come, praying that no American would pass us by, warning myself over and over again *to stay out of it and not to interfere*, not to remember the crusts and the smell of burned men I had already seen in hospitals."

For twenty minutes a reporter for *The New York Times* crouched alongside the road, waiting to watch American soldiers burn to death in an ambush, cautioning herself all the while to "stay out of it and not to interfere."

The mission failed, but through no fault of Emerson's. A "sleepy" GI drove by in a truck. "There was that second when I could have screamed, yelled, rushed forward to warn him, given the plan away," Emerson wrote long after the event. But the "student" moved too fast, and with bad aim; his bag of gasoline splattered harmlessly against the windshield, and the GI drove away before he could be incinerated.

If Gloria Emerson had any moral qualms about being a silent witness to murdering American soldiers, such is not expressed in her memoir.

Emerson alarmed her Saigon bureau chief, Alvin Shuster, on another occasion when she did a story about the availability of heroin in Vietnam. With an interpreter, she easily purchased $40 of heroin and brought it to the *Times* bureau, as if engaging in a journalistic show-and-tell. Shuster recoiled as if physically assaulted. For the love of God, he told Emerson, *The New York Times* is the most unpopular newspaper in this whole goddamned country, and you walk in here with *heroin*. Can you imagine what the South Vietnamese secret police would do to us if they came in that door right now? You and me and everyone else would go to jail, and *The New York Times* would not exist in Saigon any more. You've played your fuckin little game, *now get rid of it.*

Chastened, Emerson flushed the heroin down the toilet. She thought Shuster unduly nervous.

Emerson's emotional involvement with the war became so intense she could no longer report for the *Times*. She had many complaints. For instance, the *Times's* copy desk used the adjectives "bitter" or "fierce" in describing battles. She preferred "ghastly" or "fearful." So she left the paper, and she became an active participant in the peace movement, and she marched with veterans on the Capitol in Washington, and elsewhere. She sheltered military deserters in her Paris apartment.

In talks with friends and others Gloria Emerson denounces Abe Rosenthal for "having a viewpoint" on the world and its issues. In the mid-1980's she was foremost (but anonymous) in a grouping of former

Times reporters who criticized Rosenthal for "politicizing" *The New York Times.*

But one point is important: Whatever his qualms about Emerson's reporting, and her techniques, Rosenthal left her on assignment. That she had chosen sides in the Vietnam War did not disturb him sufficiently to bring her back to New York.

Rosenthal's *Times* of the early 1970's was combative in other areas as well, eager to seek out malfeasance wherever it was sensed, in business as well as government. Rosenthal seemed determined, in fact, to show his independence from pressures of any sort, from any source. In 1972 the paper went through intricate negotiations for permission to open a permanent bureau in Peking.* President Nixon's surprise visit to the People's Republic of China raised the prospect of normalized relations with the United States, and the *Times* desired a permanent presence in the country. Several correspondents had visited there, but under limited short-stay visas. Just as the negotiations showed signs of success, the *Times* ran an advertisement from the Chinese Nationalist regime describing its exile government as the "Republic of China." The Peking government lodged a formal protest with Rosenthal. As Iphigene Sulzberger noted in her memoir, "Abe, in good *Times* tradition, replied that there was nothing morally objectionable to the ad, and that what a foreign government chose to call itself was its own affair and not the *Times'*."

The protesting Chinese official next told Rosenthal, "You want to get a correspondent in, don't you?"

Rosenthal replied that the *Times* did not intend to alter its coverage to court favor with any government. He saw to it that the paper published a story about the Peking protest, further aggravating the situation. As Mrs. Sulzberger commented, "Perhaps the incident could

*While he was the *Times* correspondent in New Delhi, Rosenthal spent months trying to obtain a visa for travel to China. Aided by officials of Prime Minister Nehru's government, he spoke many times with persons in the Chinese Embassy. Secretary of State John Foster Dulles mooted the issue by stating that even if the *Times* obtained a visa, the United States government would not sanction travel to China, even by a correspondent. Then-published Arthur Hays Sulzberger stopped efforts for the visa. The Chinese irritated Rosenthal by stating they would prefer that a more illustrious correspondent, someone of the stature of James Reston, be their first *Times* visitor.

have been handled more tactfully, but the *Times* wanted to make clear that it couldn't be bribed."

Rosenthal seemed determined to show that the *Times* had no favorites—that business, even *Times* advertisers, were subject to the same muckraking that reporters did on government. The consumer advocate Ralph Nader was in the paper so often, with his many "raider reports" on business, that persons in the Washington bureau joked about covering the "Ralph beat," as if this one person warranted the attention given, say, the Pentagon.

The *Times'* barrage of attacks on supposed shoddy business practices pleased even such longtime critics of the paper as George Seldes, whose half-dozen books on the press had been unstintingly critical of its previous devotion to big business. Seldes marvelled at the *Times's* willingness to report on Catholic attempts to change the state's liberal abortion laws, and its friendly treatment of the Consumers' Union, an organization tacitly ignored by most of the American press because of its critiques of advertisers. As Seldes summarized the *Times's* changed attitude in his book *Even the Gods Can't Change History*: "In 1972, writing the first draft of this chapter, I found something in almost every daily issue to document the view that the *Times* had begun to publish all the news, whether it would have been fit to print or not according to its previous decisions." Seldes ticked off more than half a page of stories he found pleasing as an old muckraker; among them:

> A Federal Trade Commission report criticizing misleading painkiller ads, naming as offenders Anacin, Bayer Aspirin and Exedrin.
> "Reader's Digest Accused of Bias."
> "Korvettes Charged in Detergent Sales."
> "G. M. Is Accused of Hiding Dangerous Cadillac Flaw."

Seldes praised the *Times* for reporting that large advertisers including Gimbels, Bergdorf-Goodman, and Lord & Taylor, among others, had been "charged with bilking charge account customers of more than $2,800,000 in credit insurance," and were bargaining consent degrees with the FTC. For four straight years, from 1969 to 1972, the *Times* won the New York Newspaper Guild's citation for "best example of a crusading newspaper," a designation that would have been unthinkable even a decade earlier.

On the surface, Rosenthal liked the *Times's* new image of toughness, and the attention the hard stories brought his paper. Rosenthal is not a man who enjoys jokes at his expense, and Ben Bradlee's quip after the Washington *Post*'s Watergate Pulitzer ("Eat your heart out, Abe Rosenthal. . . .") rankled for years. But the anomaly was that he had no true philosophical commitment to crusading journalism. What he permitted the *Times* staff to do, during the first part of the 1970's, was to make a temporary splash with investigative reporting—not because he cared for it, but because he wished to prove that the *Times* could beat the *Post* at its own game. This he did—but only temporarily, and to satisfy his ego. And in many instances he violated journalistic ethics without hesitation, even though he hurt such friends as Ed Korry, the one-time ambassador to Chile.

Hence these years rank as Rosenthal's worst as an editor, because he put the full majesty and power of *The New York Times* behind stories of dubious validity. He permitted the *Times* to damage reputations of individuals and institutions. He permitted a good reporter, Hersh, to use methods he at once deplored and condoned. And when staff persons complained of mistreatment, Rosenthal ignored them. The 1970's were not Abe Rosenthal's finest years.

Punch Sulzberger, who through the early 1970's displayed little significant interest in what his newspaper printed each day, implicitly endorsed Rosenthal by doing nothing to curb him, a classic instance of mismanagement through non-action. Sulzberger can be defended, in a fashion, on the grounds that he is not a very smart man. In those years, he paid far more attention to what was printed in his account books than in his newspaper. His attitude was to change later, and in significant fashion. But as publisher he bears ultimate responsibility for Rosenthal's—and the *Times*'s—excesses.

Rosenthal's irresponsibility was not uniformly applauded within the paper. Younger reporters and editors enjoyed the relatively permissive reportorial license granted by Rosenthal. Yet more seasoned persons, those whose enthusiasm for gathering news was leavened with a keen sense of ethics, felt (and said privately) that *The New York Times* was squandering its reputation for fairness. Credibility is not easily achieved by an American newspaper—but it is easily lost. And prominent among the senior *Times* persons disturbed by Rosenthal's approach was John Oakes, editor of the editorial page, and a member of the modern *Times*'s founding family, the Ochs-Sulzbergers.

ELEVEN

"Terribly Opinionated, Terribly Subjective"

As a child in the 1920's John Oakes loved to ride the clanking old elevator to the tenth floor of the Times Building and skip down the long hallway to the southwest corner, into the office of his father. George Oakes, a brother of Adolph Ochs, edited a *Times* subsidiary called *Current History* magazine, founded during the First World War to offer an instant history of the conflict. George Oakes would run his fingers through the wiry mass of curls of his son's hair and then give him a quiet spot in the corner, where young John would read through the myriad exchange papers from around the country. George Oakes (fierce anti-German sentiment caused him to change the spelling of his name during the war) made his early journalistic reputation on his own, as editor of the *Public Ledger* in Philadelphia. When familial ties inexorably tugged him back to 43rd Street, the position of publisher was definitely passing to the Sulzberger end of the family, to Arthur Hays Sulzberger, husband of John Oakes's cousin, Iphigene. This was a decision George Oakes accepted without visible rancor, for his brother controlled the Times Company, and certainly was entitled to choose his own successor as publisher. Nonetheless, in the Ochs/Oakes-Sulzberger melange, the founder's direct descendants always seemed to be shoved aside.

Such was what happened to John Oakes, who more than half a century later had his own office on the tenth floor, a few feet distant from where his father once worked. *The New York Times,* to its paternalistic credit, can be kind to persons forced into premature or unwilling retirement; there are no *gulags*. Oakes works (as a "consultant") in a spacious room with a northern exposure; it is chockful of books and the stacks of paper that seem to slosh around a newspaperman's office regardless of how tidy he tries to be. A memory of George Oakes is also in the room—a massive oaken desk his son took when he began to rise to authority within the newspaper. But in 1986 John Oakes had no authority; he wrote an occasional column, on the environment or Cuba; he sent occasional memos to Punch Sulzberger. Given that he wrote editorials for 27 years, the last fifteen as editor-in-chief, he had thought successor Max Frankel might seek his advice. During a full decade, not once had Frankel called. Frankel was pleasant when they met in the hall; he would nod and smile and sometimes pause to offer a pleasantry. But he wanted no guidance from John Oakes.

John Oakes, in essence, was a non-person at *The New York Times,* due to a deliberate decision by his second cousin, Punch Sulzberger. And why this became so explains much about what Punch Sulzberger did with the newspaper in the mid-1970's.

John Oakes always knew he wanted to work for the *Times*; someone in the family used to jest that *Times* ink was injected into Ochs/Oakes-Sulzberger babies at birth. As did his father, he wished to prove his talent in a non-family setting. After graduation from Princeton (1934, *magna cum laude*) and Oxford as a Rhodes scholar, he went to Trenton, New Jersey, to the *State-Gazette.* That paper folded within a year and he moved across town to the Trenton *Times,* where he covered the legislature. Next the Washington *Post*; on the police beat, and to fire engines and ambulances. But he was good, and soon he was the swing-man at Congress and the Supreme Court, and he covered part of President Roosevelt's 1940 campaign. When war came, as a lieutenant he trained Southern boys in Arkansas. "An absolutely shocking experience. For the first time in my life, I saw grownup Americans who could not read or write; they signed the payroll with an X." Later, as an editor, Oakes wrote frequently about illiteracy. Because he spoke fluent French, he went to the Office of Strategic Services, and spent two years in France and Germany on counterintelligence missions he does not wish to discuss, even at four decades removed. Oakes took a secrecy oath, which is important to him. In 1946 he was ready for the *Times*, and he took a job on the News of the Week in Review, under Sunday editor Lester Markel.

This background is recited at length to point up something significant about John Oakes. By the time he arrived at the paper, he was a man of varied experiences who had done reportorial street work at enough levels to know the news business. Lester Markel learned something else about Oakes. Oakes did not nod approval of whatever a superior said. He and Markel had sufficient problems that Markel eventually took him to lunch at Sardi's to discuss "our situation."

Oakes, characteristically, was direct. "I think, Mr. Markel, what you want around you is 'yes men,' and I'm not a yes man."

Markel sighed deeply and shook his head. "Well, John, the trouble with you is that you are a *'no man.'*"

Soon thereafter publisher Arthur Hays Sulzberger repeated an offer that Oakes join the editorial board, and so in 1949 he became an editorial writer, under Charles Merz.

Editor since the late 1930's, Merz under Arthur Hays Sulzberger transformed the *Times* editorial policy from mainstream Democrat to right-of-center Republican, provincial conservatism that meant opposing Presidents Roosevelt and Truman, and reflecting what one *Times* writer called "pretty much the business community viewpoint." Merz desired to hear no editorial voices other than his own. Even dissenting letters received careful screening. Yet Merz avoided taking strong stands, and often the intrusive phrase, "But on the other hand . . ." punctuated his editorials. Merz did what the publisher wished.

When Orvill Dryfoos became publisher in 1961 his first act was to promote John Oakes to editor of the editorial page, with a mandate to revitalize the page. This Oakes did with enthusiasm. Oakes did not hesitate to state opinions, and strongly. Under Merz the editorial page had been a boneyard for worn out reporters, with the average age above sixty. Oakes found even quieter pastures for these men and recruited his own staff. He persuaded A. H. Raskin, the veteran labor reporter, to become his deputy. He brought onto the editorial staff both the first woman, Ada Louise Huxtable, and the first black, Roger

Wilkins. He lured the talented William V. Shannon away from a comfortable position as Washington columnist for Dorothy Schiff's New York *Post*. Many of the twelve new persons he hired were in their thirties, meaning a needed infusion of new ideas into the paper.

As noted earlier, when Orvil Dryfoos died in 1963, and Punch Sulzberger became publisher, Oakes felt a pang of perhaps justifiable anger. He had far more substantive experience than his aimless second cousin. He had convictions. Punch, conversely, seemed an arrested adolescent with no appreciation for the *Times* tradition. These feelings Oakes suppressed; as one man who worked for him said, "Johnny would rather be drawn and quartered in Times Square than say a disloyal public word about the newspaper." What Oakes did not realize, could *not* realize, was that events of the next decade were to put him on a fatal collision course both with Sulzberger and with Abe Rosenthal. These events were complicated, and interlocked; they involved both personal and professional hard feelings. Rosenthal, however talented, to Oakes was a rude, loud outsider, not the sort of man to be given control of the most crucial part of the family business, the news operation. Professionally, Oakes challenged what he considered the intrusion of editorial comment into Rosenthal's news columns, to him an unpardonable breach of the so-called "church-state" wall that separated the *Times*'s editorial page from the news department. Perhaps most important, Punch Sulzberger in the mid-1970's decided to call an abrupt halt to *Times* crusading, be it in the news pages or in editorials. As shall be seen, Sulzberger arrived at this decision gradually, then abruptly executed it overnight. Rosenthal adjusted, and he survived. Oakes did not, and he was suddenly out of his job.

This complicated interplay of personalities and philosophies had results that shaped the *Times* to the present, both in its news columns and in its editorials—in essence, the very core of the paper.

In reconstructing byzantine events, one is not always confident at pointing to a particular episode and calling it The Beginning. But as accurate a starting position as any came in 1961 or 1962 when Oakes told Dryfoos of a problem he was facing. "I said to him one day, 'I'm kind of bothered about something. Somebody sent me an article I thought was interesting. But it was longer than a letter [to the editor] ought to be, and too short for a Magazine piece. Hence I find there is no place to publish it.' " The New York *Herald Tribune* provided a spot on the editorial page beneath the daily cartoon for non-staff articles. But the *Times* format had no such space. As Oakes explained,

"One of the things I wanted to do was to have a substantial editorial presence, five or so separate editorials a day, with the rest of the page devoted to letters and the regular *Times* columnists. So we had no room for this kind of article."

He suggested to Dryfoos a separate page for articles written by persons other than members of the *Times* staff. These articles would be substantially longer than letters to the editor, and they would not necessarily be tied to a specific editorial or a current news story. Opinion would be permitted, even encouraged. Oakes saw the page as a forum for differing views.

Where in the paper would you put the page? Dryfoos asked. Oakes suggested opposite the editorial page, where the *Times* then ran obituaries. Dryfoos felt this was too drastic a change to impose on his own, so he talked with retired publisher Arthur Hays Sulzberger. A few mornings later, as the men walked to work through Central Park, Dryfoos said, "Look, John, you better forget about this idea because AHS [they spoke of the former publisher by his initials] would never agree to removing the obituary page from its present position. He would have a fit."

After Dryfoos died, Oakes broached the idea to Punch Sulzberger from time to time. Sulzberger appointed a committee to study the idea, and at its meetings Oakes found strong opposition from both the news and the Sunday departments, who argued the page would "encroach on news space." Here naïveté worked against Oakes, by his own admission. He was not attuned to internal *Times* politics. (For instance, he says he was not even aware of the fight over the aborted appointment of James Greenfield to head the Washington bureau until it ended.) As Oakes says, "Only towards the end . . .[did] somebody wise me up to the thought—which I had been too innocent or dumb to realize—that the opposition was not that the op-ed page was a bad idea, but that the news department did not like me controlling it." Rosenthal's stated objection was that the lost space would come from his share of the paper. To succeed, he felt (incorrectly) the op-ed page would feature non-staff writers. Oakes laid proprietary claim to control, since the page was his idea. The talks dragged through late 1969 without resolution, until Oakes decided to break the impasse.

I finally went to Punch one day. I said, "Look, I understand there is a problem about who the op-ed page should belong to. By rights, because this is an opinion page, it ought to be under the control of the editor of the editorial page. Opinions, even if not our opinions, are the issue.

But if control is the issue, I yield right now to the news department. I'd rather have an op-ed page under the news department than no op-ed page at all.

Punch made a sharp decision. He came down on the side of the editorial department controlling it, which I thought was great.

Rosenthal did not. Coming on the heels of his humiliation over the attempted Greenfield assignment, the loss to Oakes cut him deeply. So did what happened next.

Sulzberger now did some politicking of his own. For more than a year he had fretted about what use to make of Harrison Salisbury, who had effectively been sidelined in the news department since his controversial Hanoi trip. He decided to put him in as the op-ed page's first editor. "This was not my first choice," Oakes said, "but it was pretty good." Although Salisbury would have daily control, he would report to Oakes.

There was one final dispute. Oakes wanted the new page to be free of ads, for he considered it an extension of the editorial page. "But Punch was beginning to worry about the economics of the *Times,* and he felt we should have advertisements to help carry the costs." Again Oakes was pragmatic. "I surrendered right away." Punch did agree the ads should be institutional, low-key and in good taste, "No 'Bargain Day' types of ads."

The first page appeared in September, 1970, and the lead editorial that day, by A. H. Raskin, attacked United States Steel's position on a labor matter. Oakes remembered with glee, "Who do you think had the first op-ed page advertisement, in the right-hand corner? A very dignified institutional ad from U. S. Steel. This gave me a huge laugh, although I neither knew it was coming—or cared." The juxtaposition, to Oakes, was a "very good omen."

In fact, that this situation brought mirth to Oakes turned out to be a very *bad* omen, for it foreshadowed an ultimately fatal clash with Sulzberger.

Although Oakes insisted on his editorial page maintaining a strict independence from the news operation, he did not hesitate to com-

ment, critically and often, about what he considered to be lapses in
news judgment. And ironically his chief complaints concerned *Times*
coverage of the Vietnam War.

To the public—and to the Johnson White House—Oakes and his
editorial page were the most authoritative voices in all of America in
opposing the escalation of U. S. military force in Vietman. *Times* editorials gave legitimacy to the anti-war movement, for the *Times* spoke
for the American establishment. Oakes felt his first qualms about the
war when President Kennedy went on television, with a map and a
pointer, and talked about what must be done in Indochina. Oakes
sensed that United States was heading towards a repeat of the disas-
trous French experience in Indochina, and the eventual involvement
of American combat troops. So Oakes wrote against support of the
Diem regime and its successors, and he opposed trying to win
through escalation of military force. Oakes's mail swelled with letters
accusing him of being a handmaiden of Communism, or a Russian
stooge, or worse. The actual story is more complicated.

"One of the major factors in making me more and more opposed
was our own news stories from Vietnam," Oakes said. "I began to
think that this escalation was more and more dangerous, and counter-
productive, fruitless. But I have to tell you that I felt some of those
reports we published were terribly opinionated, terribly subjective.
Some argue that in such circumstances there was no alternative. That
well may be. But this illustrates my rigidity on objectivity. The material being reported was vitally important. But it moved me to opposition, first to escalation [of the war], then the whole thing."

Oakes argued that opposition should be expressed on the editorial
page, not through slanted reporting. "I felt so strongly I protested to
Turner Catledge and to the publisher on one or two occasions in writing. The reporting was one-sided, on *my* side; it was making the
points I was basing my editorials on. I still thought it should have
been done more objectively."

Oakes faulted editors in New York as much as he did field reporters. He cited the famed photograph of a South Vietnamese officer
shooting a captured Vietcong guerrilla during the Tet offensive of
February, 1968. The *Times* that day had available photographs of
gruesome Vietcong atrocities committed during the offensive. These
pictures received less conspicuous play, either below the fold or on
inside pages. Oakes's complaints were not well received in the news
department. "This sort of thing does not make you popular with news

executives. But I squawked. I felt this was really a bad thing to do, for the *Times* to publish this kind of picture when Vietcong atrocity pictures were also available."

By happenstance, Oakes and Rosenthal had the opportunity to attempt to discuss their differences because of a decision by Sulzberger to involve yet another outside consultant in his attempts to understand how the *Times* worked internally. The first attempt, by the Yankelovich research organization, in 1966, succeeded only in infuriating Rosenthal; eventually this group left. In the late 1960's, Sulzberger invited Dr. Chris Argyris, a management specialist from Harvard University, to do in-depth interviews with *Times* executives in an attempt to lessen internal tensions within the paper. Argyris, a patient man, spent three years meeting with *Times* executives, singly and in groups, trying to understand how the paper functioned. Sulzberger concluded the experiment was contributing to the very problems he had hoped to solve, and he halted Argyris's work in midcourse. Argyris published his study in a book, *Behind the Front Page*, in which he disguised the *Times* as *"The Daily Planet"* and used coded letter designations when quoting what various persons said to his tape recorder. (Argyris never said publicly his study concerned the *Times*; that it did was confirmed to me by Rosenthal, Punch Sulzberger, Oakes and others on the paper.)

To anyone with even cursory knowledge of the *Times*, Argyris's "code" proved about as secure as a cryptogram that comes in a child's box of Cracker Jacks.* The interchanges between Rosenthal ("R") and Oakes ("T" and "Q") bristle with mutual hostility. Oakes's chief argument was that Rosenthal permitted too much editorializing in news stories; if he ran the news department, he would be stricter on reporters.

"You believe that I'm steering the news the wrong way," Rosenthal answered. "I'm just as sensitive to this as you may be sensitive to criticism of editorials. . . . You think we're making the paper too much like a magazine, that we're not giving enough attention to what happened yesterday, et cetera."

"Yes, I think you've put your finger on it—since you raised it,"

---

*Oakes was infuriated when Sulzberger permitted Argyris to publish the study, even in veiled fashion. He banged his fist on his desk when he first saw galleys; he felt Sulzberger had permitted a betrayal of the *Times* and its employees. Oakes insisted that he be shielded through not one but two letter designations, used alternately.

Oakes said. "You're damned right I believe that too much attention is being paid to sociological developments and trends. I feel there is too great a degree of subjective interpretation." Oakes bridled at comments he heard from the news department that "our editorials are dreamed up and unfounded." Oakes would be happy to meet with reporters, singly or in a group, to hear criticisms of his page. "I would rather get it directly than behind my back, and I know that some of it goes on behind my back."

Rosenthal acknowledged he did not like criticism, even in such a setting as the Argyris meetings.

> "When I hear criticism about myself or the department, even though it may be low-key, it sounds like it's on a loudspeaker, it sounds profoundly important.
>
> "For example, you jibe at me by calling the newspaper a 'magazine' and I go home and get mean to my wife. We have strong reactions, I mean it. You say one word and I spend a whole weekend brooding about it, trying to get it off my mind. After the weekend is over, I realize that it was childish."
>
> "And I feel the same way when you use the word 'shrill' regarding editorials," Oakes replied.

Rosenthal spoke at length about his worries over his control of his own staff, and the general drift of the entire newspaper. He was "terribly concerned that the paper, in the last few years, had gone toward the left politically." As Rosenthal put it, "This has bothered me more than anything else in my professional life. And I would feel equally strong if it went to the right. The editorial page has gone toward the left, the columnists are liberal to liberal left, and many of the bright reporters have come out of an atmosphere of advocacy. All of us— something has happened. At times during the Chicago business [the 1968 Democratic National convention] I felt that the paper was in trouble. I felt that my job was to pull it back to center. This paper should not be politically discernible." [sic] Rosenthal was under pressure from younger reporters to permit "more subjective analysis" in news reporting, demands he resisted as a "dangerous trend in the news."

Here Rosenthal and Oakes found themselves on common ground. "I feel just as strongly as you do that reporters should not become editorial writers," Oakes said. "Indeed, I would fire some of those bastards." (Oakes told me this statement sounded stronger than intended; that what he meant was that straying reporters should be schooled in objective writing; if this did not succeed, then he would "fire *the* bastard.")

Rosenthal's protestations about advocacy reporting surely reflected his inner concerns; repeatedly he worried that his *Times* would lose its reputation for objectivity. Nonetheless, for several years past the Argyris sessions he permitted *Times* reporters to continue the very things to which he objected.

Yet in another phase of the Argyris sessions, Rosenthal surely sensed a growing skepticism on the part of Punch Sulzberger about Oakes's liberal editorial policies. Oakes's view of his own authority vis-à-vis Punch seemed ambivalent. The publisher's views would ultimately be expressed on the editorial page, and Oakes "had no interest" in challenging Sulzberger's "right to this influence." Nonetheless, Oakes asserted the "obligation" to influence Sulzberger's opinion. Sulzberger should not disregard serious disagreements by the editorial board. If a view violated "the paper's mission," it should not be published. Here Oakes seemed to be arguing against himself, that although the publisher might be autonomous, the editorial board could be "right" on policy questions. Oakes felt the *Times* should side with the "public good" regardless of the impact on the paper's earnings. He went so far as to argue that the *Times* should take "correct" positions even if they harmed the corporate well-being of the New York Times Company.

Had Oakes listened closely, he might have heard the death rattle of his career when he made that statement. Sulzberger responded with a hypothetical question. Suppose New York City proposed a tax on advertising that would hurt the paper financially. Would it be proper for him, as publisher, to write a letter to the editor opposing the tax?

Certainly, Oakes replied. The publisher could even go to City Hall and work against the tax, even if the paper supported it editorially. In any event, the editor of the editorial page should not be an officer of the New York Times Company. (None has ever held an office.) This independence would relieve any conflicts in making editorial decisions affecting the company's financial health.

Sulzberger strongly disagreed with Oakes on the advertising tax issue. "I should do about any goddamn thing to stop it," he said. "That's the difference between you and me."

"But," pleaded Oakes [Argyris's characterization of his voice], "what is more important than any tax or bill is the reputation of the paper. There are no sabbaticals on integrity."

"I understand you, but we have to keep the corporation going, and so we have to perform some very dangerous balancing acts," Sulzberger said. As the New York Times Company continued to grow, Sulzberger said, perhaps the jobs of corporate president and publisher should be divided. (Sulzberger as of 1987 continued to hold both positions.) His disagreements with Oakes, he admitted, were few, "but I think as the paper grows, it will be tougher to let them ride. I don't think it makes much sense to say that I can't put an idea in the editorial page [but must write it] in the form of a letter to the editor."

Oakes talked about his concept of an editorial page. A newspaper with a conscience best served a community by being critical. "We're helping our city by being critical of all the things that are wrong with it. I think that the best way to help the city is to be critical. Of course, this is different from the typical booster view."

"Are you anti-business?" Sulzberger interrupted.

"No, I'm not," Oakes replied.

"The editorial page could give some people the idea we're anti-business," Sulzberger said.

"That's because businessmen didn't like some of the criticisms that we made," Oakes said. "I would say that we're as critical of big labor as we are of big business."

Intervening, Argyris suggested the issue was not what Oakes wrote, but his tone. Oakes could not remember any particular anti-business expressions, although he did "try to get editorials that use some vigorous modes of expression." He explained:

> I grew up with the paper, and for years I thought the editorials were awfully flabby and never said anything. I was determined that if I made the editorial group, I'd begin writing editorials that said something. For years, I felt that our editorials were so damn low-key that no one read them.
>
> The paper for years had a reputation of being a great paper except for its editorial page. I think maybe what I consider to be vigorous and definitive is what you would call angry, and what Rosenthal considers shrill, which is a word I don't appreciate but use because he did so.

Argyris asked Sulzberger, "Do you believe there is shrillness and stridency in the editorials?"

"Yes, sometimes, and that concerns me," Sulzberger said.

Oakes defended himself. "I don't think they're shrill at all."

"I think they are, on occasion, and my associates feel it more than I do," Sulzberger said. He was not happy when he came into a *Times* board meeting with outside directors whose companies had been attacked editorially by the *Times*. "None of these men would even think of trying to influence our position," Sulzberger said, "but they might say, 'You are certainly entitled to print anything you wish, but how on earth did you arrive at such-and-such a position?' "

Roger Wilkins, who watched the on-going struggle from the vantage point of an editorial writer who was intimate with Oakes, felt that much of the problem came because "Punch runs around with a bunch of businessmen who are not much brighter than he is. They're always bitching at him about anti-business bias of editorials." Another editorial writer of the era stated, "What we didn't understand was the extent to which Punch enjoyed the company of other big businessmen." Each autumn Punch went to Detroit to help *Times* executives sell advertising to the Big Three auto companies. Invariably he would hear complaints about Oakes's editorials attacking auto pollution or lack of car safety. "This would make Punch squirm, because he was trying to get General Motors and Ford to take out ads." Punch visited each summer the Bohemian Grove resort near San Francisco, "surrounded by businessmen all raising hell about the *Times* being left-wing," the former editorialist said. "The editorial page embarrassed Punch, and he kept wanting to tone it down."

Reflecting on Oakes in 1986, Sulzberger suggested his cousin did not think through his editorial positions to their ultimate consequence; that his ideas, while attractive theoretically, ignored realities. "I once wrote John a letter pointing out that he had come out against overhead power lines, and against strip mining of coal to supply fuel for power plants, and against the use of nuclear energy for power. What am I supposed to say, I asked John, when Consolidated Edison calls up and says, 'At eleven o'clock tonight we are shutting off your presses, because we've run out of electricity.' " Sulzberger said the letter did not amuse Oakes.

During the last years of Oakes's editorship Sulzberger wearied of defending the *Times* when social and business friends attacked the paper. Although their criticisms had justification, "I reacted like you do when you are an American abroad and some one begins attacking your country. I got defensive."

Nonetheless, "in only a few instances" did he ask Oakes to change an editorial; further, few appeared that he did not see in advance that he would have changed. Sulzberger says, matter of factly, "The ultimate decision on what goes on the editorial page is that of the publisher, for the editorials speak for *The New York Times.*"

Sulzberger's position is that the early 1970's was not a politic time for the *Times* to be needlessly antagonistic to the business community. Several men who worked under Oakes as editorial writers, including Roger Wilkins, insist, "Punch paid more attention to the balance sheet than the newspaper." Indeed he did, and what he was reading in those years was not encouraging. The *Times* was but a short slide away from a financial bloodbath and possible bankruptcy, and Sulzberger's master plan for revival of the paper did not include an anti-business editorial page.

Rogers Wilkins of the editorial staff first sensed that Oakes was in serious trouble in early 1976, when his friend David Schneiderman, an associate editor of the op-ed page, reported a peculiar luncheon conversation with Max Frankel. Frankel, the Sunday editor, aspired to greater things. Frankel knew Schneiderman worked closely with the editorial staff, and could give an underling's appraisal of the talent there. Over lunch Frankel asked a question that Schneiderman decided was more of an assertion: "Isn't it true that the only people on the editorial board who are worth a damn are Silk, Huxtable, Shannon, and Wilkins?* Wilkins, no stranger to power politics, felt Frankel had loosened a trial balloon which he wished to land in the proper tree; that he was using young Schneiderman to announce that if a change was made in editors, certain persons would be protected.

The Frankel-Schneiderman lunch was in the spring. A few months later came the Democratic primary election to choose a candidate for the United States Senate, to oppose incumbent Republican James Buckley. The major contenders were Daniel Patrick Moynihan, the U. S. representative to the United Nations; Representative Bella Abzug; and Ramsey Clark, the former attorney general, Wilkins' former boss and close friend. According to Wilkins, who made clear his own preference, "If you had taken a formal vote of the editorial

---

*Frankel balanced his ticket with the skill of a Chicago political boss. Leonard Silk is Jewish. Ada Louise Huxtable was the first woman editorial writer, Wilkins the first black, William Shannon a Roman Catholic.

board, the breakdown would have been ten for Ramsey, two for Abzug, and one or maybe none for Moynihan." Both Wilkins and Oakes strongly opposed Moynihan. Wilkins and Fred Hechinger, another editorial writer, argued against any endorsement of Moynihan. They wished the strongest possible candidate against Buckley. "We wanted to get Buckley out of there," Wilkins said.

By August, according to Wilkins, "John [Oakes] thought he had an agreement with Punch that the *Times* would not endorse anyone in the primary. He went off to the Cape, and an editorial comes down from the publisher's office endorsing Moynihan." During his five and a half years as an editorial writer, Wilkins remembered no other "from the publisher" editorial. "It was clear that Max Frankel had written the editorial, although no one admitted it."

An angry Oakes, by long distance telephone, asked Punch that the editorial be withdrawn; denied, he asked that he be permitted to publish a dissenting letter the same day, lest the editorial be taken for his own opinion. His letter was a thousand words or so of strong rebuttal; Punch let him publish only the first two sentences. To further aggravate the situation, James Reston in a column suggested that if blacks understood their best interest, they would support Moynihan.

"Who the fuck was Reston to define the 'best interest' of blacks?" Wilkins demanded. He wanted to write a letter of rebuttal. No, Oakes said, "there's an iron rule that staff members can't write letters to the editor."*

But Oakes offered a sly suggestion. Editorial board members rotated the writing of a Tuesday column on the op-ed page. "Why not write me a column rather than a letter?" Oakes said. "I'll run it on primary day. And this is 750 words versus 250 in a letter."

By Wilkins' own description, his column was "pretty stinging." He accused Moynihan of racism for his study of the 1960's blaming the collapse of black families on paternal indifference and suggesting that "benign neglect" could resolve racial problems. Oakes played fair. He knew the subject was sensitive, and he showed the column to Sulzberger the day before it was to be published. "John told me he had never seen the publisher so angry," Wilkins said. "He quoted Punch, 'I agree that Roger Wilkins' column is quite perceptive and I

---

*The *Times* granted Abe Rosenthal an exception for a letter protesting the obituary of former Polish dictator Wladyslaw Gomulka. The man was a tyrant, and should have been called one, Rosenthal wrote.

am willing to let it run—any time after Tuesday,' " In other words, after the primary election. Moynihan won over Abzug by a narrow margin. A decade later Wilkins still felt his column could have changed the outcome.

Oakes took cousin Punch at his word and published Wilkins' column the day after the primary. Intended or not, the belated publication caused much harmful gossip about the *Times*. Wilkins said, "The whole town quickly recognized what Sulzberger had done. Why the hell run it on a Wednesday, when a day earlier it could have made a difference? This made Punch look like a fool *and* a tyrant." Wilkins feels that Sulzberger was angered not at him for the column, but at Oakes for making him a public laughing stock. "As I said about John, he never gives up, he keeps coming at you," Wilkins said.

The circumstantial evidence suggests that the Moynihan editorial episode, reported in the journalism review [*MORE*] and elsewhere, to Sulzberger's embarrassment, forced a decision already in the publisher's mind. Sulzberger and his executives realized drastic changes were needed in the *Times*; otherwise, slipping circulation and advertising could soon kill the paper. The "new" *Times* required a unified news staff, with the split between Sunday and daily ended, in fact as in promise. Sulzberger's survival plan meant the *Times* must make amends with the business community. Corporations paid for the advertisements that supported the *Times*. Sulzberger had heard enough of the gripes that the *Times* was "anti-business." Purging the paper of Oakes would symbolize his new attitude.

Removing Oakes would also help Sulzberger solve a nagging personnel problem. Max Frankel, when brought to New York as Sunday editor, carried in his baggage the notion that he might one day become executive editor. He recognized Abe Rosenthal as a competitor, yet he felt a good performance in the Sunday department would attract Sulzberger's attention. Any such ambition, according to Rosenthal, was Frankel's private dream; if Frankel thought he might become executive editor in the 1970's, no one else at 43rd Street shared the secret. Once Rosenthal acquired the title of managing editor, he ran the newspaper. The several years that no one had the title of executive editor—from 1969 to 1976—were meaningless, in terms of authority. As managing editor, Rosenthal was the *Times*. He did not want the title of executive editor, even for symbolic reasons; as a newspaperman, he thought managing editor best described his job. One reason for accepting the change was to give Seymour Topping a title without "deputy" attached to it. When Rosenthal became executive editor, Topping moved into the managing editor's position.

But in 1976 the demands of producing a different *Times* meant that the Sunday and daily papers must be brought under one editor. Abe Rosenthal logically should be the single editor. So what must be done with Frankel? He must be given a job of substance, otherwise he might bolt the *Times*. Roger Wilkins feels that Sulzberger saw the editor's job as a consolation prize. "He sees this editor cousin who persisted in baiting his business friends, and who was being stubborn and obstinate in other ways. So Punch says to himself, 'OK, we'll get rid of my cousin and give Max that job.' "

Two obstacles remained. First, Punch wanted Frankel to feel he had received "fair consideration" for the executive editorship. So he directed both Frankel and Rosenthal to write memos stating what they felt should be done to revitalize the *Times*. Frankel considered this exercise a challenge match, that if he bested Rosenthal he would have the job. Such was not the case, according to Rosenthal. He could have had the title five years earlier if he wanted it, which he did not. The outcome, pre-ordained by Sulzberger, was the offer to Frankel of the position of editor of the editorial page. (Rosenthal argued briefly that the editorial job go to Seymour Topping; this would have made possible the promotion of his old friend Artie Gelb as managing editor. Sulzberger refused.)

The selection of Frankel put Sulzberger square against the second obstacle. Oakes was 63 years old, and not due to retire until April, 1978. Further, he liked his job, and he gave no signs of wanting to leave it.

Sulzberger, however, is not a man to let personal feelings interfere when he wishes something done. In October he summoned Oakes to his thirteenth-floor office and put it directly: he wanted him out. He could stay on until January 1, 1977, but then Sulzberger intended to make Frankel editor. Oakes realized the futility of arguing with his cousin once his mind was made up, and he remembered the pre-emptory manner in which Lester Markel had been fired in the 1960's. Neither man will discuss what was said, but indications are that harsh words were exchanged.

Oakes broke the news to his twelve-writer editorial board at a luncheon (Sulzberger graciously offering the use of his private dining room for the occasion). Wilkins said, "John acted with great dignity; he never bitched or moaned about the publisher. He told us, 'Everything will be fine.' But everyone knew John had been skewered." Another editorial writer recollected, "It was like announcing a death in the family." Some of the writers began worrying about their own futures. Harry Schwartz, the Soviet expert (Wilkins dismissed him as a "250-pound four-year-old"), went around the office moaning, "What is to become of *us*? What is to become of *us*?" Wilkins and others worried more about what would happen to Oakes. (Punch gave him an office and a job as "consultant"; he retained both a decade later.)

Schwartz's question, however, proved prophetic, for within days rumors circulated about sweeping changes in the editorial board. Sulzberger's purge apparently was not to end with Oakes. Wilkins went to Sydney Gruson, by now an assistant to Sulzberger, and told him, "Some of the guys are worried about what will happen to them." If changes were to come, announce them, and end the uncertainty. Yes, Gruson said, there would be changes. "If you are going to do it," Wilkins counselled, "you must do it clean, and look them in the eye, and have places for them."

Nothing happened. A day or so later Wilkins encountered Sulzberger and Gruson in the elevator. It was balky, and Gruson said, "We've got to get this fixed." Irked, Wilkins said, "You guys are fiddling around with human lives, and you worry about fixing elevators?" He shook his head in unconcealed disgust. Punch suggested they go upstairs to his office and talk. The thrust of the conversation was that any decisions about personnel would be made soon, and be announced publicly. "Well, they didn't do what they said they would," Wilkins said, bitterness uncalmed by the passage of a decade.

As Wilkins feared, word of what would happen leaked before any announcement. He came into the editorial office one morning to find colleagues standing in mournful clusters. Eight of the twelve were being moved out. The only survivors were to be Silk, Shannon, Huxtable and Wilkins. Wilkins thought back to Frankel's peculiar statement months ago to Dave Schneiderman about these very persons being the only ones "worth saving." Frankel told several persons, "I had nothing to do with it [the shifts], my hands are clean." Wilkins wrote him a letter recasting the quotation "Conscience doth make cowards of us all." He continued, "In your case, Max, ambition doth make cowards of us all," He never mailed the letter.

Even the four holdovers did not survive long. Bill Shannon, who had written a brilliant history of the Irish in America, accepted President Jimmy Carter's appointment as ambassador to Ireland in January, 1977. Silk started writing a column for the business-finance page. Huxtable returned to her first love, architecture writing. Wilkins went to the news department to write an urban affairs column. The other editorial writers, men in their forties and fifties, were scattered throughout the paper. Within a very few months Max Frankel decimated the editorial board John Oakes had so carefully assembled.

Deep bitterness remains among those purged and their former associates, directed both at Frankel and Sulzberger. How could judgments be reached about individual editorial writers who worked in anonymity? The general specialties of each writer was known, yet the daily product was collegial, often with extensive consultation between Oakes and the writer. "Unless you worked directly with the person, you didn't know what or how he contributed," one former editorialist said. This man resented the "unfairness" of Frankel arbitrarily ridding the editorial board of two-thirds of the staff Oakes had assembled. He simply did not believe that Oakes could have been wrong on such an array of persons.

Frankel held his first editorial conference in January, 1977. He had tried hard the previous day to write his first-ever editorial for *The New York Times*, and he admitted he found it difficult. The last time he wrote an editorial, he said, was as an undergraduate editor of the Harvard *Crimson*.

One holdover writer sat in a mixture of bemusement and anger. He thought, here is a man who had become editor of the editorial page of *The New York Times*, the most powerful editorial position in newspapering, and he had no experience at his profession. "You can imagine the effect upon the alumni group," he said of the Oakes loyalists.

The final irony of Oakes's displacement came two years later. The hallway on the eleventh floor of the Times Building, leading to the Publisher's Dining Room, is lined with photographs of *Times* men and women who have won the Pulitzer Prize. Only one editorial writer was among them, Edward Kingsbury, who won in the 1920's for the ultimate non-controversial editorial, on the 100 Neediest Cases, the *Times*'s annual Christmas campaign to persuade fortunate citizens to help feed starving children. Just how the Pulitzer board overlooked Oakes year after year baffled persons at the paper. On Vietnam, from the mid-1960's on, Oakes was the most influential anti-war voice in the nation. Other anti-war editorialists took heart from Oakes, for the *Times* stand gave legitimacy to their cause. Oakes also applied his passionate personal interest in the outdoors to editorials on preservation of America's environment. Such a congeries of individuals and groups worked on environmental issues that no one deserves sole credit for the legislation passed during the 1960's and 1970's. But as one of Oakes's former associates asserts, "The environment had been a somewhat kooky issue on the par, say, with the single tax, and John Oakes played a major role in moving it towards the respectable center."

But within two years of joining the editorial board as Max Frankel's deputy, Jack Rosenthal won a Pulitzer for "general editorial excellence," and his picture went up on the eleventh-floor hallway. One former *Times* person familiar with Pulitzer politics suggests a reason. Given its strong national and foreign staffs, the *Times* (along with the few other significant big-city dailies) is always an odds-on favorite to win Pulitzers in those fields. But each daily in the country, regardless of size, can boast an editorial page, and these papers compete for the sole prize within their reasonable reach. According to this man's theory, Abe Rosenthal and Turner Catledge, both of whom served on Pulitzer panels, lobbied other judges, saying in effect, Give us the news Pulitzers and ignore the *Times* editorial page; let the papers in Podunk have that Pulitzer. As this man states, "I always thought this was part of the deal that Max Frankel made for the editorial page—put me back there, but let us have our chance at the Pulitzer."

Frankel, however, gave Punch Sulzberger the sort of editorial page he desired. The attacks on business ceased; Frankel took stands, to be certain, but in far less forceful language than that used by John Oakes. But as one former Oakes associate stated, "Punch can go to '21' or the Bohemian Grove and never be embarrassed."

With the perceived anti-business voice of Oakes now banished from *The New York Times*, Sulzberger could proceed with a major reshaping of the newspaper, to transform it into an advertising medium attractive both to readers and corporate America.

TWELVE

"This Jars Me"

Several years after he retired as publisher of *The New York Times*, Arthur Hays Sulzberger sat next to advertising director Monroe Green on a flight to New York from Detroit, where executives had made their annual presentation to auto advertising buyers. Sulzberger was disturbed. Last Sunday's *Times* had weighed three pounds. Was not that size getting too much for readers to handle comfortably?

Green replied, "When we reach the point where circulation begins to fall off because of too much advertising, or where individual advertisers start pulling out because they feel they are lost in the crowd, then is the time to think about whether we're too big. I can't think of a more pleasant way to find out."

Sulzberger chuckled, and he said no more of the "problem."

Punch Sulzberger, unfortunately, by the mid-1970's had the "problem" put before him in reverse fashion. Although he had tinkered with management and internal procedures his first years as publisher, he had been unable to attack the basic problem confronting the paper: increasing production costs, both for labor and materials. Although revenues rose steadily from the 1960's into the mid-1970's, higher costs tugged down profits.

Two sets of figures illustrate the *Times*'s profit dilemma. In 1969 the company had total revenues of $284.7 million and a net income of $19 million. In 1975, revenues rose to $392 million, yet net income dropped to $12.7 million. In other words, while revenues *rose* $106.3 million, income *dropped* $6.3 million. Competition from television and suburban newspapers chipped at advertising revenues. Distributing papers printed in Manhattan became increasingly costly and difficult.

An even more damning figure was Wall Street's assessment of the New York Times Company as an investment. In 1968, just before President Lyndon B. Johnson's guns-and-butter Vietnam budgets sent the nation reeling into a recession, *Times* stock sold for $53. Then it commenced a steady slide downward, to less than $15 in 1976. Even such editorial coups as the Pentagon Papers did not help the *Times*. Since the Sulzberger family and its appendages owned 70 percent of the company's stock, the drop struck directly at their pocketbooks. Other persons in publishing wondered how long the family would stick by the *Times*. The chain publisher S. I. Newhouse, sensing a possible bargain for the grabbing, approached Sulzberger about buying the paper but was rebuffed. Newhouse told his friend Wes Clark, dean of the journalism school at Syracuse University, "They'd never sell to a kike like me."* Newhouse's implication was that the Sulzbergers might listen to a more respectable buyer.

The market for the *Times* was not encouraging either. After World War Two much of the middle class abandoned New York City, and business and industry joined the exodus to the suburbs. The economic foundation of the city rapidly eroded. The city seemed to have lost control of its own destiny. As one *Times* executive stated, "The combination of strong unions and weak city leadership led to nightmare economics: huge raises for civil servants, a systematic increase in featherbedding, exorbitant overtime payments, large and early pensions—all of this paid out of money that the city hoped would come in tomorrow or the day after tomorrow." The mix of problems exacted a toll from the New York press. At the end of the war eleven daily newspapers were published in the city; by the 1970's the field

*Quoted in *Newspaperman: S. I. Newhouse and the Business of News*, by Richard H. Meeker. Tio Knor & Fielbs, 1983, p. 239.

had shaken down to three—the *Times*, the *Daily News* and the New York *Post*, all ailing. No longer did anyone worry about the *Sunday Times* being so heavy.

Sulzberger recognized from the outset that restoring financial strength meant breaking the stronghold that the production unions held on the paper. Because the Times Company relied on the paper for the bulk of its revenues, the unions used strikes (or the threat of them) to prevent any serious negotiating on cost-cutting automation. The 1970 contract with the International Typographical Union cost the *Times* a staggering 42 percent increase over three years. (Oakes's editorials, ironically, were criticizing other industries for agreeing to even smaller raises.) According to Sulzberger's estimate the *Times* was forced to employ about 50 percent more production workers, on a comparable basis, than competitive newspapers. To challenge the unions, to take a strike if necessary, the *Times* needed to broaden its revenue base.

Sulzberger's first significant move towards diversification came in 1970 when he purchased fourteen properties from Cowles Communications for $52 million in *Times* stock and the assumption of $15 million of debt. The key parts of the package were *Family Circle* Magazine, five Florida newspapers in thriving cities, and a Memphis TV station. Sulzberger felt good about the Cowles deal from the start. The night before its consummation he dined with his family at the Sun Luck Imperial, his favorite Chinese restaurant. His fortune cookie read, "Prosperity in the family circle." Punch thought of the name of the magazine he was buying, and smiled; he felt a blessing had been passed on his deal. The framed fortune slip remains in his office.

In the following years the *Times* accumulated other odd properties—*Golf World, Golf Digest, Tennis* and *Hockey*; a batch of medical and dental publications, more daily and weekly newspapers, chiefly in Sun Belt cities, and three book companies. Slowly these diversified revenues added strength to the Times Company.

Sulzberger added strength elsewhere as well, to *Times* management, in the person of Walter Mattson. A stout, seldom-smiling man who reputedly has only hearsay knowledge of vacations and relaxation, Mattson learned about newspapering commencing at age nineteen as a printer in his native Boston. He came to the *Times* production department as a manager and in his early thirties was selected to head the paper's unsuccessful West Coast edition. Sulzberger recognized that Mattson had an insider's grasp of the intricacies of producing a newspaper. Both men are mechanical buffs, a common interest that deepened into friendship. By 1974 Mattson was general manager of the paper, and he told Sulzberger, in so many words, that the *Times* had either to change its product or face the serious prospect of going out of business. Mattson did not profess any special knowledge of the *news* business; he did claim to know something about the *newspaper* business. And the newspaper the *Times* published had lost its appeal to advertisers and readers alike, as witness stagnant or declining figures in both categories.

Here Mattson received strong support from another new talent in *Times* management. John Pomfret had covered labor at the Milwaukee *Journal* during Punch Sulzberger's brief stay there in the early 1950's. The men struck up a friendship that continued after Punch returned to New York. Through coincidence, the *Times* Washington bureau hired Pomfret in the early 1960's, first to cover labor, then the Johnson White House. "A very good reporter, a hard worker," Tom Wicker, then the bureau chief, said of Pomfret.

Pomfret became concerned in 1966 when an American Newspaper Guild strike put bureau members on the picket line. He thought both sides could handle the negotiations better. As Wicker stated, "Pomfret, who was both a labor authority and a Guild member, finally said, 'To hell with this.' "

Pomfret telephoned Punch Sulzberger. "You really fucked this up," he said.

"You're such a smart ass, come on up here and straighten it out," Sulzberger replied. As Sulzberger says now, "Well, John did." At Sulzberger's invitation Pomfret left news for management. "He is a tough, smart guy and he wended his way upward," Wicker said. Pomfret allied himself with Mattson early, his value being a knowledge of the news side of the *Times*. With Pomfret as a coach, Mattson could talk knowledgably when he began to press Abe Rosenthal and other news executives for what he considered to be necessary changes in the paper.*

---

*Pomfret's decision to leave the news department for management made much financial sense. In 1987 he earned $335,000 in salary, $190,950 under an executive incentive program, and another $146,300 under a long-term performance program for executives, for a total of $672,250. This is somewhat more than is earned by Washington bureau reporters.

A.M. Rosenthal. (AP/Wide World Photos)

Turner Catledge.
(AP/Wide World Photos)

Arthur Ochs ("Punch") Sulzberger.
(AP/Wide World Photos)

Clifton Daniel.
(AP/Wide World Photos)

James ("Scotty") Reston. (AP/Wide World Photos)

Sidney Gruson.
(AP/Wide World Photos)

Harrison Salisbury talking with a Chinese journalist at a writers'
conference in Peking. (AP/Wide World Photos)

Iedrick Smith. (AP/Wide World Photos)

Sydney H. Schanberg.
(AP/Wide World Photos)

om Wicker. (Gene Maggio, New York Times Studio)

Max Frankel. (AP/Wide World Photos)

Seven *Times* employees who charged the newspaper with discrimination against women: front row, left to right, Nancy Davis, classified; Andrea Skinner, then children's fashion editor; Grace Glueck, then art editor; back row, from left, Betsy Wade, then of national desk; Eileen Shanahan, formerly of Washington bureau; Louise Carini, accounting; Joan Cook, metropolitan desk. (Photo courtesy Joan Cook)

Molly Ivins.
(Courtesy Molly Ivins)

Katharine Balfour.
(Courtesy Katharine Balfour)

A.M. Rosenthal
and Shirley Lord,
on their wedding day.
(Ron Galella)

John Oakes. (AP/Wide World Photos)

Arthur Gelb. (AP/Wide World Photos)

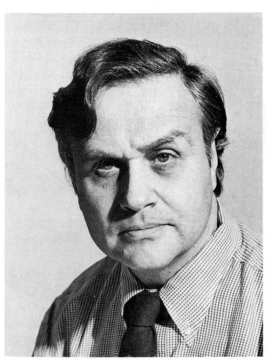

Richard Severo. (Courtesy Richard Severo)

Walter E. Mattson. (AP/Wide Wocrld P

The core decision pushed by Mattson and Pomfret was to convert the *Times* into a four-section paper five days of the week (Monday through Friday) and offer specialized coverage targeted for particular readers and advertisers. The *Times* had experimented with special sections in the past, particularly a section designed for Brooklyn/Long Island/Queens. As Rosenthal told *Business Week* in 1976, "It was a disaster—cheap and shoddy. The business people carried the day on that one, and I think they lived to regret it." So in planning the new sections there was considerable interplay between the news department, the production people, and an enhanced advertising and research crew.

Indeed, so many persons were involved in working out concepts for the new sections that exact parentage of each is lost in a welter of irreconcilable claims. Sulzberger himself admits that who did what on each section has become more and more "cloudy" as the years pass. By his own estimate, "this was a 50-50 judgment, news and business." He gives Mattson equal billing with Abe Rosenthal, and he prefers to stress "the perfect blending of talents."

Mattson, however, stands as the executive who made possible the physical production of the expanded paper. Prior to 1976, the *Times* was a two-section paper on weekdays, with the printing done on West 43rd Street and at a small satellite plant on the upper West Side. At Mattson's urging, Sulzberger invested a very dear $35 million in another satellite printing plant in Carlstadt, New Jersey, just across the Hudson River from Manhattan. Sulzberger had to scrape deep to find that money; Mattson, however, convinced him the *Times* needed more capacity (and better technology) than it had at the Manhattan plants. Carlstadt meant the *Times* now had the press capacity to publish four sections daily, up to twenty-eight pages each, as well as a vastly larger Sunday edition plus special magazine and other sections. Now the news department's challenge was to produce sections to meet the capacity.

What the *Times* wished was to publish sections that would attract new and affluent readers who, in turn, would attract advertising from businesses who wished to sell to them. Clay Felker's *New York* Magazine had demonstrated that a market existed for publications stressing service features—the best-buy reviews and advice on how to make life easier in the city. The *Times*'s first new section, Weekend, to be published on Friday, was to a degree a newspaper version of *New*

York Magazine, but with some significant differences. Given the *Times's* traditional emphasis on culture, arts and leisure—the Sunday Arts & Leisure Section is hefty enough to give a bass drummer a hernia—Weekend had to take a different approach without becoming trivial. Another decision was control. As is true of any large bureaucracy, the *Times* abounds with empire builders, and both the business and advertising departments made early runs at dictating how Weekend should be shaped. They cited the commercial reasons for the section's existence.

Here Rosenthal drew the line. He accepted only grudgingly the arguments for the new sections, for he feared they would detract from the dignity and integrity of the *Times*. Leave that sort of crap to *New York* Magazine, he said; if Clay Felker wants to sell lists of ice cream parlors, more goddamned power to him. But Rosenthal soon realized he had lost this argument; the sections were to exist, and so the issue was control.

Rosenthal made his case to Punch Sulzberger with a fusillade of profanity. "The *Times* is a newspaper, not a goddamned advertising throwaway. Give these sections to a bunch of goddamned advertising people, they'll fuck it up, and the rest of the paper in the process. *Times* readers expect quality; give it to them, and they'll buy." Implicit in this strong language was that Abe Rosenthal did not intend to work for a newspaper vast portions of which were beyond his editorial control. By several accounts Rosenthal did not exactly *threaten* to quit, but he certainly left such an insinuation floating in the air for Sulzberger to study.

Sulzberger really had no choice. Rosenthal unarguably was the most brilliant editor around, and the new sections had to be done right. "You've got them," he finally said, "now give us something that we can sell—and that we can be proud of as well."

So the team of Abe-and-Artie commenced yet another reformation of *The New York Times*, one even more important than their transformation of the metropolitan desk in the early 1960's. And once again Artie Gelb did the scut work of creation, converting broad concepts into specific stories and layouts. To Gelb the long yellow legal pads he clutched under his arm are the tools of office. Whatever Gelb's flaws might be, stupidity is not among them. Gelb is the consummate newspaper technician—the man who can make the pages run on time, if you will—and Rosenthal more or less gave him his head during months of planning. As his shirtsleeve allies Gelb had James Greenfield, who now carried the rank of assistant managing editor, and Louis Silverstein, a gifted designer who for several years had been subtly modernizing the gray face of *The New York Times*. Silverstein's role was very important, because Gelb wanted the new sections to *look* like something different from the everyday newspaper. This meant a certain freedom of design gimmickry — outsized photographs and drawings surrounded by moats of white space; a melange of type sizes on headlines and varying column widths; odd little boxed items scattered over pages for variety. Gelb gave Silverstein freedom to work out the new designs, but at the same time he reserved veto power. He would be the arbiter: if he felt a concept was "right," it would be used; otherwise, Thanks, Lou, but let's try it again. And Gelb in turn deferred to Rosenthal as the final authority.

By Gelb's account these were trying times in the truest sense of the word. Several times he, Greenfield and Silverstein had dummies made of the Weekend section which they felt were satisfactory; several times Rosenthal rejected them with the vague objection, "You're not quite there; give it another try. I don't know exactly what is wrong, I just don't like it." So Gelb would sigh and retreat to his office with his yellow pads, and try once more. Rosenthal described his role: "I became what we Jews call 'the ladle in the kettle.' I tasted, I stirred, passing from one desk to another, almost always listening to what they were telling me, reflecting, giving suggestions. In my opinion, a good editor is one who succeeds in communicating."

The basic problem was to produce what was essentially an Arts & Leisure section without duplicating what the *Times* was already publishing on Sunday under that very name. The solution Gelb ultimately hit upon was to do the Friday section in the form of a guide to the arts of the city and its suburbs to tell readers what plays and exhibits were scheduled, and the when-and-how to find them. This the *Times* would do with its customary thoroughness, listing events in the affluent suburbs as well as in the city itself. The accompanying feature stories would be considerably lighter in tone than the reviews and profiles featured in the Sunday paper. The movie column, for instance, would choose an interview with a kooky starlet or director over a ponderous examination of the oddity currently in vogue in the French cinema. The thrust of Weekend was to be a service calendar and guide to help readers enjoy the city.

Gelb finally met Rosenthal's expectations, and the first Weekend appeared in April 1976. To Gelb's surprise, persons in the newsroom received the section with absolutely no reaction whatsoever other than a few muted mutters of "Good section, Artie." Obviously his colleagues intended to wait for public reaction before offering any praise of what many still considered to be an ill-fated experiment. Curiosity got the best of Gelb at midweek, and he began calling some friends he knew as avid *Times* readers, persons such as Mike Wallace and Garson Kanin, and asked what they thought. They loved it. Gelb breathed a bit easier. Yet the business department withheld judgment. "We couldn't get the right vibes right away," Gelb said. But the market spoke. Friday sales jumped immediately by some 60,000 copies, and settled down for a permanent gain of 35,000 new readers—and young ones, according to *Times* marketing surveys.

"Imagine what that means to a newspaper," Gelb said. "Thirty-five thousand new readers who had the same demographics as your old readers, but who for some reason were not reading *The New York Times*. They had the same income, the same lifestyle, as other readers, and Weekend was bringing them in." The *Times* and the yuppie generation had discovered one another.

Gelb produced the next few issues of Weekend, then Rosenthal told him, "OK, that takes care of Friday. Now let's get on with another day."

This day happened to be Wednesday, and this time the advertising department dictated the emphasis, if not the presentation. The theme would be food. That the *Times* had never actively pursued food advertising was one of the many anomalies about his own newspaper that Sulzberger never understood. "We'd never had food advertisements. Presumably, *Times* readers did not eat." One man who was an advertising executive early in Sulzberger's tenure as publisher offered a reason. "Food advertisements don't look nice, what with all that black type," he told the publisher. "That's the sort of thing you see in the *World-Telegram*." As Sulzberger said, "That sort of attitude did not make it easy to go for grocery advertisements."

Food sections of most American newspapers are clipsheets of recipes produced with less thought than is devoted to the basketball scores, boilerplate material to fill the chinks around supermarket advertising. Here again Rosenthal demanded something beyond the routine. Gelb suggested, "Let's put Wednesday's culture news in the back of the section." Once readers realized the book reviews and TV commentary were in the nether reaches of Living (as the section was called) they might pause to read articles encountered along the way—provided the articles were any good.

Gelb made a special effort on Living, for Weekend by comparison was a snap. He went to the Hamptons and persuaded the food writer Craig Claiborne to come out of retirement and write again for the *Times*. He pitched Claiborne's friend Pierre Frenay, formerly chief chef at Pavillon.

"Pierre," Gelb said, "my wife has a wonderful idea. As a working woman she can spend only thirty minutes preparing dinner. It would be wonderful if you'd write a thirty-minute gourmet feature."

Frenay thought a moment, and he said, "I can't do it in thirty minutes, but I can in sixty, and very well." The "Sixty Minute Gourmet" column became a popular (and often-clipped) feature of Living.

The first Living section featured an article by Claiborne, "Cooking Along With the World's Greatest Chef." The bottom of the page had paired articles (Gelb commissioned them) by Mike Wallace and William F. Buckley, Jr., under the headline:

Of Wives and Their Skills,
Of Men and Their Dreams

Two celebrity bylines in the premiere issue brought out Gelb's critics in full voice. Was the *Times* degenerating into a supermarket tabloid? Was Artie Gelb using the food section, of all places, to publicize his friends? As other name writers appeared, the criticisms continued. To Gelb, this was journalistic aversion to new ideas. Newspaper people talk much about change but don't particularly like it.

Gelb thought about the credibility problem. "Damn it," he decided, "I'm going to make my point." If he could persuade the novelist John Cheever to write for Living, "this would shut up the troublemakers." So he swallowed some nervousness and telephoned Cheever and said, "I would regard it as a special favor if you would write a piece for our Living section."

Cheever thought a while on the telephone. Yes, he had noticed the section; as a longtime *Times* reader, he thought it "interesting."

"How about something on Thanksgiving dinner, and what it means to you?" Gelb said. He stressed that a Cheever article would "help the section"

Cheever asked for "some thinking time," and he called Gelb that evening and said he would do the article. "I pinched myself," Gelb said. "Imagine, John Cheever writing for Living!" As Gelb states, "Anyone of intelligence who had any doubts about the Living section had to change his mind.*

Gelb dealt with dissension on the *Times* staff as well. Jane Brody did not want to write a personal health column. "I'm a science writer," she told Gelb. For many days Gelb argued the popularity of such a column, and finally he had to tell her, point-blank, that she *would* write it, for "it's important to the paper." The column "Personal Health" and the book spinoffs brought Brody both international repute and a good sum of money. (And she and Gelb remained friends.)

Two other sections followed with little controversy. Home, on Thursday, was a sop to furniture retailers. Sports Monday was the *Times*'s way of handling the gush of scores from the weekend. Rosenthal gave Sports Monday cursory attention because he cared not a whit about sports, and he did not understand why other people did. In the 1980's, Yankees owner George Steinbrenner had Rosenthal as a guest for several games. Rosenthal neither understood nor enjoyed what happened on the field. When he hired Michael Janofsky as a football writer, Rosenthal told him, "We don't care about sports here." Gelb had the same attitude. "I learned everything I need to know about sports in two weeks," he told a *Times* sportswriter. A writer who worked in sports for more than five years remembered Rosenthal coming to the fourth floor (which houses that department) only twice.

The most serious confrontation between Rosenthal and the advertising department came over the Tuesday section. The ad people insisted upon a section to be called Fashion Tuesday, arguing that it would attract high-dollar advertising from designers and clothing manufacturers. Rosenthal thought differently. Science fascinated him, and he loved stories that could explain its mysteries in direct lay language, in articles of 1,500 words or less. He had several persons in the news department with science backgrounds write memoranda outlining how such a section could be developed. (One of the memo writers, Bill Kovach, who studied science in college, was so caught up

*Cheever did not respond to a written query as to why he wrote the article. Yes, Gelb said, Cheever was also mindful that he controlled *The Times Book Review* as well as Living.

in the concept he begged Rosenthal to let him edit the new section. Rosenthal declined; Kovach went on to become chief of the Washington bureau.)

Rosenthal quietly put together some dummy sections of what he wished to call Science Tuesday, and he laid the package before Sulzberger, Mattson and Pomfret. Rosenthal cited the *Times*'s long tradition of attention to science, from the Byrd expeditions to the South Pole to the opening of King Tut's tomb and the exclusive coverage of the development of the atomic bomb. Rosenthal prevailed. "Go ahead, Abe, turn your longhairs loose," Sulzberger said. Sulzberger now says he had serious doubts as to whether Science Times would generate enough ad revenues to support itself. But because of what Sulzberger called "a wonderful coincidence," the home computer came along at the right time, and with this advertising the section flourished from the start.

Thus did *The New York Times* present a totally different face to its readers five mornings weekly—splashy typography, line drawings, a plethora of photographs, much white space to give the appearance of openness. A bit of the new design even slopped over onto the front page, which changed from the traditional eight-column format to six columns. Such a sweeping change in the appearance of a publication, be it magazine or newspaper, is risky business. Editor Clay Blair, Jr., for instance, did an overnight redesign of the old *Saturday Evening Post* in 1963 that flopped so badly the magazine turned belly up within three years. Wary of offending readers, Rosenthal made the *Times*'s changeover proceed at a deliberate pace.

James Greenfield, who worked closely with Gelb and Louis Silverstein in designing the sections, felt at times as if they were striving for an undefined goal. They would show a mockup to Rosenthal, who would reply, "This jars me, this doesn't fit what we are trying to do."

Just what *are* we trying to do?" Greenfield once asked.

"Beats me," Rosenthal said, "but keep working. When we have it, we'll know."

Nonetheless, the "new" *New York Times* startled many readers to the point of anger. As one New York educator said, "It's as if someone came into your living room and started moving the furniture around without asking permission or telling you why. Those of us who've read the *Times* all our lives feel rather proprietary about the paper. Reading the new paper the first months was akin to seeing the Queen come out of Buckingham Palace in a dayglo-orange miniskirt."

The "new" *Times* was edited for an upbeat, affluent audience with a strong emphasis on self-indulgence and high-ticket consumer goods. The *Times* brimmed with features on the best places to buy Scandinavian furniture and *pâté* and imported coffee and Givenchy scarves or whatever. Asked by Stephanie Harrington of *New York* Magazine whether the remaking had been influenced by Clay Felker, Rosenthal replied, "You bet your sweet life!" He called Felker, *New York*'s founding editor, "the best originator of service material I've ever seen. He used to drive me out of my mind."

But as many readers asked themselves, Did the city really need another *New York* Magazine, in the form of major sections of its leading daily newspaper? Advertisers apparently thought so, for they crammed the new sections with offerings of such things as wicker furniture (a chair and an ottoman for $3,000; $5,850 with the cushions); dyed, etched and acrylic-encased easter eggs at $49.95; and Bloomingdale party dresses for $6,995 (sequins included).

The sections in themselves are harmless, and indeed frequently entertaining and informative—although non-New Yorkers learn to skim past the how-to-redo-your-loft perennial in the Living Section. No one forces a reader to go through these sections; they are there for the advertisers and for the customer curious about yet another way to cook asparagus or what's playing at the dinner theater outside New Haven. That Rosenthal won the Science Times argument was fortunate, for that section clearly is the strongest and most intelligent of the five. The front part of the section for July 22, 1986, contained a not untypical mix: William J. Broad writing from Moscow about advances in the Soviet space program. Sandra Blakeslee on a new surgical technique for reducing the muscle spasticity of young people with cerebral palsy. Archaeological studies on how and when the first humans entered North and South America. Daniel Goleman on psychological studies on the rationality of love. Lindsey Gruson on the unrecognized high incidence of illiteracy. Each Tuesday the *Times* offers readers the equivalent of a science magazine.

Further, the new sections gave the *Times* the desired financial rejuvenation. Advertising revenues in 1975, the year before they commenced, had been $195 million. By 1977, revenues were up to $254 million, and net income increased the same years from $12.7 million to $25.8 million. In 1987 revenues for the newspaper group were $1,364,293.000, with an operating profit of $271,595,000. Clearly Sulzberger and Mattson made a business decision that stopped the paper's headlong slide into ruin.

Gelb feels that critics who accused the "new" *Times* of "lowering the tone of the *Times*," overlooked some fundamental facts. The thousands of new readers attracted by Weekend and Living did not spend all their time in those pages; they also read the Washington report, and the foreign coverage, and most everything else in the paper. Hence the previous audience expanded dramatically, and in the form of high-earning, highly-educated persons who had always been the core of the *Times* readership. Further, he adds, *The New York Times* is still in business.

Several years after the change of the "new" *New York Times*, Rosenthal sat at a dinner party one evening and listened to a man— someone from outside communications—lament at length the death of the New York *Herald Tribune*. "Best-written paper that was ever published in New York City or anywhere else," the man said. "It's too bad that other papers don't pay any attention to what it did, and how. All of us really liked the *Trib*." If the man was aware of Rosenthal's acute sensitivity towards even an implied criticism of the *Times*, he did not show it.

Rosenthal was content to listen in silence, then he rummaged in his pocket and produced a quarter and handed it to the man. "Here," he said, "go buy me one. I'd like to read one right now." Puzzled, the man asked, "Read what? What are you talking about?"

"That *Herald Tribune*, you've been talking about it being so good all evening. Go buy me one, I'd like to see what they have on the front page tonight," Rosenthal said.

The man protested, "But the *Trib* has been out of business for years. Surely you know that!"

Rosenthal grinned, a not very pleasant grin. "Sure I know that. Sure the *Trib* was a great newspaper. But you sure the fuck ain't agonna buy it at the kiosk at West 43rd and Broadway tonight."

THIRTEEN

"No Effort to Sell to the Mob"

In a ghostwritten foreword for Abe Rosenthal's book *Thirty-Eight Witnesses*, on the Genevese case, Punch Sulzberger had glowing words about *The New York Times*'s commitment to New York City. "It is often forgotten—*I think sometimes by ourselves*— that we are above all a community newspaper," Sulzberger stated. "Our readers are people who live in the city or its suburbs and although they are interested in foreign and national affairs they are quite as interested, perhaps more, in what takes place in the City Council as in the Security Council. Sometimes we suffer from Afghanistanitis—the theory that what happens in exotic places is somehow more appropriate than what happens in Queens."

Those words appeared in 1964. A dozen years later, the "new" *New York Times* proceeded to make a mockery of Sulzberger's credo. The *Times* had written enough gloom-and-doom stories about the city. Selling the new sections to advertisers required optimism about New York. Forget about the near-bankruptcy of the mid-1970's. Portray

New York as a vibrant, prosperous city; the warts, if ignored by the *Times*, do not exist.

So at Abe Rosenthal's direction the *Times* commenced a major retrenchment on local coverage. Bureaus in the four boroughs outside Manhattan were closed. A joke arose in the newsroom—unfortunately, it was true—that a *New York* newspaper now had more correspondents in Africa than it did in Queens, which represented one-third of the city's population.

The official explanation by Rosenthal, a lame one, was that No, we're *not* abandoning coverage of those boroughs, we're just doing it differently.

Instead of working in the boroughs, reporters would look for "trend" stories affecting the entire city. The old beat reporter, who gave the *Times* a physical presence in an area, was not necessary. Rosenthal's theory, a goofy one, was that reporters working from the City Hall press room in lower Manhattan, or from the third floor of the Times Building on West 43rd Street, could somehow get better information than someone who had an office in Staten Island or the Bronx. Rosenthal's new system did produce a steady flow of "soft" articles about the city. But features comparing, say, bicycle couriers in Queens with those in Manhattan do not substitute for a reporter watching a borough government on a daily basis.

The unadmitted reason, of course, was that residents of the four non-Manhattan boroughs did not fit the demographics of the "new" *Times*. The target audience now were persons with incomes in the upper five-figures and beyond, and these people did not live in the South Bronx. So the *Times* withdrew. The only honest explanation was offered, apparently unwittingly, by a *Times* senior vice president, Donald Nizen, in a 1981 interview with *Editor & Publisher*, the newspaper trade publication.

"We make no effort to sell to the mob," Nizen said.

What local coverage continued was of sharply changed tone. The "new" *New York Times* emphasized the upbeat side of the city. Welfare mothers, rotten housing, messy city finances, dirty subways, garbage on the street—under Rosenthal's direction the *Times* now looked for the positive features of troubled New York City. Constantly telling readers they live in a deteriorating city does nothing for civic morale. Circumstantial evidence suggests the *Times* felt its own financial future at stake as well—that the paper demanded an affluent market, and that constant carping about urban horrors would not encourage upper-income families to stay in the city. Perhaps. But by giving only fleeting attention to very real problems facing the have-nots of the city, the *Times* did not encourage their correction.

A striking example is the ramshackle Carter Hotel across the street from the Times Building, two hundred feet from the door through which Sulzberger and Rosenthal go to work each morning. Ragged, hungry-eyed children always seemed to be playing outside the Carter, or on cold days in the lobby. They were an incongruous presence on Times Square. In early 1986 the CBS program "60 Minutes" revealed the Carter was a "welfare hotel" where the city and federal governments paid upwards of $3,000 a month to house each poor family in single-room squalor. Newsman Mike Wallace skewered Mayor Ed Koch for criticizing inadequate housing programs while a member of Congress, and of doing nothing as mayor to correct conditions at the Carter and other dumps. The *Times* got around to the story a few weeks later—but did not point out the differing statements made by Koch when he held different offices.

Abe Rosenthal once wrote:

> There is a great deal of turning away in _____, even more of simply not seeing. There is an explanation: if _____ reacted to all the misery they see about them and which so many of them are a part, they would find their day-to-day lives shaken emotionally to an almost unbearable point. It is easier to shrug and turn away, and _____ do both. Among _____ upper class there is depressingly little realization of the responsibilities that go with wealth and position. . . .

Rosenthal wrote those words in *Foreign Affairs* in July, 1957, reviewing a book entitled *Mother India: Thirty Years Later*. The blanks referred to India and Indians; commencing in 1976, New York and New Yorkers could be substituted, by the standards of *Times* journalism.

Many persons on the staff recognized with dismay the direction in which the *Times* was turning, and these reporters collected their own files of horror stories—of incidents and happenings the *Times* deliberately chose not to report. Some of these persons remain at the *Times*, unhappy but unwilling to abandon the comfortable life that comes with the newspaper's salary, and the retirement security offered by the *Times*'s employee stock purchase program. Others—many others—decided professional honor would not permit them to continue what they considered to be essentially dishonest work; they quit, often with no better employment opportunity in sight or in hand.

One defectee was John Hess, who worked at the *Times* for almost twenty years. Hess had been a rewriteman when Rosenthal returned to New York as metropolitan editor, and he welcomed the fresh approach to city coverage. In the 1970's Hess worked from the Paris bureau. He is an independent-minded man who prefers his own drummer, and he was not pleased when he learned that Flora Lewis, Sydney Gruson's ex-wife, was arriving as bureau chief. James Greenfield, then the foreign editor, stated, "John called. He had met Flora several times over the years and did not like her. Hess told me he didn't want to report to her, that he wanted to report to New York. I told him, 'If you want to report to New York, do so—come back and work right here.' " So an unhappy foreign correspondent found himself doing city reporter's work again. (Greenfield says Hess's unhappiness stemmed from this reassignment; Hess says such is not true.)

In any event, Hess found things much changed on city coverage. He attended a City Council finance committee hearing, and a member exclaimed, "You are the first *Times* man we have seen in years." At a staff meeting Hess questioned how the *Times* could claim to be covering the city when it had, say, no reporters in the Bronx. Seymour Topping, presiding, turned to Mitchell Levitas, then the metropolitan editor, who shrugged and offered no comment. "Well, we have more readers in Suffolk County," Topping said. Well, Hess retorted, the *Times* had correspondents in Dallas and Dublin, but they're not for the readers who live there—they are there to report. Topping did not continue the argument.

From his City Hall beat Hess found smells of corruption in city government. He came upon one story which he felt indicated criminal liability in the financing of one of Mayor John Lindsay's campaigns. He worked days on the story; he turned it in; it never got into print. An editor told him, "We couldn't find space for it." He could not interest editors in a study of why Consolidated Edison had rates considerably higher than other major cities, or how city tax policy actually encouraged industries to leave New York. "These are the sort of questions the *Times* should have asked. But under Rosenthal, most of the best investigative work was done out of town. Those are the pieces that won the prizes," Hess said.

By the argument of Hess (and many other persons, including the writer Martin Mayer, in a long *Columbia Journalism Review* article) the *Times* misreported the single most important city story of the 1970's—the threatened bankruptcy of New York's government. "The *Times* dismissed the bankruptcy story as an argument over arithmetic between Mayor [Abe] Beame and the city controller, [Harrison] Goldin. The *Times* reported what the politicians said about one another, rather than explaining why the richest city in the world should be broke." Hess stated he had the core of the story early: that the city "quite likely was guilty of fraud, in selling bonds to the public on the basis of phony records of anticipated revenues." Hess documented, to his satisfaction, that city revenues would not be sufficient to redeem the bonds. The *Times* would not print his story. Some weeks later Marion J. Epley, a young partner in the Wall Street superfirm of White & Case, came upon the scam while reviewing the city's documentation for a client who was involved in the bond issue. His disclosures—which John Hess had weeks earlier—almost toppled New York City into bankruptcy. There were other unprinted Hess stories as well, of corruption in contracts ranging from trash hauling to nursing homes. "These accounted for millions of dollars of city funds," Hess said. "The *Times* didn't want to know what was going on; it stuck its head in the sand while the city went to pieces."

To Hess, the most egregious smear on the *Times*'s journalistic integrity came on the day when City Hall made simultaneous announcements. It was cutting back on funds for day care centers for children of working mothers, most of them poor. It was also giving a multi-million dollar grant for the renovation of Yankee Stadium. The Yankee story ran; the day care story did not. (Rosenthal is a chum of George Steinbrenner, the Yankees' owner. Introducing Steinbrenner at a meeting of the American Society of Newspaper Editors in New York in 1979, he praised him as a man who "gave the city not only a winning baseball team, but he also gave it a shot in the arm, a lot of zest.")

Hess preferred journalism to a "lot of zest," and he became so unhappy that he eventually quit. Hess wrote a harshly critical article about the *Times* for the magazine *Grand Street* in early 1985, and his former superiors at the paper dismissed him as an embittered old crank who, variously, "couldn't make the grade," or was "so obstinate you couldn't work with him." Hess indeed makes no secret of his hard feelings about Rosenthal and what he did with the *Times*. Nonetheless, the *Times* felt well enough of the man's work to give him responsible jobs, both in New York and abroad, for two decades, a tacit endorsement of his talent.

Hess is unique in several respects. He realized, earlier than most persons, the new reportorial direction of the *Times*; further, he is one of the few people now away from the paper willing to speak candidly of the changes. One man who did *not* realize what was expected of him was Sydney Schanberg, who until the late 1970's seemed on a career track that well could have put him in the executive editorship. Schanberg came from hard times. He was born in 1934 in Clinton, Massachusetts, to blue-collar parents. A scholarship enabled him to attend Harvard. He did a medley of hard-work, low-pay jobs to pay bills: waiter, bartender, hod carrier, canning machine operator, sorter of dirty laundry. After the army he became a copy boy at the *Times*, in 1969, and a reporter a year later. When Rosenthal returned as metropolitan editor he recognized Schanberg as one of the talented men with whom he could reshape *Times* coverage. Schanberg received good assignments. He ran the *Times* bureau in Albany, he went to New Delhi (a move of symbolic significance, given Rosenthal's happy days there) and then to various Southeast Asian countries. Cambodia became Schanberg's special fascination, for the country was in the last throes of a savage civil war between the government and Communist guerrillas, the Khmer Rouge.

As did many other journalists working in Indochina, Schanberg was outraged by the inconsistencies between what he was told by the U.S. Embassy and the realities of what he witnessed when he went into the field. "Inconsequential accidental bombing" of a village, he discovered by personal reporting, actually involved the deaths and mutilations of scores of civilians. Schanberg felt that manipulations by Secretary of State Henry Kissinger and other Nixon Administration officials had drawn Cambodia into a war not of its making. (Given the use of Cambodia as a sanctuary and supply base by Vietnamese Communist insurgents, American strategists argued, the country inevitably would be drawn into the war, regardless of what Washington did.)

Schanberg's disillusionment with American policy spilled over into his copy, in angry rhetoric. He dismissed administration fears that the Khmer Rouge, if victorious, would wreak vengeance on its domestic opponents. On March 13, 1975, the eve of Khmer Rouge victory, Schanberg wrote in the *Times* that "unlike administration officials in Washington . . . most Cambodians do not talk about a possible massacre and do not expect one." He concluded in another dispatch that for "the ordinary people of Indochina . . . [it] is difficult to imagine how their lives could be anything but better with the Americans gone." He felt that "Cambodia, being a country blessed with rich agricultural land and a relatively small population, can be revived without any major reconstruction program as would be necessary in an industrialized nation. . . ."

When the Communists seized Pnomh Penh, the Cambodian capital, Schanberg realized to his horror that the Khmer Rouge indeed had vengeance in mind. He ignored orders from 43d Street and remained in Cambodia to report the first days of Khmer Rouge rule. His photographer-assistant, Dith Pran, was arrested immediately and taken to a "corrective camp."* Schanberg managed to get out of the country through the good offices of the French Embassy. And in a two-page article in the *Times* on May 9, 1975, he wrote about the "maniacal behavior" of the Khmer Rouge, and their massive violations of human rights. For his work, Schanberg on May 3, 1976, received a Pulitzer Prize for international reporting.

Unfortunately for Schanberg, critics of the *Times* for a decade bedevilled and reviled him with quotations of the line about how Cambodian lives could not be "anything but better" with the Americans gone. The sentence appeared as an overprint on gruesome photographs of piles of skulls of Khmer Rouge victims. In the right-wing gallery of journalistic horrors, Schanberg was given a niche alongside Herbert L. Matthews, whose 1957 reportage from Cuba brought world attention to the moribund revolution of Fidel Castro. Schanberg remained sensitive about these accusations, and the fact that they overlooked his later stories about Khmer Rouge atrocities. At least twice he and his lawyer hinted at libel actions against publications which considered publishing articles suggesting he was sympathetic to the Khmer Rouge (specifically, the *Accuracy in Media Report*, and *Policy Review*, a journal of the Heritage Foundation).

If Abe Rosenthal had any reservations about Schanberg's reporting from Cambodia, he did not express them at the time. The very day Schanberg received his Pulitzer, Rosenthal appointed him deputy metropolitan editor; a year later, in 1977, after the necessary refamiliarization with the city, Schanberg became metropolitan editor. These appointments suggest that Schanberg enjoyed Rosenthal's

*Schanberg wrote of Dith Pran's experiences in the camp and eventual escape in a *New York Times Magazine* article which became the 1985 movie *The Killing Fields*.

confidence. In January, 1986, Rosenthal had a different appraisal. After pausing a moment to organize his thoughts, Rosenthal said, with obvious deliberation, "Schanberg was brave and courageous in Cambodia, but in retrospect he was wrong about the Khmer Rouge."

Rosenthal soon realized that Schanberg did not understand the approach the "new" *New York Times* took towards local coverage. During Schanberg's previous years on the city side, the *Times* had gone after stories about the dispossessed, the persons victimized by the imperfect society that is New York City. Now Rosenthal found Schanberg's ideas about coverage unnecessarily negative. For instance—this is Rosenthal's example—if a report showed that 25 percent of pollution had been taken out of the Hudson, Schanberg's view would be that 75 percent remained. Nor did Rosenthal like the way Schanberg ran his staff.

With Schanberg as an editor, Rosenthal said, "Art and Top [Gelb and Seymour Topping] and I spent all our time playing backup catcher. Stories came through for the paper that contained opinion, unsubstantiated statements, innuendo, the sort of stuff that I will not permit to be published in *The New York Times*. That is a quirk of mine. I want to run a fair newspaper." Rosenthal felt Schanberg had a blindness for what he called the "hook story," one which put two unrelated facts together and presented them as news. Rosenthal offered a highly-hypothetical example of what he meant: "Joe Goulden, a friend of the publisher, is getting a job at *The New York Times*."* Rosenthal depended upon the metropolitan editor to train reporters because this department is a traditional point-of-entry for new hires, yet by his account Schanberg "could not teach because he did not know himself the right way to do things." Throughout his time as editor Rosenthal worried about "red-flag reporters," whose reliability is so questionable that everything they write must be examined carefully. Yet Schanberg could not—or would not—infuse these reporters with Rosenthal's concept of objectivity.

Such is Rosenthal's account of why he soured on Sydney Schanberg as a working journalist. Others involved on the metropolitan desk at the time tell a different story—that Schanberg got into Rosenthal's ill graces (most uncomfortable territory) by insisting on a warts-and-all approach to city coverage. "Syd was still doing 1960's reporting, with his bleeding heart right out there on his sleeve for everyone to see,"

---

*Rosenthal frequently uses variations of this example, usually employing the name of the person with whom he is speaking.

one of his reporters said. "Syd never realized the game had changed, and that all his stuff about starving welfare children didn't go well with the Bloomingdale ads."

In 1980 Rosenthal had had enough; Schanberg had clearly jumped off the career track in the news department. "I asked Punch to take him off my hands," Rosenthal said. "He said, 'OK, but you got to take so-and-so back down in the news department to get him off *my* hands.' " (Rosenthal declined to identify Sulzberger's "so-and-so.")

"That's the way it is?" Rosenthal asked Sulzberger.

"That's the way it is," Sulzberger replied. So the swap was made, in September, 1980, and Schanberg moved to the op-ed page to begin writing a column about New York. He now would be answerable to the op-ed page editor and to Max Frankel, editor of the editorial page, and ultimately to Sulzberger. As far as Rosenthal was concerned, Schanberg was not his problem.

With Schanberg hopefully out of his way Rosenthal insured that his new metropolitan editor understood the realities of the "new" *New York Times*. He chose the ever-faithful Peter Millones, who had held various jobs over two decades at the paper, last as Rosenthal's deputy for administrative and personnel affairs. Millones is the one underling who, with the possible exception of Artie Gelb, is most keenly attuned to Rosenthal's wishes. Rosenthal's cardinal rule of management, according to James Greenfield, is "Don't surprise me." This rule Millones followed to career-promoting perfection. He had worked only briefly, and not too well, as a street reporter. His view of news was insular. As a bureaucrat who worked most of his career in the office, only a few feet distant from Rosenthal, he was content to let superiors shape his view of the world, without getting emotionally excited about issues, as did Schanberg.

Rosenthal did give the deputy's job to a harder-nosed newsman, the veteran Nicholas Horrock, who had worked on the defunct Washington *Daily* news before coming to the *Times* as a national investigative reporter. Horrock recognized the mandate, that he and Millones were to "correct" the course set by Schanberg.

As Horrock related, no further explanations were necessary. Most days Rosenthal did not issue specific orders as to what he wished done, in terms of coverage. But he would hold what Horrock called "thought meetings" with editors, and his suggestions carried the impact of direct orders. "If Abe would say, 'We've got to get back to New York communities,' naturally, if you're not stupid, you lean on that end of your reporting for a while," Horrock said. Such a directive would lead to a profusion of what the *Times* calls "talkers," articles headlined, "The Talk of Maplewood, New Jersey," or "The Talk of Brownsville," featurish profiles of communities, usually upbeat.

Such mini-profiles fit Rosenthal's concept of explaining America on an on-going basis, yet their brevity prevents them from having other than passing interest. Further, according to one former *Times* editor, readership surveys show they have "insignificant interest" to anyone outside the profiled area. Horrock objected to the proliferation of "talkers" because they diminished the amount of space available for hard news. Rosenthal prevailed. Rosenthal also prevailed when he insisted that the metropolitan desk develop a column of New York trivia entitled "Day by Day" modeled after the successful "Washington Talk" column. Millones joined Horrock in protesting the loss of a column of space. The column runs.

In one sense Horrock felt he and Millones succeeded in obtaining better coverage of the suburbs and the regions beyond that are the responsibility of the metropolitan desk. "Syd was pretty much a city guy" he said of Schanberg. But, in retrospect, "we took it too much the other way, and I was not comfortable [with the style and emphasis of coverage] when I left. But it *was* more balanced." (Horrock left the *Times* in 1983 to report in Washington, first for *Newsweek*, then for the Chicago *Tribune*.)

Arthur Gelb, who acted as Rosenthal's surrogate on metropolitan desk affairs, was not nearly so subtle. Gelb once sorted through a collection of pictures of New York residents for a feature display on the front of the metropolitan page. An editor who must remain nameless felt the best picture showed some Puerto Ricans, but Gelb kept shoving it aside in favor of pictures of whites. Why? the assistant editor asked.

We can't show *them*, Gelb replied, making obvious he did not want to discuss the matter further.

Them? What do you mean, *them*? the editor asked. "I wanted to make him say it," he said.

Puerto Ricans, Gelb said, with some anger. *You know what I mean*. The pictures of the whites ran in the *Times*.

Rosenthal could be specific, very specific, when he felt an issue important. The mayoralty of Abe Beame ended in 1977, with the city near bankruptcy, and much of the country feeling it would never recover. The *Times*, with its new sections, was eager for a new start. At the first front-page meeting after Edward Koch's election to succeed Beame, Rosenthal said, "Let's give this new mayor a chance to show his stuff before we lay into him." One subordinate says Rosenthal confided that he felt the *Times* had been unduly harsh on Beame. Rosenthal's order gained momentum as it came down the line of command, with each editor making the admonition a bit stronger. By the time it reached Molly Ivins, then the City Hall reporter, "Nobody could go picking on the mayor unless we caught him fucking dead goats. This was never intended by Abe, of course, but reporters at City Hall would not criticize Koch; they feared what Abe might think or do."*

Ivins soon saw the go-soft policy in operation. She covered a Koch appearance at a Black community meeting in a Brooklyn school where one of the mayor's flip remarks about race relations almost started a riot. She wrote it that way. An editor changed her lead to state that "an incident almost occurred." An *incident*, not a *riot*. The difference was significant, and Ivins roared into the office the next day to protest.

"They don't want you to say things like that," the editor told Ivins. (She declined to name the man. "Poor fellow has to live with himself already; why let the rest of the world know what a toad he is?")

"Who are *they*?" Ivins demanded, determined to embarrass the editor into giving an answer. The editor gestured towards the ceiling, as if indicating higher-ups. (He pointed the wrong way; Rosenthal's office is on the same floor.)

Ivins looked at the ceiling and walked around in a circle, her neck craned. She turned to the editor with a mock puzzled expression. "Honey, I don't see anything up there but acoustic tiles."

Koch was to receive tender treatment through his first two terms and beyond. Although City Hall reporters collected literally dozens of inconsistencies in his statements over these years, few got into print. In private conversations with Katharine Balfour and other intimates, Rosenthal called the flamboyant Koch, a *"schmuck"* and professed to detest him. But when he dined at Gracie Mansion, the mayoral residence, Rosenthal behaved like a charmed guest. New York City recovered financially under Koch, and Rosenthal and the *Times* overlooked his foibles. When Koch published his autobiography *Mayor!*

---

*As shall be seen, Ivins' penchant for pungent speech eventually got her into terminal trouble with Rosenthal.

in 1984, Jack Newfield of the *Village Voice* counted a "howler"—i.e., a glaring misrepresentation—once every 1.7 pages. The *Times* review, on the front page of the Sunday book section, was written by Gay Talese, a friend of both Koch and Rosenthal, and he performed the improbable feat of being even more enthusiastic about the mayor than was Koch himself. Koch boasted to more than one person that "I've got the fuckin' *Times* in my pocket!" (The critical study, *I, Koch!*, by several City Hall reporters, including the *Times*'s Michael Goodman, was dismissed with a *Times* review 2.7 inches in length, versus 44 for Talese on the mayor's book.)

Given the *Times*'s soft treatment of Koch, cynical New Yorkers looked for sinister motives behind the rare hard investigative stories written about city government. Their question was, "How does this help Ed Koch?" A striking example came in January, 1985, when the *Times* ran an extraordinary four-part series—455 column inches, almost 38 feet in length—attacking the city medical examiner, Dr. Eliot Gross. The examiner was an embarrassment to Koch as he faced re-election. Gross had not performed well in reporting autopsy findings in the death of a young Brooklyn black man, Michael Stewart, who died in police custody after his arrest for scrawling graffiti in a subway station. The case was medically complicated, and much of the confusion came from Gross's verbal fuzziness when he announced preliminary results that stopped short of affirming that Stewart had been choked to death, as some witnesses claimed. (Gross blamed equally fuzzy reporting of what he actually said.)

In any event, *Times* reporter Philip Shenon, a newcomer in his mid-twenties, used the Stewart case and other examples to brand Gross as an incompetent coroner. The net effect of the articles was to shift criticism of the Stewart case away from the police department, which Koch controlled, to a single appointed official who could be shoved out of office. Such is exactly what happened: Gross went on leave to start the laborious task of trying to clear his name before several investigative forums.

To readers the Shenon articles seemed journalism at its best. He quoted Gross's detractors by name, and he referred frequently to official documents. But despite the length of the stories, Shenon did not mention some interesting background material on two of Gross's chief accusers: Dr. Robert Wolf, a professor at Mount Sinai Medical Center in New York; and Dr. John Grauerholz, a New Jersey forensic pathologist. Both had been hired by the Stewart family to monitor Gross's autopsy.

In 1974 a federal court jury in New York convicted Dr. Wolf of eight counts of evading $65,000 in taxes for failure to report some $130,000 in fees received from 1966 to 1969. Testimony showed that he deposited these funds in six separate accounts, including one in Switzerland. The judge sentenced Wolf to two months in jail, fined him $4,000 and put him on probation for 22 months.

Dr. Grauerholz also had a background that conceivably should have been of interest to *Times* readers, had Shenon reported it. Grauerholz was the personal physician of the political extremist Lyndon LaRouche and an active member of three of LaRouche's groups—the Fusion Energy Foundation, the Anti-Drug Coalition, and the National Coalition of Labor Committees. He ran for Congress in New Jersey on a LaRouche ticket in 1984, at the same time Shenon was interviewing him. During that period Grauerholz testified in LaRouche's behalf in a libel suit LaRouche brought against NBC News in United States District Court in Alexandria, Virginia. Grauerholz said he was attracted to LaRouche initially because of their common interest in fighting drugs by "eliminating the financial and other infrastructure that underlies it." He "probably put in about 84 hours a week" on various LaRouche activities and did his private practice at the same time. NBC attorney Thomas Kavaler cross-examined Grauerholz about the drug industry on October 22, 1984:

Kavaler: Do you think *The New York Times* is part of the drug lobby?
    Grauerholz: I think they are: I think people in the *Times* are connected to it.

Kavaler: To save a little time, who else is part of the drug lobby that perhaps other people might consider to be a major institution in America? What about the Washington *Post*? Is that part of the drug lobby?
    Grauerholz: My understanding is that there are people connected with the *Post* who are connected to certain organizations involved with that lobby, yes.

Kavaler: Did you hear Mr. LaRouche say Walter Mondale is a K.G.B. agent?
    Grauerholz: Yes.
    Kavaler: Do you think that's correct?
    Grauerholz: I think there's evidence that would support that, yes.

Gross and his attorney, Howard Squadron, soon after the articles appeared offered a point-by-point rebuttal of many of Shenon's allegations; a precis of their statement appeared in the *Times.* Grauerholz's peculiar testimony in the LaRouche trial was also mentioned—in the fifty-seventh paragraph of a followup story. Two years later Gross remained mired in a series of inconclusive official investigations. Regardless of the outcome, the *Times* series ended his New York career.

The demonstrated flaws aside, Rosenthal continued to think highly of the Shenon series. Asked in May, 1986, about *Times* investigative reporting, Rosenthal immediately cited the Shenon work. "He heard a mild tip, and he came up with good source stories," Rosenthal said. That Shenon did not tell more of the background of these sources did not disturb Rosenthal.

Something else, however, did cause Rosenthal problems: the continuing presence of Sydney Schanberg, who used his urban affairs column to critique the *Times*'s coverage of New York. To Rosenthal's discomfort, the exiled Schanberg regularly blistered the city staff for neglecting or misreporting major stories. Schanberg hectored Koch for promise-performance gaps. He poked at the real estate mogul Donald Trump, treated with awe elsewhere in the *Times.* A *New York Times Magazine* profile of the *wunderkind* developer in 1985 was prose any subject would be proud to show mother. Schanberg saw Trump more skeptically. When Trump tried to squeeze tenants from a rent-controlled building on Central Park South to make way for more expensive apartments, Schanberg's column provided the only *Times* coverage. These persons' rent was a fraction of the open market price, and Trump might have been right; nonetheless, the *Times* simply ignored the issue. The same months metropolitan editor Peter Millones covered a dispute over possible sale of the Zabar delicatessen empire on upper Broadway with the seriousness newspapers used to reserve for world wars. Schanberg and Millones clearly entertained different priorities on uncountable issues.

Rosenthal came to so detest Schanberg that he could not speak his name without a scowl or curse; he called him alternately "our homegrown St. Francis" or "the Commie." Two years running Schanberg was not invited to sit at the *Times* table for the Inner Circle dinner for the city's political reporters. Schanberg did not concern himself with Rosenthal's mutterings. He had other problems. His marriage ended in the early 1980's, victim of, among other things, years of journalistic stress. He became ill; he underwent heart bypass surgery. The first months of 1985 friends worried about Schanberg; he looked gaunt of face, and he acted increasingly remote. He knew that he was not pleasing Sulzberger and other powerful executives, but he did not care. He made a decision. If he ever felt himself succumbing to self-censorship to please Abe Rosenthal or Sulzberger, he would move back to Massachusetts and work in the mills or as a fry cook. The *Times* might have taken a quarter of a century of Schanberg's life; it would not capture his integrity.

The days before he went on vacation in July, 1985, Schanberg in successive columns wrote about subjects sensitive to the *Times*. On July 20 he attacked Koch's announced intention to limit debate during his re-election campaign. The press should not permit him to get away with it, Schanberg argued. ". . . [T]he media—newspapers and television—should be asking him the tough questions, because the answers about the housing shortage, the weaknesses in the school system, the growing numbers of homeless people and the conditions of the subways are important to the city." Next Schanberg criticized the proliferation of high-rise office and apartment buildings gradually bringing "daytime darkness" to the city.

What proved to be Schanberg's last column for *The New York Times* ran July 27, 1985, under the headline, "Cajun Flies and Westway," and it was an explicit attack on Abe Rosenthal's news judgment.

"As I leave on vacation," Schanberg wrote, the front-page story was Koch's intervention to permit Cajun chef Paul Prudhomme to open a Columbus Avenue restaurant despite Health Department objections.

> This is big news? Yes, as a matter of fact, it *is* big news in a city where the newspapers have shrunk to four in number and suffer from frequent bouts of sleeping sickness—and not just in the soporific summertime.

Other items of current press interest, Schanberg noted, were the "black book" of a madam the tabloids called "the Mayflower Madam" and the slow market for summer rentals in the Hamptons. (The latter was featured on the *Times* city page, July 23.) Schanberg did not object to covering these stories.

> We all need trivia on our newspaper pages to leaven the serious stories that weigh down the mind. But if trivia begins to dominate, the mind can become air-headed.

With that prologue, Schanberg got to the business at hand: the *Times*'s decision to give minimal coverage to procedural scandals on the Westway superhighway along the west side of Manhattan from the Battery to 42d Street. Developers and politicians loved Westway, for they felt it would vitalize a Manhattan backwater, and provide thousands of construction jobs. Westway opponents pointed to other factors. New York City could put the federal transit funds to better use, to upgrade subways. Westway landfills would obliterate Hudson River spawning grounds for many species of fish. The *Times* and other New York newspapers supported Westway editorially, but by the summer of 1985 allegations were being heard in federal court in Manhattan that Westway backers had falsified their case, to the point of perjury.

Westway was doubly sensitive for the *Times*. The city's power structure, including Mayor Koch and the major real estate developers, supported the project. Westway supposedly would revitalize the West Side of Manhattan, including the *Times*'s 43rd Street building. Another factor was not revealed to *Times* readers.

As deputy metropolitan editor in the late 1970's, Nicholas Horrock had a crew of reporters go through land records along the entire Westway route and contiguous areas, looking for land speculations by parties who might have had advance knowledge of the highway plans. Right away the reporters found a visible New York Times Company holding—some 66 acres above West 57th Street, between Eleventh and Twelfth Avenues, adjacent to CBS's West Side studies. The *Times* bought the property decades ago to off-load newsprint shipped in via the New York Central Railroad. By the 1970's the *Times* received newsprint by truck delivery, and the West Side tract was used as a parking lot for circulation trucks.

The article developed by reporters working under Horrock listed the *Times* property. The article never ran. Soon thereafter the New York Times Company sold the tract.

Schanberg dealt with more immediate matters. As he wrote in the column:

> Our newspapers, oddly, can't seem to find space for Westway and its scandal. The lone exception in the region is the Newark *Star-Ledger*, which has lately provided first-rate coverage. It is hard to understand the silence. . . . [S]candal has oozed out at the latest court battle over the Federal permits for Westway—more unbelievable testimony by pro-Westway government officials, more documents indicating that

the political fix was put in by senior officials in Washington to bring the Corps of Engineers and other Federal agencies into line. . . .

The city's newspapers, like the big politicians, have . . . ignored most of the scandal. The New York dailies, strangely asleep, run only occasional bland stories, sometimes just snippets—rarely anything about the chicanery. That, too, is part of the shame of Westway.

Max Frankel, the editorial page editor, sensed trouble when he read the column before publication, and he talked about it with Sydney Gruson, Sulzberger's assistant. By one account, Frankel suggested to Schanberg that by attacking the *Times* directly, he was getting out of bounds. Frankel did not direct that the column be withdrawn; to do so would be censorship. Sulzberger was in Alaska on a fishing trip when the column appeared, so Gruson took the initiative. He called Schanberg.

"I asked him to come in and chat with me. He was going on vacation, and he said he would see me when he returned. I told Syd, 'I just want you to know there is considerable unhappiness up here [on the executive floor] with that last column.' " Schanberg did not react to Gruson's veiled suggestion the column could cause him trouble and should therefore be changed or withdrawn. It was published as written.

Gruson called Sulzberger in Alaska and read the column to him. "He told me what he wanted done." This meant taking Schanberg off the column. They discussed timing. Sulzberger would cheerfully dismiss Schanberg himself, but he did not wish to interrupt his fishing trip. Nor did he want the column to be his last before the deadline. That straw broke the camel's back. "Now you can say anything you want about *The New York Times*." The *Times*—i. e., Gruson—chose to offer no reason because he did not wish to argue the and/or facts of each of Schanberg's columns; better to cut him off cold, and remain silent.*

Here the *Times* displayed an hypocrisy common in the American press—an unwillingness to discuss internal editorial decisions that are important to its own readers. The Schanberg dismissal was an acute example, for it involved a popular and controversial columnist. The *Times* was not hesitant to discuss controversies elsewhere in the me-

*Gruson said this on October 29, 1985, with the stated hope that Schanberg "deserves maybe an asterisk" in any book about the *Times*.

dia. Eighteen days after Schanberg's sacking, the *Times* media columnist Alex S. Jones did a reprise on "Joe Bob Briggs," a pseudonymous
writer who reviewed drive-in movies for the Dallas *Times-Herald,*
and who was fired when his red-neck satire slopped over into what
blacks perceived as racism. That the *Times* would comment on a distant paper's problems with a columnist while ignoring the controversy at 43d Street is explicable only when one accepts a core fact: the
Times is so arrogant that hypocritical conduct is accepted there as a
matter of course. Nor does the *Times* grant other large media enterprises immunity from discussion of personnel changes. In the weeks
immediately following Schanberg's ouster, for instance, the *Times*
carried numerous stories on job eliminations and early retirements at
CBS News; a major shakeup at Doubleday & Company, Inc.'s book
division; and office politics at another publisher, Arbor House.

The *Times* endured enormous professional criticism for not only
the dismissal of Schanberg but also for its refusal to offer any explanation.

Newsday: "Falling Out of Step With the Times."
Columbia Journalism Review: "Shutting Up Schanberg."
Washington Post: "The Journalistic Double-Standard: The Squashing
   of Sydney Schanberg."

But the Schanberg affair hurt the *Times* in more lasting fashion than
some unfriendly headlines. It soiled the *Times*'s reputation for credibility, and for giving free voice to columnists of *opinion.* There is a
word for shutting up a writer because he is disagreeable; it is censorship, and it is one of the dirtiest terms that can be said in a newsroom.
By this time Rosenthal was notorious in the newspaper trade for being a mercurial tyrant who ran a very unhappy ship. Although
Rosenthal had no direct role in the Schanberg matter, journalists
elsewhere saw it as but another example of the way the *Times* handled its own people. John Finney, whose duties in the Washington
bureau included hiring, had several prospects cite Schanberg during
interviews as a reason they would not consider joining the *Times.*

Schanberg did not wish to leave 43rd Street, and he talked with
Gruson about a variety of jobs—a national reporter for the *Times* magazine, or an executive position with the New York Times Foundation,
the company's charitable arm. But all offers seemed dead ends, and

so he left, to write an urban affairs column for *Newsday*'s New York
edition—the sort of writing censored by *The New York Times*. And in
February, 1986, at a dinner meeting of the reformist New Democratic Coalition, he gave a succinct reason for his dismissal: "Sometimes you get fired by people who become annoyed at you for
noticing that they have no clothes on."

By the 1980's the *Times* had essentially stopped covering city government. Through attrition Rosenthal gradually rid the city staff of
the veteran reporters who had done the hard investigative work in
the past. In their stead he hired younger men and women content to
do the sort of writing now demanded by the *Times*. Many of these
persons were bright, yet they spent inordinate time searching out the
soft features that filled the metropolitan section. Hard news suffered.
In terms of City Hall coverage, the *Times* skipped along the visible
peaks—a mayor's ceremonial appearances, City Council votes on major issues. But the *Times* stayed out of the important valleys containing the minutiae of city government—who received contracts,
and why, and how they performed; the influence of the Democratic
city organizations in the five boroughs on City Hall; the interplay between campaign contributors and politicians. Rosenthal never cared
much for the workings of government and politics; to him these were
"insider stories" of interest only to the actual players. He was wrong.
He missed the fact that events must be monitored closely, even on a
daily basis, to make sense to the intelligent reader.

Newspapers cover government for two reasons. First, of course,
they desire stories, for news sells newspapers. The other reason is
more subtle. The press's claim to privileged status under the First
Amendment is rooted in the assertion that it monitors government on
behalf of the public. This *The New York Times* failed to do for the
citizens of New York City.

Covering a City Hall anywhere in the United States means much
scut work, chiefly that a reporter study at least a portion of the city
contracts awarded each year. There must be spot checking: for instance, who are the principals in Sunshine Enterprises, Ltd., which
received a half-million dollar contract for replacement of manhole
covers? What are the connections of these principals, if any, to the
city's politicians and office-holders? And what links exist between the
councilman who pushes a particular bill and the parties who benefit

from it? Newspapers *should* seek this information as a matter of course, even if stories do not turn up every day. (Few papers do, alas.) The knowledge that someone outside government is monitoring contracts discourages thievery.

Such was not done by *The New York Times* or any other media in the city during the 1980's. While the *Times's* watchdogs sought out the ten best places on the Upper West Side to buy *gelato* ice cream, and trends in yuppie exercise salons, New York politicians gleefully looted the city of uncountable millions of dollars in questionable contracts. The first hint of these scandals came not from a New York reporter, but from a free-lance journalist named Gaeton Fonzi, who lived in Fort Lauderdale, Florida. Investigating the 1975 disappearance of a local heiress, Fonzi discovered that a man implicated in the case had been arrested elsewhere, and then vanished behind a screen of sealed court files. Fonzi poked a bit, and an alarmed FBI agent asked him to desist, confiding that the man, one Michael Raymond, was helping in a scam operation involving bribes to politicians and officials in four cities—including New York. To keep Raymond from being killed, Fonzi held the story for months. Then he went to an old friend from Philadelphia journalism, Gilbert Spencer, editor of the *Daily News*, which on January 7, 1986, covered its front page with the headlines: "SLAY SUSPECT DEALS FOR FBI." Fonzi wrote that one of Raymond's companies, Systematic Recovery Service, Ltd., was based in New York and had contracts there to collect parking tickets and other accounts.

The story would have alerted any tolerably attentive city editor that something was amiss in New York government. *Times* metropolitan editor Peter Millones did not pursue it, even to the point of the *Times* running its own version of the *Daily News* story.

Three days later, early on the morning of January 10, one of the city's most powerful politicians was found near-dead in his car, blood gushing from a slash of his wrist. Donald Manes was both borough president and Democratic chairman of Queens, the nation's fourth largest county. During Democratic administrations, he was a frequent White House visitor. He held veto power over judicial appointments; he controlled Queens patronage in city government. He was powerful in state politics, a true kingmaker, for fourteen years.

The *Times* had to introduce Manes as if he were a visitor from outer space; in his fourteen years of power Manes's name appeared in *The*

New York Times index a score or so times annually, but the vast majority of these mentions were fleeting. Never had the *Times* paused to explain why Donald Manes was an important figure in the city.

Four days after Manes's attempted suicide (he succeeded in killing himself in a second attempt, in March) one of his protégés was charged with taking a $5,000 bribe from Systematic Recovery Services, Ltd., the firm named in Fonzi's first story. With the FBI scam now unveiled, a cascade of indictments followed in many sections of New York government. And belatedly *The New York Times* began covering what one columnist called "the greatest municipal scandal in this city since Jimmy Walker was mayor."

The *Times* was lost from the outset. The scandal revolved around links between city departments and borough Democratic organizations ("clubhouses," in local parlance). In trying to explain the "clubhouses" the *Times* sounded like Marco Polo describing the Chinese to a European court. As one reporter discovered in a Manes-related story on January 14, the "Adlai E. Stevenson Democratic Club storefront is plainly visible from the Long Island Expressway in the Flushing area." Subsequent stories did not show any significant gain in sophistication. By contrast, the *Village Voice*—with a budget minuscule in comparison with the *Times's*—seldom lets a week pass without a story about nefarious clubhouse chicanery. Ignoring the clubhouses when reporting on New York politics, as the *Times* attempted to do, is akin to writing about football without mentioning the players, only final scores.

That the *Times* performed so poorly on the city scandals caused Rosenthal no admitted concern. That the clubhouse bosses had influence in city government was certainly known; what the *Times* did not realize was that the "influence extended to corruption." Rosenthal had a lame rationale: "It's possible that we all took the same attitude toward 'influence' that the Mayor [Koch] did. Everybody knew about influence, but no one made the connection between influence and corruption." Rosenthal's explanation sounded lamer as he continued talking: "So was it possible for a newspaper to bust this? Yes. But the fact that no newspaper did—not us, not the *Daily News*, not the *Post*—does not imply a lackadaisical attitude towards government.

"Those who expect the press to reveal all the ills of society are self-delusionary. And these are the same people, by the way, who usually criticize the press. *Remember also these contracts went through the [city] auditors, and they didn't catch them either."*

But is a city audit agency responsible for noting that contracts are going to someone with strong political connections? No. That is the job of the press. And that is the job *The New York Times* failed to do for its readers.

FOURTEEN

"Burst In . . . Foaming At the Mouth"

With power came affluence, and the means for Abe Rosenthal to enjoy the upbeat New York City promoted so assiduously by his newspaper. Rosenthal's income rose into the six figures, and started a steady march upwards that ultimately would bring him, in salary and executive bonuses, a shade more than half a million dollars a year. Publisher Punch Sulzberger was generous with *Times* stock, and Rosenthal accumulated a portfolio that rose along with the fortunes of the Times Company until his net worth was well more than a million dollars. (The sharp rise in *Times* stock during the 1970's brought respectable wealth to a number of employees. Reporter Nicholas Gage bought a block at the employees' price before going to Europe on assignment in the 1970's, and forgot it for three years. When he returned, he was pleased to find the increase in value enough for him and his wife to buy a house.)

The Times Company was generous in other ways as well. Rosenthal and wife Ann had gone through a succession of apartments on the West Side, none quite big enough for the three boys and the entertaining they now wished to do. He found two co-op apartments on Central Park West in the Eighties that could be joined. The *Times* loaned him $96,000, $70,000 of it at an interest rate of 4 percent versus the then market rate of 9 percent, and Abe and Ann finally had the urban equivalent of a dream home—a dozen high-ceiling rooms overlooking the park, with a penthouse.

Somewhere Rosenthal acquired a passion for plants, and now he spent summer evenings and some of his weekends puttering on his new patio. As his advisor he commandeered the expertise of Joan Lee Faust, the *Times*'s gardening writer, and she came to expect at least one call each spring weekend when a high-pitched voice would say, "Hey, Joanie, I'm sorry to bother you, but I have a problem with my . . ." and Rosenthal would go into a long discussion of whatever plant he was potting that day.

Rosenthal renewed an old friendship with Theodore White, and they had put together their own informal luncheon group, "The Boys' Club." The group was eclectic, intellectually and politically—William F. Buckley, Jr., the writer, editor and columnist; John "Jack" Chancellor of NBC News; Dick Clurman, longtime chief of correspondents for Time-Life; and Osborne Elliott, the editor of *Newsweek*.

Teddy White felt that the Boys' Club was a good outing for Rosenthal, because "no one in the office would speak to Abe as imprudently as we do."

White thought that Rosenthal came to rely upon the Boys' Club for the friendships he could no longer enjoy at the *Times* because of his rank there. "He wants to get out of that cloistered, imperial atmosphere that goes with the *Times*." The schedule was informal; once each six weeks or so, with members rotating as host; Rosenthal would take the group to the executive dining room at the *Times*. "We all air our problems, and those of the universe in general," White said. For instance, when White was planning his book on the 1972 election, Watergate remained the looming unresolved issue. Yet for contractual reasons the book had to go to press in July, 1973. The Boys' Club's collective advice was that he should do this book on the election, and then return to Watergate. This he did.

Yet the unspoken rule is that the Boys' Club does not grant members any special treatment from the *Times*. In 1977 one of Buckley's family oil companies got into trouble with the SEC. The *Times* ran the story under a two-column head on the front page, and Rosenthal did not say a word to Buckley in advance.

White had his own experience in 1982. "The very worst review a book of mine ever received was in the *Times Book Review*." He referred to *America In Search of Itself*, the summation volume of his *Making of the President* series. "That prick Bob Sherrill savaged me, in a vicious and idiotic fashion." Rosenthal read the review in advance and he suffered. But White recognized his dilemma. "You assign a review, you can't change it, or you get murdered by the *Village Voice* and the literati," White said.

"I was boiling mad for forty-eight hours, then I said, 'Shit, you can't give up a friendship over this sort of thing.' But it did cost me a fortune." Sulzberger, whom White had known in Paris, sent him a copy with a note, "I love this book, Teddy, would you autograph it for me?" As White says, "This was graciousness; Punch was saying that no matter what they said on the front page of his book review, he cared for my book."

Rosenthal discovered social New York, and hostesses initially loved to have him at a dinner party. One woman called Rosenthal "a joy to be around. He could talk about anything. He would get so engrossed in good conversation he would not even eat his dinner." This was when he was sober. A few too many drinks—Rosenthal never learned to drink whiskey, or how to stop shy of his limit—and his speech would slur, and he would drop obscenities into his conversation. Another woman said, "I gave him one 'free night' when he got drunk and made an ass of himself; I figured that he might have been tired. When he did it the second time, I drew a line through his name. He has not sat at my table again."

Even these social friends learned that Rosenthal could transform a chance remark into a conversation about *The New York Times*. "Nice weather we've been having," a hostess once said to him. As she recounts: "He started talking about this great weather story someone had written in the *Times* science section a few weeks back. EGO. Eyes-gloss-over. Boredom." Worst yet was when someone would speak disparagingly of the *Times*, even by indirection.

A friend was at the Dick Clurmans' one evening when Shirley Clurman, a producer for ABC News, and a most intelligent woman, talked about the libel trial General William Westmoreland was waging against CBS. She ventured that the Philadelphia *Inquirer* reporter was doing the best coverage of any journalist, and she suggested that Rosenthal should hire him. Abe sloughed off the suggestion and managed to change the subject.

The same person happened to be present several evenings later at a party which again included both the Clurmans and Rosenthal. Midway through dinner he glanced across the table at Shirley Clurman and said, "By the way, I thought the Philadelphia *Inquirer* didn't do all that good a job covering Westmoreland." Then he turned to another subject, leaving most of the guests totally baffled. The remark, as this witness said, "came totally out of left field." Shirley Clurman suppressed a grin and reminded herself *never* to criticize the *Times* again.

That Rosenthal was most unhappy in his marriage was apparent to most of his new friends. Ann Rosenthal's weight became enormous, and she seemingly did not have the will to do anything about curbing it. One longtime acquaintance called her a "two-handed eater. She goes after *hor d'oeuvres* on a tray as if they are her last meal on earth. The woman does not snack, she *attacks*." Rosenthal would sometimes sit quietly and look at the prettier and far more gracious wives of fellow members of the Boys' Club—women such as Pat Buckley and Shirley Clurman—and one person who watched him closely sensed, "Abe is saying to himself 'Why don't I have a wife like that?' " His relationship with Katharine Balfour remained a closely-held secret these years, to the women in his social circle at least.

In time his drinking came to cause public embarrassment, to him and *The New York Times*. At "21" one evening he got into an angry shouting match with Alexander Haig, the former secretary of state, for reasons no one present could ever quite understand. He went directly from work another evening to a reception at the New York Public Library; he sensed a slight in the way he was received, and he left in a rage, snarling obscenities and profanities.

Now the testiness and ill manners that had long marked his personality became dominant. Rosenthal had succeeded in gaining control of *The New York Times*, but he had felt resistance (or so he thought) at every turn. Now he no longer had to be courteous or falsely jovial with persons whom he considered fools. Only one word can describe the way Rosenthal behaved towards persons subordinate to him on the paper—mean. Sarcastic mean.

Rosenthal chose his targets carefully—the young reporter, for instance, who said something Rosenthal considered silly. The older man, the editor who relied upon Rosenthal's good will for his job. The press agent or writer who depended upon the good grace of Rosenthal's *Times* for a livelihood. Even an old friend who unwittingly said something about the *Times* which offended Rosenthal. Richard Cohen, a CCNY classmate of Rosenthal, now a New York public relations man, once passingly complained that the ink used by the *Times* rubbed off on his raincoat; couldn't the production department find a better quality ink? "Buy a black raincoat," Rosenthal snapped, without a trace of a smile. "He was really offended," Cohen said.

Cohen could grimace and turn away; he saw Rosenthal only once or twice annually, in a social setting. Other persons were not so fortunate. These were people who worked under Rosenthal at the *Times*; when they fell under the lash of his tongue, or his savage sarcasm, they could only grimace and keep silent. In November, 1981, for instance, Rosenthal spent more than a week touring Texas with David Jones, the national editor; and a couple of regional correspondents. At breakfast the talk turned to the *Times*'s new national edition. Jones casually mentioned something he thought should be included.

"Dave, when I want your opinion, I'll ask for it," Rosenthal said with a frown.

"I just assumed you would welcome the opinion of your national editor on your national edition," Jones replied.

"Oh, I do," Rosenthal said. "I welcome your opinion—once."

Jones swallowed and said nothing, but the exchange embarrassed other persons at the table. Rosenthal had rudely slapped down their boss. To do so in the presence of other correspondents let them know who ran the paper (as if there could be any question anyway). But one of those persons could not help but wonder, "Was that really necessary?"

That he would subject David Jones to such petty humiliation was all the more striking because, as national editor, Jones was totally loyal to Rosenthal. Rosenthal had an inflexible rule with sub-editors such as Jones. They were never to pass on to the correspondent or reporter the fact that Rosenthal had an interest in a story, or to issue instructions in his name. "Dave played by the rules," a former national reporter said of Jones. But he and other astute national correspondents learned to sense when Jones did something at Abe's bidding. "Jones would call and say, 'I want you to do a story on such-and-such,'" the former reporter said. "I would reply, 'That's the dumbest thing I ever heard of; this must be coming from Abe.' 'No, it's my idea,' Jones would say. 'I want you to do this right now.' But you could tell the source. You developed a knack after a while."

As he gradually accumulated more rank within the *Times,* Rosenthal chose larger targets for his outbursts, and old animosities that had festered inside him for decades would gush forth seemingly without provocation. Rosenthal always blamed C. L. "Cy" Sulzberger for the years it took him to get on the foreign staff. He frequently told the story of the misplaced travellers' checks in the Paris hotel at the UN conference in 1948, and how Sulzberger used "this shitty little episode" as a claimed excuse for not letting him work abroad. By the time Rosenthal became managing editor, Cy Sulzberger's power at the *Times* had ebbed. His nephew Punch did not like Cy Sulzberger. Here, too, some old slights were involved. Uncle Cy had not liked the idea of "having this idiot nephew foisted off on me" in the late 1940's, when he worked from Europe and the neophyte Punch was sent to Paris as a reporter. Cy snubbed the youngster, and, aside from the obligatory social gestures one must give to relatives, kept his distance. Now, in the 1970's, Punch ran the newspaper, and he thought Cy's foreign affairs column hopelessly outdated and conservative. Punch's cousin, John Oakes, was unhappy about running Cy's column on the editorial page, but neither man was willing to risk starting a bitter inter-familial quarrel attempting to depose him. Cy Sulzberger, for his part, had a low opinion of both Punch and Johnny Oakes. As a man who knows the three principals intimately has said, "Cy was used to supping with kings, and in his later years he began to confuse himself with presidents and prime ministers. He certainly had no time for a left-wing editor or a kid publisher who was the second-choice of his own family."

Rosenthal knew of these strains in the family; he realized that Cy Sulzberger no longer was a magisterial figure within the *Times,* but simply an aging columnist who was serving out his time. The evidence suggests that Rosenthal was eager for the opportunity to let Cy Sulzberger know, and in humiliating fashion, that a new order now prevailed at *The New York Times.* Cy Sulzberger could write what he wished in his editorial page column; once he got into the domain of the news department, however, he would answer to the "little Jewish kid from CCNY" who had been snubbed in the 1940's. The inevitable explosion came in March, 1971.

Despite his differences with Punch, Cy Sulzberger retained a more or less open mandate to report wherever he happened to be. For decades his speciality had been the long, on-the-record interview with heads of state who would make themselves available to no other reporter. One person who had eluded him was President Richard Nixon, who had granted several non-attributable "backgrounders" to journalists, but no extensive on-the-record interview. Hence Sulzberger was happily surprised when the President told him at the start of a conversation at the White House, "This is on the record, ask what you want." Sulzberger talked several hours with Nixon, and he felt pleased with himself when he returned to the Washington bureau and commandeered a small office.

"I was in the middle of typing my news story, some thousands of words of which had already moved on the Washington bureau's line to New York, when Abe Rosenthal . . . burst in, white as a sheet, and as close to anyone I have ever seen to foaming at the mouth.

"The burden of what he had to say was, 'Who the hell did I think I was working for, myself or *The New York Times*,' et cetera, laced with cursing. I told him it was a nuisance for me to write news stories of this sort but I was always requested in the most urgent way by the publisher to do so.

"What goddamned right did I have to see the President without seeing him first? Wryly I said I saw no reason to tell him. When did I know I was going to see him? About three weeks ago. That sent him. I then explained that the appointment had been made three weeks ago, but I didn't have a clue that it was going to turn into an interview until I was actually with the President.

"Well, I still goddamn well should tell him when I was going to see anybody. How would I feel if someone came to Paris [Sulzberger's home base at the time] to see the French president and didn't tell me? It had already happened, I said, but I couldn't care less.

"I had no right to see people on a secret basis, said Abe. I did not agree and I refused to change my methods. I had spoken to six presidents of the U.S.A. and many other world leaders, and when they wanted to talk on a confidential basis I respected their wishes; this is what kept open my access to them. I refused to tell him; in fact I never even told my wife. Eventually he stormed out with a face like a festering pear that had been left in a dark cellar all winter."

The exclusive interview with Nixon ran; not even Rosenthal was dumb enough to forego such a story to satisfy a petty quarrel. But Rosenthal did exact his revenge for the supposed slight to his authority. The White House had photographs made of Sulzberger talking with the President, and they were transmitted to New York. "The *Times* cut me out of the photograph published, leaving only Nixon who, because of the artificial amputation, looked something like a stunned character out of a comic strip. . . ." The deletion amused Sulzberger as the ultimate demonstration of the smallness of Rosenthal's mind; as he has joked, he was reminded of Stalin's practice of cutting "non-persons" such as Trotsky out of photographs and paintings. Rosenthal's tantrum scene had no impact whatsoever on Cy Sulzberger's work habits; as he told one acquaintance, "Yapping little dogs should be kicked, not heeded. The smaller the dog, the louder the yap. Good heavens, should I be forced to work under the direction of that man, I would run away to sea, or even become a movie actor."

Rosenthal apparently realized that temper fits do not impress personages such as C. L. Sulzberger. Sulzberger and his wife Marina happened to be in New York in 1972, and Rosenthal somewhat sheepishly asked them to his home for what Cy Sulzberger called a "lavish and cordial" dinner. Late in the evening Rosenthal offered a contrite apology. He had been emotionally upset the day of the incident because he had attended the funeral of a friend; he was also affected "by drinks served subsequently to the mourners." Sulzberger accepted the apology, but he did not change his opinion of Abe Rosenthal. In latter years, with a deep sign he would gaze into space, eyes lidded, and he would say, "*The New York Times* run by *that man?*" He would then shake his head slowly and wrinkle his nostrils, as if something unpleasant were around.

During his first years of power Rosenthal, intentionally or not, reserved his most vehement outbursts of rage for persons on the paper. He would savage the occasional cab driver or slow waitress, but the dark side of Abe Rosenthal seldom was seen outside the newsroom. People outside the *Times* who witnessed these emotional squalls wrote off Rosenthal as the classic New York nut, the ranter who is shouting at enemies unseen by the rest of the world. He was known to the public neither by face nor by name. After an especially ugly taxi scene one evening a subordinate editor tried to make peace with the driver. "Just who is that little shit?" the cabbie asked. Being told, he blurted, "You mean that guy works for *The New York Times.* Sweet Jesus!" He shook his head and drove away with a grinding of gears. But as Rosenthal grew in prominence he became even less restrained in his public behavior. The scenes that had long been commonplace in the relative privacy of the *Times* newsroom now spilled out into public places.

In the early 1970's Rosenthal made one of his periodic attempts to determine whether reporter Douglas Robinson had come to like him as a man. Robinson had been one of the few surviving people on the staff to look Rosenthal in the eye, as metropolitan editor, and say, No, I don't like you. Robinson by then was a roaming reporter who specialized in trials and racial strife. (That Rosenthal let him be assigned to cover riots in Illinois, South Carolina and New Jersey, Robinson did not necessarily see as a compliment to his professional ability. "I had the idea Abe had this mental picture of me lying in the gutter bleeding from a head wound.")

But this particular evening Robinson was in New York, and after work Rosenthal swept him off to Sardi's. "Abe was talking to me, trying to see if I liked him. Almost immediately, we were surrounded by a knot of people from the paper, wanting to be seen hanging around with Abe." Robinson smiled inwardly and sipped his Scotch. A young general assignment reporter walked over, a lady in tow, and Robinson described what happened:

"Abe, I'd like you to meet Miss So-and-So, she's managing editor of Bantam Books," the reporter said.

Rosenthal looked up with a frown and considered the woman and shook his head. "No, she's not," he said.

Nonplussed, the reporter continued. "Yes, she is, she is the managing editor." He attempted a smile, as if trying to figure out what game Rosenthal was playing this evening. (As was often the case in instances of his public boorishness, Rosenthal had been drinking Scotch.)

Again, Rosenthal shook his head, this time more emphatically. "No, she's not." When the reporter tried to speak again, Rosenthal silenced him by raising his hand. "No, managing editors are *only* on newspapers. You don't find managing editors around publishing companies."

As Robinson related, "Abe said this in a loud tone, enough to embarrass the woman, who was really an innocent bystander. The reporter dragged her away in embarrassment. This was a bit of unnecessary cruelty on Abe's part. But that's Abe. He doesn't think of anyone else's feelings."

Rosenthal and Doug Robinson, incidentally, never made peace. Robinson kept out of his way as much as possible, for a while under the protectorship of Gene Roberts, with whom he served in Vietnam and again on the national desk. After work as a combat correspondent in Vietnam, Robinson went to the Washington bureau. Even at that distance, Rosenthal would unexpectedly paw at him from time to time. He tells another story. Clifton Daniel, then the Washington bureau chief, called Robinson into his office one day with a solemn expression.

"Well, you've done it again," Daniel said. "Abe wants to fire you as an example."

"An example of what?" Robinson asked bewildered. "What have I done?"

"Well, someone was here from New York and overheard you say something about Abe. He's so mad he wants to fire you."

"What did I supposedly say?" Robinson asked.

"I don't know."

"Who reported this 'slur' to Abe?"

"I don't know that either," Daniel said. "But don't worry about it. I've convinced Abe that I'll handle it administratively here." He told Robinson to go back to work and forget the matter.

To Robinson, the episode said much about Rosenthal and the atmosphere he created at the *Times*. That Rosenthal was willing to fire a veteran reporter because of an alleged slurring comment in a newsroom—without even asking the intended victim his version of the episode—was the act of "a borderline psychotic," Robinson said. That a colleague would carry back casual banter—Robinson went through some of the things he *might* have said about Rosenthal; none of them were nice, but he remembered nothing out of the ordinary— indicated "the kind of place Abe has turned the *Times* into, a nest of fear." When Gene Roberts and Clifton Daniel left the *Times*, within a relatively short span, Robinson realized his days were numbered there. "My rabbis were gone. I was at Abe's mercy. The word was that I would be sent out to Connecticut as the third reporter. I felt I had learned a bit in the business, and I thought I could serve myself, and the paper, by not taking that kind of insult."

So after twenty-two years, Robinson resigned from the *Times*. After sending Rosenthal the letter, he went home emotionally drained. "This was like a divorce. I was terribly depressed—twenty-two years, down the drain." That Robinson was unhappy was no secret in the journalistic world, and Philip Nobile of *[MORE]* Magazine called him that very day.

Robinson had kept his complaints about Rosenthal in-house. He would grouse with colleagues, but not with other persons. This day freedom loosened his tongue, and he spoke with Nobile, candidly, for forty-five minutes and he said, "Yes, you can quote me, put my name on it." The thrust of Nobile's article was that Rosenthal intended to use Hedrick Smith, Daniel's replacement, as a straw boss while he ran the bureau from New York. *[MORE]* illustrated the story with a caricature of Smith on Rosenthal's knee, à la Charlie McCarthy.

Nobile's article did not please Rosenthal. By one eyewitness account that reached Robinson, Rosenthal walked out of his office and saw a stack of copies of the magazine on a desk, awaiting forwarding to correspondents outside New York. Rosenthal supposedly grabbed handfuls of *[MORE]* and tore them to shreds, shouting obscenities all the while. (Rosenthal still seethed at the mention of Nobile's name more than a decade later. He said in March, 1986, "He reached the height of his career. He runs a sex magazine." Rosenthal referred to *Forum*, one of the Penthouse group of publisher Bob Guccione. To Rosenthal's considerable dismay, Nobile even managed to find grounds for a *Times* article in *Forum*, on sexual pruderies at the *Times*.)

Again, Rosenthal was to have the last word. By the time the *[MORE]* article appeared, Robinson was well along towards taking a job as assignments editor in the Washington bureau of the *Los Angeles Times*. Bureau chief Jack Nelson, and old friend from civil rights reportage days in the South, had taken Robinson to lunch twice. "At the same time *[MORE]* came out, with my comments on Abe and the *Times*, Bill Thomas [executive editor of the *Los Angeles Times*] called Abe to check me out. As I was told later, Abe told Thomas, 'Don't hire that son of a bitch,' and proceeded to fill his ears with the stories of my ineptitude. I was suddenly persona non grata at the *Los Angeles Times* bureau." So Robinson followed a well-worn path from the *Times* to the Philadelphia *Inquirer*, where he happily rejoined Gene Roberts, first as city editor, then as state editor.

Something about his resignation letter still amuses—and perhaps rankles—Robinson. Rosenthal received the letter weeks before learning he had talked to Nobile and *[MORE]*. Nonetheless he never received even a perfunctory acknowledgment. "Twenty-two years, zip," he says. "Not even a thank you note for Vietnam and all those riots where mobs were trying to bust my head. Let me put it straight: Abe Rosenthal doesn't give a shit about people, unless they do things his way, and snuggle up to him. Bah."

These stories could be told in endless succession; after listening to them for months, one hears a certain sameness—of a hair-trigger-tempered editor whose disposition was not improved by alcohol, and who was hypersensitive about himself and his newspaper to an extent that any pathological explanation must come from other than a lay-man. Rosenthal prided himself on professional toughness; he ex-pected the same of the people who worked for him. When Seymour Hersh would come to his office with stories of how he had tricked or frightened someone into talking to him, Rosenthal would howl with appreciative laughter. Rosenthal has called himself, in uncountable forums, a "First Amendment absolutist," that is, *no* barriers should be placed on free speech.

Such is what Rosenthal says at seminars on freedom of the press and such journalistic lodge meetings as the American Society of Newspaper Editors. Such is not the standard Rosenthal uses at his own newspaper. Joseph F. Sullivan, a city reporter, was at his desk one day when Rosenthal walked through the newsroom and said casu-ally, "Hi, Jack." Sullivan, quite content with the name given him by his parents, quipped back, "Hi, Al, how're things going?" Rosenthal stopped and glared at him, and within the month Sullivan was as-signed to New Jersey. New Jersey is purgatory for most reporters even though the state undoubtedly has good features that the rest of the world eventually will discover. In this instance Sullivan came out the winner. He lives in New Jersey, hence he was spared the com-mute to 43d Street, and he eventually became chief political corre-spondent for the state for the *Times*. He does not pretend that Rosenthal intended any such happy outcome. He does not intend to swap flip remarks with Abe Rosenthal in the future.

Equally fatal can be a suggestion that a person has business more demanding than a conversation with Abe Rosenthal. Elliot Fremont-Smith is a good case history. Fremont-Smith reviewed books for the *Times* from 1961 through 1968, and during those years he had only one contact with Rosenthal, one that began in disturbing fashion but ended amicably. Reviewing the Lawrence Durrell novel *Tunc* Fremont-Smith mentioned that *Newsweek* had explained the title in *its* critique, without stating that it referred to a jumbling of the letters of the vulgar word for the female genitals. Fremont-Smith relates, "Two days later, about five in the afternoon, I was sitting at my desk in my enclosed office when suddenly the door burst open. There stood this little man with a beet-red face. It was Rosenthal. We had barely met. He was waving a piece of paper and shrieking, 'Does this mean what I think it means?' I could not understand, for the life of me, what he was saying.

"His idea was that I'd tried to be naughty and get a dirty word into the paper without anyone knowing it. What saved me was my obvious surprise." But he marked Rosenthal as a man who did not wish games to be played in the columns of *The New York Times*. Fremont-Smith after the *Times* moved to Little Brown as editor-in-chief for "a day less than three years." An intellectual, Fremont-Smith found only bafflement in profit-loss statements and the like, and he decided he must return to the literary end of books. "I thought naturally of the *Times*, and I talked with Gelb. He asked whether I would be interested in being the second-string movie critic. I had done some movies and theater in the past, but my thing really was books." So this contact came to naught. Nonetheless, "Gelb supposed that I would leap at the opportunity, any opportunity, to return to the *Times*."

Fremont-Smith did other things for several years and in 1976 he was invited to a publication party at the *Times* for Tom Wicker's book on the Attica prison riots, *A Time to Die*. The affair was a homecoming for Fremont-Smith, and he handshook his way through the crowd, chatting with old colleagues he had not seen for years. Someone tugged at his elbow. He turned to face Rosenthal.

"Come on, I want to talk to you," Abe said, "Let's get a drink."

Given the contact with Arthur Gelb, Fremont-Smith felt Rosenthal wished to talk about a return to the *Times*. As he moved to follow Rosenthal, he felt hands clasp over his eyes. "Guess who!" trilled a woman's voice, and Fremont-Smith looked over his shoulder to see a woman who had worked with him in the *Book Review*. They exchanged a few seconds of pleasantries and then as he moved along to rejoin Rosenthal, he heard a harsh voice. "Well, if you don't want to talk with *me* . . ." and he watched Rosenthal stride away with angrily stiff steps.

Fremont-Smith related, "I found this very upsetting. I said to myself, 'There went a job.' It was most bizarre. There was no possible way I could have given offense." In the rational world, such is perhaps true. In the world of Abe Rosenthal, Fremont-Smith had committed the ultimate error, that of fleetingly giving attention to someone else.

Some time later Fremont-Smith did a *Village Voice* review of *Good as Gold*, a Joseph Heller novel. "I put it down hard. I did not like it." Hence he was surprised the next time he encountered Gelb, whom he knew to be a close friend of Heller, and through the *Times Book Review* a strong promoter of his works. To Fremont-Smith's surprise, Gelb was most cordial. "Come to lunch sometime," Gelb said.

Fremont-Smith felt he must be candid with Gelb. He told him about the party incident, and said he felt certain he was *persona non grata* at the *Times*.

"Well, Abe is like that sometimes," Gelb replied. "You shouldn't think anything of it." They shook hands and Gelb hurried off. Gelb, a decade later, still had said nothing further about the suggested luncheon.

What Fremont-Smith experienced at the Wicker party illustrated a core truth about Abe Rosenthal. He cannot conceive that any person could have business more pressing than talking with Abe Rosenthal, or doing whatever else Rosenthal chose. A *Times* national reporter, a man no longer at the paper, once spent two months away from his home in another state while working on an investigative article. He flew into New York to do the final writing and editing; he intended to fly home for the weekend, to see his family for the first time in two months, and then return to New York on Monday to resume work. Rosenthal called to invite him to a dinner party at his house that night.

"I explained that while ordinarily I'd love to come I had plans to spend the weekend at home and would have to take a raincheck," the former reporter stated. "There was a frosty silence, then he mumbled about how of course he understood." The reporter learned later Rosenthal told several persons he was the "only *Times* correspondent who had ever turned down an invitation to dinner at his house."

The episode apparently continued to rankle Rosenthal several years later when he encountered the same reporter at a social function away from New York. Again, Rosenthal asked the man and his wife to join him and a party for dinner; again, the man already had other plans, with out-of-town relatives. "He did not seem to understand that I was saying I had an unbreakable prior commitment. 'Just tell them you've changed your mind and you're coming with me,' he said, as though it would be the most natural thing in the world to want to have dinner with A. M. Rosenthal.

"I tried again to explain that I simply couldn't, but Abe wouldn't give up and kept insisting we come. His mood was also getting a little uglier (he had had a number of drinks but certainly wasn't drunk). The dinner itself had ceased to be of importance to him. Now it had become a contest of wills. It was only after my third or fourth refusal that he finally frosted over and stalked off. I could see the rejection he felt, but also his total inability to understand that he wasn't being rebuffed, that it wasn't personal."

Rosenthal reacted sharply as well when he felt he was not being treated with the respect due a person of his standing. During a trip to Texas in the 1970's he went to Scholtz Garten, the famed outdoor beer garden in Austin, and found himself at a table with some strange politicians and non-*Times* reporters. As a former *Times* correspondent stated:

> I can't remember who had invited them or even who they were, and I think a few of them were a little unclear about who we were. They knew we were from the *Times*, and that Abe was somebody important, and not precisely who. The whole thing was a little awkward.
>
> Somebody, trying to straighten things out, turned to Abe and said pleasantly, 'So you're an editor at *The New York Times*.'
>
> All conversation stopped. After several seconds of silence, Abe turned to the poor fellow and said, as if speaking to a half-wit, 'I . . . am . . . THE . . . editor . . . of . . . *The* . . . *New* . . . *York* . . . *Times*.'
>
> If looks could kill, that poor man would be dead.

Acting silly before a table of beer drinkers in Austin, Texas, surely causes no permanent harm to the reputation of *The New York Times*; Texans expect their journalists to behave oddly. But boorish behaviour at a Nieman Fellowship seminar at Harvard is another matter. The Niemans are working reporters and editors in their late twenties and early thirties, the best of their generation. Rosenthal thought little of the Nieman or any other fellowship, for he felt the *Times* was the best training grounds for *his* people. Since most fellowships require a leave of absence, Rosenthal discouraged applicants by saying, "Fine, go ahead, but you don't have a job here anymore."

Rosenthal showed his contempt for the Nieman program the evening of April 30, 1985, when he met with the 1985 group at Walter Lippmann House, near the Harvard campus. Howard Simons, the program director and a former managing editor of the Washington *Post*, presided. This particular program was designed to let the fellows have conversations of substance with the nation's foremost journalists.

Rosenthal got off to an unusual start during the buffet dinner by complaining about the cheapness of the wine. But the supposed poor quality did not prevent him from drinking many glasses. Things got much worse the next hours. According to Nieman fellow Mike Pride, editor of the Concord (N. H.) *Monitor*, "usually our guests made remarks, either off the cuff or prepared; then took questions. Rosenthal said only that he was glad to be there and it was our show. Of all the exchanges we had with guests in the Lippmann seminar room, and that spans perhaps 100 sessions, this was easily the least cordial. We had tough, adversarial sessions, but Rosenthal had not come to debate or discuss."

Early in the question-and-answer period, someone asked about the *Times*'s attitude towards its people applying for Niemans. "His answer wasn't even a non-denial denial; it was simply contradictory," Pride stated. Rosenthal at first denied such a ban existed, then he said, "We're going to change that." As Joel Kaplan of the Nashville *Tennessean* said, "The damage was done. He was answering questions like a goddamned politician who is lying to you."

The talk then turned to what Rosenthal called the " 'ah-ha' school of journalism," which he defined as reporters who take circumstantial happenings and "make them to be sinister." He gestured towards James Greenfield, the *Times* associate managing editor, who was with him, and he recited a hypothetical lead to illustrate the point: "James Greenfield, a close friend of *New York Times* executive editor A. M. Rosenthal, today was appointed deputy managing editor of the *Times*." An instance, Rosenthal said, of two true things being put together to produce an untruth; that the coupling suggests Greenfield got his job because of his friendship with Rosenthal.

As a true-life example, Rosenthal talked about an Associated Press story that said William Casey, the director of the Central Intelligence Agency, had access to economic and financial intelligence, yet continued to make personal investments. That kind of writing did not appear in *The New York Times*, Rosenthal said, and the reporter "who wrote that kind of thing" would never be hired by the *Times*.

"Give me *your* lead," suggested Joel Kaplan.

"I'm not a journalism teacher," Rosenthal snapped in reply.

Pride's overall impression of Rosenthal during this exchange was arrogance: "There is a lot of gray area here, as his own examples indicated, but to him it was black and white. Such questionable linkages might appear in shabby newspapers, but *never* in *The New York Times*.

The nastiest exchange of the evening began when Ed Chen of the *Los Angeles Times* asked Rosenthal if he had read a recent *New Republic* article by Fred Barnes saying *The New York Times* had become neo-conservative. Rosenthal said he had not read it, then he "flew into a tirade about how no one had called him, and how dare anyone venture an opinion of the *Times* without talking to him," Mike Pride recollected. Howard Simons sent for a copy of the article, and Rosenthal skimmed part of it, then returned to his previous theme. This guy never talked to me, he repeated, and we would never do a thing like this in *The New York Times* without talking to the head guy. This kind of journalism would never appear in *The New York Times*.

To the surprise of most persons in the room, Pride spoke up. The other fellows considered him the most mild-mannered member of their group, the unlikely person to challenge Rosenthal, especially given Rosenthal's visibly mounting temper. But Pride had heard enough.

"It occurred to me that what he was saying was absurd. I said to him, 'Hey, wait a minute, your newspaper runs play reviews, book reviews, without talking to the authors. You run political commentaries, opinion pieces, without talking to the principals. Although I haven't read the Barnes piece, it seems to me the *New Republic* is a journal of opinion and commentary. . . .

"I don't think I got all this out before he turned on me. His denunciation was loud and personal. 'Maybe that's the way *you* do it at *your* newspaper,' he said. 'Maybe *you* run that kind of story in *your* newspaper, but we *never* allow that kind of crap in *The New York Times*.'

"I tried to restate my question, but he shouted me down, so I just sat back, a little red-faced, and clammed up. . . . [T]here was a moment of uncomfortable silence before Howard Simons jumped in to cool things down and change the subject."

The evening broke up, and several fellows commiserated with

Pride. "I didn't see much reason to take Rosenthal seriously. He had no basis for criticizing me or my paper." Simons called the next day. "He said Abe had asked him to apologize to me. Howard said Rosenthal knew he had gotten out of hand and wanted me to know he was sorry I had borne the brunt of it. I thanked Howard and told him I wasn't losing any sleep over it.

"For me, the editor of a 21,000-circulation newspaper in the rock and ice of northern New England, this was a humorous outcome worth the moment of discomfort the night before. Here was the former managing editor of the Washington *Post* calling the editor of the Concord *Monitor* to apologize for the executive editor of *The New York Times* about an argument over an article neither of us had read." Pride, Kaplan and others wrote off Rosenthal's appearance as a failure. As Pride put it, "It was a performance rather than an honest discussion of *The New York Times*, journalism ethics, or any other issues of common interest to the group."

Such outbursts as the Nieman fellows experienced did incalculable damage to *The New York Times*. The group consisted of a coming generation of American journalists, the pool from which the *Times* had traditionally drawn to supplement its own training program. Even those persons not tempted by the prestige of working for the *Times* continue to be opinion leaders in their own newspapers and beyond.

Joel Kaplan was one of the persons approached by *Times* recruiters after his Nieman year. Although not quite thirty years of age, the *Tennessean* reporter had already won numerous awards for reporting on corruption in Tennessee state government. Kaplan definitely was a reporter ready to move to a more challenging arena than Nashville. John Finney of the Washington bureau asked for clips, and suggested he come up for a visit. Kaplan did; what he heard in Washington bore out what he had surmised on his own from Rosenthal's performance. He did not wish to work for Abe Rosenthal's *Times*. A few months later he took a job with the Chicago *Tribune*.

For persons no longer with the *Times*, such horror stories were circulated as journalistic curiosa, cumulative evidence that, whatever his professional brilliance, Abe Rosenthal lacked many of the qualities normally found in a decent human being. Those still with the paper, however, had to contend with yet another Rosenthal phenomenon— "Abe's Shitlist."

William Farrell, one of the more irreverent reporters ever to work for *The New York Times*, once had a splendid idea. That Rosenthal maintained a shitlist was an existential fact. People got on it for reasons petty and grand, and they stayed there until they either worked their way back into Rosenthal's good graces or they decided to work elsewhere. People on the shitlist suffered. One day they would be writing the stories that *ipso facto* commanded space and display in the paper. Then something would happen to put them upwind of Rosenthal, and they would find themselves studying the subway maps for the best way to ride upty-ump miles farther into Queens to cover something that might warrant two paragraphs in the inner reaches of the paper.

Bill Farrell was not an orderly man. By his own admission he spent more time in saloons than is recommended by any family physician, and a chaos of lost laundry and neglected hotel bills trailed in his wake when he travelled. But Farrell did not like to be poked in the ribs by uncertainties. And one thing that nagged him literally to the time of his death in late 1984 was that Rosenthal's shitlist was amorphous. Farrell's logic ran something as follows:

The *Times* newsroom is infested with sycophants and assorted nervous Nellies who spend more time trying to decipher the wildly swinging moods of Abe Rosenthal than they do in producing the world's greatest newspaper. Rosenthal would growl at a three o'clock meeting that he had it up to fucking-here with that fucking jerk so-and-so in Washington, and why does his fucking stuff still appear in the paper in such fucking shape. (Removing the F-word and its close associates from Rosenthal's vocabulary would significantly extend the life expectancy of his vocal cords.) Abe's functionaries would hear this remark, and for the next days so-and-so would disappear from the paper. The bad news would self-multiply as it spread through the newsroom, the victim often not knowing exactly what he had done to make himself a pariah.

Then, just as suddenly and capriciously, Rosenthal would restore the poor fellow to grace. "Where's so-and-so been the last couple of months? I used to think he did a good job with Q Heads on Congress. Why the fuck isn't he in the fucking paper more fucking often? If you fuckers put him on special assignment, you fucking well should have told me." And so-and-so would find himself hoisted back into the paper without a semblance of an explanation.

Having endured several stays on the shitlist himself, some of them directly related to adventures involving John Barleycorn, Bill Farrell had an idea. The shitlist, he loved to tell his friends, should be updated daily, in writing, and posted prominently on one of the pillars in the newsroom at 43d Street. Farrell's reasoning was that a public announcement would end the is-he/isn't-he paranoia that panicked Abe's underlings. Changes in the ratings would indicate whether a person was rising or falling in Rosenthal's estimate. "Hey, old Jonesy was in the twenties yesterday, and this morning he's all the way up to number seven. Boy, he's going fast; at this rate he'll be off the staff by the weekend. . . ." Similarly, Farrell would have periodic "erasure ceremonies," so that editors would know when it was safe to treat an underling with decency again.

Farrell, alas, died before he did anything more concrete about his plan than talk about it in bull sessions at Sardi's, Gough's and elsewhere. But behind his black humor was the fact that Rosenthal frequently made career-threatening decisions about a person's work capriciously and without bothering to seek an explanation as to why something was done a certain way.

—One bitterly cold day a city reporter wore a ski cap to work. Rosenthal thought the cap undignified, and he snarled something nasty to a subordinate editor. For two years the man was not given an assignment that permitted him to leave the newsroom. No one around Rosenthal would take responsibility for challenging what they obviously considered to be an order.

—In the 1960's reporter Joseph Lelyveld had a string of front-page and first-front stories about racial violence in New Jersey. After the first edition deadline one night he telephoned insert material which he, as the reporter on the scene, felt should be worked into the earlier story. The editor handling the story disagreed, and Lelyveld made the mistake of arguing too long. He received the dread news: "You're now on Abe's shitlist, and you're going to stay there a while." Lelyveld felt no guilt, for such editor-reporter arguments occur perhaps a dozen times daily on any city desk in the land. Lacking any appeal, he set out the next day to cover a classic shitlist assignment, a Quaker anti-war demonstration. By happenstance, construction workers broke up the march, and the non-assignment turned out to be a front-page story. Lelyveld breathed a small sigh of relief; the near-miss taught him to keep his arguments without bounds.

—A news clerk innocently stopped Rosenthal in the newsroom one day and asked him a casual question about something in the news.

The youth did not realize that underlings approach Rosenthal by invitation only, and that he is not fair game for interruptions by anyone who happens to catch his arm or his eye. Rosenthal glowered and said, "Why bother me with that?" The clerk stammered, "Because you are managing editor, I thought you . . ." Rosenthal cut him off with a shout. "I'm the *executive* editor, not the *managing* editor, and you are too stupid to be on this paper." This particular clerk's tenure on the shitlist was brief; he left the *Times* that very day.

Other habitués of the list, arrived there by more involved routes. One reporter who came to view her contests with Rosenthal as an ongoing war of wits was Molly Ivins, who was in and out of his graces so often during her brief stay on the paper that "I thought about having little stickers printed up with my name on them so that it'd be easier for the editors to either paste me on or pull me off." Although Rosenthal was initially suspicious of Ivins because of her editorship of the left-wing Texas *Observer*, their first substantive contacts went well. But there were continuous cultural and other clashes. Ivins's speech sounds like a rough-draft of country-western music lyrics that you wouldn't play during the young'uns' listening hours. She loves laughing at herself and anyone else in range. She does not take to supervision. At the Texas *Observer*, she answered to no one directly and to absentee publisher Ronnie Dugger only distantly. "I was not trained according to the sacred canons of *New York Times* objectivity. But hell, honey, I'm a professional writer—I can slice your baloney any way you want it sliced, just tell me. I can write *New York Times* prose as dull as any kiddie on the block. But I admit I prefer to tell readers what happened and why."

Ivins' career began nicely. She worked on the metropolitan desk briefly, "long enough to prove I'm not a wild-eyed Commie," and then national editor David Jones, an admirer, picked her up for the Rocky Mountain bureau, based in Denver and responsible for nine states that cover all that blank space on maps. The distances involved in her beat were an enormity many New York editors never seemed to grasp. "I got tired of explaining from Carlsbad, New Mexico, that yes, I know Bismarck, South Dakota, is in my territory, but since it's now eight in the morning, I just might have trouble getting up there by noon to cover a story."

But Ivins's irrepressible spirit eventually got her into fatal trouble. It started at a chicken festival in a small town in New Mexico. "Everyone in this little place seemed to be a commercial chicken grower, so they put together their own festival. They get together and kill and pluck and dress the chickens, and listen to music and drink beer and have all sorts of fun. It's sort of a chicken version of the old-timey barn raising."

When Ivins dictated a story to New York she could not resent calling the event a "gang pluck," a phrase she never expected to see in the *Times*. "I used to have fun with the editors on the national desk. I'd throw in one of these fun-lines, and they'd get a chuckle before they took them out." Unfortunately for Ivins, this line was so good that although it did not get into print, it was laughed about around the newsroom, and eventually came to Rosenthal's attention. Rosenthal was not amused in the least. "I was abruptly recalled, told to report to New York for reassignment *immediately*. So I go dragging back to New York; I'm no longer to be working in the mountains."

Ivins sighed and told David Jones she might as well quit for she did not think she could survive a permanent transplant to New York. "Hell, you ask for chicken-fried steak in that town, and they point you to the nearest Colonel Sanders."

Rosenthal called her into his office. "He talked nice—for about forty-five seconds. He appreciated how hard I had worked for the *Times*, all that territory I had covered in the west. I knew he was getting ready to snap my butt, so I just smiled and said 'Thank you,' real nice like."

Rosenthal continued, "But the problem you have, Molly, is your tendency to stick your thumb in the eye of *The New York Times*."

"Abe, this is not true," Ivins protested. She said she did not "try to flout the traditions of the *Times*," but sometimes she honestly did not know the acceptable limits. She reminded him of what he said during her hiring interview, that he wanted vivid, descriptive writing in the paper, and especially from national staff reporters who were attempting to explain their territories to a wide audience. Time and again, Ivins said, she felt that insensitive editors had cut good lines from her stories.

An example, Rosenthal demanded, give me an example.

"This didn't require much of a head-scratchin' on my part. I told him about writing about this old Western boy who 'has a beer gut that belongs in the Smithsonian.' An editor changed that one to a 'man with a protuberant abdomen.'"

Rosenthal, however, had more important issues on his mind than descriptions of beer bellies. "But you wrote this story about the chicken slaughter," he said.

"That I did, Abe."

"You called it a 'gang pluck,' " Rosenthal said. He paused, and he repeated the words. "A gang pluck."

"Yes, I did, Abe. I thought it was a good line, you know, a play on words."

Rosenthal's face darkened. "You, Molly, were trying to make the readers of *The New York Times* think of the words 'gang fuck.' "

Ivins shook her head in mock exasperation. "Damn, Abe," she said, "you're a hard man to fool."

She had to leave his office in a hurry, for by now Rosenthal was spluttering with rage. "He said some things that compare unfavorably with 'gang pluck' but as a delicate Southern maiden I dare not repeat them in the presence of a man lest my blush spoil my complexion permanently and make you think dirt of me." She could continue working at the *Times*, but only on the metropolitan desk, and she had best mind her manners—and her language.

Ivins sort of liked the *Times*; to her it contained the most fascinating montage of psychopaths, confidence men, sycophants, neurotics and some decent people that she had seen since she covered the Texas Legislature. Besides, she wanted the job, even though she realized she was now at perhaps the very top of the infamous Abe Rosenthal shit list. "The problem is that I am congenitally irreverent, incurable. Best doctors in the land have treated me; gave up on me, to a man. I'm classic. Abe, unfortunately, does not like irreverence at all, especially when directed at *The New York Times*. This is like putting a whoopie cushion under the Pope at a High Mass. But there's nothing I can—or care to—do about my condition. I like Molly the way she is."

Colleagues told her not to despair. "Stick with it," she was told. "You'll work you way off the shitlist. Dozens of people here have come back to favor."

Ivins wasn't sure she wished to make the effort. She was thirty-seven years old. "I didn't have that much time left in my life that I wanted to spend it miserably for reasons that are crazy to begin with." She was assigned to City Hall. She wrote stories, she sent them to 43rd Street, few appeared in print. Clyde Haberman, another City Hall reporter, commiserated with her. He also had fallen afoul of

Rosenthal while a stringer at City College of New York. Retyping a seemingly endless list of commencement prize winners he inserted a spoof:

BRETT AWARD to the student who has worked hardest under a great handicap—Jake Barnes.

Haberman thought the line was funny and that anyone who read it would get a chuckle out of his reference to the Hemingway character. Rosenthal awoke him with a phone call the next morning and under questioning Haberman admitted to a "moment of silliness." Rosenthal replied, "Well, that moment finished you in newspapers." He let Haberman resign as an alternative to being fired. Not until almost three years later did Rosenthal relent and let Haberman return.*

Now Ivins and Haberman talked about *her* problem, and what she could do to win her way off the shitlist. For one glorious day they laughed about this wonderful idea. When they wrote stories that evening, Ivins would sign Haberman's copy, and he would do the same with hers. The "Haberman" articles would appear, while Ivins's would be spiked. Both reporters had the essential sobering thought at about the same time. Haberman had already suffered for one prank and been forgiven. To be caught in another one, and with Molly Ivins as an accomplice . . . well, perhaps the idea wasn't that jolly after all.

Once the word circulated at the *Times* that Ivins was in Rosenthal's disfavor, she found any number of editors almost reflexively hostile to her and her work. She came to realize that fear of Rosenthal—and even worse, *anticipation* of Rosenthal—was omnipresent, and self-expansive. She used an analogy. The news is a football field, and Rosenthal orders that the news—the game—be played without anyone encroaching into the end zone. "The first editor down the line says, 'All right, just to make sure nobody wanders into the end zone by accident, I'm setting my own limit at the ten-yard line.' The next guy says, 'I'll keep it within the twenty-yard line.' And so forth. But

---

*Gay Talese gives a lengthy account of the Haberman story in his *The Kingdom and the Power*, casting it as an example of Rosenthal's determination not to permit "tampering" with the news columns. Such harsh discipline was necessary lest other reporters be similarly tempted, Rosenthal said. Several persons at the *Times* suggest that Talese's account, although sympathetic to Rosenthal's position, led the editor to decide he had overreacted, and for that reason he brought Haberman back.

shit, honey, at the working level, you're moving around the fifty-yard line and no place else. This drives you crazy."

Ivins made one last try. She did extensive research on a self-initiated series on poverty in the city. "I realized that either me or the *Times* was out of touch with reality when the *Times* ran a 1,200 word piece at the top of a page announcing that place cards were now 'in' for formal dinner parties and that hostesses could use either the old-fashioned holders or some of the new glamor stuff. Whew! A golden island in the sea of misery, and the *Times* gives *its* attention to the island."

So she wrote the articles on poverty, and passed them along to Peter Millones, the metropolitan editor. Ivins deliberately did not write in traditional *Times* style. "This didn't have all the *Times*-sort of quotes from the ranking sociologists and the government whoop-de-doos and that sort of thing; it was about poor people." Millones came to Ivins shaking his head. "This is fascinating stuff, Molly," he said, "but I don't know what to do with it."

"How about printing it in the goddamned paper?" Ivins snapped. ("My typical smart-ass answer, but spoken from the heart.")

The series did not run. Ivins instead was asked to do one of the "neighborhood" pieces by which the *Times* finds nice things to say about almost every conceivable area of the city. (To some *Times* reporters, the "neighborhooders" are known as "diamonds in the dung heap.") Ivins drew the line. "I didn't give a shit about a New York neighborhood as seen by *The New York Times*. I was tired, was ready to leave, and I left."

Rosenthal did not bid her farewell. Indeed, he never spoke to her from the time of the "gang pluck" interview. Ivins now writes a column for the Dallas *Times-Herald* from Austin, and she is one of the most widely-read commentators in a large state. Although she left the *Times* with a sour taste in her mouth, she retains a semblance of admiration for Abe Rosenthal, if not for the system that he engendered at the *Times*. "Abe Rosenthal admires good writers, I really think he does. But the *Times* system beats the good writing out of you. I felt like a horse trapped in a stall with somebody, an editor, hanging over the sides saying to me, 'I can hear you kicking in there, and we're not going to let you out until you stop kicking.'" Molly Ivins now does her kicking—and it is good kicking—for a more pleasurable newspaper.

Abe Rosenthal and friends can explain away a Molly Ivins as a journalistic odd-ball, a flip-talking, flip-writing Texan whose particular (and often peculiar) talents cried out for a more permissive outlet than *The New York Times*. Would, say, Flora Lewis and Dolly Parton charm the same dinner party? Ivins came to be a sore point with Abe Rosenthal, and for a time he matched her bad-mouth for bad-mouth. Vulgar. A reporter who created quotations. "All the people in her stories talked alike." A left winger whose politics finally got the best of her, so that she wrote excessively about the supposed looting of the environment of the West. And, finally, a reporter who was not *fair*. To Abe Rosenthal, that fault was the ultimate condemnation.

The downside of Rosenthal's shunning of Ivins as an oddity is the fact that he did even worse to a man he once considered a personal and professional friend. Sidney Zion, as noted earlier, created an innovative legal beat for Rosenthal in 1964-65, and wrote well for the *Times* through 1969. Rosenthal loved Zion's wit and wise-guy knowledge of New York, the sense of the street he had never developed as an editor. They drank much Scotch together at Sardi's, and Rosenthal chose Zion as a confidant on many personal matters, including his deteriorating marriage and his increasing interest in other women. Rosenthal was not discreet but he did recognize Zion as a non-threatening repository for his private thoughts. Zion was the rare foil for Rosenthal, the sort of friend who would listen to the other man's problems—or preachings—for a decent period, then be able to say, "Hey, jeeez, Abe, that's damned interesting, but let me tell you about this." Zion was one of many people in New York who came to doubt that Abe Rosenthal could ever have true friends, in the sense of an equal-give/equal-take relationship.

Appropriately, Zion's initial break with the *Times* came through circumstances over which Rosenthal had no control—and, indeed, in which Rosenthal argued his reporter's case. After scandals forced Justice Abe Fortas to resign from the U.S. Supreme Court, Rosenthal and Arthur Gelb assigned Zion to search for improprieties elsewhere in the federal judiciary. The Fortas story, broken by Bill Lambert of *Life Magazine*, left the *Times* scrambling to catch up; much of what it wrote about the case was lifted from other publications. As Zion was to note later in *Scanlan's Monthly*, "This may not have been well known to the general public, but it was the raging snicker among newsmen . . . and since papers are edited for other editors, the *Times* was more than a little embarrassed."

Zion spent many weeks tracing instances of judicial bias by U.S.

District Judge Henry J. Friendly. Zion realized he might have problems getting the story into print, for Friendly had intimate ties with the *Times*. Louis Loeb, for four decades the paper's counsel, was one of his closest personal friends. James Reston, then the executive editor, had described Friendly in a column as "the most respected judge in the lower federal courts."

Look, Zion told Gelb and Rosenthal, I don't want to bust my butt for a story that might be killed for "policy reasons." Forget that sort of stuff, they said; write the story and we'll print it.

Zion wrote the story, Rosenthal and Gelb approved it, and James Reston killed it, flat. Zion went in to argue his case with Reston. Look, he said, this guy is being talked about as a Supreme Court justice. What would we do with the story if he's nominated?

"Print it, of course," Reston said.

"Why then and not now?" Zion asked.

"Because it would then be up to the Senate and it would become our responsibility to print it," Reston said.

Reston's logic left Zion scratching his head. There were other fits and starts about the story but the bottom line was that it never got into print. Zion by this time had had enough of *Times* journalism, and he left to join rogue journalist Warren Hinckel in launching a new magazine called *Scanlan's Monthly*. Circumstantial evidence suggests Rosenthal realized Zion was a crusader who needed looser editorial reins than the *Times* permitted, and hence he did not argue seriously about his decision to leave. (Gelb and Rosenthal, however, for years went through a ritual of periodically asking Zion why he *really* left, and telling him that had he stayed, he would be covering the Supreme Court.) The important point is that both men continued to consider Zion a friend, a drinking buddy with whom they shared gossip and laughs at the Sardi's bar.

Zion left the *Times* in November 1969 and did *Scanlan's* and freelance work. The afternoon of June 15, 1971, he went to the *Times* to read old clips for background material for a story on crime he was writing for the *Times Magazine*. While he was there the *Times* received word that U.S. District Judge Murray Gurfein had enjoined the paper from continuing publication of the Pentagon Papers, which had begun two days earlier. Zion joined a group of reporters in banter as to where reporter Neil Sheehan got the papers. Someone suggested that not even Rosenthal knew. Zion disagreed; Rosenthal would never run such a story without knowing its source. "I thought Abe looked a little smug today and he should be smug. He knows something I don't know and I consider that an outrage, it's intolerable. I'll find out and I'll tell you all tomorrow." His boast having been made, Zion laughed along with everyone and went home.

That evening he began calling friends in the peace movement. He established early that the source of the leak was known to these persons; although they would not tell him on their own, they would confirm it if Zion found the identity on his own. The next morning someone in Washington told Zion the list of names of persons the Washington *Post* had established had access to the Pentagon Papers. Zion realized the leaker would not be someone of prominence, such as former Defense Secretary Clark Clifford or Nicholas Katzenbach, the former under secretary of state. No, the leaker would be a working-level bureaucrat. Zion began running the secondary names on the list past his "confirmers," and sure enough, three of them told them that Daniel Ellsberg was the man.

Zion recognized he had a major news story on his hands. He tried repeatedly to call Ellsberg, but got only an answering service operator, who confided that *Time, Newsweek*, the St. Louis *Post-Dispatch*, "everybody keeps calling." Zion tried to market his story in London, but since he could not name his source editors there feared libel. Finally, in desperation, Zion called radio broadcaster Barry Gray, who ran a late-night radio talk show, and told him what he had. Be here in twenty minutes, Gray said; I'm bringing in the press as well.

A group of reporters watched through a glass window as Zion revealed Ellsberg's name over the air. When the broadcast ended, *Times* reporter Murray Schumach came over to Zion and said, coldly, "Arthur Gelb asked me to tell you that you are never to enter *The New York Times* again."

"Well," Zion said, "you tell Gelb for me that I don't give a damn, as long as his writ doesn't run to Sardi's bar."

Next commenced personal abuse that left Zion stunned, hurt. Jack Newfield of the *Village Voice*, whom he had known for years, called to denounce him as a "rat bastard" and a "criminal." Peter Hamill used his New York *Post* column to denounce Zion as a "shyster lawyer" and "scrummy." The press questioned Zion's motives until he exclaimed,

"What the hell are you doing? Since when does one reporter ask another his motive in writing a legitimate news story? Come on, the St.
Louis *Post-Dispatch* published its own story the same night; why not
jump their ass?" Slowly the truth dawned on Zion:

> What bedeviled the press was the fact that I wasn't working for a paper
> or a TV station. I don't know how much of it was conscious, but the
> clear-cut feeling was that you don't go around breaking stories unless
> you've got a job.

That Zion indeed was on Rosenthal's shitlist came clear within
hours. *The New York Times Magazine* sent word that "under the circumstances" his assigned article on crime would not be published.
Two months earlier, Zion had reviewed Stephen Birmingham's *The
Grandees*, on rich Sephardic Jews in America for the *Sunday Times*.
The review drew much mail, and Sunday book editor John Leonard
told him over drinks, "Our pages are open to you anytime you want."
The day after the Ellsberg disclosure, Leonard told his staff, "Zion
will never write for us again." Nor did he, as long as Leonard served
as book editor. When Zion went into Sardi's, *Times* people dining
there studiously examined their plates, avoiding eye contact; none
wished to be seen acknowledging a pariah. Gerry Walker, one of the
editors of the *Times Magazine*, was bold enough to take Zion aside for
a private alert. "I now know what the Salem witch hunt was about,"
Walker said. "The whole paper is going nuts over this, the elevators
are buzzing. I'm sorry to tell you this, I think it's a disgrace, but I
thought you ought to be forewarned."

What especially hurt Zion was that the blacklist order came from
men he considered his friends. The prime mover, he felt, was
Rosenthal, so at first he did not take the ban seriously. "Abe is an
emotional man," Zion was to write later, "he gets mad on the spot,
but he's ultimately reasonable and is possessed of a good and sweet
character." But not for months was Rosenthal to change his mind. In
the interim, Zion suffered. The *Village Voice* and *New York* Magazine
declined his request to print his side of the dispute; ultimately Jim
Brady of *Women's Wear Daily* bought (for $300) an article in which
Zion struck back at his critics. "The *Times* has treated me to lectures
on morals and ethics, which is like learning about love from Attila the
Hun." Zion suffered financially. To keep up appearances, he bor-

rowed money. He took a $10,000 advance to write a book on the *Times* (and told people it was $50,000; again, appearances). A smart friend counseled him to let this project slide. He had "bumped into *The New York Times*," just as some persons bump into history; once the emotional heat had died, he would be back. But "if you write this book . . . if you go after them that way, they'll never forgive you. Then you'll be dead, then you'll have to go back to law or whatever you come up with. And you'll be unhappy the rest of your life."

Zion did as advised; he abandoned the project. He struggled, but he survived, and after a year Rosenthal grabbed his arm as he walked past the Sardi's bar and said "*Genug*," the Yiddish word for enough. Zion ordered a drink and he and Rosenthal clinked glasses. "I forgive you," Rosenthal said, and Zion put down his glass and began to walk away. Rosenthal pulled him back. "You tried to drive *me* out of journalism. Now you forgive *me*?" Zion asked.

"Are you asking me to apologize?" Rosenthal asked. No, Zion said, "I just want to get out of here." Rosenthal pulled him back to the bar, and he confessed what Zion had felt for months: had Zion written *for a newspaper* that Ellsberg was the source of the Pentagon Papers, "nobody would have objected, they'd have given you prizes." Rosenthal said that he realized he was wrong when he read Zion's article in *Women's Wear Daily*. As Zion wrote years later: "I thought to myself, What took you so long to tell me this? But I stifled myself. It was time to leave well enough alone. What took me so long to get that?" Rosenthal formally took Zion off the shitlist by sending word to editors of the magazine, the book review and the Week in Review that he no longer objected to him writing for them, and in fact suggesting that he be given assignments. But because these departments remained under Sunday editor Max Frankel, the word from Rosenthal did not suffice. Zion's financial and professional struggle was to continue for several more years. As late as 1978, in fact—seven years after the Ellsberg story—Zion visited Egypt with a group of American Jewish leaders to interview President Anwar el-Sadat. A wire service sent a picture of the group to New York; Zion was standing in the middle. A picture editor took it to Rosenthal. Was it OK for him to run it, or was Zion still on the shitlist? "Let him in the paper," Rosenthal said.

Yet the bottom-line remained that Rosenthal's unjustified rage at a friend effectively cost Zion seven productive years of his life.

And ironically, concurrent with this injustice, Rosenthal was conducting a major campaign to convince both his staff and the general public that *The New York Times* intended to handle the news fairly, and to acknowledge mistakes and to correct them in print. Here again a well-meaning idea went astray because of Rosenthal's mercurial nature, and what could have been a true journalistic innovation succeeded only in causing more embarrassment for *The New York Times*.

FIFTEEN

"Violated the *Times*'s Standards of Fairness"

Speaking to the American Society of Newspaper Editors in 1983, A. M. Rosenthal told of the origins of a unique *New York Times* news feature. "The other day I walked in the office smoking from the ears," he said. "There was something in the paper that bothered me very, very much. We had a little story about the book publishing world. The headline was unfair, the story was unbalanced, and so on.

"I approached a couple of cultural editors, prepared to have a heart-to-heart conversation. I found they shared my feeling. They thought the story was lousy, the headline was lousy, and that we had done an injustice to the book publishers. So I said, 'We all dislike something that took place in this paper and we don't tell anybody.'

"They asked what we could do. I said, 'Well, we will start a new department in which we will report those things to the reader which disturb us.'

"We already run corrections, as most papers do. We run them fairly prominently. But this was to go beyond corrections. We all know there are some stories that bother us terribly—unfair headlines, distortion, artful juxtaposition in the lead, everything true but the totality. . . .

"So, I said, 'Let's start a new policy now. We will tell the reader when we feel we have done something that bothers us. It may not bother them, but it bothers us.' They said, 'Okay, when do we start?' I said, 'Tomorrow morning.' 'No meetings, no committee?' one asked. I said, 'No, because this obviously has been cooking in me for some time.' "

The initial "Editors' Note" ran in the index section at the bottom of the metropolitan page, with the italicized explanation of purpose: "Under this heading, the *Times* amplifies or rectifies what the editors consider significant lapses of fairness, balance, or perspective. Corrections, also on this page, continue to deal with factual errors." The first note set the record straight about the publishing story that had offended Rosenthal; to his surprise, "it was greeted with enormous silence. Nobody saw it, apparently, not even the staff." So he sent a memo to department editors telling them they were responsible for such notes about unfair stories which they originated. "I didn't get any response from that so I sent out a nastier note."

The next published note, on April 22, 1983, definitely caught the attention of both the staff and the public—and led to the first of what came to be recurring charges that Rosenthal used the column to chastise persons (including his own staff) who used the *Times* to criticize his friends. The item in question was a review by Frank J. Prial of the cultural staff concerning a segment of "Inside Story," public television's weekly critique of broadcast and print journalism, that dealt with the controversial CBS report, "The Uncounted Enemy: A Vietnam Deception." The central figure in the CBS program, General William Westmoreland, former commander of U.S. forces in Vietnam, was suing the network for libel. Rosenthal had severe problems both with the PBS production narrated by Hodding Carter, Jr., and the prominence given the review, and the Editors' Note said so, and directly:

> The debate over CBS's documentary has long since been detailed in the *Times*. And yesterday's *Times* article quoted Mr. Carter as saying that "Inside Story" had turned up no new information about military operations in Vietnam—only a "lot of old information that was not included in CBS's documentary."
>
> Nothing in the *Times*' account suggested that the criticism of CBS by "Inside Story" was fresh, substantive or otherwise newsworthy.

Nevertheless the *Times* devoted some 700 words to "Inside Story" displayed across six columns at the top of a page. By its length, the *Times* article seemed to imply that the criticisms of CBS were fresh or newly substantiated.

By the *Times'* standards of new judgment and fairness, the article was too long and too prominently displayed.

Oddly, Rosenthal wrote the Editors' Note without even taking the time to view the PBS show, a video tape of which was available in the *Times's* cultural department. Several editors suggested that he do so before rendering such a harsh judgment on the Prial review. He refused. Hodding Carter angrily suggested that Rosenthal's friendship with Mike Wallace, who did the questioned CBS documentary, led to the correction, a charge heatedly denied by both Wallace and Rosenthal.

"Had the *Times* story been too long?" *Time* magazine's press critic Thomas Griffith asked. "Over on the food page, critic Craig Claiborne often gets as much space to describe the place and circumstances where he discovered a fish sauce. Was there nothing new in Hodding Carter's critique? It added about as much, or as little, to public knowledge as had the original Westmoreland broadcast." Journalists suddenly were astir at the sight of a newspaper taking a rare step in the direction of self-criticism.

To Rosenthal, the surprising lesson of the reaction was that "candor is very hard to accept, particularly in our own business," and he repeated his belief that the Prial review was not right "simply because it didn't tell anything new. It was journalism by water torture—you have the same story repeated over and over again, get one new fact, and everything else is background.

"That's okay when you are dealing with asparagus cooking or something. But when somebody is the target, to have the same story repeated over and over again with one new paragraph, I always felt that was unfair."

So the Editors' Note became an accepted feature of the *Times*, albeit a sporadic one. No formal policy established when one should be run; such was left to the whim of Rosenthal or an editor who felt so moved. One note, for instance, apologized for the *Times's* failure to run a story about an ethnic day parade. "There are lots of parades in New York. We have a new assistant city editor. He decided, the hell with it, he wouldn't run this one. Hundreds of thousands of people saw it, hundreds participated in it, millions saw it on TV. The phone rang all day long . . . I just picked up the phone and said, 'You are right,' and hung up.

"The next day we said we should have printed it."

Yet regardless of whatever good intentions Rosenthal had at the outset, the Editors' Note degenerated into something of a journalistic joke, with the "intended correction" often causing more embarrassment to the subject than the original item. The style of the Editors' Note is highly susceptible to parody. Henry Kissinger, for instance, felt a spoofing item in the Briefing column on the Washington Talk page in December, 1984, offended his dignity. He called Rosenthal, and then sent a protesting letter, setting out his version of what actually happened at the dinner marking the seventieth anniversary of the *New Republic*. The *Times*'s apology to Kissinger read:

> The report said that the audience included many liberal politicians and journalists and that Mr. Kissinger, as if to demonstrate what he had in common with them, introduced himself as a "member of an extinct species," a Rockefeller Republican.
>
> The report recalled that Mr. Kissinger, while a Harvard professor in the 1960's, was hired as a foreign affairs consultant by Nelson A. Rockefeller, and that when he accompanied Governor Rockefeller to the 1968 Republican National Convention in Miami, he took with him dozens of cardboard boxes full of foreign affairs position papers. Finally, the report noted that Mr. Rockefeller lost the nomination to Richard M. Nixon and that in time Mr. Kissinger went to work for Mr. Nixon.
>
> In two respects, the dinner quotation lacked necessary context.
>
> First, because the *Times*'s notes were incomplete, it failed to recall that Mr. Kissinger, rather than having sought to reassure his audience, said at one point, "Let's face it. This is not my normal constituency. This evening has been traumatic for me. I have been photographed with so many liberals, my semi-annual visits to the White House will now be even less frequent."
>
> Second, the report should have acknowledged that intra-party job shifts are common in politics—particularly in foreign affairs—when there is a common ideological ground, as in the case of Mr. Rockefeller and Mr. Nixon.

Thus did the *Times* state some obvious truths about politics—surely ones known to anyone with enough interest in the subject to be browsing on the Washington Talk page—just to soothe the ruffled ego of Kissinger. (Kissinger by reliable account did not like the omission of his prized title "Dr." in the note, but he heeded a friend's suggestion that he pursue the matter no further.) Three public relations specialists were asked separately whether they thought Kissinger gained or lost from the note; they were unanimous in stating he made himself ridiculous by focusing attention on an innocuous item.

Another powerful figure who felt offended by the *Times*, and who was annointed by an apologetic Editor's Note, was the real estate mogul Mortimer B. Zuckerman, whose company in July, 1985, paid $456.1 million for one of the most valuable pieces of Manhattan real estate existent, the New York Coliseum on Columbus Circle. John Vinocur, who had just returned from Bonn to become deputy metropolitan editor, decided the city needed to know more about the 48-year-old tycoon, and he assigned Jane Perlez to explore the roots of his fortune and explain how he suddenly became prominent not only as a developer but as owner of *The Atlantic Monthly* and *U. S. News & World Report.*

Perlez is a diligent reporter but she had trouble with the Zuckerman article from the start. He insisted that she spend much time with his partner, which she did. When he told her she must visit his major developments to get a grasp of what he did, she went on the road. But after all this groundwork Perlez received only a perfunctory interview. Vinocur did not like the first draft. "Turn up the throttle," he said, "make it stronger." Perlez found that many Zuckerman critics were unwilling to speak for attribution; with Vinocur's approval, she used quotations anyway, although she knew Rosenthal frowned on such a practice. Vinocur did the final editing.

On Saturday night, August 3, Rosenthal was in the Hamptons with his good friend Shirley Lord, and they dined with Zuckerman and his then-companion, the writer Gloria Steinem. Rosenthal had met Steinem in India in the 1950's when he reported there for the *Times*, and she came through New Delhi as a student. Zuckerman apparently charmed Rosenthal. He, too, is a native of Canada, and they joked about "two Canucks making it in the United States." Rosenthal told a friend the next day, "Mort is quite a guy, he has ideas and he knows how to get what he wants."

On Monday, August 5, Perlez's article ran on the metropolitan page under the headline: "Mortimer Zuckerman: a Developer Who Thrives on High-Stakes Dealing." Perlez recounted some of the hassles Zuckerman had encountered in Boston and elsewhere, and called him a "man of great ambition whose desire is to be everywhere," and who "seems always to be looking for more."

Rosenthal came into the *Times* at ten o'clock that morning quivering with anger, and in a sharp voice he ordered Millones and Vinocur into his office. He closed the door, and he berated them at length. By the account the two sobered editors gave other *Times* reporters later, "He chewed them two new assholes. He ordered Millones to start writing an Editors' Note." Later that day he established to his satisfaction that Vinocur was the villain, and he called him for yet a second lecture. Rosenthal did some revisions on Millones' note and ordered it printed. The note was tantamount to an assault on Perlez's professionalism.

> . . . Through opinionated phrases and unattributed characterizations, the article established a tone that cast its subject in an unfavorable light.
>
> Describing Mr. Zuckerman's real estate acquisitions, the article uses the phrase "more than five years of plotting." It said he had befriended people "in an effort to win a place in their world." His latest major purchase . . . "does not sate him." When he was young, he went to work for a private firm . . . "instead of taking a public policy job."
>
> Without naming sources of criticism, the article described Mr. Zuckerman's "architectural taste" pejoratively. It attributed to "friends"—unnamed—a statement that he "seems always to be looking for more." And it allowed one person, "who declined to be named," to question Mr. Zuckerman's truthfulness about the purchase price of *U. S. News & World Report.*
>
> The article violated the *Times*'s standards of fairness. The paper's policy is to avoid such opinionated wording in its news columns, and to omit personal criticism by sources who insist upon anonymity. The pejorative phrases and anonymous criticism created an unbalanced portrait. They should not have appeared.

Perlez took the rebuke hard, and especially because she had followed Vinocur's direct order to "turn up the throttle." Yet hers was the byline that appeared on the article, and hence she felt she had been singled out for unjustified criticism. Several friends told her she should quit the paper in protest. "What would that accomplish?" she asked. "Why give up a career just because they are unprintables?" (The episode did no immediate damage to her career, her hurt feelings aside. She spent much of the rest of 1985 reporting from upstate

New York, and in the spring of 1986 Rosenthal assigned her to cover New York City schools with a direct order to strengthen the beat.)

Soon after the Zuckerman matter Edwin Diamond, the media critic for *New York* Magazine, had a researcher do a systematic study of the Editors' Notes. As he expected, the anonymous citizen brushed by the majesty of the *Times* had little chance of solace. Diamond wrote, ". . . [A]n analysis of 105 Editors' Notes over the last two and a half years shows next to nothing about the Blatzes of the world, while Kissinger has benefitted from two Notes. The parties who get two or three paragraphs of an Editors' Note are almost always public officials, influential people, or institutions. Once in fifty times an ordinary party appears—for example, a high-school coach said to have been unfairly characterized."

Through periodic broadsides to his staff, and speeches to journalistic lodge meetings, Rosenthal has spoken so often of his ambition to keep the *Times* "fair" that he is obviously sincere about it. As he wrote to his department heads in September, 1984, "Everyone of us agrees that the most important thing in our professional lives is to keep the *Times* straight and clean."

The Editors' Note feature, flawed though it might be, goes a significant step beyond the corrective mechanisms found in the majority of American newspapers. But it essentially provides fairness by whim—it is the *Times*, and not impartial outsiders, that determines whether a citizen or an institution has been mistreated. And here lies the crux of the fairness issue for the American press. What recourse does the offended person have other than suing an editor for libel, or visiting him with a horsewhip? Little.

Someone in the newsroom once asked Rosenthal how he edited the paper, and without hesitation he replied, "With my stomach," which is a pretty good answer. "When you read a story that has a knife in it, that has an unfair twist, it makes you uneasy to read it." He gives new reporters a lecture. Take out the name of the person you are writing about, and substitute your own. The story might hurt—but is it fair, and free of innuendo? "If you can't read it with that conclusion, don't do it that way."

Rosenthal's ongoing campaign during his last decade as executive editor was to curb the use of unnamed sources in the paper. Here he draws a distinction between the use of unnamed sources for hard news and the use of unnamed persons who wish to denounce other people. As he stated in a staff memo, "Obviously, this is not a rule that can be applied one hundred percent. We would hardly expect a Chinese peasant or a Russian worker to state his middle initial when criticizing his government." He continued:

> But when reporting in this country, there is hardly ever a reason to give somebody who attacks another person or an institution the cloak of anonymity. Yes, this does make reporting more difficult. This means that sometimes nice juicy quotes cannot be used, or that we have to work harder to get at reality.

Tom Goldstein, who covered legal matters and the courts for the *Times* in the 1970's, considered the doctrine fair but unduly limiting, and in a manner that denies the reader full information in instances "when a public official really is monstrous . . . and those in a position to criticize him intelligently are unwilling to do so on the record. In writing profiles of judges, for example, I found myself constantly hamstrung. Few colleagues wished to incur the wrath of a judge they privately felt wanting. . . ." Similarly, lawyers are not going to say bad things about jurists who will be hearing their cases. Rosenthal's enforcement of the rule seems uneven. For instance, on July 23, 1986, the *Times* carried a story from Washington about a federal appeals judge in Chicago writing a letter describing Daniel Manion, a nominee for his court, to be unfit. Senator Paul Simon, an Illinois Democrat opposing the Manion appointment, released the letter but said the judge who released it "declined to be identified publicly." The *Times* ran the anonymous charge anyway on the eve of Manion's confirmation vote, which he narrowly won.

Rosenthal, however, insists the rule is workable. In May, 1986, he read an article in the *Times* that said, "A spokesman for the mayor who refused to be identified . . ." Rosenthal said, "I almost had a heart attack. This is not the goddamned CIA. He is a civil servant who works for the fucking Mayor. He shouldn't try such a thing, and we sure the hell shouldn't let him get away with it." What Rosenthal demands is that reporters and editors, when an unnamed source is used, narrow down as tightly as possible the person's position or viewpoint. If quoting a "foreign observer" in a capital, for instance, is he Western or non-Western? Communist or non-Communist? "You find that if you push hard enough, you get closer. If we can't get some things on the record, OK, we'll miss the story. But I'd rather miss it than have it full of fuzz."

Thus the Washington bureau, in reporting the debate in 1985-86 over nuclear arms policy, would report that a document was leaked to the press "by a Senate staff member who advocates prompt resumption of the Geneva talks." With the motive of the source, if not his exact name, a matter of record, the *Times* felt free to use the document.

But the bottom line is that Rosenthal wishes the *Times* to speak with unchallenged authority; that when it states something as a fact, it does so with the knowledge that the ground is firm beneath its feet. "The *Times* should be a paper of demonstration, not assertion," Rosenthal stated.

Which leads again to the classic unsolved problem of newspapers in the United States: if the public is conditioned to believe everything it reads in *The New York Times*, what happens when the information is demonstrably untrue or so distorted as to have no relation to reality? The *Times* and other major media have opposed bitterly any attempt to establish an outside monitoring agency. The grounds are the ever-useful First Amendment on freedom of the press; and the cherished notion that what happens in America's newsrooms is no one's business.

Indeed, Rosenthal opposes any monitoring of press performance even if the oversight group is of the press itself. As he told the American Society of Newspaper Editors in 1983, "I do not believe in any form of regulation by the press of the press as a unit. I do not believe, for instance, in a National News Council.* I'm quite chilly on codes of ethics, because sooner or later . . . they may be started with all the best intentions in the world . . . but I do not believe we should regulate each other. . . . I think the idea is ridiculous."

Finding episodes where persons and institutions claimed to have been damaged by inaccurate or biased reporting by the *Times* is not difficult. Discovering the ultimate truth is. But three instances illustrate vividly the nigh-impossibility of persuading *The New York Times* that it should confess error on a story and set the record

*The NNC was formed in 1973 to review complaints against the media. Persons filing complaints waived the right to sue, and a panel of lay persons and journalists would review the dispute and issue public findings. Punch Sulzberger dismissed the idea. "As we view it, we are being asked to accept what we regard as a form of voluntary regulation in the name of enhancing press freedom." Other media took the same attitude, and the NNC folded after an ineffective decade.

straight. One involved a relatively obscure Greek investments adviser living in Washington. Another concerned a Fortune 500 company. The third involved a distinguished American scientist whose honesty was challenged. Each suffered in his own way at the hands of *The New York Times*. And their stories show the impact the *Times* can have on persons who are not given the forum to respond to charges, and thus defend themselves against questionable accusations.

Elias Demetracopoulos had reason to be suspicious one fall morning in 1977 when David Binder of the Washington bureau of *The New York Times* called for an interview. Long active in leftist Greek politics as a journalist, Demetracopoulos had fled Athens a decade earlier when a military junta deposed an elective government. Demetracopoulos devoted those years to establishing himself in Washington as an adviser to the Wall Street firm of Brimberg & Company, and doing what he could from afar to goad the ruling colonels.

Demetracopoulos took naturally to exile lobbying. He established himself in a small, austere room in the fashionable Fairfax Hotel on Embassy Row, and made a broad range of contacts with both Democrats and Republicans, and he argued strenuously that Washington should suspend aid to Greece until the junta surrendered power. During the Nixon years, however, the United States wished to keep friendly relations with the colonels, and eventually Demetracopoulos began to annoy the State Department and the White House. Attorney General John Mitchell went so far as to have his Justice Department look for a way to prosecute him.

Even more alarming was information suggesting that the CIA was running a covert operation bent on discrediting Demetracopoulos. In January, 1977, a journalist named Russen Warren Howe published a book on foreign lobbyists in which he used material supposedly from CIA files that was critical of him. Demetracopoulos had known Binder when both worked as journalists in Athens, and he knew Binder had strong CIA connections. Demetracopoulos had worked successfully in 1977 to stop the appointment of an ambassador to Greece who was friendly to the junta, and he sensed that Binder was about to make another run at him with smear material compiled by CIA.

So the two men sat in Demetracopoulos's file-crammed hotel room for some two hours, talking before the Greek's tape recorder. Demetracopoulos is a document-hoarder; he had discovered the

Freedom of Information Act, and used it to obtain literally thousands of pages of documents compiled about him over the years both in Greece and the United States. He answered all of Binder's questions as best he could, and when he got a transcript of the recording he sent it to Binder.

Two months passed, and no story appeared, and Demetracopoulos began to breathe easier. Surely the *Times* was too sophisticated a newspaper to be taken in by disinformation. His previous relations with the *Times* had been good, and indeed an editorial on December 30, 1970, on his work against the dictatorship referred to him as a "respected, self-exiled Greek journalist."

Then on Monday evening, December 5, 1977, a friend telephoned him from New York and said in an excited voice, "Elias, my friend, there is grave news."

Demetracopoulos gulped. "Read it," he said.

Under the headline "A Ubiquitous Hand Guides U. S.-Greek Ties," Binder essentially called Demetracopoulos's entire life a lie. The journalist the *Times* had lauded editorially seven years earlier as "self-exiled" was now "self-styled." Quoting liberally from what he claimed were CIA documents, Binder challenged Demetracopoulos's wartime service with the Greek resistance helping escort downed fliers to freedom. Other CIA records, Binder wrote, showed Demetracopoulos attempting to go to work for the agency in 1951, and later becoming "associated with both the Yugoslav and Israeli intelligence services." Many assertions Binder presented as facts had not been raised during the two-hour interview. Binder even picked up the CIA's supposed misspelling of his name—"Ilias Dimitracopoulos."

"Sheer malicious gossip—and inaccurate gossip at that," Demetracopoulos said. Now commenced the nightmare of trying to get a correction—to show that documents in his possession refuted what the CIA papers supposedly said. He had known Seymour Topping, the *Times* managing editor, for years. Topping refused to speak to him. Through a secretary, Topping referred him to a deputy foreign editor, who in turn referred him to the Washington bureau. The ultimate decision by the *Times*: "Write a letter to the editor, we'll consider it." Demetracopoulos did, and the *Times* published a highly-truncated version that did not begin to correct the inaccuracies contained in the article.

Demetracopoulos is a determined man, and for years he pursued the truth. Singly and in batches he obtained more CIA documents under the Freedom of Information Act. In 1979 his situation was one of several addressed during Senate hearings on CIA conduct. The first three days of the hearings, John Crewdson of the *Times* wrote long stories. The fourth day, when Demetracopoulos's case was detailed by Morton Halperin of the ACLU, the *Times* used a United Press International story. Demetracopoulos's mistreatment by the *Times* was discussed in the story as transmitted; those paragraphs were deleted from the version that appeared in the *Times*.

Demetracopoulos pushed on, and finally in June, 1983, Representative Wyche Fowler, of the House Intelligence Committee, wrote William C. Casey, the director of central intelligence, noting the man's "five-year effort to clear his name." Fowler asked for a declassified confirmation that nothing in CIA files supported allegations that Demetracopoulos had ever worked for a foreign intelligence service. Casey replied no such files existed; further, he said, the CIA had no record that any of its employees had ever talked to the *Times* about Demetracopoulos.

Demetracopoulos took a xerox of the Casey letter—and several pounds of backup documents—to Bill Kovach of the Washington bureau. Kovach was immediately sympathetic, and the bureau filed a story stating that the record supported Demetracopoulos. Demetracopoulos looked through the *Times* Sunday morning, September 25, 1983. On page two the index contained a listing:

C.I.A. review backs Greek's
denial of report on him   12

Demetracopoulos turned to page twelve, thrilled that he had finally won. No story. He leafed through the entire paper, thinking the index had erred. No story. He called Kovach, who was "really mad, really cursing," that the story had not appeared. Not until Thursday did the article finally appear. Demetracopoulos immediately saw the reason for the delay. Rather than the *Times* admitting error and apologizing for smearing him with bogus information, the article simply spoke of a "new Central Intelligence Agency review of his case that refutes the allegations against him."

But, as Demetracopoulos says, "Even getting this sort of back-handed retraction cost me approximately $100,000, and six years of my life, six years that I could have devoted to other more important

things. But I'm a Greek, and we Greeks are tough when you touch
our honor."

Another challenged story, ironically, marked the end of the first
phase of Seymour Hersh's career at *The New York Times.* In 1977
Hersh realized his era was fading at the paper. The soft-news approach of the "new" *New York Times* meant Rosenthal had less interest in involved investigative pieces. Hersh was now working out of
43rd Street while his wife completed her medical training, and so he
began looking for corporate and other corruption. With Jeff Gerth of
the Washington bureau he did a long series on a Los Angeles lawyer-
businessman with supposed links to organized crime. The *Times* gave
the articles good display, but Hersh sensed that Rosenthal and other
editors were uneasy with the work. Kicking around a government is
one thing. Going after private citizens is another. Nonetheless,
Rosenthal did not object when Hersh hurried into his office one day
and said, "Hey I've got a lead on a helluva story on Gulf & Western
Industries."*

To summarize a most involved story: a lawyer named Joel Dolkart
for years had been both counsel and confidant of Charles Bluhdorn,
the industrialist and capitalist who put the G&W conglomerate together. In 1974 it was discovered that Dolkart had systematically em-
bezzled at least $2 million—and possibly three times that sum—from
his then law firm, Fried, Frank, Harris, Shriver & Jacobson, and a
previous firm, Simpson Thacher & Bartlett. Facing enough criminal
charges to imprison him for several lifetimes, Dolkart began accusing
G&W and chairman Charles Bluhdorn of a wide range of securities,
tax and other crimes. This information flowed to Robert Morgenthau,
the Manhattan district attorney, and to Stanley Sporkin's enforcement division of the SEC—and, ultimately, to reporters Hersh and
Gerth.

Hersh played rough when questioning present and former G&W

*Here a recitation of a multi-tiered conflict of interest on my part concerning this
episode. Stanley Sporkin, then the enforcement chief of the Securities and Exchange
Commission, was one of the persons involved in Hersh's reporting, which reflected
the SEC viewpoint. I have known Sporkin since the 1960's, and in his official capacity
he helped me with two of my earlier books; his daughter did research for me on another book, on the Korean War. Martin Davis was executive vice-president of G&W
at the time of the Hersh articles; I have known Davis since the early 1960's, when he
worked for Paramount Pictures, now a G&W subsidiary. And, lastly, I know Hersh
socially.

employees about points covered in Dolkart's accusations—so much so
that G&W executive Martin Davis sent a series of complaints to
Times managing editor Seymour Topping that Hersh, "in the guise of
seeking information about Gulf & Western and its executives, is
spreading lies, although he bluntly asserts them as facts—lies of the
most vicious kind, including flat statements that we have committed
crimes." Davis listed some of the Hersh statements reported to him
by past G&W employees:

> "You better see me. Otherwise, you are going to jail with the others.
> [G&W executives.]
>   "Every transaction they enter into, they do so with tax fraud in
> mind.
>   "I have a *prima facie* case of tax fraud.
>   "G&W is a piece of shit—garbage.
>   "I am repulsed by their lack of morals.
>   "Bluhdorn is friendly with Mafia members.
>   "They tried to bribe tax agents."

Davis asked for a meeting with Topping. "I want to document for you
the evidence we have which we believe clearly shows that . . . we are
being investigated by a man whose repeated statements must lead us
to believe that he is, in his own words, 'out to get us.' " Topping refused, saying, "I do not think that it would be appropriate for us to
meet at this time." In a later complaint, Davis accused Hersh of freely
exchanging information with SEC investigators about the G&W
probe. Again, the *Times* refused any substantive discussions.

The *Times* investigation spanned six months, and indications the
paper intended to publish damaging information about G&W became
widespread on Wall Street. Short sales of the company's stock—
trading in anticipation of a drop of price—increased dramatically the
month before publication. From May 15 through June 15 there had
been short sales of 49,352 shares. From June 15 through July 15,
short sales jumped more than fourfold, to 218,244 shares. The Monday after the first of three page-one articles appeared, G&W was the
most actively traded stock on the New York Stock Exchange, 938,000
shares, compared to the average of 30,000.

The Hersh-Gerth articles accused G&W and its chairman, Charles
Bluhdorn, of a wide range of misdeeds ranging from tax evasion to
perjury and failure to disclose significant information to shareholders.

The articles used strong language. They claimed the SEC "is in the midst of one of the most intensive investigations in its history" and spoke of a "separate criminal investigation" by the Manhattan district attorney. As one G&W official stated years later, "These articles had devastating impact on everyone in the company, from Bluhdorn on down. The *Times* was calling us criminals and thieves and shyster businessmen on the front page, three days running. People tend to believe what they read in *The New York Times*, and a lot of people I considered good friends gave me funny looks when I would encounter them on the street. Was I one of Charlie Bluhdorn's crooks? That hurts."

Many persons at G&W felt Sporkin used the *Times* in an attempt to bludgeon the company into a consent decree, which meant the SEC would not have to prove its case in court. Bluhdorn refused; once the articles appeared, his reputation was on the line, and he knew the charges being made by Dolkart were bogus. And in November, 1979, more than two years after the *Times* articles, the SEC finally filed a much watered-down complaint. Three years later, after G&W spent uncounted millions of dollars in legal fees, the SEC essentially abandoned the case. G&W signed an agreement to abide by existing corporate bylaws that required three outside directors and an independent audit committee. The agreement did not mention returning any of the massive sums allegedly misappropriated, or correcting supposedly fraudulent financial statements. In sum, the case was a total bust for the SEC.

Yet the collapse of the SEC's "most intensive investigation" in its history went virtually unnoted by the *Times*. The charges that scandals permeated G&W were published on the front page. The refutation of the charges ran in a brief item on the inside pages, and even here the *Times* erred, calling the agreement a "consent decree." Nor did the *Times* say that the "criminal investigation" by the local prosecutor came to naught.

In 1986 Hersh insisted he did a "fair and square" investigation of G&W; further that "G&W and that bastard Marty Davis played rough with me and Gerth, investigating us when we were working on the story, taping our conversations, the whole smear." But Hersh did acknowledge the series marked a distinct cooling of Rosenthal's attitude towards both him and his style of investigative reporting. "The *Times* wasn't nearly as happy when we went after business wrongdoing as when we were kicking around some slob in government."

Hersh was to leave the *Times* in 1979 to write a book about his longtime adversary Henry Kissinger (published by Summit Books, a G&W subsidiary). He wanted a leave of absence; Rosenthal refused, although he had permitted other *Times* reporters time off for similar work. Hersh declined to speculate whether the *Times*'s unhappiness with the G&W fiasco contributed to Rosenthal's decision. "My relationship with Abe has always been really complex," he said, "and there's some things I'm not going to talk about."

But the shallowness of Rosenthal's claim that he wants to "keep the *Times* straight" is best illustrated in an episode involving the physicist Dr. Edward Teller. Here some background is in order. For some five decades Teller had been a major figure in the American scientific community. Although he disdains the title "Father of the H-Bomb," it was at Teller's insistence that the Atomic Energy Commission in the late 1940's and early 1950's pressed development of the weapon. In doing so he pushed aside many opponents, notably Dr. Robert Oppenheimer, with whom he had worked on development of the atomic bombs used against the Japanese to end the Second World War. But Oppenheimer and other scientists then had qualms of conscience and urged that future atomic work be for "peaceful purposes." Teller, however, argued successfully that the United States should have no illusions that the Soviet Union would abide by any such restraints. Teller prevailed, but the American left thereafter cast him as a true-life Dr. Strangelove, whereas Oppenheimer was an innocent victim of the arms complex. Such depictions defy reality and reason— nonetheless, such is "reality" as created by the media.

On April 28, 1983, barely a month after President Reagan first proposed his Strategic Defense Initiative of space-based anti-missile systems, *The New York Times* published a lengthy front-page article that in effect accused Dr. Teller of using his position as an informal science advisor to the White House to enrich himself financially. The article, by Jeff Gerth (Hersh's associate on the discredited Gulf & Western story) charged that Dr. Teller, because of his ability to influence the Reagan Administration, had been "given" a large block of stock in Helionetics, Inc., a small California firm that was developing a laser that could be used in the space-defense program. Further, Gerth alleged, Teller had helped Reagan prepare his speech of March 23, 1983, announcing the initiative. Gerth "reported" brisk trading of Helionetics stock just before the speech, implying that insiders were enriching themselves because of Dr. Teller's advance information of a project that would benefit the company.

Gerth's story, unfortunately, had a basic flaw: it was demonstrably wrong. Teller had not been "given" the stock; he had bought it, on the open market, in 1980, before President Reagan's election. The laser being developed by Helionetics was for communications purposes, not for space defense. And, finally, Teller had no role in writing Reagan's speech, and indeed he did not even know of it until two hours before delivery. Helionetics executives explained the activity in its stock as related to reported record first quarter sales and profits.

Stung by the *Times's* accusations against his honor, Dr. Teller wrote a long letter of rebuttal, which the paper refused to print. Nor would Gerth do a follow-up story giving his explanation. Finally, Teller's friend Dr. Reed Irvine of Accuracy in Media, the press monitor group, spent $13,000 for a full-page advertisement in *The Wall Street Journal*, stating the facts in the contrived episode. The headline read, "I Was NOT the Only Victim of *The New York Times*," and Teller denounced the *Times* for publishing "misinformation masquerading as news."

The *Times* absolutely refused to acknowledge error. Its only reaction was a short item—on page D-3—some three weeks after the original Gerth article, stating that the White House had "cleared Dr. Teller of charges he acted improperly."

One of Dr. Teller's friends who knew Rosenthal socially sent him a copy of *The Wall Street Journal* ad, with a polite note asking, in effect, "What's going on here? Why isn't the *Times* giving both sides of what is obviously a complex matter?"

Rosenthal replied, in a curt two sentence note, "I am tired of people badgering me about the esteemed Dr. Teller. Our article of April 28, 1983 speaks for itself."

SIXTEEN

"Hey, Jim Is Bored"

The metropolitan desk, sited only a few feet from Rosenthal's office, readily adapted to the *Times*'s new style of reporting. "If Abe didn't like something he would be out with arms flapping," a former editor on the desk said. But the Washington bureau had major symbolic importance to Rosenthal. Control of this important outpost, which produced more page one stories than any division of the paper, caused Rosenthal's only stumble during his climb to power, when James Reston and others persuaded Punch Sulzberger to rescind the appointment of James Greenfield as bureau chief. Rosenthal bided his time during the tenure of interim chiefs, Max Frankel and Clifton Daniel, each of whom got the job because of *Times* politics beyond Rosenthal's immediate control. Thus Rosenthal surprised many persons on the *Times* in 1975 when he finally made his first unfettered choice for a bureau chief—Hedrick Smith, who had been hired by Reston for the *Times*, and who spent his formative years as one of "Scotty's boys."

Rick Smith is the physical and intellectual anthesis of Abe Rosenthal. A strapping six-footer and everyone's idea of an Ivy Leaguer (actually, he went to Williams College, where the Ivy League is considered déclassé anyway), Smith wears a starched collar and a necktie even on Saturdays. He worked briefly for United Press International before joining the *Times* in the early 1960's, and he learned Washington reporting around the State Department. He was a valued participant in the Pentagon Papers project, and he did well in Cairo and even better in Moscow, winning a Pulitzer Prize for distinguished foreign reporting. Smith came back to New York as a deputy national editor, his book on the USSR made the bestseller list, and in 1975 Rosenthal sent him to Washington as bureau chief. Rosenthal now felt so confident of his own power—and of Reston's decline—that he did not hesitate to promote a man whose career began at the knee of his former rival.

Smith was told the new ground rules: Washington would no longer be autonomous; he would work directly under New York, and he would follow directions. Further, Rosenthal gave Smith a "hit list" of people he wanted out of the bureau as rapidly as possible—Edwin L. Dale and Eileen Shanahan, the financial writers; Richard Madden, who covered New York's Congressional delegation; and Howard Schmeck, who covered science. Each of these persons had offended Rosenthal in one way or another.

Discretion dictates that a new boss settle into a job, and let underlings become comfortable with him before he starts making drastic changes. Smith, however, did not hesitate: almost from the day he arrived he went after the targeted persons. He shifted assignments of many persons within the bureau, with little consultation. One man initially a friend of Smith's said, "Rick acted as if he were determined to establish how tough he was from the outset. He turned off a lot of people he needed to succeed."

Nor did Smith perform nearly so well as could have been expected of a man with his news experience. He developed the reputation of being a "story hog," someone who commandeered the day's top story to assure himself a prominent byline. Smith decided to write the main stories on the Strategic Arms Limitation Treaty (SALT) negotiations, shoving aside diplomatic correspondent Leslie Gelb. Infuriated, Gelb resigned to join the State Department. (He returned to the *Times* when administrations—and bureau chiefs—changed.) When Smith joined a 1976 Carter campaign trip in mid-course, a reporter already aboard glanced at his size twelve-plus shoes and cracked, "Well, here comes Big Foot." He was not offering a compliment, and the word "big foot" is now in Washington journalistic jargon for a pundit or bureau chief who moves in on a story with a heavy tread when it becomes important. Within the bureau Smith was criticized for writing "one-source" stories, relying on one or two interviews for a Q Head analytical article. (The name "Q Head" comes from the Times style book designation for the type of headline used on the articles.) For stories about the U. S. Senate, for instance, he relied heavily upon Dick Clark of Iowa for the Democratic view and Howard Baker of Tennessee for the Republican. Unfortunately for the *Times*, politicians quickly learned Smith was acutely susceptible to leaks, so they used him to float ideas they wished publicized. Smith acquired another uncomplimentary nickname: "Hydrofoil Smith," for a tendency to skim over the surface of a story.

Most grievously, Smith, a married man, had the misjudgment to become romantically involved with a young woman who worked in the bureau. They vanished into Smith's office, with the doors closed, and reporters and deputy editors fretted, waiting an interlude so they could talk business. The two also enjoyed long lunches, from which they returned dreamy-eyed.

A reporter saw Smith and the woman clutched in a standup embrace in the busy terminal of Washington National Airport before the seven o'clock shuttle. Discretion should have curbed ardor, this man felt. "After all," he reasoned, "the bureau chief of *The New York Times* is not an anonymous figure, and he was doing this in full view of the shuttle crowd." To the further distress of colleagues, Smith invited the woman, a non-journalist, to staff meetings and solicited her views on how Washington should be covered.

Smith realized his marriage and his career were falling apart, and he lamented to a senior reporter, "I'm having a mid-life crisis."

"You *can't* have a mid-life crisis," the man replied. "You are chief of the Washington bureau of *The New York Times*, and you are just going to have to wait for your crisis."

Extramarital affairs surely did not disturb Abe Rosenthal (he was well into his liaison with Katharine Balfour by this time) but only so long as the people involved did their work. Here Smith was vulnerable. Equally important to Rosenthal, perhaps, was Smith's increasing independence from direction by 43rd Street. The first months he ran the bureau, Smith did defer to Rosenthal. Bureau news editor Douglas Robinson heard Smith on the phone with Rosenthal one day, asking, "Is it OK if I let Dave Burnham cover the House assassinations committee?" This appalled Robinson, for previously New York had no voice—or interest—in details of assignments.

But as if determined to be his own man Smith began arguing with Rosenthal about coverage. As the editor on the scene he insisted he knew more about Washington than editors in New York. Rosenthal's dissatisfaction was such that one of Smith's friends telephoned him a warning.

"Look, Rick, Abe is about to bounce your ass out of Washington," he said. "He's already scouting for a replacement. He hasn't made his mind up definitely yet, but if you want to keep your job you better start listening to Abe."

Smith ignored the warning.

Now Rosenthal's interference became even more direct. He shackled Smith by forbidding the *Times* to pursue what had been legitimate stories in the past. The consumer advocate Ralph Nader, for instance, found the *Times* no longer interested in writing about his studies of shortcomings in government and industry. Several times, Nader states, he was told, "We do our own investigations. Your work is advocacy, not reporting." Perhaps, and many Nader reports *are* flawed by the overzealous work of college students working as summer interns. Nonetheless, ignoring Nader deprived *Times* readers of a major source of information. To Nader, the *Times*'s tacit boycott meant "closing a gate of access to the public." Nader's view was that newspapers had a public obligation to present readers with a full menu of news, and let the individual choose what he wished to read and/or believe.

Having reported from Cairo, Smith understood the Arabs' side of the endless Middle East conflict; while not anti-Israeli by any means, he came under constant criticism from Rosenthal (and other editors in New York) for supposedly "slanting" bureau stories towards the Arabs. "New York was whip-sawing poor Rick," a deputy editor said. "There seemed to be days when whatever he did couldn't please the guys up north. Then he had all that mess in his personal life." The bottom line was that Smith could not adjust bureau coverage to get into step with the tone of Rosenthal's "new" *New York Times*. But Rosenthal, who did not know Washington, could not tell Smith from afar just what he *did* want. So the bureau drifted, and morale became exceedingly low, even by newsroom standards of grousing.

Rosenthal's meddling in bureau personnel affairs—often with direct brutality—made Smith's job more difficult. One victim was James Wooten, a very religious southerner who came to the *Times* as a protégé of the then-national editor, Gene Roberts. Wooten had recurring problems with Rosenthal, and when Roberts left to become executive editor of the Philadelphia *Inquirer*, Wooten followed, as a columnist. But Philadelphia proved too slow a track, and Wooten rejoined the *Times*, in the Washington bureau.

Wooten was a bright, innovative reporter, and with Terry Smith he was the chief impetus for the Washington Talk page inaugurated in the *Times* in the mid-1970's, one of the paper's most popular features for readers in the capital. Because Wooten had covered Jimmy Carter as a governor of Georgia, he knew the crowd well, and he was dispatched to the White House to cover the new administration in early 1977.

Having known the Carter people for years, Wooten did not take them nearly so seriously as they felt they deserved, and from the very beginning they complained about his coverage. Early in his office President Carter had problems communicating with the public in general, and with the press in particular. So the President took public speaking lessons. Wooten learned of them, and wrote a witty article about a President learning oratory after reaching the White House. Someone at the *Times* killed the article. (Wooten could never confirm that Rosenthal gave the order.) Why? Wooten asked, in sincere puzzlement. "You are not being respectful of the office of the President," Wooten was told. Wooten fumed.

Soon afterwards Rosenthal visited Washington, and Wooten and several other persons in the bureau joined him for dinner. Over drinks, Rosenthal asked, "How are you doing, Jim?"

"Frankly," Wooten replied, "I'm a little bored."

"Tell us why you are bored, Jim. After all, it's only the White House you are covering."

Wooten did not rise to Rosenthal's bait. Two weeks later, he was taken off the White House beat, and soon thereafter he was reporting for ABC News. He has told several persons that as a civilized man and as a professional he did not intend to waste his life working under someone capable of such oafish conduct as Rosenthal was. That Rosenthal pounced on Wooten during the course of a casual conversation did not surprise one of the *Times* reporters who witnessed the episode. "Rosenthal has a vindictiveness—he'll jump on you for a chance remark if you let your guard down for a minute."

Something else nagged at Abe Rosenthal during the 1970's—his hatred of Ben Bradlee, the executive editor of the Washington *Post*. Bradlee's people killed the *Times* Washington bureau during Watergate. Bradlee was the physical man Rosenthal could never be— lithe, attractive, relaxed, and respected and *liked* by editors of other newspapers. Rosenthal would go to a convention of the American Society of Newspaper Editors, and he seemed on the fringe of the crowd. Bradlee, conversely, knew everyone, and people laughed at his jokes and enjoyed him as a person. Whatever attention came to Rosenthal seemed *ex officio*; that if he were not executive editor of *The New York Times*, he would be ignored.

There was also Sally Quinn, the talented and pretty woman who had gone from *Post* feature writer—the best of her genre—to Bradlee's live-in friend and third wife. Rosenthal thought of his own wife, Ann, increasingly burdened by weight and arthritis, and he would look across an ASNE function room and see the glowing Bradlee and Quinn, and he would grimace. In a cab ride after a Gridiron Club dinner in Washington Rosenthal said to a companion, "I have to get me one of those."

Puzzled, the companion said, "One of *what*?"

"One of those blondes," Rosenthal said. "Did you see the tits on that thing Bradlee had along tonight?" He sighed and fell silent.

Rosenthal was explicit in telling Rick Smith that so far as the *Times* was concerned, the Washington *Post* was the only competition. Let's don't get our ass kicked again, he told Smith. If a story starts, I don't want to read it first in the Washington *Post*. So now Smith dealt with a wide range of pressure—from an executive editor who shouted at him over the telephone several times daily; from a floundering marriage; from a restive staff dissatisfied with his performance; and from Rosenthal's compulsion not to be beaten by the *Post*, at any cost.

That things were out of kilter in Washington was sensed early on by young Wendell Rawls, who joined the bureau in early 1977 from the Philadelphia *Inquirer*. Rawls had done investigative work for the *Inquirer* that was to bring him a Pulitzer Prize later that spring, so he felt he knew a bit about that form of reporting. But Rawls realized his first day in the bureau that the *Times* was run somewhat differently from the *Inquirer*.

An editor showed Rawls to his desk, and briefed him on office procedures, and asked, "What is your first story going to be?"

"Shit," Rawls replied, "I just got into town." Since he had never worked in Washington, he suggested a day or two might be required for him to find the "first story." "Oh," the editor said.

Rawls started with a rush. His first week he led the paper several times with the story of the fight over the nomination by President Carter of Theodore Sorensen, a lawyer and former counsel to President Kennedy, as director of central intelligence. The military objected to Carter's appointment of a Second World War conscientious objector to head the intelligence community. There were questions also about Sorensen taking classified material from the White House to use in his memoir of the Kennedy Administration. "I had a really good run the first ten days there." Rawls said. "I was holding a hot hand."

One person with whom Rawls came to immediate odds was the senior investigative reporter, Nick Horrock. Rawls stated that Horrock "jealously guarded his sources, as did everyone else in the bureau." To Rawls, this attitude was nonsense. From his own experience, he knew that the best investigative teams are just that—teams. One example among many is Jack Nelson and Bob Jackson of the Washington bureau of the *Los Angeles Times*. At times Rawls wanted to stand in the middle of the bureau newsroom and shout, "Hey, goddamnit, we work for the same damned newspaper, remember?" In Rawls's estimate, the lack of cooperation was a major factor in the *Times*'s inability to produce good investigative reporting from Washington.

The story which led to Rawls's ultimate breach with the *Times* was one which neither 43rd Street nor the Washington bureau originally accepted as serious. This was what came to be known as the "Bert Lance affair." The episode began quietly. The Carter Administration had taken office with many trappings of probity, including a President who vowed, "I shall not lie to you." But several months into office the White House sent a letter to the Senate asking that President Carter's close political friend, Bert Lance, the budget director, be permitted to be let out of an agreement to sell certain Georgia bank stocks. To William Safire, a columnist who worked out of the Washington bureau (and who had honed his practical politics as a speechwriter for President Nixon), "The letter was artful—I remember that kind of writing—and had, to me, the unmistakable clang of falsity." Safire wrote several questioning columns. No one else, in the *Times*, the Senate, or elsewhere, shared Safire's concern that something was gravely amiss at Lance's former banks in Georgia.

Senator Abraham Ribicoff of Connecticut held hearings, and by Safire's words, "was extraordinarily sympathetic to Lance and scornful of those who found his story unbelievable. In his testimony, responding to softball questioning, Lance seemed to demolish the points I had made about his finances. I felt sick." But Safire kept writing about Lance, "convinced he had broken the law." What privately infuriated Safire was a feeling that both the *Times* and the Senate were permitting conduct in the Carter Administration that would have been roundly condemned under Nixon.

After several weeks in which the columnist outpaced his news staff on a story that would not die, Rosenthal asked Safire what specific law he thought Lance had broken.

"18 United States Code 656," Safire replied, "misapplication of bank funds. Abe, the President's best friend could be going to jail."

Safire and Rosenthal had talked in the latter's third-floor office on 43rd Street. Rosenthal left Safire and walked out into the newsroom, and he ordered that an investigative team be unleashed to find the truth about Bert Lance's banking affairs.*

The *Times*'s main effort, through the Washington bureau's "investigative cluster," went for the trusted official sources, Justice Department officers and bank examiners going through Lance's affairs. Working on a hunch, Rawls took a different tack. He flew to Atlanta and "began working the Lance crowd, men who wanted to get out their side of the story." For reasons he still cannot explain, other than "one Southerner liking a fellow Southerner" (hominy drips from Rawls' voice on demand), Rawls cultivated a man named Tommy Mitchell, one of the trustees of the blind trust Lance had created when he entered government.

Rawls's deal with Mitchell was basic journalism. Mitchell would talk, but he would not be identified as a source, even in oblique fash-

---

*Rosenthal was irritated that the goad of a columnist was required to get the Washington bureau moving on the Lance story. He told several people in New York he felt the bureau was being overly friendly to the new Democratic administration.

ion. "He was loading me up, but I was protecting his name," Rawls said of Mitchell. Mitchell was irked with Lance, because he had discovered stocks in Lance's portfolio that were not disclosed to the Senate during Lance's confirmation hearings. Mitchell's name had also been used in Lance stock transactions without his knowledge.

The partnership worked, and with Mitchell as a solid but unnamed source Rawls produced front-page stories which no other newspaper had. "I had a great source, and they [the *Times*] realized that," Rawls said. Circumstantial evidence suggests that Rawls's success, as a newcomer, irritated some older members of the bureau. As the story grew, an editor (Rawls would not name him) asked that he introduce his source to Jeff Gerth, another reporter working on the Lance matter. "The deal was that Gerth had some good information, but he needed confirmation before he could go with it. Would I introduce my guy?"

The request made Rawls uncomfortable, for he had built a good relationship with Mitchell which he did not wish disturbed. Too, he did not trust the sudden insistence that all reporters "must cooperate," for such had not been true when he was the reporter needing help with sources. Rawls recognized Gerth as an aggressively ambitious reporter who prided himself on being "a new Seymour Hersh," and who did not let niceties get between him and a good story. But Rawls finally agreed to the introduction, with caveats. Mitchell's anonymity must continue to be guaranteed, and the agreements Rawls had made with him were binding on Gerth and the rest of the bureau. Gerth agreed.

The two reporters met Mitchell in New York for dinner at the Plaza Hotel, then had drinks at the Oak Bar there and later at the sidewalk cafe of the St. Moritz. In Mitchell's presence, Rawls once again told Gerth the ground rules: You can use the information, but you cannot identify this man. Gerth said nothing to indicate any reservations or disagreements.

During the hours-long conversation Rawls realized that Gerth, if indeed he had information for which he needed "confirmation," was not sharing it. Instead, he was probing Mitchell for details on a wide range of matters. "He was fishing for leads. I kept thinking he would come up with some stuff [of his own]. He never did." Later, as the reporters walked south on Sixth Avenue back to their hotel, Gerth exclaimed, "God almighty, that's really good stuff."

"Yeah," Rawls said, "but it occurs to me you didn't have any good stuff until he gave it to you."

Back in the bureau Gerth set out to write a story which was to appear under an italic box identifying it as a joint effort. "Horrock wanted to get into the act also, so he rewrites the first two or three paragraphs, so that his name goes into the box also. Nick kept saying, 'Dynamite stuff, a landmark piece.' "

When Rawls read the article, he was horrified to see Tommy Mitchell quoted by name, and at length, contrary to the promises he had made. "You've burned his ass," he told Gerth. "You can't do that. You promised to protect him." Rawls was hot. He felt betrayed.

Again to his surprise, Horrock sided with Gerth. "We can't use blind quotes. This is too important a story." Well, Rawls said, you should have thought about that earlier, rather than go around changing the rules at your own goddamned convenience. Hedrick Smith took the same attitude as did Horrock and Gerth. On such a story, the *Times* needed more than one source, or else independent confirmation. Hence Mitchell must be identified for the story to be usable.

Rawls fought a long, painful and ultimately losing battle. Rawls is an old-fashioned man, in the best sense of the word; to him, a gentleman does not lie, nor does he quibble. He had given his word directly to another man, and he had brought Gerth into the scene upon Gerth's acceptance of certain terms. Rawls's own integrity was at stake, and he made plain, most plain, that he did not like what was happening.

Gerth had a rationalization. No, he *himself* had no understanding with Mitchell. "Did he [Mitchell] ever say this was off-the-record?"

That's not the point, Rawls countered. He had made sure Gerth understood the relationship, and Gerth had acquiesced. "Now you've got *me* lying and going back on my word."

The argument went on for a long time, more than an hour. To Rawls, Rick Smith and Gerth seemed determined to find an excuse for what he felt was a deliberate decision by *The New York Times* to break its word of honor. Smith kept returning to a central point: "Some stories are just too important to protect a source like this," he told Rawls. The story would run.

So Rawls sighed and performed the distasteful talk of telling Tommy Mitchell that the *Times* had broken its word. "Tommy was a gentleman about it. He didn't shout or holler. He just said, in his quiet Southern way, 'You have ruined me. I can't trust you. I'm not going to talk to you any more. I want nothing else to do with you or with *The New York Times*." Then Mitchell added something that cut Rawls to the quick. "They must not think much of you, or of your word."

Mitchell told his friends around Bert Lance of the betrayal, and whatever sources Rawls had among them dried up overnight. The *Times* reverted to its Justice Department and other official sources. "The *Times* thereafter was not doing investigative reporting; it was reporting on an investigation." But Rawls was effectively out of the Atlanta end of the story. "I couldn't get a smell at that point." In hindsight Rawls sees a couple of options he could have—perhaps should have—pursued. First was to take his name off the story. This would have been meaningless, however, for "Tommy Mitchell knew I was involved in it." The second, and most drastic, was to resign on principle, and say, "If that's the way you guys do business, goodbye." He rejected this decision as an "empty, dramatic gesture." Rawls called his friend Gene Roberts and told him what had happened. "Me and *The New York Times* don't gee and haw the same way," he said in the dialect of a Southern mule driver. Roberts chuckled. He knew exactly what Rawls was talking about.

Rawls was to stay at the *Times* for another six years, chiefly as a correspondent in the South and in Texas, before going on to write books. But the Tommy Mitchell episode effectively told him he did not wish to work for *The New York Times*.

Rawls faults Rosenthal only indirectly for the Tommy Mitchell fiasco. Rosenthal was pushing Rick Smith and others to "stay out front" on the Bert Lance story, and Rawls feels the pressure caused the bureau to cut ethical corners. And indeed once the Lance affair sputtered to a close, Rawls was called upon to do little true investigative reporting.

Such was true of other reporters in Washington, particularly those writing about controversial subjects. David Burnham, in the Washington bureau, in the 1970's, wrote frequently, and critically, about problems in the nuclear power industry. The thrust of Burnham's articles, and there were many of them, was that the industry was on untested ground, and that society owed itself the obligation to monitor closely a technology that had the potentiality for great damage. Burnham realized from comments by Washington editors his stories were not always appreciated on 43rd Street. There were many arguments about space and wording and fairness; eventually, however, most of what he wrote appeared in the paper, even if sometimes in truncated form.

Burnham developed a reputation in journalism as the reporter to seek out to offer a story about nuclear dangers. To use a nuclear analogy, once such a reputation is established, it is self-sustaining, a chain reaction where one good story brings in tips on a dozen others. A reporter could work without such tips, but the faraway people who know of a story and volunteer information are the feedstock of journalism. Hence it was to Burnham that officials of the Oil, Chemical and Atomic Workers Union turned when they learned a young woman named Karen Silkwood suspected faulty fuel rods and falsification of Atomic Energy Commission reports at the Kerr-McGee complex in Oklahoma. Burnham agreed to meet her in Oklahoma; she was driving to the rendezvous when her car mysteriously swerved off the road, killing her. Because of the peculiar circumstances, Ms. Silkwood's death focused national attention on nuclear safety, and provided Burnham a run of good stories.

Nonetheless, Rosenthal frowned at his efforts. Burnham happened to be in New York one day, and he encountered Rosenthal in the newsroom. Abe looked at him, and made a gesture with his hand as if pointing to something not quite clean. "Here comes Johnny-One-Note," he said, in a voice loud enough for other editors to hear.

Abe Rosenthal's world runs on an intricate system of signals via which his displeasure can be expressed on several levels, in several voices. In some instances he berates publicly, and loudly, and obscenely; in others he brings the offending editor or reporter to his office for a private dressing-down, and then offers absolution in return for a promise of undying fealty to Abe Rosenthal and *The New York Times*. The third form, the most subtle one, is to rebuke someone in public with a remark that can be innocuous when put into cold print, but that is intended to send a clear signal to persons within earshot. Such is what happened to Burnham.

Rosenthal's underlings quickly scented that Burnham was in disfavor. The news editor, Allan M. Siegal, sidled up to Burnham, took him by the arm, and pulled him to a quiet corner. "You know," he said, "you'd get more of your stories on page one if they didn't have that tone about them."

"What tone?" Burnham asked. He was determined to force Siegal into specific objections, not generalities.

"You know what I mean," Siegal said.

"What do you mean?" Burnham asked.

"I don't have time to look it up right now," Siegal said, and he broke off the conversation and hurried away. Burnham did not need further notice to know he had arrived on Rosenthal's list.

Writing stories that a reporter knows in advance are to be unpopular with editors is a debilitating experience. "It really gets you tired," Burnham stated. "When you have a good editor, like Arthur Gelb, the story gets better." But now Burnham had no such attentive editor. This can be dangerous. Lacking editorial support, and knowing he is in disfavor, can cause a reporter to opt for self-censorship, and to write stories intended to get him past the perceived trip wires; the result is compromise and second-guessing. Burnham, a spunky fellow, avoided this trap, but he was not happy.

Then something remarkable happened to cause Abe Rosenthal to do a 180-degree turn on nuclear energy and its attendant dangers. Jane Fonda starred in a movie, *The China Syndrome*, loosely based on the Karen Silkwood story. A cultural editor asked Burnham to attend the press screening of the movie and do an article on how Hollywood adapted a factual situation to the screen. Burnham warned he was on "Abe's shitlist" for nuclear energy, but the editor insisted.

Rosenthal came to the viewing with Gelb, and Burnham looked at him periodically during the showing. "Abe was genuinely upset by it," he decided, based on Rosenthal's facial expressions. Other problems then developed. At the *Times* the next morning the cultural editor, William Honan, told Burnham that an unspecified "they" did not want him to do an article. This touched off a series of yelling matches between Burnham and, first, Honan, and then Gelb; the end result was that he did the requested article, and he received a private audience with Rosenthal to discuss nuclear energy.

Rosenthal expressed strong doubts about nuclear energy. "Well, we should abolish all nuclear power plants, shouldn't we?" he asked Burnham. The reporter could only sigh at a situation rich with irony. Rosenthal, the quintessential newspaperman, had put more credence in one hundred minutes of Hollywood glitz than he had in years of solid factual reporting by his own staff member.

When Burnham left the office after half an hour, Artie Gelb came close and said approvingly, "Abe thinks you are wonderful."

Which is somewhat of an overstatement, for Burnham symbolized what Rosenthal thought was wrong with the Washington bureau—a reporter who wasted the paper's time writing critically about a scientific development which Rosenthal felt was essential to the national interest. He was not excited about Burnham's other area of expertise, threats to citizen privacy because of the proliferation of computerized government files. Rosenthal's feeling was that Burnham invested far too much time in stories in which he, as an editor, had minimal interest. He felt the same about several other reporters in the Washington bureau, men "so caught up in the mechanics of the damned agency they are covering that they are writing for themselves and other insiders." (Burnham was to leave the paper briefly to write a book; he returned only to resign again in 1986—this time for good, he avows—because "it was no longer fun working in the *Times* Washington bureau.")

So Rosenthal had to admit that Rick Smith, his first hand-picked chief of the Washington bureau, had failed. He was unwilling to make a public admission of error. Instead, he sent veteran national reporter and editor Bill Kovach to Washington with the contrived title of "editor of the Washington bureau," and announced that Smith would thereafter be known as "chief Washington correspondent." The obvious intent was to suggest that Smith was actually getting a promotion, rather than being shoved aside.

Smith and his wife had just moved into a new house in the Maryland suburbs, and he was called upon to host a cocktail party for Kovach, marking the transition. To several bureau reporters the affair was a case study in multi-faced hypocrisy. "Here was a guy being deposed hosting a party honoring the guy who was deposing him," one of these men said. A couple of Smith's four children milled through the crowd around the swimming pool, offering trays of canapes. (Ann Smith had no stomach for the event and refused to participate; a short time later the marriage ended.) Rosenthal, Seymour Topping and other New York editors stood with drinks and easy smiles, oblivious to (or uncaring of) the fact no one present was being fooled.

Kovach was in his late forties when he took control of the Washington bureau, a taciturn man who kept clear of office politics and personalities. His boyhood ambition had been to be a marine biologist, and he studied science in college. But part-time jobs at the newspaper in his hometown of Johnson City, Tennessee, changed his love to journalism. He eventually made his way to the Nashville *Tennessean* and wrote about politics and corruption in government. He also wrote many letter to *The New York Times* about a job there, all of which were ignored.

Thus he was surprised one day to receive a letter from the *Times* asking him if he *would* apply for a job. Kovach did some checking and found that James Reston, in his brief tenure as executive editor, had asked editors of the respected smaller papers throughout the country to give him a list of the most talented journalists working in their area. Kovach's name was at the top of a list of Southern reporters submitted by an editor in Atlanta. So when people asked later how he got his job at *The New York Times*, he would reply, "pure dumb accident."

Kovach is a Southerner of an entirely different type from the garrulous Turner Catledge or the patrician Clifton Daniel. He is a small man with graying tight curls who has the good reporter's knack of being a better listener—and questioner—than talker. Kovach is also very shrewd, and during the first weeks of the Watergate scandal he had performed two reportorial feats that mightily impressed Abe Rosenthal.

Kovach was reporting from Boston at the time of the break-in, and was one of several national reporters sent to Washington to help Max Frankel's beleaguered bureau try to catch up with the Washington *Post*. One story the bureau had been unable to obtain was an interview with maids who worked on the seventh floor of the Howard Johnson Hotel across from the Watergate, where the burglars established their command post. Kovach took a taxi to the hotel, signed the register as being from the "Massachusetts Tool & Die Company," and sheepishly admitted to the desk clerk that he was superstitious. When he stayed in hotels he always wanted to be on the seventh floor. The clerk obliged, and Kovach unpacked his bag and took his key to the Washington bureau and dropped it on Frankel's desk and said, "Here. This will get you to the room right next to where the Plumbers stayed that night." Thus did the bureau obtain the maid interviews.

Kovach also went calling on Lawrence O'Brien, the Democratic National Chairman and P.R. man for Howard Hughes whose office had been the burglars' target. Kovach knew O'Brien from Boston, and he was surprised that the *Times* had not been interviewing him, for the chairman is talkative perhaps to a fault. "For Christ's sake quit passing all your stuff to the Washington *Post*," he said. "You need the *Times* with you too."

O'Brien shook his head. "Honest to Christ," he said, "the *Times* never called me." Kovach immediately made an appointment for someone from the bureau to see him that very day. No story quoting O'Brien appeared for three days, so Kovach called him again, to find no one from the *Times* had ever appeared.

Kovach's suggestion that the bureau contact O'Brien was stated much stronger now, and he was finally interviewed, and became a good source for future stories. Rosenthal learned of what Kovach had done, and he began moving him up through ranks, eventually to the position of deputy national editor.

Kovach carried several directives with him to Washington. Most important was Rosenthal's insistence that the bureau work much closer with editors on 43rd Street. This Kovach accepted. Although he had worked briefly in the bureau earlier in his career, he had no philosophical commitment to the Krock-Reston tradition of bureau autonomy, and he felt coordination made sense. So Kovach had a speaker-phone rigged in his office so that he and deputies could participate personally, so to speak, in the 3:15 and 5:15 P.M. "front page meetings" at which each day's editions are shaped.

John Finney, longtime news editor in the bureau (he retired in January, 1986) felt this step of immense practical value. "This permits us to offer our own comments, and for them to ask questions about our stories. This is also psychological; it makes people think we are part of the whole operation. It also eliminates the sniping that would go on if Washington was not 'present' at the meetings." After an event such as a Presidential press conference, there is free-wheeling discussion on how stories should be broken out for coverage, and how they should be written. Previously, Washington would decide on its own, and send a budget of stories to New York.

Rosenthal also insisted on much tauter writing from Washington. Twenty years ago, when Finney covered the old Atomic Energy Commission, he could routinely crank out a column-and-a-half story and think nothing of it. The space was there, and the *Times* gave it to him. Now any story of that length or more must be approved personally by either Rosenthal or Seymour Topping, the managing editor. The result has been a mechanism for tighter New York control. "Each time you sit down to do a take-out, everyone gets involved." The necessity to go through channels means a quantum jump in the number of editors tempted to tinker with a story, to suggest a different approach or to cut a section.

A third major change in Washington was Rosenthal's insistence that the *Times* no longer attempt to be a "paper of record" for everything that happened in town. Rosenthal realized that the vast majority of the public, even *Times* readers, now relied on television for what he likes to call "the top of the news." So what he demanded of Washington were deep background stories explaining why a particular situation developed. Here the *Times* is blessed with such men as Bernard Gwertzman and Leslie Gelb, who on short notice can write a lucid explanation of the meaning of some change in Middle East or arms control policy.

But Kovach was to live with two problems throughout his years in Washington—Abe Rosenthal's temper, and his constant tampering with bureau personnel affairs. During the last years of his marriage to Ann Burke, Rosenthal made his periodic trips to Washington alone. He would do his business at the bureau and perhaps lunch with an old friend, and then insist on taking a half dozen or so editors and reporters to dinner. Invariably Rosenthal and Kovach would start drinking martinis after dinner, and talking about the bureau, and invariably there would be a nasty argument. Rosenthal used these meetings to say savage things about persons working in the bureau, and their work, and he would also jab at Kovach, as if seeing if he could pick a fight. Sometimes he did, and on at least one occasion, Kovach told a friend, "After we finished yelling at one another, I went home thinking I'd probably talked my way out of a job." But Rosenthal seldom seemed to remember arguments the next day; if he did, he would pass them off. "That was the martinis talking, not Abe Rosenthal." Kovach did not believe this statement for a moment, for he knew that liquor stripped away the thin mask of civility that concealed Rosenthal's true feelings about situations and personalities.

But personnel matters gave Kovach even more headaches. As an executive who managed an important bureau, he felt he should have a strong voice in choosing the people who worked there. Twice he found strong prospects who wished to come to the bureau, persons he truly wanted. Each of them he sent to New York; each was vetoed by James Greenfield, the deputy managing editor for administration, without Rosenthal even giving them (or Kovach) the courtesy of a personal interview. This Kovach, resented, for he felt Greenfield was undermining his authority.

Kovach also became most upset with Rosenthal's handling of a gifted young reporter named David Shribman, considered one of the better political journalists in the bureau. In 1984 Rosenthal called Shribman and told him to move to New York, that he was being assigned to the United Nations. Shribman protested. His wife, Cindy Skrzycki, had just taken a responsible job at *U. S. News & World Report*, and a move now would disrupt her career. Take the job or else, Rosenthal retorted.

Shribman appealed to Kovach, who pleaded with Rosenthal not to insist on the transfer. Look, he said, you're going to be up against two-career couples frequently. If we intend to hire good people, and keep them, we've got to find a way to accommodate them. Kovach did not feel Shribman's transfer was all that essential.

Rosenthal would not yield. Shribman resigned from the *Times* and moved to the Washington bureau of *The Wall Street Journal*. (Al Hunt, the *WSJ*'s bureau chief, told the *Washington Journalism Review*, "The *Times* may be the most anti-family newspaper in America. Their policy has the effect of breaking up families. They want people not to care primarily about their families, and I think in the 1980's you can't deal with people that way.")

Rosenthal faced the two-career dilemma twice in 1985 in more complicated form. Two Washington reporters he wished to transfer to foreign bureaus both had wives who worked for the Washington *Post*. When Phil Taubman pressed Rosenthal about an assignment to Moscow, Rosenthal agreed—but on condition that his wife, Felicity Barringer, not do any reporting for the Washington *Post* while there. Living conditions in Moscow are so confined that Taubman could not possibly keep his work secret from a rival reporter, regardless of how they tried. So Barringer resigned from the *Post* so her husband could take the assignment. (Some months after the move she got the necessary Soviet credentials to permit her to work as a journalist, and she had several bylined articles in the *Times*.) In the instance of the other reporter, Steven Weissman, being sent to India, Rosenthal negotiated an agreement with Ben Bradlee of the Washington *Post* that permitted Elizabeth Bumiller to write feature stories—but no hard news—while they lived in New Delhi. But each of these situations required intricate negotiations in which Taubman and Weissman were told directly that their very careers depended on their wives not passing any bootleg information to the rival *Post*.

Rosenthal's harshness with David Shribman, and the strictures he put on Weissman and Taubman, caused much gossip among Washington media people, little of it favorable to him or the paper—or helpful to Kovach's continuing struggle to hire the people he wanted. His ideal hire would be a person with good political experience in a medium-sized city, who could bring an insider's knowledge of a region or an issue to the bureau and do productive reporting from the start. Instead, time and again Rosenthal used Washington as a promotion for the bright kids who had impressed him working on the metropolitan desk. "Abe's yuppies," bureau veterans came to call these young newcomers. And as products of the soft-news format of the 1980's *Times*, they often were of little use to the sort of bureau Kovach was trying to run.

For instance, one major problem Kovach faced in 1985 was covering the tidal wave of spy stories—from the John A. Walker ring to the peculiar case of Vitaly Yurchenko, the KGB officer who defected to the West, and then fled back to the Soviet Union. Phil Taubman had covered the intelligence community handily for five years. But during the "year of the spy" he was on leave studying Russian in preparation for his transfer to Moscow. So Rosenthal insisted that a major part of the "spook beat" be given to Philip Shenon, the metropolitan reporter who had done the intricate but gravely-flawed articles on Dr. Howard Grossman, the city medical examiner, in early 1985. "Phil's a nice kid and he might be a good reporter—some day," a *Times* veteran said of him. "But to throw him onto such an intricate beat was cruel." Consequently, the *Post* regularly ran ahead of the *Times* on intelligence stories.

So Rosenthal had no choice: he picked up the phone in the spring of 1986 and telephoned Seymour Hersh, who had just finished a book on the Soviet downing of a Korean airliner. Come bail me out, he said, I'll give you a lot of money. I need you for six months. (Rosenthal had originally intended to take Hersh on for only three months; however, Leslie Gelb of the bureau insisted that developing intelligence stories of any consequence required twice the time.) Hersh agreed, and as Rosenthal told a couple of friends with glee, "I feel like I just hired the toughest gunman in the West to go shoot up Washington for me."

What Rosenthal did not seem to understand was that the *Times* system he had fostered, in Washington and elsewhere, did not encourage the development of other Hershes.

On a bright December morning in 1985, John Finney sat in a book-crammed office at the rear of the *Times* bureau at 1000 Connecticut Avenue NW in downtown Washington. He talked about being hired by Scotty Reston in the 1950's, specifically to cover the AEC, and how the AEC chairman, Glenn Seaborg, once told other reporters when asked some arcane question, "Hell, I don't know—I have to go to John Finney to find out what is going on."

But no longer is a *Times* reporter accepted by his editors as an autonomous expert. More and more he is part of an operation in which he must satisfy a group of editors. Reporters no longer enjoy the freedom of the Reston era. Although Finney sees some of the advantages of the Rosenthal system, "This carries a price, in terms of one's satisfaction with the job, and with morale."

Finney fiddled with his pipe a bit, and he looked out a rear window as if he really saw something of interest on the rooftops. "You know," he finally said, "when I go out that door for the last time on January 1, that's the end of it. I'm the last of 'Scotty's boys' in the entire bureau."

Which is exactly what A. M. Rosenthal wanted—a Washington bureau of his own creation, and under his control.

SEVENTEEN

"Don't Pull a Syd On Me"

The summer of 1982 was a harrowing time for Thomas L. Friedman, bureau chief in Beirut for *The New York Times*. For two months the Israeli army had the city under sustained attack, trying to dislodge the Palestine Liberation Organization. Many nights Friedman sat in his office and watched artillery shells and bombs burst in the city, and more than once his own building shook with the impact of an explosion. Despite the danger, he stayed at his post. A. M. Rosenthal had told him when he took the assignment, "Don't get yourself killed, but you are in a damned important position." Friedman was determined to report the Israeli incursion to its conclusion regardless of the risk.

Friedman realized he was in a professionally precarious position as well. The festering Middle East conflict evokes more raw emotion in the United States than perhaps any other foreign issue. The *Times*, because of its Jewish ownership and preponderance of Jewish sub-editors, is watched closely by both parties, and over the years nuances of reporting have been seized upon as evidence of bias. When Zionists were fighting to create the State of Israel in 1946, publisher Arthur Hays Sulzberger publicly opposed them. Referring to Zionist fund-raising tactics, he said, "I dislike the coercive methods of Zionists who, in this country, have not hesitated to use economic means to silence persons who have different views."

The same year Sulzberger refused to publish an ad submitted by the American League for a Free Palestine, which raised funds for the Irgun, an underground group fighting the British. Sulzberger felt Irgun was terrorist, and that charges the ad laid against the British were not true. Jewish department store owners launched a brief but expensive advertising boycott. Sulzberger still refused the ad, but over the years he came to peace with the concept of an Israeli state, and the paper became generally supportive of the Israeli position in disputes with the Arab world. But in the late 1970's the support began to slip, chiefly in reaction to the hardline tactics of Prime Minister Menachem Begin. The *Times* gave front-page publicity to Begin's opponents who urged concessions to start talks with the Arabs on ending the long struggle. The *Times* also began writing stories about supposed Israeli atrocities in occupied West Bank territories.

At a Jewish women's convention in New York in 1978 an Israeli vice consul charged that the *Times* "has mismanaged news, failed to reflect the basic difference between Israel and the Arab world, permitted its editorial policy to determine its portrayal of news and presented its readership with a thoroughly unrealistic picture of Arab policies and motives." The *Times*, he concluded, "is the most dangerous enemy of Israel in the United States."*

Although Rosenthal in private conversations made no secret of his deep love for Israel, he stressed to Friedman and other correspondents in the Middle East that its Jewish origins and ownership made the *Times* especially suspect to Arabs. Hence they must be extra careful to report with objectivity.

The first five days of August the Israelis sensed they had the PLO on the brink of capitulation, and the bombardments intensified. Friedman no longer recoiled when a bomb or artillery shell thudded into a building a few hundred yards from where he worked. Finally, on August 5, he wrote a story describing the Israeli bombing, and in the very first sentence he called it "indiscriminate." He hesitated

*For sharply divergent studies of *Times* policy in the Middle East, see *Bad News: The Foreign Policy of the New York Times*, by Russ Braly, Regnery Gateway, 1984, which argues the paper is virtually a PLO adjunct; and *The Zionist Connection II*, by Alfred M. Lilienthal, North American, 1982, which accuses the *Times* of a strong Israeli bias.

about using such a charged subjective adjective, but based on what he had seen he felt it justified.

Several hours after Friedman filed the story the Telex machine in his office brought a message from the foreign desk: the word "indiscriminate" was editorializing, and editors had deleted it. The cable went on to praise Friedman for good work under dangerous conditions.

Friedman stomped around the office the better part of an hour, muttering nasty things about editors, wondering why he risked his neck for a newspaper that would not accept his on-the-spot judgment about what was happening. Then he sat down and wrote one of the more indicting messages the *Times* ever received from a correspondent.

Friedman wrote he had been careful "to note in previous stories that the Israelis were hitting Palestinian positions and if they were hitting residential area to at least raise the possibility that the Palestinians had a gun there at one time or another." He had used a "strong word" because he had spent the day going around Beirut with William Branigin of the Washington *Post*, and he had concluded that "what happened yesterday was something fundamentally different from what has happened on the previous sixty-three days" of the siege. The "newspaper of record should have told its readers and future historians" about the Israeli terror bombing, he said. For it was "the very essence of what was new yesterday. . . ." The bombing had the "apparent aim of terrorizing its [Beirut's] civilian population." His editors had been "afraid to tell our readers," something he thought "thoroughly unprofessional."

Friedman concluded the angry cable with a cry of true anguish. "What can I say? I am filled with profound sadness by what I have learned in the past afternoon about my newspaper."

Because of a communications complication Friedman sent this particular cable to 43rd Street via a wire owned by Reuters, the British news service, and hence it was exposed to many outside eyes before it reached Rosenthal's desk.

Rosenthal read the cable in a rage. Not only had Friedman challenged the judgment of superiors, but he had done so tartly, and in a manner that exposed the dispute to persons outside the *Times*. Rosenthal cabled Friedman, ordering him to return to New York immediately. As Friedman told a friend, "I flew home expecting to be fired."

In New York he telephoned Rosenthal's office, and he was told to be at a certain restaurant at two o'clock sharp for lunch. Rosenthal came in looking unhappy, and he stood and glowered at Friedman for at least a minute before slipping into his own seat.

"First," Rosenthal said, "you are receiving a $5,000 raise. Second, tell me what happened."

Friedman literally shook with relief, and for more than an hour he told Rosenthal about the war in Beirut, and the troubles he had reporting it. Rosenthal told some stories of his own days as a correspondent, and by the time the last glass of wine had been drained, both men were weeping.

As they arose to leave Rosenthal stepped closer to Friedman and his face darkened again, and he wagged a finger directly in the reporter's face.

"But if you ever pull a stunt like that again, you are fired. Understand?"

"I understand," Friedman replied.

Given his reporting experience abroad, Rosenthal pays particularly close attention to the workings of the *Times* foreign service. Here is an area where he feels true expertise. Rosenthal is an inveterate traveller, and he loves to make hurried trips to areas where big news is developing. In December, 1985, for instance, he became curious about the Philippines, and he flew to Manila to talk with President Ferdinand Marcos and his challenger Corazon Aquino, and in doing so he helped make important news. This came during the Aquino interview, when Rosenthal realized, to his astonishment, that the woman was not familiar with even broad parts of the platform on which she was running. She had no specific program, "the only thing I can offer the Filipino people is my sincerity. . . . What on earth do I know about being president?"

Rosenthal and the *Times*'s resident correspondent in Manila, Seth Mydans, realized Aquino had spoken nonsense, and that she had not the slightest grasp of what she intended to do if elected. So how was this confusion to be conveyed to readers? Ordinarily, the *Times* would publish excerpts from the interview transcript, highlighting the main points. In this instance, Rosenthal decided to "write it exactly as she said it, to let her words speak for themself. Hell, the reader would have no problem figuring it out." The *Times* did just that, quoting Aquino at incomprehensible length.

"This landed like a bombshell in Washington," Rosenthal said. "The State Department had been moving towards supporting her. They got on the phone to her and her advisers and they said, 'This is a disaster, this can't go on.' " Later, Rosenthal said, he heard from Secretary of State George Shultz that the *Times* interview was a turning point in Aquino's campaign, for although an immediate disaster, it forced her to stop talking in generalities and get down to the issues of the campaign, and especially how to cope with the insurgent New People's Army. (Aquino had told the *Times* "I don't feel I am that competent" to deal with the NPA.)

Rosenthal's account of the State Department's reaction to the Aquino interview points up the importance of the *Times*'s foreign coverage in shaping Washington's decisions on how to deal with foreign policy issues. Policy makers must cope with public perceptions of an issue when addressing it. And the *Times*, because of the importance it places on foreign coverage, does more than any other print media to inform the serious American about what is happening in the world.

Persons who have worked on foreign news under Rosenthal, both as reporters and editors, give a fairly uniform composite of what he demands from a correspondent. Foremost, the correspondent must be versatile and have a broad range of interests, for Rosenthal demands that a reporter write about the totality of a country, not just spot news. William Stockton, who became the *Times* Mexico City correspondent in late 1985, within the space of a month wrote about the horrors of driving in that country; on the piquancy of *mole* sauce; on *pastoleraias*, the Christmas folk festivals; and on the walled-in architecture prevalent in Mexican housing. Seeking out such features, Rosenthal feels, helps a correspondent learn about his country in a hurry.

Another characteristic demanded is political "objectivity" that borders on the conservative. As he told one man being sent to Latin America, "Don't go down there and get excited by the leftists and pull a Syd Schanberg on me," referring to Schanberg's reportage from Cambodia. Rosenthal can talk at profane length about Herbert L. Matthews and Harrison Salisbury, "goddamned ideologues," he calls them, for their controversial reporting, Matthews on Fidel Castro, Salisbury from North Vietnam and other places. Rosenthal flinches when reminded of the poster that was a favorite of American conservatives during the 1960's. It depicted a smiling Fidel Castro and the caption, "I got my job through *The New York Times*," long a subway-card advertising slogan of the paper. "There'll be no fucking Herbert Matthews while I'm at the paper," Rosenthal has said.

But Rosenthal does have two conspicuous blind spots in his "objectivity." One is the Middle East, where the *Times* has shielded Israel from the probing criticisms directed at other countries. (Tom Friedman's experience over the "indiscriminate" Israeli bombing of Beirut was unique in that he was a rare correspondent who momentarily overlooked his implicit marching orders.) Another area is South Africa, where Rosenthal's hatred of apartheid and the racist system there long blinded him to Communist domination of the major black opposition group, the African National Congress. Not until prodded by such conservative critics as Reed Irvine of Accuracy in Media did Rosenthal order, in the spring of 1986, a full take-out on the Communists in the ANC. (The information had been publicized in Senate subcommittee hearings four years previously, and the Central Intelligence Agency had circulated unclassified reports on such ANC figures as Joe Slovo, the terrorist director, to anyone who asked for them.) Here Rosenthal's revulsion with the South African regime caused him to overlook the nature of the so-called "legitimate opposition."

Ignoring the ANC, however, was an aberration, for the *Times* is alert for signs of failures of leftist causes and governments abroad—for instance, the "Green Peace" anti-nuclear movement in West Germany, and the socialist Mitterand government in France. Further, the *Times* does not hesitate to correct itself (although in unacknowledged fashion) if it gives an unwitting boost to socialism.

On June 2, 1985, the veteran correspondent Henry Kamm wrote from Athens, "To most Greeks, the election . . . is a referendum on the nation's first experiment in Socialism." The accompanying headline read, "Greek Vote Today Seen as Test of Socialism."

The following day, Kamm did a curious turn-around. Under a headline "Socialist Victory Appears Certain in Greek Election," he wrote, "In effect, the elections were more of a test of the personal popularity of Mr. Papandreou and Mr. Mitsotakis [the socialist candidates] than a clash of party programs and divergent proposals on major issues."* *Times* readers were left to cope with inexplicably differing versions of why the Greeks voted the way they did.

Another characteristic of a successful foreign correspondent is that he learns quickly to play upon Rosenthal's emotions and prejudices. Rosenthal hates Germany, because he can never forgive the massacres of Jews during the 1930's and 1940's. When based in Europe he resisted any suggestion that he be forced to work in West Germany, even temporarily, and several letters he wrote to his boss Turner Catledge state his detestation of Germans in strong language.

John Vinocur, a strapping former college athlete whom Rosenthal hired away from Associated Press in the 1970's, knew of Rosenthal's virulent hatred of the Germans, and when he was assigned to Bonn he wrote a series of stories best summarized by two headlines:

"Hitler's Alpine Hideaway is a Tourist Town's Gold Mine"
"Visit Tests Emotions of Jews Driven From Germany."

The journalist Jan Reifenberg, in a contribution to a book on press coverage of U. S.-European relations† felt that "both stories reflected Vinocur's feelings towards Germany: a constant, nagging doubt as to whether today's Germans have really overcome a sordid past. . . ." Vinocur kept alert for signs of revival of Nazism, on the one hand, and for signs of Communist influence on the anti-nuclear movement on the other. And in 1985 Rosenthal rewarded him with promotion to the job of metropolitan editor, tacitly thrusting him into competition to be his successor as metropolitan editor.

Given Rosenthal's attention to the foreign service, and its importance to the reputation and success of the paper, it is a matter of some irony that one of the *Times*'s greatest embarrassments of the 1980's came from the reporting of an uncredentialed reporter who somehow

---

*If Kamm had any complaints about the change of emphasis, he kept quiet about them, for correspondents gripe about editing at their peril. In 1982 a Paris stringer named Adress Freund complained to Rosenthal about what he considered to be unwarranted tampering with his stories. Rosenthal cabled back, "We will not be addressed in this offensive manner" and fired Freund. Whereupon Freund sued the *Times* for wrongful discharge and won $20,000 and severance pay from a French court.

†*Reporting U. S.-European Relations: Four Nations, Four Newspapers.* By Michael Rice et al. Pergamon Press, 1982.

slipped through the careful screening required of correspondents. Whatever the heat of the controversies over the reporting of such figures as Herbert L. Matthews, Harrison Salisbury, David Halberstam and Sydney Schanberg, the *Times* could argue from the professional high ground that each of these men was an experienced reporter, with an established reputation and journalistic training before joining the paper.

Such was not the case with Raymond Bonner, who in the early 1980's had a brief but controversial stint as the *Times* correspondent primarily responsible for covering El Salvador. How Bonner came to the *Times*, the way he worked while there, and his ultimate disposition by Rosenthal is a case study in how the newspaper behaves when under attack—and how the quality of the information that has been presented to readers became of lesser importance than preserving the self-imputed infallibility of *The New York Times*.

The son of dirt-poor Minnesota farmers, Bonner was only vaguely aware of *The New York Times* until he entered Stanford Law School. He was a marine officer in Vietnam; he worked briefly for one of the myriad Nader organizations in Washington, doing one book on the lack of benefits for Vietnam veterans (*The Discarded Army*) and helping on another (*The Transformation of American Medicine*). He worked as a prosecutor in the San Francisco district attorney's office, but he found the law too harsh. He did not like putting people in jail; many, he felt, were products of a system that had failed them socially and economically. Equipped with a knowledge of Spanish and a vague notion he would like to be a foreign correspondent, Bonner set out for South America, offering his services to any news organization that would hire him.

Here a word about the journalistic foot soldier known as the "stringer." Newspapers such as *The New York Times* are able to cover vast territories because of stringers. These are part-time employees who live and work in the world's backwaters. They must have the journalistic skills to cover routine stories, and the sense to tip the home office when a major story is looming, so that a staff reporter can be dispatched. A permanent stringer receives a modest monthly stipend, plus extra pay for exceptional work. Another category of stringer is the roving free-lance who must produce to be paid. The roving stringer receives the journalistic equivalent of letters-of-marque to roam an area; if he finds a story, he writes it, and he receives money. The better the story, the better the numbers on the check, and hence the stringer is always watchful for something deserving the front page.

Stringing is scut work, and the people who do it must be prepared to live (and often smell) like goats. The stringer lives in the back-alley *pensiones*, not the big international hotels. When he goes to the country, he rides the bus, or a trader's truck, not the chauffeured limousine. The stringer's hope is that his country somehow becomes a big story. And then a staff correspondent arrives on the mid-afternoon plane to pick the stringer's brains, interview his sources, and claim the byline.

Nonetheless, stringing is a gateway to big-time journalism. Stories, not credentials, count the most. This Bonner knew, and he managed to be places that produced news. He was in Bolivia at the time of a military coup, which he reported for the Washington *Post* and *Newsweek*. His work impressed Warren Hoge, then a *Times* correspondent for Latin America, and he did some brief string work for the *Times*.

Hoge wanted Bonner as a full-time correspondent, and he wrote numerous letters to 43rd Street. But no one there wanted to hire a former lawyer with no journalistic background. So Bonner continued roaming. In late 1981, in Mexico, he encountered Alan Riding, the *Times* correspondent there. Riding had problems. Although based in Mexico, he bore responsibility for covering El Salvador, and rightists there had put his name on a death list. Riding offered Bonner a deal. Bonner would spend a week each in Guatemala and El Salvador; if he proved himself, Riding would recommend that the *Times* hire him full-time.

Guatemala proved unfruitful, so Bonner moved south to El Salvador, arriving on a Sunday. On Tuesday four American nuns were kidnapped by men wearing military uniforms, and repeatedly raped and then shot to death. Bonner wrote this story, plus other accounts of the growing violence in the country. In less than six weeks, he was receiving regular bylines, and in December, 1981, he made a three-day trip to New York to meet for the first time with Abe Rosenthal, Seymour Topping, the managing editor, and Jimmy Greenfield, then the foreign editor. Bonner impressed the editors. A strong-bodied man in his late thirties, Bonner eschewed the beard and scuffy clothes of the vagabond journalist. He opted for a neat suit and a trim hair cut. Whatever politics Bonner had he kept to himself, and Rosenthal and the others agreed he had a firm grasp of the politics of El Salvador. So Bonner was hired. For logistical purposes, he would be assigned to the metropolitan desk, for Rosenthal recognized his lack of journalistic training. But he would be sent to El Salvador as needed and should consider that country his more or less permanent assignment.

Here the *Times* went counter to its own practices, something that in hindsight Rosenthal acknowledges was a mistake. Regardless of what Rosenthal and others say of the importance of the metropolitan desk, and how all *Times* reporters should be considered equals whether they cover the White House or rewrite press releases for the Real Estate Section, the foreign service is the crown jewel of *Times* reportage. *Times* practice does not call for unschooled reporters to be sent abroad. It was obvious in 1981 and 1982 that Central America was at the flash-point of crisis, for the Sandinista government of Nicaragua had begun a massive flow of arms to Communist rebels in El Salvador and elsewhere. Bonner's considerable energies notwithstanding, he was an amateur journalist—and yet the *Times* chose him to cover an incipient civil war in Central America.

Rosenthal admits now this was an error. Of Bonner's dispatch to Central America, he says, "He was available. He spoke Spanish. He was a stringer on the spot. We exploited him." After Bonner was taken on staff, Rosenthal notes, he *was* brought back to New York and assigned to the metropolitan desk. But each time a crisis occurred in 1982—and there were many—Bonner was hurried south to cover it. Consequently, as Rosenthal states, "he never really got to learn the job."

This was unfortunate, both for the *Times* and Ray Bonner, for within months the young correspondent was embroiled in controversies that cast doubt on both his credibility and that of the newspaper.

From the very beginning Bonner adopted the skeptic's role in El Salvador. He challenged the efficacy of the government's land reform program, conducted under American advisers. He chronicled the murders of peasants and labor leaders by death squads which he linked to the Salvadoran government. The overriding theme of Bonner's stories was that the U.S. effort to help the faltering Salvadoran government was failing. One person assigned to the U.S. Embassy at the time states, "Bonner was an adversary from day one.

Lord knows but we had problems there, but Bonner would not even listen to arguments for the sake of discussion. His attitude was, 'Since you work for the Embassy, you are a liar.' After a while we pretty much washed our hands of him. Hell, he *wanted* the Duarte government to collapse and the other crowd, the commies, to take over."

Within a month of arriving in El Salvador as a full-time correspondent, Bonner found himself facing two major challenges to his credibility. The first episode, the most serious one, came in early January, 1982, when Bonner wrote a long story claiming that eight U.S. soldiers acting as advisers to the Salvadoran army stood by passively as military men tortured two teenagers suspected of working with the guerrillas. Bonner's sole source was a young man named Gomez, who claimed to have deserted from the Salvadoran army because he was sickened by such atrocities. Bonner found Gomez in Mexico City (through sources he has never discussed publicly) and wrote what he said about the torture sessions. The account was gory, with the soldiers allegedly tearing the skin off a fourteen-year-old boy in strips, and then gouging out his eyes. John Crewdson, another *Times* reporter who happened to be in Mexico City at the time, met Bonner late one night in a coffee shop and went over the article line by line. Crewdson saw a major shortcoming.

"You've got to go to El Salvador and get comments from the government," Crewdson said.

"You *know* what they're going to say!" Bonner replied.

"Yeah," Crewdson said, "but let them say it—that's what a newspaper has to do; that's reporting, that's fairness." That Bonner was seemingly unaware of this fundamental rule of reporting was something for which Crewdson blamed the *Times*. "But Rosenthal is blinded by impact and personality. Ray *looked* like a *Times* reporter in that Brooks Brothers suit, so that was enough." Further, Crewdson suggests, the *Times* should have put an early rein on Bonner's enthusiasm, which at once made him an aggressive reporter but someone who must be monitored closely. Crewdson admired what Bonner did for the *Times*, but with a qualification: "Ray brought his prosecutor's mentality to the *Times*. He wrote articles like he was drafting an indictment."

The first of several versions of Bonner's story arrived at the *Times* foreign desk at 11:05 A.M. on December 21, clicking into a wire machine at the west end of the newsroom. The opening paragraph read:

MEXICO CITY, Dec. 20—A former Salvadoran Air Force soldier said that American military advisers were present during training sessions when young Salvadoran guerrillas were tortured and that the Salvadoran Army frequently dropped victims while still living into the sea from helicopters.

The story aroused suspicions of editors immediately, chiefly because it was "single-sourced," that is, based on the unsubstantiated statements of one person. Although John Crewdson had urged that Bonner obtain comment from the U.S. Embassy in El Salvador and the Salvadoran government, no such comments were in the article. Copy editors began poking through the story with sharp questions. A copy editor with military experience pointed out two inconsistencies. Bonner wrote that the American soldiers, supposedly Special Forces, wore the distinctive "green berets." They were clad also in camouflage fatigues. But as this editor pointed out, Special Forces soldiers then in Central America wore neither the berets nor the "cammies." "This is a fact," the editor said, "for I knew guys who were down there, and they were not wearing the berets anywhere outside the United States."

Craig Whitney, a deputy foreign editor, had enough reservations that he told Bonner to return for a second interview with his source. The revised lead, filed on December 31, took the informant out of the "Air Force" and identified him simply as a "former Salvadoran soldier," and dropped the reference to the American advisers wearing green berets. Whitney also asked John Finney of the Washington bureau to obtain Pentagon comment. "Finney sent it back a day or so later, that it was 'bullshit and garbage,' " a foreign desk editor said. There was more editing; Bonner did a third lead. Although several assistant foreign editors argued to Whitney that the story was "inherently wrong," he replied, "The bottom line is that we believe it." So did Robert Semple, the foreign editor, and the article was published, on page two of the *Times* of January 11, 1982. Several persons who challenged the article thought this placement peculiar and reflected doubt.

Rosenthal was away from the office during all this debate, and the first he knew of the article was when he read it in the paper. According to an editor, "Abe was furious. If the story was true, it should have been on page one. If not true, it should not have been printed.

Putting it on page two admitted the *Times* had questions about a controversial story." Rosenthal summoned Whitney and Semple into his office and "chewed them out."

Upon close examination, by U.S. diplomats and reporters from other newspapers, Bonner's "exclusive" turned out to be built on a most shaky foundation. For starters, his single source, Gomez, had been offering the story around Mexico City for a full eight months before encountering Bonner. Only one paper credited him enough to print it—*Uno Mas Uno*, which is leftist, anti-American and partially financed by the Cuban intelligence service. Gomez claimed that Salvadoran national guardsmen had murdered his parents in May, 1981. Persons in his village stated that the parents had died long before then, and of natural causes. Gomez had problems remembering the number of brothers and sisters he had. Gomez claimed to have made a dramatic escape from a Salvadoran military jail, during which two soldiers were killed. But Salvadoran records showed he had gone on a two-day pass and not returned.

In a war with political overtones, as was the case in El Salvador, it is inevitable that the press and the diplomatic corps become adversaries. Given its attempts to civilize the Salvadoran military the American embassy reflexively would attempt to discredit a charge of an atrocity involving U.S. advisers. The *Times*'s uncertainty about its own story did not help the paper's position. And several persons, including Crewdson, thought it unseemly that the *Times* faulted Bonner for a multi-tiered error. As he put it, "The stories that caused all the trouble were read by seventeen persons. But the blame was all put down on Ray."

Less than three weeks later Bonner published another atrocity story which brought denials from the U.S. Embassy. A major political struggle was waged in Washington in December, 1981, and January, 1982, over whether Congress should give the Salvadoran military more aid to combat the insurgency. Central to this effort was a required certification to Congress by President Reagan that the government of President Duarte had made significant strides in stopping human rights violations. During January Bonner and Alma Guillermoprieto of the Washington *Post* spent two weeks travelling with guerrillas in Morazán province. On January 27 the *Post* published a front-page story by Guillermoprieto about a supposed massacre of civilians by Salvadoran troops in the village of Mozote. The story was datelined January 14, the day of the murders. The *Times* published a similar account by Bonner the next day, January 28, on page 12. Administration supporters were outraged that these stories appeared just as Mr. Reagan was telling Congress that Duarte had made human rights gains, for they seemed timed to undercut the President.

That something awful happened in Mozote was beyond dispute, for both reporters counted scores of bodies, many savagely mutilated. Bonner put the number of deaths at either 926, the count of the Human Rights Commission of El Salvador, or 733, a count by residents of Mozote and adjoining hamlets. Bonner wrote vividly of one woman's remembrances: "Somewhere in the carnage were Mrs. Amaya's husband, who was blind, her nine-year-old son, and three daughters, ages five years, three years and eight months. Mrs. Amaya said she heard her son scream, 'Mama, they're killing my sister. They're going to kill me. . . .'" Bonner did write he could not confirm independently how many persons died or who killed them. (He did *not* report that one of his cited sources of the casualty figures, the Human Rights Commission of El Salvador, was Marxist-controlled, and that the State Department had categorized it as "an insurgent propaganda vehicle.")

Embassy officers disputed Bonner's reportage. Thomas O. Enders, the assistant secretary of state for inter-American affairs, told a House subcommittee that although a battle had occurred between government troops and guerrillas around Mozote in December, "No evidence could be found to confirm that government forces systematically massacred civilians in the operation zone, nor that the number of civilians killed even remotely approached the 733 or 926 victims variously cited in press reports." Enders noted the *total* population of Mozote was estimated at only 300, and that a "good number of persons still lived there." This testimony was not reported in the *Times*.

Bonner also accepted at face value—and the *Times* printed—guerrilla claims that they received no material assistance from either Nicaragua or Cuba. Much of a three-part series he wrote after the conducted tour of Morazán cast the guerrillas as a Latin version of Jeffersonian Democrats who loved Christ, their farms, and freedom, and who set up schools, hospitals and clinics. These statements Bonner reported without a flicker of skepticism. Max Frankel's editorial page echoed guerrilla denials about Soviet or Cuban help for the guerrillas. On February 5 a *Times* editorial stated, "No Cuban 'advisers' or sizable caches of Soviet weapons have been seen by American correspondents in El Salvador."

For Dr. Reed Irvine, the combative president of Accuracy in Media, the press monitor group, the *Times*'s editorial was the figurative last straw. As Irvine commented tartly, "Does he [the editorial writer] really think the guerrillas are going to introduce Cuban advisers to Ray Bonner?" Irvine had written several letters to Abe Rosenthal over the years, protesting the accuracy of *Times* coverage in many areas; Rosenthal ignored him. Now, unfortunately for Rosenthal, Irvine attracted the attention of Punch Sulzberger. And it was through the conduit of Punch Sulzberger, rather than Rosenthal's news department, that Irvine and AIM shamed the *Times* into a turnaround on its coverage of Central America and other areas.

Although press executives such as Benjamin Bradlee rail at Irvine as a "self-appointed critic," the jibe is not taken as the intended insult. Irvine is proud that he started AIM on his very own, for he believes in individual citizen initiative. Irvine came to press criticism in round-about fashion. A Phi Beta Kappa graduate of the University of Utah, Irvine served with the Marines in the Second World War and afterwards as a Japanese linguist. He was a Fulbright Scholar at Oxford and then joined the staff of the Federal Reserve Board in Washington, becoming a senior officer in the Division of International Finance. During the 1960's Irvine became disturbed about media reporting of unrest in America, for he felt that uncritical coverage often caused excesses—the press, in essence, incited mobs for more visual stories.

Irvine became a letter-writer. He would retire to the basement of his suburban Maryland home and write what he considered to be reasoned critiques of media coverage. The media ignored him; "I was naive in those days; I really thought journalism was a profession that prided itself on accuracy and fairness. Well, I had a few things to learn." So Irvine conceived of a formal organization, chaired by a respected media figure, who would monitor the press systematically—not as an adversary, but as an outside voice to evaluate performance.

Irvine did not think the proposition revolutionary. "The media have been reviewing books, films, plays, and what have you for decades," he said. "What I wanted was to apply the media's own process to the media itself." If the media truly was interested in "self-policing," such a group—run by a media person—could be an objective vehicle. Irvine asked Arthur Krock, the former *New York Times* bureau chief and columnist, to head his group. Krock liked the concept but he declined; inevitably the *Times* would be criticized, and he had too much institutional loyalty to publicize his many misgivings about the paper. Other media figures told Irvine to forget it, that the press did not want outside voices "nit-picking and carping at us."

Irvine changed course. Why not form a group to permit media *consumers*—that is, readers, listeners and viewers—be the critics, rather than media *producers?* With $200 donated by a friend, Irvine in 1969 started Accuracy in Media, which put his complaints on a formal letterhead and in 1972 a newsletter, The AIM Report. As Irvine has stated, "I naively thought that if Accuracy in Media's criticisms were just, accurate and well documented, we would be able to prevail over those who were responsible for unfair and inaccurate reporting. Surely in those great media institutions we would be able to find men and women who would see the justice of our complaints and who would insist that corrections be made and remedial action taken to prevent repetitions of the flawed reporting.

"It didn't work that way. . . . While they were willing to mouth their devotion to truth and accuracy, they tended to follow the practice of standing by their stories even when they were manifestly wrong."

Most of the media dismissed Irvine as a meddlesome outsider with an ideological axe to grind. Irvine in fact is unabashedly conservative; and many of his attacks are directed at the liberal bias of the national media. Nonetheless, he is painstakingly careful to marshal his facts when he goes after a perceived distortion of the news. But Irvine began to notice a pattern: the media replied to his detailed critiques not with factual rebuttal, but with polemics. By labelling him a "right-wing extremist," Irvine was dismissed as unworthy of debate or serious rebuttal.

Irvine tried yet another tack. AIM bought token shares of stock in major media companies, and Irvine and an associate, an old-line non-Marxist socialist and labor figure named Murray Baron, attended annual shareholder meetings and asked questions. They first confronted the *Times* in 1975, and the presiding Punch Sulzberger uncomfortably referred their questions to Abe Rosenthal and Jimmy Greenfield, sitting in the front row as news executives. Rosenthal essentially gave brush-off "I'll get back to you" answers; neither he nor Greenfield ever appeared again at a shareholders meeting. Irvine pressed on, at subsequent meetings, and finally in 1978 Sulzberger said he had had enough.

"Look," Sulzberger told Irvine, "you come in here and pop these questions to me, and I'm not prepared to answer them. Couldn't we do this in a different way?" A deal was struck. Each year Irvine and Baron would send a detailed letter to Sulzberger's office, and several weeks later they would meet with Punch and Syd Gruson, his *eminence grise*. Irvine's only stipulation was that the sessions be on-the-record; what Sulzberger told him, he could print in the AIM Report.

Thus commenced an extraordinary series of meetings—confrontations initially, then increasingly civil discussions—during which Sulzberger came to the conclusion that Irvine had truly found serious flaws in *Times* coverage. At the first meetings Sulzberger would defer to Gruson, who as a former newsman reflexively defended the news department. But as the years passed Irvine noted a subtle change in Sulzberger. "He seemed more confident in his own convictions; he did not defer to Syd for answers. He listened to us. He asked questions." And one area where Sulzberger seemed especially interested was Central America. Here Irvine could make a strong case.

The *Times* was slow to report on the degeneration of the Sandinista "revolution" into imposition of a Marxist state upon the people of Nicaragua. In 1981, on the second anniversary of the overthrow of Somoza, the Sandinista government announced sweeping confiscations of farms and private businesses. The Washington *Post*, the Washington *Star*, and *Diario de Las Americas* carried lengthy accounts of these seizures; a lengthy story was dispatched by UPI and available to the *Times* foreign desk. The *Times* story, a small one, reported only that the Sandinistas had staged a rally in Managua and that half a million persons attended. It ignored the confiscations of property.

Nor did the *Times* heed high-level defectors from Nicaragua—luminaries such as Jose Francisco Cardenal, former Vice President of the Council of State; Jaime Pasquier, Managua's Ambassador to the United Nations office in Geneva; and Nevardo Arguello, the third-ranking official in the Justice Ministry. Cardenal and Pasquier warned that the Sandinistas were a step away from declaring Nicaragua a communist state. The *Times* did not publish these warnings. Nor did the *Times* pay attention to the defection of Eden Pastora, who won worldwide fame in 1978 when, as the Sandinista "Commander Zero," he held the Nicaraguan congress hostage. Pastora commanded the *Times* front page as a Sandinista; his defection drew silence.

Irvine and Murray Baron raised these omissions in a meeting with Punch Sulzberger on July 23, 1981. According to a transcript of this conversation, Sulzberger said the *Times's* failure was a question of manpower, that no reporters might have been available to cover Cardenal and Pasquier. The answer did not impress Irvine, UPI filed a story available to the *Times.* Sulzberger did not explain why the *Times* did not cover the property confiscations and the other defections.

The important point was that when Bonner's articles began to appear, AIM's criticisms had prompted Sulzberger to watch Central American coverage closely. Irvine gave him a direct analysis of Bonner done by the journalist Daniel James, who had reported from Latin America for three decades. James learned from his Cuban and Sandinista experiences how "reformers" can mask their motives behind propaganda. James analyzed 23 articles on El Salvador, mostly by Bonner, published in the *Times* between January 11 and February 2, 1982. James termed sixteen "perceptively pro-guerrilla" and the remaining seven "pro-junta" or "pro-U.S.," although two of the latter were only "marginally so." (With perhaps unwitting candor, the left-wing *Village Voice* gave its verdict on Bonner's reportage in February: "It's clear that, at least for the time being, the Administration has lost the propaganda war.")

But the most crushing attack came from *The Wall Street Journal,* whose editor, Robert Bartley, grew disgusted with the *Times* for giving Bonner such license in his "reportage." In an editorial on February 12 that stretched two-thirds of the way down a page, the *Journal* attacked Bonner for being "overly credulous" and warned the *Times* against "journalistic romanticizing of revolutionaries." The *Journal* pointedly reminded the *Times* of Herbert Matthews' espousal of Fidel Castro, and Sydney Schanberg's failure to recognize that the Khmer Rouge victory in Cambodia would result in one of history's most odious genocides. ". . . [Y]ou would think that after being burned enough times serious editors would start to appreciate how such stories tend to end. John Reed's 1917 love affair with the Russian Bolsheviks had no room for any fear that a Stalin might emerge from among its heros. . . . Are we going to have to watch this script replayed again in El Salvador, or can we in the press succeed in bringing some perspective of the story?" The Duarte government had attempted land reforms and was attempting to hold elections. "The press will have failed if, in the whirlpool of confusion, these realities are lost."

By the rules of Establishment journalism, the editorial was a rare public dressing-down of another newspaper, in essence a calling-to-account not only of Bonner but his superiors, Abe Rosenthal and Punch Sulzberger. The criticisms bothered Sulzberger, for they bore out the same points he heard from Reed Irvine.

The morning the *Journal* editorial appeared Rosenthal received a telephone summons from Nancy Finn, Sulzberger's secretary. "He wants you up here right away," she said, "and he's a little upset about something; I thought I'd warn you in advance."

Sulzberger asked Rosenthal, in essence, "What the hell is going on down there? Who is this kid Bonner? My own read is that he is pretty much off base."

The Wall Street Journal editorial upset Rosenthal, but Sulzberger's complaint, polite as it was, was something entirely different. Sulzberger was saying, in his own rambling, round-about way, that he was unhappy with Bonner, and that he wanted Rosenthal to correct the situation. Subordinates remember Rosenthal having a clerk retrieve from the *Times*'s computer system every article Bonner had filed from Central America. He questioned editors who had handled his copy, comparing his as-filed stories with the edited versions that appeared in print. Rosenthal later claimed "outrage" at the Gomez "atrocity" story because he felt it poorly-sourced. The fact remains, however, that Rosenthal did not order a corrective story. He asserted much later his doubts about letting Bonner continue in Latin America, but he uncharacteristically did nothing to translate thought into action. However, at the very time that Reed Irvine and AIM and others forcefully attracted Punch Sulzberger's attention to Ray Bonner's reportage, there came what seems to be a remarkable coincidence that Rosenthal claimed "set my mind to thinking." By Rosenthal's account, his transformation began one quiet Sunday morning in March 1982 at a Quaker meeting house in lower Manhattan.

Rosenthal delighted in spending quiet Sundays roaming around New York, ducking into the odd book store or restaurant, or finding a new gallery. This particular day someone asked if he would attend a meeting at the Friends Meeting House at 221 East 15th Street. Rosenthal was surprised to find bulletin boards in the lobby cluttered with an array of clippings from *The New York Times* about civil wars in Central America. Rosenthal skimmed over them. Those from El Salvador seemed hostile to the Duarte government. Rosenthal looked over the crowd of mostly upper middle class persons. "I thought this strange, that these particular people would be so hostile to the elected government of El Salvador, and also to attempts by the United States to help it against a Communist insurgency."

Quaker "meetings" are non-structured. There is no leader. Persons sit and contemplate until something comes to mind they wish to say, and then they arise and speak. During the period of enforced contemplation, Rosenthal's thoughts kept returning to the lobby display. "I started thinking. The people who put up those clippings are our readers. Maybe they are not getting the total picture. Then I asked myself, How come you've never been to El Salvador? You have two to three people there, and it's only a few hours away. And our people are getting shot there." When he left he was going to Central America, and within forty-eight hours he was there.

The visit, which lasted ten days and included stops in Nicaragua and Guatemala as well as El Salvador, was viewed within the *Times* as an "inspection tour" to see how well his reporters were performing; Rosenthal told me this was not the case. As editor and a former foreign correspondent, he feels professionally handicapped unless he has seen a country and the people who are important there at first hand.

"A day in a strange country is not as good as two days, and two days aren't as good as a week, or a week as good as a month. But even a day is better than nothing." Whatever Rosenthal's motive, Bonner felt his boss had come to Central America to check on him, and also to see what the American Embassy felt about his work. Rosenthal lunched with Ambassador Deane Hinton, who criticized Bonner's work harshly. Rosenthal accepted embassy assertions that Bonner had downplayed Communist aid to Salvadoran rebels. As Rosenthal told *Editor & Publisher* magazine after his return, "I have no doubt the Russians, Cubans, and Nicaraguans have been sending material" to El Salvador, and "possibly to the PLO" as well.

Rosenthal also gave credence to his own reportorial instincts. To Rosenthal, Nicaragua had the Marxist trappings of the post-Stalinist

Communist dictatorships he saw in Poland and elsewhere in East Europe during the 1950's. Bonner argued with Rosenthal on this point. Rosenthal said Nicaraguan society was self-eloquent in its Marxism. Bonner demurred, "Abe," he said, "the simple fact is that we look at it differently. I don't see Nicaragua as any sort of paradise. But it's a fuck of a lot better than El Salvador. In Nicaragua, reporters don't spend their spare time driving around on 'body hunts,' looking for *campesinos* and students left in the road with their heads chopped off. Each of us brings our own baggage to a story. In Nicaragua, at least, I felt safe. No cop or soldier was going to shoot me and leave my corpse with my balls in my mouth just to make a point."

Rosenthal's main decision upon his return to 43rd Street was that the *Times* would no longer cover Central America on an *ad hoc* basis, with reporters flying in to cover each crisis. *Times* people would stay in Central America permanently, "not just when people were shooting at one another."

In a letter to Reed Irvine of AIM, Sulzberger conceded that the *Times* erred in giving the "green beret" torture training story prominence, since the charges lacked any corroboration. As Irvine has written, this admission of error by Sulzberger was the "closest thing to a retraction that AIM has ever received from the *Times*."

Rosenthal's attitude was entirely different. What he said about Bonner in public, and what he did to Bonner in private, say much about Rosenthal as an editor. In public Rosenthal was aggressively protective of Bonner. Rosenthal mentioned AIM in an interview in *Editor & Publisher* on April 10, 1982. Charging that the American press had credibility problems for its Central America coverage was a "phony issue" and a "political red herring," Rosenthal stated. "Credibility is a word used by people who are partisans [sic]. AIM criticizes the press for political motivation. It's pure agit prop, just as the communists use agit prop. They seize on a point and carry on a propaganda campaign against the paper or the individual."

Having thus likened Reed Irvine and AIM to the communists, insofar as communications techniques are concerned, Rosenthal in his next words conceded that the *Times* in fact had been wrong on the torture story. He said, "I felt that story was overplayed. That story was worth only a few paragraphs or nothing because there was only one source. Legitimate criticism of that story can be well taken, but that is not how it's being used. It's being used, ignoring everything else the man and the paper has done, as a matter of so-called credibility. The only people who have no credibility as far as I'm concerned are the AIM people. Absolutely none."

Rosenthal also implicitly endorsed Bonner by including him on a panel he chaired in April at the American Society of Newspaper Editors meeting in Chicago. The same month, Rosenthal gave Bonner a merit raise.

Such was Rosenthal's public defense of his reporter. In private, however, his attitude was a polar opposite. After the spring 1982 elections which put Napoleon Duarte into the presidency in his own right, Bonner wrote an analysis for the Sunday News in Review Section stating, in his later paraphrase, "the war ain't over yet." The lead four paragraphs were changed to depict the elections as a "big defeat for the left," which as Bonner has said, "was not what I wrote." (History proved the edited version more accurate, the Salvadoran war subsided dramatically after Duarte's election.) In another area, for months Bonner wrote stories about flaws in the electoral system, the thrust of which was that even if Duarte won, he would do so by fraud. Warren Hoge, who became foreign editor in early 1982, at first ran these stories. Then he passed along a Rosenthal order: "I don't want to see any more of Bonner's pieces on electoral fraud." (Outside observers credited Duarte with a clean win in one of the more honest elections in the history of Central America.) Bonner's reportage had its anchor in perceived failures of American policy in El Salvador. By mid-1982, the policy seemed to be working, and Abe Rosenthal began a swift disengagement from Bonner.

Bonner heard few complaints directly; he could best judge 43rd Street's dissatisfactions by the changes made in his copy, or by stories that were not printed. By late 1982 he realized that his reportage displeased Rosenthal. He tried to find the exact nature of the complaints. He ran into blind alleys; what editors would say behind his back they would not repeat personally. Craig Whitney told people, "Bonner is not a leftist; he's a lawyer, an advocate, he pushed his viewpoint but not necessarily the Commie one." Bonner heard of this statement. He bearded Whitney, and he demanded, "Show me a story, give me an example." Whitney denied making any such characterization. Bonner came to look on Whitney with disgust, as a man who was afraid to confront him directly.

There was another episode, even more ugly. Rosenthal came to

Washington for the annual dinner of the Gridiron Club, the journalistic lodge. During the weekend he took several Washington bureau
people to dinner. Rosenthal was tipsy when the dinner began; he got
drunker as it progressed, and he talked about "fascists on the right,
and fascists on the left." Why, Rosenthal asked, had not "the great
Ray Bonner" given as much attention to "the Commie murderers" as
he had to the so-called "death squad" killings by the Salvadoran military. His voice slurring, Rosenthal referred to the fascists as "shit,"
drawing out the word until it seemed four or five syllables long. Bill
Kovach, the Washington bureau chief, seemed uncomfortable as did
his wife Linda, who sat near Rosenthal. At each utterance of the barn-
yard expletive, Rosenthal turned to Linda Kovach and said, "Sorry,
that slipped out, forgive me, little lady, it won't happen again."
Kovach listened in seething silence. He told another man the next
day, "If he did that one more time, I had decided to stand up and
dump the table in his lap."

In August, 1982, Rosenthal recalled Bonner from Central America
and told him he would work on the business-financial desk. Rosenthal
had no problems with Bonner's reportage; the reassignment would
school him in the "*Times* system." Rosenthal denied that he considered Bonner an "advocacy reporter," as Bonner had heard from several persons. Once Bonner completed "training," he could expect assignment to the Washington bureau. Four years later, however,
Rosenthal gave a significantly different reason: "I brought him out because he didn't know how to be a correspondent."

Bonner began writing a book about El Salvador, and his career at
the *Times* slowly sputtered to a close. As a business writer he turned
his attention to the Philippines, and how loans from the World Bank
and the International Monetary Fund supported the tottering government of President Ferdinand Marcos. Two of these stories got into
print, in the inner reaches of the paper. Other, harder ones did not,
and the biz-fin editor, John Lee, would give Bonner no logical excuse. One of Rosenthal's underlings, a man named William Borders,
finally broke the expected news. No, he would not be going to Washington. Borders said this with an uneasy smile, as if sorry to bring bad
tidings. Bonner thought even less of Borders when he heard something the man said about him behind his back. "I hope," Borders told
another *Times* editor, "that Bonner's book is not going to be another
leftist tract."

Bonner went on a leave of absence to write his book about the Salvadoran government being beyond salvation. (Actual events proved the opposite; three years after Bonner's doom forecasts Duarte remained in power with growing support.) After finishing his book Bonner did not wish the limbo of the *Times*. He turned his attention to the Philippines, and the Marcos government. He made perfunctory inquiries at the *Times*; no, if he returned, it would be to metropolitan or business-finance, not to the foreign desk. There was another factor. Bonner was in love with Jane Perlez, an Australian-born *Times* city reporter and he did not want his problems to hurt her career, even indirectly.

So Ray Bonner went to 43rd Street as his leave ended and told Craig Whitney he was quitting. Rosenthal was away; Whitney suggested he wait until he returned. No, Bonner said, his mind was made up. He repeated his decision to Seymour Topping, the managing editor. Topping said, "Such a rash decision, such a surprise." But the charade was too much for Topping, and he joined Bonner in an outburst of honest laughter.

Bonner left a note for Rosenthal. He was sorry he could not say farewell in person; he would nonetheless like to talk to him "at your convenience." Bonner never heard from Rosenthal.

Times Books Company, then the publishing subsidiary of the New York Times Company, prepared promotional material for Bonner's *Weakness and Deceit*. The ads pictured Presidents Carter and Reagan, and the headline asked, "Have they been telling you the truth?" The text, in essence, stated that "now we know Ray Bonner is telling the truth," that he was giving the "true story" of El Salvador, because of the previously classified documents which comprised the core of his book. Max Frankel wrote a hot memorandum of protest to Roger Straus, the book company president. The implication, Frankel argued, was that the *Times* had not been telling the truth. Times Books changed the ad.

The *Times*'s review of *Weakness and Deceit*, written by Latin American specialist Abraham Lowenthal, was unfavorable; by one reliable account that reached Bonner, the original version was even worse. But Ned Chase, Bonner's editor at Times Books, passed along some office talk that did not surprise Bonner. If any other author had written the book, Chase said, the harsh language of the review would have been softened even further. "But you are no friend of Abe Rosenthal's."

Rosenthal's final disavowal of Bonner came in early 1985, when he hired as a Latin American correspondent Shirley Christian, who had long covered the area for the Miami *Herald*. Christian is good; in 1981 she became only the second woman to win the Pulitzer for international reporting. She had been on the "death lists" of Salvadoran death squads. But to Bonner and his friends, Christian was anathema because of an article she published in the *Washington Journalism Review* in 1982 entitled "Covering the Sandinistas: The Foregone Conclusions of the Fourth Estate." The thrust of Christian's article was that reporters for *The New York Times* (including Bonner's mentor, Alan Riding), the Washington *Post* and CBS spent more space on the barbarities of the late General Anastasio Somoza than on what the Sandinista National Liberation Front intended to do to the country. In her reportage Christian looked beyond revolutionary slogans to record that the Sandinistas were imposing a police state worse than that of the deposed Somoza.

Rosenthal met Christian during his trip to Central America in 1982, and he tried to hire her then. But correspondents Warren Hoge and Alan Riding argued she was so aligned with conservatives as to be unreliable. After the Bonner experience, however, Rosenthal decided to try again. So to Bonner's enormous irritation, Shirley Christian took the job he had wanted for himself: assignment to the *Times* Washington bureau, with broad responsibility for coverage of Latin policy stories. His pique goes back to her critical article in the *Washington Journalism Review*. His thesis: "You don't attack one of your own. Reporters working together in the field on the same story should not challenge one another's motive. And then for the *Times* to turn around and hire someone who has attacked a reporter on the paper—bad news."

Christian's thesis is the opposite. Once the media and the tone of its coverage become a part of the story, as it did in Central America, the media should be subject to the same critical analysis that it applies to the other parties.* The press—and especially the *Times*

---

*Christian's book on Nicaragua, *Nicaragua: Revolution in the Family*, was published in early 1985, soon after she joined the *Times*. Seemingly she indulged in some self-censorship, for she did not repeat her criticisms of press coverage of the Sandinista revolution.

and Bonner—did not hesitate to criticize the U.S. Embassy, the Salvadoran military and President Duarte. Why, then, should the press be exempt from the same examination?

Easily overlooked in the arguments over inadequate or biased press coverage of a significant event is that the loser is not an editor or a newspaper whose reputation suffers transitory professional embarrassment. The loser is the reader. Persons who pay the *Times* for news rely upon the paper to tell what is happening, in accurate and intelligible fashion. And if what subscribers are told in previous months has been wrong, why not say so, and set the record straight? The bulk of the evidence is that in Raymond Bonner, the *Times* had a reporter whose energy and political conclusions far exceeded his journalistic qualities. Bonner burned the *Times* twice (the Gomez "atrocity" and Mozote). Nevertheless the *Times* left him in place for many more months, and did nothing to alert its readers that perhaps there was more to those articles than they had been told—that in fact Green Berets may not have witnessed the torture of Salvadoran teenagers, and that the pillage at Mozote may not have been a deliberate slaughter by Salvadoran soldiers.

In this instance Rosenthal displayed what is arguably his worst quality as an editor—his inability to admit that *The New York Times* could err on a story, and once having done so, to set the record straight for readers who trust the *Times* to bring them accurate news. Insofar as El Salvador was concerned, Rosenthal did not approach his oft-stated goal, "to keep the paper straight."

EIGHTEEN

"Arthur Is a Newspaper Fool"

An assumed truth around the *Times* newsroom—for most persons, in any event—was that Arthur Gelb spoke for Abe Rosenthal, regardless of the issue involved. Gelb would state that he wanted such or such an article done; if the writer resisted, Gelb would continue, with a helpless sigh and an I-don't-like-this-either shrug, "Abe *wants* this done." He uttered these words with assurance. Given the long relationship of the two men, a friendship so deep it was a part of the *Times* legend, few persons offered challenge. Thus Artie Gelb made wide use of his implied and assumed power, in apparent comfort that no one would call his hand. To a skillful conniver, maintaining the *illusion* of authority can be as valuable as the *reality* of authority.

Artie Gelb's claimed mandate as Abe Rosenthal's surrogate was especially important at the *Times* once the newspaper began the special-section expansion of the mid-1970's. Given Gelb's intense interest in cultural and arts news, he assumed broad responsibility for choosing what stories went into these "soft sections," and how they were written. That Gelb did not always seem as versed on music, the theater and books as he tried to demonstrate was really of no matter to him. He would make the choices as he saw them, and he did not entertain argument.

Besides, he could always fall back on his stock clinching argument, "But Abe wants this done. . . "

Intellectually and professionally, Gelb was absolutely subservient to Rosenthal. A woman acquaintance reports asking Gelb casually at a dinner party, "Artie, have you *ever* disagreed with Abe on anything?" She states, "Without a flicker of hesitation, he replied, 'No.' He didn't even have to think about it. He knew the answer."

Nor did Gelb pretend to possess the cleverness—much less the pride—to show even a semblance of independence. Two episodes, among dozens, illustrate his eagerness to please Rosenthal, to the extent of abandoning his own position in mid-course, or giving his superior credit for his own idea. Frank Prial developed a reputation as a superb wine writer at the old New York *Herald Tribune*; when he came to the *Times* the decision was made to send him to the Paris bureau. There was a long interval between the assignment and the actual departure date. Gelb called him to his office and asked, "What are you doing to prepare for Paris?"

Prial explained he was studying French at Berlitz and taking courses in French history and literature at the New School.

"Frank, that's stupid," Gelb said. "That's not the way to prepare for a job as a foreign correspondent. Get your tickets and go to Paris and write a story and get it in the paper—that's the way."

Rosenthal wandered in about this time, and he repeated Gelb's very question. The sequence worried Prial; was he being set up for something? He decided to offer the some honest answer, but with some trepidation given Gelb's advice. Rosenthal heard him out, and he exclaimed, "That's exactly right! The French do not respect people who don't speak their language or know their history and culture."

Gelb threw his arm over Prial's shoulder. "I wanted you to hear it from the man himself," he said. Prial never quite trusted Gelb after that moment.

A graduate of the University of Michigan law school, Roger Wilkins had served in the Justice Department in the early 1960's under Attorney General Ramsey Clark, then with the Agency for International Development, the Ford Foundation, and the Washington *Post*, the latter as an editorial writer. While in school Wilkins had lived in the same dormitory as Marvin Siegal, one of Gelb's assistants. One day in the newsroom they fell into conversation about Michigan's upcoming Rose Bowl football game. Gelb happened by, and Wilkins stopped him.

"Artie," he said, "you are deputy managing editor. If you had any imagination, you wouldn't send just any sports writer to the Rose Bowl; you'd send Marv or me, 'cause our hearts are made of Michigan blue."

Wilkins said this as a joke; covering college football was not on his agenda those days. But Gelb took him seriously. ("Gelb had no sense of humor unless it's Abe telling the joke," Wilkins said.) He suggested that Wilkins do a retrospective piece for the sports section about Michigan and the Rose Bowl. Wilkins shrugged; why not? "All this for kidding with Artie."

As it turned out, the article was a success; it was picked up by one of the Detroit papers, and reprinted in the Michigan alumni bulletin. When Wilkins commented on the piece later, with the aim of crediting Gelb for asking him to do it, Gelb said without hesistation, "You know, that was Abe's idea."

These and other episodes convinced casual observers in the news room that the relationship between Rosenthal and Gelb flowed two ways; that Rosenthal so respected Gelb as a newsman, and his faithful subordinate, that he gave him broad license to do as he wished with the "soft sections." Being a sycophant does not necessarily destroy a person's ability to function as a newsman; supporting exhibits are sprinkled liberally throughout the American media. But only rarely did an outsider see a hint of any discord in the Abe-and-Artie partnership. Hence an episode Mimi Sheraton witnessed one night at dinner in 1977 was all the more shocking to her—both at the time, and at a distance of more than a decade.

Mimi Sheraton is a confident woman, a food and restaurant critic sure of her own tastes and judgments, and willing to test them in the market of public opinion. At *New York* Magazine beginning in the late 1960's she acquired the reputation of a writer who considered the diner and the food buyer her ultimate audience. She recognized editor Clay Felker's core idea that service-oriented magazines are for the reader, not for the advertisers who rent space. Satisfy the reader, the magazine will succeed. There was no particular magic to Sheraton's formula, only logic. She would visit a restaurant, write intelligently about the food and service there, and go on to the next place. Readers trusted her. And she "felt a responsibility to all those folks who drove in from Jersey or the Island, and depended on me to tell them the best place to spend $50 or $75 for their night on the town." So when the *Times* began constructing its own service sections, Mimi Sheraton was the logical candidate for restaurant critic.

The *Times*, through several editors, had flirted with Sheraton earlier, to no avail. Rosenthal seemed serious when he brought her in for a talk in 1975. He wanted her for his "new" *Times*. He professed to have no problems with her reputation as a "strong," outspoken critic," for such was what he wanted. Rosenthal had only one caveat: "If a product or a restaurant is no good, say so. You slap a man in his face, but you don't have to cut him with your ring."

Rosenthal then told a story which Sheraton interpreted as a broad mandate on how she should do her work. A previous *Times* critic (Sheraton politely declined to give his or her name) wrote a long and supposedly informed story about how food in a certain country had "improved." But the critic had not visited the country previously; his "comparison" was hearsay. "It's horrible to do a story on hearsay," Rosenthal said. "Never write about anything you haven't tried."

Sheraton happily went about her new job, writing a variety of stories for the new sections—restaurant reviews, trends in food, how-to pieces on cookery. Gelb had working authority over the sections and on a day-to-day basis Sheraton answered to him. Very early she realized that she and Gelb had divergent ideas on how her job should be done—and also the hollowness of his claim, "Abe wants this done."

The first direct conflict came over a "round-up story" run each Wednesday in the Living Section. "I'd list the best butcher shops, or the best places to buy coffee in the city," Sheraton said. "Artie comes over and says I must also do all the suburbs—the best place to find coffee in Scarsdale, in New Jersey, in Nassau." Sheraton protested. She worked alone, with no researcher, no secretary. "It's impossible," she told Gelb. "It's hard enough to do Manhattan."

Sheraton's objections did not bother Gelb. He suggested that she go through the phone books and whatever other directories she might have and make her choices. "Can't you make a few phone calls?" Gelb asked.

Incredulous, Sheraton responded, "You mean, get recommendations without actually *going to the place*?"

"Yeah, yeah, that's it, make a few phone calls," Gelb said.

Sheraton protested even louder. She remembered what Rosenthal had told her during the hiring interview, that a critic should not write about things she or he had not experienced. As the argument heated, Gelb became adamant.

"Abe wants you to do this," he stated.

Sheraton wondered. Was Gelb really speaking for Rosenthal, or was he invoking Rosenthal's name as a false trump card to intimidate or impress a reporter?

Sheraton chose to call Gelb's bluff, "because I was not afraid to go to Abe. In fact, it was the only thing that I could do." So she recounted the conversation to Rosenthal, who replied, "Oh, Arthur's crazy. That's not what I said. Why do people misinterpret me all the time?"

This particular storm passed without further ado, but the significance was not lost on Sheraton, who is not dumb. As she saw the ploy, "See how far you can push her, and let the other guy take the burden of making the demand."

Another episode, a most ugly one, called into more vivid focus Sheraton's doubts about Rosenthal's true feelings about his supposed friend and most-trusted aide. After Sheraton had been at the *Times* about a year, she and her husband, Richard Falcone, joined Abe and wife Ann for dinner one evening at the Coach House, a popular Village restaurant. Four bottles of wine were served during the evening, and Rosenthal did much of the drinking. "He was drunk," Sheraton says of Rosenthal. The talk turned to the special sections, and Rosenthal said they had "saved the paper."

"I understand you are making a fortune on them," Sheraton said.

"Who told you that?" Rosenthal demanded.

"Why, Arthur Gelb," Sheraton said.

"Arthur told you they are making a lot of money? Making a fortune! It took so much money to get them started, it will take a long time to get it back," Rosenthal exclaimed. Gelb knew nothing about the finances of the new sections, he said.

Rosenthal then began talking about Gelb as a person. "Arthur is stupid," he said. "I love him, he is my brother. But he will always be stupid."

As Sheraton and her husband listened in embarassed silence, Rosenthal continued denouncing Gelb. "Arthur is a newspaper fool. He is one of those people who work on newspapers all their life and never understand what they are doing or what is happening in the world." Rosenthal seemed to like the words "newspaper fool," and he repeated them several times with relish.

Recalling the incident, Sheraton said, "I was turned to stone, listening to him. My own feeling is that Arthur would kill for Abe, and Abe would sell Arthur down the river if push ever came to shove." Although Sheraton realized that Rosenthal was "*very* drunk" that evening, his statements were so emphatic they could not have been random. That he would say such things about a man reputedly his friend in the presence of other persons unnerved and disgusted Sheraton. (Later, she wrote a memo about the incident, to preserve it for her memory.)

Rosenthal never mentioned the evening again, nor did he ever criticize Gelb in such harsh words in Sheraton's presence. Indeed, the food critic and the editor seemed to have a smooth relationship, for the most part. Sheraton quickly picked up on the small things that made Rosenthal happy, the among-friends gestures that appealed to his broad sense of family. She knew he doted on Indian and Japanese foods, and when she found an especially good restaurant she would send him a note several days in advance of her review, so he could enjoy it ahead of the crowds. (Rosenthal does not hesitate to use his title to command a table. "I want a good table," he once told Sheraton. "I've earned that through the years." To a *maître d'hotel* who inquired, "Are you with *The New York Times*?" Rosenthal replied, 'I *am* the New York Times.")

Rosenthal exuded delight when he went to the Carnegie Delicatessen a few days after Sheraton wrote that the place had the best corned beef in New York. "It was a madhouse when Abe arrived," Sheraton said, "with people lined up on the sidewalk. Some had clippings of my review in their hands. Abe was delighted. When he went in he introduced himself, and he told me, 'Now I know what power is. Power is getting a cloth napkin at the Carnegie Deli when everyone else gets paper.' "

Unlike Gelb's concentration on trivialities, Rosenthal chose to argue with Sheraton over matters of substantial critical policy. During her early days at the *Times* two very expensive restaurants opened in Manhattan, with prestigious managements—Windows on the World, and a revamped Tavern on the Green. "They were very awful, very expensive, and I gave them bad reviews," Sheraton said. "This made

Abe mad. He had a big interest in the city at the time, because these were the days when New York supposedly was going bankrupt, and he felt the restaurants were an expression of confidence in the city's future. He told me, 'Mimi, you were too severe.' I told him, 'Abe, the food is terrible at both places, and they're way too expensive. I couldn't recommend either as a place to send people.'

"I think you are hard on famous restaurants and famous people, more than on the little people," Rosenthal said. "Would you be as rough on it if this was a small place?"

"If I went to a little unknown restaurant that was as bad as Tavern on the Green, I wouldn't review it at all," Sheraton said. As she recounted, "This stopped Abe dead in his tracks, and I could almost hear the wheels turning as he thought over what I said. 'This is a very good answer, and I now understand what you are saying,' Abe told me. 'If they are famous, it is in the public interest to say it is terrible, if it is, and they have publicized themselves." Then Abe added, "But if you are going to criticize a place, sound sorry about it. The Tavern on the Green, for instance, write, 'too bad it is terrible.' "

Disputes with Arthur Gelb, conversely, followed a more disturbing pattern. As Sheraton complains today, Gelb's favoritism towards friends was transparent, and he constantly probed for ways to bypass her authority as *the* food critic of *The New York Times*. As the person who carried that title, Sheraton spoke with institutional authority on restaurants. *Times* policy was explicit: the food critic had the final say over how an establishment should be rated, even if only for the brief notices that appear in "round-up" columns. The policy extended into the Travel Section, where a writer could describe a restaurant and its fare only in general terms. By Sheraton's account, Gelb frequently managed to find ways around the policy, by "engineering" stories and column items that featured favorably restaurants of his friends. One such instance she cited was Broadway Joe's, partially owned by a former Times writer and close friend of Gelb, Sidney Zion. *Times* policy for the Friday "Dining Out Guide" is firm. If a restaurant is included, the compiler of the column consults the original review and does a precis with a quote; if the restaurant has not been reviewed, it must not be listed in the Guide. Broadway Joe's was an exception, one that irritated Sheraton. And when she finally visited the place she did not like it, and she said so in a manner that "was very rough on the restaurant and Sid Zion personally." Gelb was on vacation when she submitted her copy. "Abe laughed and didn't change a word," Sheraton said.

Sheraton dined out seven nights weekly; the job confined her to New York. Contract restrictions kept her from writing about food elsewhere, and forced her to publish her books through Times Books Company ("a horrible publishing house, in terms of getting behind a book and really promoting it"). Her problems with Gelb intensified. "Arthur and I were at swords' point even when we were not fighting." Thus Sheraton was restless when along came *L'Affaire Alfredo*.

Alfredo's of Central Park South happened to be the favorite dining place of Arthur Gelb. The owners and staff treated Gelb attentively, and made him feel respected. Such is normal for a *maître* desiring to befriend a customer; people don't eat twice in places where they are snubbed. But Gelb's love for Alfredo's was so intense, and verbal, that people at the *Times* began to chuckle. One former *Times* reporter, a man who does not admire Gelb, said, "Artie is a hick, and he reacted like a hick when Alfredo's fawned all over him."

Eventually Mimi Sheraton visited Alfredo's, though not at Gelb's suggestion. "It was a horrid looking place, but the food could be good if they knew you. If they do *not* know you, the service could be insufferable."* Because Sheraton does not let her face be known, she was treated like any other diner in from the suburbs for a night of fun— which is to say, not too well. Sheraton wrote in effect that Alfredo's had good food but terrible service, and gave it a two-star rating. (The *Times*'s star system: none, poor to fair; one, good; two, very good; three, excellent; and four, extraordinary.) Sheraton felt the two stars would "make everybody happy."

Sometime later, Sheraton began compiling a new edition of *The New York Times Guide to Restaurants*. For many places, so much time had lapsed since her original review that she returned for a fresh appraisal. Among them was Alfredo's of Central Park South, and she found a sharp deterioration. The service was even more sluggish than before; the food was no longer as good; several old house specialities no longer were on the menu. So Sheraton downgraded Alfredo's in a new review she wrote for the daily paper, terming it only a no-star "fair." "In retrospect, I could have left Alfredo's out of the book alto-

*Amen. I stood around the entry way for twenty-five minutes one night when attempting to check Sheraton's appraisal. The *maître* seemed to have no interest in my patronage, and I left.

gether, because I did not need a confrontation." But she had reason to do the reappraisal. Gelb several times had inspired "theme" stories that included Alfredo's, and each time the two-star rating was repeated, with Sheraton as the authority. She knew the place had slipped, and she did not want her name associated with a review that was no longer accurate. "I felt the only way to squelch that was to do a re-review."

Following *Times* procedures, the review was read by editors including Gelb and Jim Greenfield as well as by house lawyers. Gelb telephoned Sheraton at her home that evening. "Abe and I are very upset by your review of Alfredo's," he told Sheraton. "We feel that it is a matter of reverse *macho*. You want to feel you are powerful enough to dump on a place the bosses go to. Why are you doing this review at all?"

Sheraton explained the changed circumstances at Alfredo's, and said that she could not help but do a re-review.

"We would like you to either drop the review, or give them one star," Gelb said. Sheraton refused.

"Abe is very upset about this and wants to speak to you first thing in the morning," Gelb said, with a huff in his voice that warned, "You are in trouble." He hung up.

When Sheraton arrived at the *Times* the next morning she telephoned Rosenthal's secretary and said, "I understand Mr. Rosenthal wants to talk with me about the review of Alfredo's. I will be here all day. Any time he wants will be all right with me." As Sheraton relates, "He never called me. He never said 'boo' about the review." The review ran as written. (Gelb was never to speak to Sheraton again at the paper, other than to tell her, "Goodbye and good luck," when she resigned.)

Six to eight weeks passed, and Sheraton picked up the *Times* one morning and saw a headline, "Recipes of My Favorite Restaurants," written by Craig Claiborne. She laughed. "I knew without looking that Alfredo's was in there. Bingo! There it was. '. . . one of my favorite neighborhood restaurants . . . ' " Claiborne lives in the West Fifties between Sixth and Seventh Avenues, and Alfredo's indeed is in his neighborhood. But Sheraton sensed that Alfredo's mention was not of immaculate origin. She knew that Claiborne is deft at playing Gelb, a "sucker for celebrities" who enjoys Claiborne's summer parties in the Hamptons. "Craig knows how to do it," Sheraton says.

Curious, Sheraton talked with Pierre Franey, Claiborne's friend and collaborator. "What is wrong with Craig?" she asked. "Is Alfredo's really one of Craig's favorite restaurants?"

"No," Franey replied, "he didn't want to do that. Arthur kept calling him, asking him to do a piece on Italian restaurants and including Alfredo's." Joan Whitman, Claiborne's neighbor in Southampton, and editor of his books, told Sheraton the same. And when Sheraton asked Nancy Newhouse, the Style Section editor, about the article, "She rolled her eyes skyward and said, 'Please, that's the week we would all like to forget.' "

There was yet another episode. The weekly "Dining Out" column, which appears in the Friday *Times*, carries no byline. When hired, Sheraton told Rosenthal that since the column consisted of capsulized, untimely reviews compiled by a clerk, she did not wish her name signed to it. Rosenthal apparently forgot this conversation, for he ordered, "I want Mimi's name on that column. She is the critic." Gelb relayed Rosenthal's order to a junior editor who compiled the column, who reminded him of Sheraton's reason for not putting her byline on it.

"You tell her [Sheraton] her name goes on, or she's fired." Gelb ordered. There was a brisk inner-office squabble. As Sheraton says now, "All I can tell you is that my name was not on the column, and I was not fired."

By the time the Alfredo matter arose, Sheraton had decided for many reasons to leave the *Times*. She wished to travel, she wanted to do books for publishers of her own choice. She saw no reason to get into yet another unpleasant scene with Gelb over Alfredo's. "But in fact that [the Alfredo's matter] was 90 percent of my decision," she said. When she told Rosenthal she intended to leave, he did not raise serious argument: "He thought I was getting too big for my britches." She signed a lucrative contract with Time, Inc., and with Conde-Nast, and the last days Rosenthal seemed to have second thoughts. He did not care for "celebrity journalists on his staff," he told her. "Be anything you want. I'll give you lots of money." Sheraton demurred. Given her options, life was too short to spend squabbling with Arthur Gelb. So she left.

Someone at the *Times* took a last slight measure of revenge. Her newest edition of *The New York Times Restaurant Guide* had been published several months previously, with promotion in numerous

Times house ads. After she left, no further house ads appeared. (The book continued selling briskly, to Sheraton's pleasure.)

Artie Gelb did not mourn Mimi Sheraton's leaving the *Times*. Indeed, to Gelb anyone foolish enough to work elsewhere surely was of no lasting talent. Several years ago Gelb became enraptured with the work of Arlene Croche, the dance critic of *The New Yorker*. He told Robert Gottlieb, her editor at Knopf, "We want to hire her. We can make her the best dance critic in America." Gelb talked enthusiastically about how the *Times* would promote Ms. Croche, with her picture on delivery trucks and large ads in the paper. "Talk to her for me, would you?" he asked Gottlieb. "I really want her working on the paper."

Ms. Croche sent word she was perfectly happy at *The New Yorker*, and she did not care to get involved in the Byzantine cultural politics of 43rd Street. And somehow having her blownup photograph on the side of newspaper delivery trucks offered little appeal.

Without a blink Gelb said, "OK, we'll get someone who's better." And within weeks he was making disparaging remarks about "that woman Croche or whatever her name is who writes all that awful stuff in *The New Yorker*."

Aside from prominent position in the *Times* news department, Arthur Gelb's chief professional accomplishment is a biography of the playwright Eugene O'Neill, written with his wife, Barbara. Understandably, Gelb's fascination with his subject continued past the research and writing of the book, which means that *Times* readers receive a diet, and a steady one, of articles pertaining to O'Neill. Indeed, a cultural anthropologist of a century hence who used *The New York Times* as his sole reference source would surely describe O'Neill as the most talented American playwright ever, based on the coverage he received in the *Times*. Some of the mentions seemed rather thin. For instance, at Gelb's insistence, the *Times* cultural staff dispatched a reporter to cover a conference of urologists at a Connecticut college for no apparent reason other than that O'Neill had been a urology patient at the hospital associated with it. A presentation of an O'Neill play in the People's Republic of China warranted a full column. A Broadway revival of *The Iceman Cometh* in 1985 brought a longish critique of O'Neill's career in the Sunday Arts & Leisure Section, bylined by Barbara Gelb. (Geoffrey Stokes of the *Village Voice* unkindly noted she cribbed vast portions from the earlier biography.)

Indeed, the *Times* has so associated the Gelbs with O'Neill over the past two decades they have come to be identified as *the* biographers of the playwright. Such is not exactly the case. Another writer became involved in the O'Neill life story at about the same time as did the Gelbs, in the late 1950's. He is Louis Sheaffer, a former drama critic for the defunct Brooklyn *Eagle*. After the *Eagle* folded in 1955, Sheaffer turned to theatrical publicity, and he did work on behalf of two O'Neill plays produced by Circle in the Square. He decided to do a biography, and almost immediately he received a call from Artie Gelb, then still a Broadway reporter for the *Times*. As Sheaffer recollects, Gelb told him, "Look, it's making it difficult for both of us [to be pursuing the same interview subjects]. Let's not sew up anybody exclusively as our source." Sheaffer did not feel any exclusive claim to O'Neill, so he agreed, and he helped Gleb arrange access to a Connecticut newspaperman named Art McGinley who knew much of the playwright's early life. But Gelb did not reciprocate as promised. "Gelb got to several people first, and I couldn't get to first base with them." Once Sheaffer realized what was happening, he stopped helping the Gelbs with his own sources.

The Gelbs did work hard, apparently. The veteran producer Jasper Deeter of Hedgerow Theater in suburban Philadelphia wrote a relative in the late 1950's that Barbara Gelb was particularly insistent. "Mrs. Gelb, not having my [home] number, calls me before and after classes in NY. She sounds like a sob-sister reporter out on a hot tip and her last insistent 'When CAN we see you?' has me lying about where I stay in NY and accepting different invitations for each Monday night. . . .

". . . [I]f it weren't for the publicity giving and withholding power of his position I think I'd have invited the wife to jump in the lake," Deeter concluded.

The Gelbs published their book in 1963, the first major work on O'Neill's life. Most persons in the theatrical world felt nothing more of substance could be said. But Louis Sheaffer continued researching, seven full years before he wrote a line. Through the Lloyds of London shipping registry he even managed to find the son of the captain of a British vessel on which O'Neill sailed from Boston to Buenos Aires in 1910; through him he obtained the captain's diary and daily log. Sheaffer's first volume, *O'Neill: Son and Playwright*, was published in 1968; it won the Theater Library Association award for the best theater book of the year. After years more research the concluding volume, *O'Neill: Son and Artist*, appeared in 1973, and it won the Pulitzer Prize for biography.

Times critical attention was interesting. The first volume was reviewed in the inner reaches of the *Sunday Times Book Review*. The daily reviewers, who answered to Gelb, ignored it. John Leonard was editor of the Sunday review when the second volume appeared, and he insisted on a front-page review. Again, there was no daily review.

Even the status of the Pulitzer did not establish Sheaffer as the recognized authority on O'Neill. Seymour Peck, then the cultural affairs editor, ran a feature article by Sheaffer when the second volume appeared. In 1973 Sheaffer wrote another article based on fresh information he obtained about O'Neill's life in Provincetown. He suggested that *The New York Times Magazine* run the article on O'Neill's anniversary date. The piece delighted the editor. "We like it, we'll run it soon," he told Sheaffer." It did not appear. Sheaffer called. The editor apologetically said that "since one of our own people" writes so much about O'Neill, using Sheaffer's article would not be appropriate. They bought it, paid for it, but didn't publish it.

Over the next years Sheaffer watched in curiosity as the *Times* continued arduous promotion of the Gelbs as "the O'Neill biographers." Measuring financial loss under such circumstances is impossible; Sheaffer was reduced to finding pride when such critics as Brendan Gill of *The New Yorker* referred to him as O'Neill's "most authorative biographer," as he did in reviewing a revival of *Long Day's Journey Into Night* in March, 1985. Sheaffer was also pleased when a committee of the Association of American Publishers chose his work for display at the Moscow International Book Fair in 1979.*

But the on-going slight has been the Theater Committee for Eugene O'Neill, organized in 1978 by the Gelbs and George White, head of the O'Neill Theater Center in Connecticut. The purpose was to organize celebrations of the playwright's birthday each year for a decade, leading up to his centennial in 1988. His Pulitzer notwithstanding, Sheaffer was not named to the committee. Consequently, the continuing publicity given the committee cites the Gelbs as O'Neill biographers, not Sheaffer. At the committee's first meeting

---

*The selection committee included John Leonard, formerly the *Times* Sunday book review editor, and columnist Tom Wicker, neither of whom care much for Artie Gelb; a consultant was Harrison Salisbury, who does not even like saying Gelb's name.

the veteran director Harold Clurman glanced along the table and asked, "Where's Sheaffer?" Someone hushed him. "Shhh. Don't mention his name here." The omission caught the attention of Oona O'Neill Chaplin, the playwright's daughter. When she was invited to the committee's first fete in 1979, at the Public Theater in New York, she agreed to attend on one condition—that Sheaffer be put on the committee. So Sheaffer was hurriedly named to an "honorary committee," which functioned only on paper.

Now in his late sixties, Sheaffer lives in a third-floor walkup apartment in Brooklyn Heights. He has had some health problems, yet he continues working on O'Neill projects, currently a pictorial biography. No, he will not admit to bitterness at the way the *Times* brushed off his work, or at the constant boosting of the Gelbs. To concede hurt or anger would perhaps give psychic satisfaction to persons for whom he has no professional respect.

Thus Sheaffer declines to get into a public quarrel with the Gelbs or *The New York Times*; he has his Pulitzer, and he has heard the praise of the theatrical professionals whom he respects. From his lifestyle one can easily acertain that he is not a man of means. But Louis Sheaffer is a proud man, and one at peace with himself; he has his pride. But what happened to this man is eloquent testimony to the "fairness" of *The New York Times*, and of the principles of the editors who permitted him to be so mistreated.

Given Gelb's background as a theatrical reporter, it is not surprising that he exercises iron control over coverage of anything to do with the stage. Being able to influence New York culture pleases him greatly, and he sees himself as both editor and kingmaker. In 1984 his friend Joseph Heller was nervous about publication of *God Knows*, his first novel in several years. Gelb told him, in effect, not to worry. Through portions of the *Times* controlled by Gelb, Heller received the newspaper equivalent of a horseracing or tennis Triple Crown: a glowing cover profile in *The New York Times Magazine*; the next Sunday, a front-page review in *The New York Times Book Review*; a day or so later, a praising review in the daily paper.

The publication party hosted by Heller's publisher seemed anticlimactic, after the *Times's* promotion. Artie Gelb was a happy guest, and he stayed close to Heller much of the evening, as if proximity would enable him to share the author's acclaim. He apparently convinced himself that the *Times's* attention had been equally as important as the literary merit of the book. So finally Gelb began assigning himself some of the credit.

"We made this book," he said to several persons. "*The New York Times* got behind this book, and we made this book."

Gelb is not modest about arts people whom he thinks have talent, and who deserve promotion. A good example is his special interest in the playwright Sam Shepherd. Other than the deserved annual feature story, Shepherd is one of the artists frequently called upon when the *Times* does round-up stories that require comments from a number of persons. Having one's name sprinkled liberally through the pages of *The New York Times*, even in casual mentions, keeps an artist's name before the public; it gives the familiarity that suggests this person is of importance. Joseph Papp, director and producer, flits in and out of grace. In 1979 he produced a play written by Barbara Gelb, *O'Neill and Carlotta*, based upon the playwright's relationship with his wife. Something then happened to shove Papp into disfavor and a long article in the Sunday Arts & Leisure Section said nasty things about him, suggesting his career was in a tailspin. But in June, 1985, he was in good graces again, and on the cover of *The New York Times Magazine*. A cultural reporter, after recounting Papp's up-and-down-and-up treatment by the *Times*, hurled a copy of the magazine across an apartment living room. "Why the good treatment? We're told Papp is bringing *O'Neill and Carlotta* to Broadway. Now that he is being useful to Barbara and Arthur, and for no other reason, he now is a fair-haired boy again."*

Gelb's attempts to promote the work of his friends did not always succeed; several times he ran headlong into *Times* reporters who simply refused to go along with him. One such case involved the iconoclastic Wendell "Sonny" Rawls, who in 1982 had fled the Washington bureau to his native South, as chief of the Atlanta bureau. Rawls was sitting in the office of his old boss, John Siegenthaler, editor of the Nashville *Tennessean*, when a graying and self-important man walked in and introduced himself as Peter Maas, a New York writer. "Surely you know my book *Serpico*," he told Rawls. Oh, vaguely, Rawls said.

---

*When *My Gene* finally opened in January, 1987, the *Times* review was done by the Boston writer Justin Kaplan. Several persons at the paper told me the cultural department did not wish the *angst* involved in having a staff person write about a play done by the boss's wife.

He knew Maas was in the claque of self-promoters that clustered around Gelb and Abe Rosenthal. Maas did a jacket blurb for Barbara Gelb's 1983 book on the New York police, *Tarnished Brass* ("A splendid and important book. I can't recall another work that better conveys the mind and character, strengths and frailties of those in the upper echelons of command in the nation's premier police department"). Maas thought enough of Rosenthal to invite him to his marriage ceremony in the spring of 1986. Now Maas was in Nashville investigating the story of a woman named Marie who had exposed corruption in the prison parole system in Tennessee. Rawls volunteered the name and direct-dial number of someone in the Justice Department's Public Integrity Section, and made an introductory call for Maas, a kindness acknowledged in his book *Marie*, published in 1983.

The next spring Maas called Rawls in Atlanta. "There's a hell of a story going on in Nashville," he said. "My book is causing a storm of controversy. People are asking why they had to wait for a book to come out to learn of it."

Rawls happened to know a bit about the "Marie" story, and its treatment by the Nashville press, and he said to himself, "Peter, this is a naked request by you to hype your fucking book." He was polite, however; he told Maas he would check it out. He was "always happy to go to Nashville," where he spent youthful reportorial years, and national editor David Jones told him to go ahead. Nothing. Rather than being lax, the Nashville papers had been aggressive in reporting the woman's charges against the former governor, Ray Blanton. Rawls spent several hours going through clippings on the story. A water haul, he said, and told Jones to scrub the story.

Maas persisted in demanding a story, and Rawls repeated what he had told Dave Jones. Maas protested. He had done radio talk shows in Nashville, and he claimed numerous callers had demanded, "Where the hell were the newspapers?" Rawls suggested these people should have *read* the newspapers rather than listening to the radio.

"The next thing I know," Rawls said, "I'm getting calls from the *Times*. 'What do I know about this story down in Nashville?' Rawls repeated, to a junior national editor named Tom Stites, what he had told Jones, and asked, "Why is this recurring?" The editor said Artie

Gelb had "received a letter from a friend who owned a newspaper outside Nashville," and Gelb had sent it to the national desk with a note asking, Can we address this somehow?

Rawls suspected deep in his heart Maas had something to do with the "letter from a friend," and he did not like being whipsawed. But he would try; as a field reporter, he knew the futility of continuing arguments with 43rd Street. Former Governor Blanton by now had been convicted of parole corruption, and his appeal was to be heard in Cincinnati within a few days. Fine, Stites of the national desk said, can we use that as a peg for the story and mention the book?

"If it's there, I'll do it," Rawls said. But the hearing produced evidence exactly the opposite of Maas's thesis—"allegations by the Blanton crowd claiming that the governor did not get a fair trial in Nashville because the *Tennessean* had run something like 241 stories that were negative about Ray Blanton. Therefore they could not get an impartial jury." Rawls called Stites and said, 'Six hundred words ought to kill this.'" He was told to include a line that publicity "continues even today with publication of the book *Marie* by Peter Maas."

"Now I've gotten the goddamned book into *The New York Times* for Peter Maas in which I consider a justifiable way," Rawls said. No, he would not have written the story had it not been for "Maas's persistence." Then Stites called. He had checked the clips, and Blanton's claims of excessive pre-trial publicity had already been published. They agreed there was no reason to run the story.

The next day came another Stites call. "Sonny," he said, "you can't believe how bad our news judgment is." The story was to be rewritten, with the reference to Maas's book moved up. Since Rawls was about to get on a plane for New York, the desk made the change, and the story finally ran.

But Maas had not finished. The next day he tracked down Rawls at the St. Moritz. "Maas tells me he really thought I was underplaying the intensity of the controversy in Nashville." Rawls had had enough of Maas's pestering. He had interviewed everyone involved, and found no continuing interest in Blanton's fall. "I don't see that *The New York Times* should be used to hype a book," he told Maas.

"You should just cover the news," Maas said.

"I'll do just that—I'll cover the news. You write the books," Rawls said, and he hung up the phone with a crash.

According to what Rawls learned later, Maas that very day visited Rosenthal. Soon Rawls's phone was ringing again, this time with a suggestion that politics kept the Nashville *Tennessean* close to Blanton, and that the "Marie" scandal stemmed from this relationship. Shouldn't he do a story telling how Maas exposed the situation? Nonsense, Rawls replied; the *Tennessean* had driven Blanton from office. Forget it, the national desk said. But Gelb was not through. Jonathan Friendly, the *Times*'s media columnist, called and said, "Gelb asked me to take a real hard look at the newspaper situation in Nashville." Rawls says, "I go through the same song-and-dance with Friendly. He could do it if he wished, but the story was nine years old." The next voice was that of *Tennessean* editor Siegenthaler. "I thought you said there wasn't going to be a story," he told Rawls. "Have you seen this story in *The New York Times* crushing my nuts?"

Friendly had written what Gelb had suggested, coming down hard on Siegenthal and the *Tennessean*, and giving prominence to Maas's book. Rawls sighed. The barbarians, he thought, finally got through the fence.

The Maas exercise in self-promotion, assisted by Artie Gelb, was trivial in itself. But its long-term harm was that Gelb enhanced a newsroom reputation of being an editor who used *The New York Times* to help his friends. Rawls is a talkative man, and he told many people at the *Times* about what he called "an attempted Artie Gelb-Peter Maas gangbang of a lowly correspondent." The Rawls-Maas episode added to a building tradition of interference by Gelb and Rosenthal in coverage of cultural affairs. John Leonard, editor of *The New York Times Book Review* during the 1970's, had recurring problems with Rosenthal because he featured books opposing U. S. policy in the Vietnam War. Rosenthal especially fumed when Leonard let Neil Sheehan fill virtually an entire issue of the *Sunday Review* with an essay-length review on war books. Leonard survived this crisis, although he was bounced to the lesser job of daily critic. A bit later he panned a Betty Friedan book on feminism, *The Second Stage*. This was a mistake. Friedan is a Rosenthal chum who served as *sub rosa* hostess to Abe and Katharine Balfour during the clandestine days of their romance. When the couple wished privacy in the Hamptons, Friedan took them in, and turned away everyone else. Now Leonard was not fired outright; he was simply cut to one review weekly, rather than two. Leonard is a good reader of handwriting, especially when it is on the walls of the *Times* newsroom, so he left.

Michael Sterne is another *Times* editor who learned the hard way. In autumn 1981, while travel editor, Sterne received an unassigned article from freelancer Lucinda Franks about blueberry picking on the farm she and her husband, Robert Morgenthau, the Manhattan district attorney, owned in Dutchess County, New York. Sterne returned the article with a polite note stating that *Times* Sunday Travel policy was not to run articles about points within 250 miles of New York City. The feeling was that such pieces are the domain of the Friday Weekend Section. "Travel" meant more than a day trip by car. (The policy has since changed; Travel's criteria now seems to be only that the place discussed is outside the city proper.)

What Sterne did not realize was that the Morgenthau-Frank blueberry patch is a legend among the couple's friends, who cherish invitations to gather their own berries. Two regular pickers are Arthur and Barbara Gelb. Sterne knew nothing of this when he turned down the article, nor would it have changed his decision, for policy was policy. He also suggested to fellow workers in Travel that he was a friend of the Gelbs himself. He left on vacation soon after rejecting the Frank article; when he returned he was told he had been replaced by his deputy of six months, Michael J. Leahy. Sterne was bounced to a lesser job within the paper, and he sadly told colleagues in Travel, "It was those damned blueberries."

Given such episodes, persons around the *Times* who don't like Artie Gelb—there are many—were psychologically prepared to believe the worst of him in 1982 with what came to be called "The Jerzy Kosinski Matter." In February *The Times Magazine* gave cover space to a long article on the Polish-born novelist, written by Barbara Gelb. The article told of Kosinski's life in a Poland dominated first by German Nazis, then Stalinist Communists. Kosinski spoke at length of Polish peasant brutality. The climax was his recounting of when, aged nine years old, he was thrown into a pool of human ordure over his head by peasants for punishment for dropping a book during Mass. The shock left him mute for several years. Kosinski was to flee Poland in 1957, and over the years he wrote *The Painted Bird, Being There,* and eight other acclaimed novels, one of which won him the National Book Award. He was elected president of the American Center of P.

E. N., which acclaimed his "imaginative and protective sense of responsibility for writers all over the world." Gelb's article, serious literary journalism, also touched on Kosinski's personal quirks, such as his love of disguises when he flitted around New York City's seamier districts. What Gelb did not explore was a systematic attempt at discrediting Kosinski's life and work by Polish intelligence that commenced upon publication of *The Painted Bird* in 1965. Loosely based on his own boyhood (although not strictly autobiographical) the novel depicted Polish peasants as unfeeling brutes who were not psychologically adverse to domination by dictatorial masters.

Oddly, the article itself attracted less comment than the photograph chosen for the cover—Kosinski in polo pants, stripped to the waist, staring enigmatically into the camera. Arthur O. Sulzberger, Jr., the publisher's son, then working in the newsroom as part of his all-departments training program, picked up an early issue of the magazine from an editor's desk and stared at it in seeming disbelief. "Of all the shit!" young Pinch Sulzberger exclaimed, and threw the issue aside. Many persons felt such a photograph was more appropriately a cover for *People*. But for the *Times Magazine*? That Kosinski was a good friend of both Rosenthal and the Gelbs—and especially of Rosenthal—was well known. There were newsroom snickers about "Abe and Artie boosting a friend." But given his leadership of P. E. N., and his outspoken support of the Polish Solidarity Movement, the article had news justification.

Then the seed so long sown by the Polish intelligence service disinformation and its outriders fell into welcome, even if unwitting, hands. Soon after publication of the Gelb article, old canards about Kosinski began surfacing around the New York literary world—that he did not write his own books, instead, he relied upon differing editors carried on his payroll as "assistant" or "literary secretary;" that the CIA spirited him out of Poland, and arranged for publication of his first books; that the CIA arranged for *The Painted Bird* to be published to discredit the Warsaw Bloc; that Kosinski was an anti-Semite; that Kosinski lived off a divorce settlement from his much-richer wife, a steel heiress (who was also eleven years his senior). Accounts of how Kosinski fled Poland were said to be fabrications.

The Polish secret service had strong motivation for discrediting Kosinski, for the novelist was foremost among writers denouncing the crushing of Solidarity. He joined the Committee for the Free World,

whose American members came from the traditional liberalism of the
old left, and who were anti-communist. He spoke against the puppet
Polish regime over the Voice of America. He denounced the new
American Writers Congress as "politically exploited" for permitting
its founding conference to turn into a forum for anti-Americanism.
For persons who take New York literary politics seriously, a writer
who adopts neo-conservatism as a creed—and talks about it as
well—is an instant pariah. So the left moved, via the pens of Eliot
Fremont-Smith, literary critic of the *Village Voice*, and Geoffrey
Stokes, who wrote at the time both for the *Voice* and *The Nation*.

Fremont-Smith told me he got onto the "Kosinski story" by journalistic accident. During his first months at the *Voice* he wrote a publishing gossip column which he signed "O. Courant." He soon
dropped it as more bother than value. At a party one evening a friend
in publishing said, "It's too bad you're not writing the column
anymore. Did you know that Jerzy Kosinski doesn't write his own
books?" Fremont-Smith's ears perked, but the man had no detail,
only what he called "wide rumor."

Soon thereafter Fremont-Smith heard the same story from another
person, Christopher Lehmann-Haupt, the *Times* book critic.
Fremont-Smith felt that Lehmann-Haupt passed on this information
out of malice, for he "despised Kosinski through his books for some
unknown reason." For several days Fremont-Smith did not connect
up the two episodes, then he realized, "Jesus Christ, you're a *reporter*, among other things, and you have heard this story from two
sources. Maybe there is something in it." So he began asking questions. He "heard" that one of Kosinski's ghosts—or editors—was
Wayne Lawson, then of *The Times Sunday Book Review*. "I called
him on a Sunday, got him at home, and told him what I was doing.
There was this long pause on the telephone, and Lawson said, 'Oh,
I've got to go, I have tickets for the opera. I'll call you back.' He never
did return the call. He had been relaxed when we started the conversation, for he knew me as a reviewer. But when I mentioned the
name Jerzy Kosinski, he got very tight, very tight."

Soon Fremont-Smith discovered that Victor Navasky, editor of *The
Nation* (which sponsored the American Writers Congress denounced
by Kosinski) had commissioned Geoffrey Stokes to pursue the same
story. But Navasky ran out of money, and so he freed Stokes to collab-
orate with Fremont-Smith, with the aim of *Village Voice* publication.

The last act was for Fremont-Smith to confront Kosinski over lunch, which he found uncomfortable. "I had known him slightly, and I liked him. He almost convinced me." Fremont-Smith concentrated on the charge Kosinski had considerable help in writing his books. Apparently Kosinski's detractors in the New York literary establishment could not accept that someone whose native language was Polish could write well enough in English to achieve such critical acclaim. Oddly, that Kosinski *does* need help is something he has volunteered. When *The Painted Bird* was published, for instance, he told a *Book Week* interviewer:

> I was not in any way ashamed to expose my manuscript to friends who would read it. I made sixteen or seventeen copies of every draft and showed them to people. I chose some people whose language was not English, and some who were Americans. I asked them to mark a little cross next to anything that didn't sound right. If enough people marked a sentence, I knew something was wrong with it.

Fremont-Smith turned his material over to Stokes, who did the actual writing. The resultant article was a direct accusation that Kosinski did not write his own work, that his supposed life story was a melange of half-truths and lies, and that the CIA had given his career a boost at several key points. But of the three persons actually named as Kosinski's ghosts, two denied any such role, and the third would not talk about the subject.

In totality, the *Voice* article tracked closely the smear campaign waged for more than fifteen years by Polish intelligence. Fremont-Smith said, "I had mixed feelings about the piece. . . . I would have done it differently. I felt guilty about hounding the guy, for what he had done was a small crime in the great scheme of things. I guess I don't have the taste for that kind of story. There was something pathetic about him, for he didn't feel that he was hurting anybody. This isn't exactly the apt metaphor, but he was a trapped rat, living with his lies, many of which he had come to believe." Fremont-Smith is insistent that "our article had *nothing* to do with what Barbara Gelb had written. But Abe saw it as a personal attack on Barbara."

Which is not exactly true. When Abe Rosenthal read the *Village Voice* article, his first reaction was revulsion. Because of his long interest in Polish affairs he knew of the disinformation campaign against Kosinski. Now the back-alley whispering had gotten into print—in a relatively small-circulation weekly, to be sure, but one widely read by literary people. Rosenthal says he made no connection between the *Voice* article and what Barbara Gelb had written for his own magazine. He told Arthur Gelb, "I'm not going to stand around and watch that guy be killed and be some kind of thirty-ninth witness," referring to his 1964 Kitty Genovese story.

Gelb went to a young *Times* cultural affairs reporter named Michiko Kakutani and asked her to review the evidence on a single question. Did Kosinski write his own books, or did he have ghostwriters? Katutani worked for several weeks, and she had problems, for "literary investigative reporting" was something she had never attempted. Katutani also became wary of Kosinski; she became convinced he was trailing her around New York as she did interviews, and she suspected an obscene message left on her answering machine came from him. Soon after Labor Day she confided her problems to John Corry, her desk mate, who had just returned from vacation, and who had not read the *Village Voice* attack.

Corry, in his early fifties, then was well into his second career at the *Times*. He had worked as an investigative reporter under Arthur Gelb in the 1960's, left for a while, and then returned, first as a columnist who lived in a single New York block for a year, writing about it weekly, and then moving to cultural news. Corry's first big *Times* story had been the controversy over Jacqueline Kennedy's attempt in 1966 to suppress William Manchester's book on her husband's death. He had worked at *Harper's* Magazine, he knew the literary crowd. Given this background, and his reportorial instincts, "I wanted the story so goddamned bad I could taste it." He also had heard the "Kosinski is a CIA agent" story before, and in the following ludicrous circumstance.

During Corry's *Harper's* days in the late 1960's, Kosinski came by for a visit one day. Editor Willie Morris, who has a peculiar sense of humor, told the staff deadpan that Kosinski was a distinguished CIA agent, and that he was so busy with spy activities he had to have someone write books for him. Morris was joking. Morris liked the joke so much, in fact, that he repeated it regularly at Elaine's, the East Side bar the *Harper's* staff used as a *de facto* second office those years. Morris would see Kosinski sitting at the end of the room, sipping red wine, and he would point to him and whisper his hoax about CIA and ghostwriters. "It was gossip, it was fun," Corry said. "No one took it seriously. And fifteen years later the goddamned things turns up in the *Village Voice* as fact, and it's picked up all over the world."

Watching Kakutani closely, Corry realized the assignment was driving her to distraction. She spent long periods in the ladies' room, and she would show signs of weeping when she returned to her desk. She complained constantly to Corry that the story was beyond her capabilities. Corry remained silent. "I couldn't go to Arthur and say, 'Get this kid off the story.' That's not fair. But that story *smelled* of politics." After six weeks Kakutani asked Gelb to be relieved. Corry said, "I asked for the story. It was my idea [to take it over]." "Fine," Gelb said.

Corry first addressed the charge of ghostwriting, by reading in successive evenings all Kosinski's novels save *The Painted Bird* and *Steps*, which he knew. To him that the same person had written all the books was obvious. "I found the same voice in all those books." Nuances of phrasing appeared time and again, as did similarities in word choice. To Corry the key element was the "voice, a quality that cannot be defined but can be detected."

Corry reviewed Kakutani's notes, thousands of words in her word processor. She had no evidence of ghosts. Joyce Hart, Kosinski's editor at Houghton Mifflin, gave what Corry felt the best summary: "Nonsense." On the CIA charge, Corry scoffed, "CIA? The CIA is not in that bad a shape." He established to his satisfaction that Kakutani's statements about Kosinski harassing her were fantasies. The "following her around" stemmed from a single episode: she encountered him walking with his girlfriend across the Lincoln Center plaza one afternoon.

Corry next addressed the attacks on Kosinski's personal background—that he fabricated incidents from his boyhood to add authenticity to his novels, and that the CIA thrust him upon the reading public. Corry talked to persons in the Polish emigre community, including many at the Voice of America, and academics of Polish literary and political affairs. A pattern began to emerge: that the disinformation campaign had its genesis in Wieslaw Gornicki, a correspondent for the Polish news agency PAP at the United Nations in the 1960s, and thereafter a ranking officer in the Jaruszelski military regime that crushed Solidarity. During intervening years Gornicki had circulated rumors about Kosinski, among Americans and others, and written frequent shrill articles for the Polish press. In 1969, to cite one of more than a dozen articles, Gornicki wrote: "Every emigre child knows that it is not Mr. Kosinski who writes so well in English, but a man called Peter Skinner—an authentic Englishman with an Oxford education, who has been hired as a ghost writer. . . . Jerzy Kosinski is the biggest literary fraud in the last several years." The Polish dossier on Kosinski was given to Jerome Klinkowitz of the University of Northern Iowa when he visited Warsaw as a state guest in 1979. On return Professor Klinkowitz wrote an article entitled "Betrayed by Jerzy Kosinski" which repeated charges that *The Painted Bird* drew heavily upon ghost work of other writers. Klinkowitz circulated his article to a number of literary friends, and he also offered it to *Atlantic Monthly, Partisan Review*, and the *Village Voice*. None published it; however, the whisper campaign surged again.

Corry holed up in his West Side work hideaway and wrote a 6,500-word article which ran up the headline, "Case History—17 Years of Ideological Attack on a Cultural Target," at the top of the Arts and Leisure section on November 7, 1982. Corry carefully traced the course of the disinformation and he accused the *Voice* of giving credence to innuendo. Corry's strong suit was his meticulous dissection of the anti-Kosinski campaign, and how it revived coincident with his pro-Solidarity activities. But what merit his thesis had was lost in a welter of complaints that Rosenthal and Gelb had "ordered" him to slam the *Voice* because of its attack on Kosinski (and, tangentially, on Barbara Gelb's work).

Here the appearance of the past counted more heavily than the realities of the present. Rosenthal and Gelb's long record of partiality towards friends precluded any rational discussion of Corry's findings. And that Rosenthal and Gelb would reflexively be accused of favoritism by much of the media—however baseless the charge—was in itself a damning indictment of their tutelage of *The New York Times*. *Publishers Weekly* charged in an editorial that "the powers that be at the *Times* certainly seem to have acted on this occasion with a degree of intemperance, using the enormous power and prestige of their paper for ends that by no means justify their extravagant means."

To the dismay and disgust of Corry, this statement was repeated as fact in such diverse publications as the Boston *Globe*, the Nashville

Tennessean, the Chicago *Sun Times*, and the Chicago *Daily News*, among many others. The general theme was that he wrote "at the request of editors to punish critics at the *Village Voice*." (None of these publications had bothered to examine the validity of the *Voice's* charges that Kosinski's entire literary career was a fraud. The bulk of any *Voice* issue is devoted to strident advocacy journalism. Peculiarly, a single answering slap by the *Times* was treated as a momentous media event. Ah, American journalism.) Corry felt other stings more directly at home. He was coming into the Times Building one day as David Halberstam, a colleague both at the *Times* and *Harper's*, was leaving.

"He shook his fist at me and said, in great and genuine outrage, 'How could you? How *could* you?' "

Years earlier Corry had been an acting deputy national editor under Harrison Salisbury. While never close, they were friendly in a collegial way. "After Kosinski, Harrison walked into the office, and he cut me dead. Not a word, not a glance.

"People stopped talking to me. I was on the 'side of the oppression.' It made me angry. It made me goddamned angry. I had expected some of that. But honest to God what I did *not* expect were the written assertions that this was written to punish the *Village Voice*, and that I was ordered to do it by Abe and Arthur Gelb. I am a smart fellow and I thought I knew a bit about journalism and popular culture." He sighed. "I've had a somewhat low opinion of my profession ever since."

The reaction to the story left Rosenthal and Gelb "beleaguered, surprised, appalled," according to a friend. Rosenthal took the criticisms particularly hard. "Reporting is his religion, and this place is his church. And suddenly he's reading in other newspapers that *The New York Times* is rewarding its friends and punishing its enemies."

Yet Rosenthal and Gelb had created the climate in which they were so readily judged. The most damning feature of the Kosinski affair was that Rosenthal and Gelb had so damaged their credibility through past favoritism that Corry's story was unjustly dismissed as another instance in which they protected a friend.

In the hard news section of the *Times*, concurrently, Rosenthal was moving the paper in even more ominous directions.

NINETEEN

"Nipples Always Pucker for Power"

Grace Glueck is a quiet woman who writes about arts and culture for the *Times* from a desk of indescribable clutter. Colleagues love her for an easy wit and offers of friendship. If, say, a new reporter has trouble finding his or her way through New York's cultural jungle, Grace Glueck volunteers as a guide, but in unobtrusive fashion. One woman says of Glueck, "She once heard me struggling over the telephone, my first week on the job, and she realized I was getting nowhere. Grace came over and sat on the corner of my desk and asked me a few questions about who I was, and where I went to school, and then she said, 'By the way, if you are trying to find out such-and-such, why don't you ring so-and-so, and tell him you are my colleague.' I did, and the person did, and I had a good story. She did this as a friend, not as a superior." This is why people at the *Times* like Grace Glueck.

Something happened in 1968 that piqued Grace Glueck's curiosity. Publisher Punch Sulzberger announced major promotions in the *Times* news management—Rosenthal as managing editor, and Arthur

Gelb and some other men as his key deputies. Why is this? she asked herself. There are women around here; could not at least one of them be given a visible job? So she wrote a polite note to Sulzberger, "congratulating him on this forward step, but asking why no women had been included." She made no fuss about the letter, although she did mention it in the cultural news department. "My male colleagues thought this was a very cute thing to do," Glueck said. "They beamed benignly, as well they might. Back came a note from the publisher saying that the point was well taken, that he would consult with 'key management executives' when they came back from vacation. But apparently they never did."

Grace Glueck shrugged and went back to writing about art news. She was comfortable in that she at least had put Sulzberger and the rest of management on notice that women were noticing disparities in promotion policies. The first rumble of anti-sexism had been heard within the *Times*.

Soon other women began to find and hoard physical evidence of sexism. For instance, Dan Schwartz, then the Sunday editor, wrote what he considered a witty memorandum concerning a woman applicant for a job in his department:

> We'll take your word on Pamela Kent, of course. What does she look like? Twiggy? Lynn Redgrave? Perhaps you ought to send over her vital statistics, or a picture in a bikini.

A male functionary in the personnel department wrote in evaluating a woman:

> Very pleasant. Good at shorthand and typing. Her chief ambition is probably to get married. Has a good figure and is not restrained about dressing it to advantage.

These memos and others were copied and distributed, in *samizdat* fashion, among female employees throughout the *Times*. Some other stories, these in verbal form, also went around the building. Abe Rosenthal, developing his reputation as a womanizer, displayed his concept of *machisimo* by telling a female *Times* reporter that he particularly enjoyed inviting a certain woman into his private office for an interview. The woman he mentioned was strikingly beautiful. Why her? Rosenthal was asked. Because, Rosenthal said with a smile, I can

sit there and fantasize about undressing her. There was also the story
about the exchange of two male editors of *The Times Book Review*
following the first lunch with Rosenthal of a newly-hired woman editor:

> Editor A. Did you see _____ when Abe passed her that cake at
> lunch? You could almost see her nipples pucker.
> Editor B. Yeah. Those broads' nipples always pucker for power.

These incidents grated on women at the *Times*. The women's
movement was astir elsewhere in the media. Female employees at
Newsweek, the *Reader's Digest* and NBC had brought class action
suits alleging discrimination in pay and promotions. Women at the
Times sensed, but did not actually know, they were underpaid. Anyone who could read the table of organization of the paper knew
women held only a handful of significant jobs. But a chance incident
in 1972 set astir the latent discontent.

Grace Lichtenstein, a breezy and inquisitive native of Brooklyn, after graduation from Brooklyn College had come to the *Times* as a promotional copy writer. She moved to writing news for the *Times* radio
station, WQXR, and then to the metropolitan desk as a consumer affairs reporter. A woman unimpressed by importance, in others or in
herself, Lichtenstein did her work well enough that she impressed
Arthur Gelb, then the metropolitan editor. "I was 'Artie's pet,' for a
month or so."

She happened to be in the newsroom when Channel 13, the public
television station, came to the *Times* to do a show about journalism on
the local level. The reporter put Lichtenstein on camera and asked,
"How would you make this place better?"

As Lichtenstein related, "They had interviewed the token Black
and an old codger and a rookie. I was the token woman. Without
thinking about what I was saying, I said, in effect, 'The *Times* is a
great paper, but one problem is that it is run by white, middle-aged,
middle-class men. It needs more women, Blacks, Hispanics, American Indians. . . .

"I had no idea, believe me, I was saying anything revolutionary. I
was excited about the women's movement, which raised my consciousness about how much of a male position the newsroom in which
I worked really was."

That Lichtenstein had been interviewed was no secret, for the camera crew worked openly in the newsroom, with the consent of management. "When I came to work the day after the program appeared, I hadn't even taken off my coat when I was told, 'Abe wants to see you.' Now, he barely knew who I was. I was one of 200 reporters, and I had not exchanged a single word with him. I went into his office, absolutely innocent.

"He lit into me. He said I was disloyal, that what I had done compared with McCarthyism, and it wasn't Gene he was talking about, it was Joe. When he finally got his foot off my neck, figuratively, I walked out in shock.

"This was my first indication that Abe Rosenthal was capable of incredible tongue-lashings against a reporter at the slightest provocation. His rage was out of proportion, I was so small potatoes. I assume that from that moment on I was labelled a troublemaker."

Grace Lichtenstein was not alone. Eileen Shanahan of the Washington bureau was unhappy about on-going professional slights throughout her career at the paper. Shanahan had covered business and economics in Washington for United Press and the *Journal of Commerce* and built a reputation as a reporter skillful at writing intelligibly about complex financial issues. Still, not until her third attempt did she succeed even in getting an interview at the *Times*. This came in 1962, when James Reston had taken the bureau from Arthur Krock and was rebuilding it with persons of his own choosing. Reston seemed cool towards Shanahan. "Everyone was saying, 'Shanahan is the best,' but he truly felt there was no place in a newsroom for a woman, that it was too rough an environment," Shanahan said. One of Reston's first acts as bureau chief was to take Bess Furman out of the White House and send her to the Department of Health, Education and Welfare. He did not want a woman even to share such an important beat.

Nonetheless, Shanahan did obtain an interview with Turner Catledge and Clifton Daniel. "Why do you want to be with *The New York TImes?*" they asked. "Because it's the best paper in the country," she replied.

"What do you want to *be* on *The New York Times?*" Catledge continued.

As Shanahan recollected, "I knew enough not to tell the truth— that I wanted to be an editor. So I simply said, 'I want to be the best reporter on the best paper in the country.' I bit my tongue, but I told the necessary lie."

Catledge beamed approval. "Good," he said, "because no woman will be an editor of *The New York Times.*"

Shanahan bit her lip and didn't respond.

In the bureau's "economic cluster" Shanahan worked as number two, behind Edwin L. Dale, who wrote heavy economic policy stories. Her forte became what she called the "interstices," such as tax policy and banking. She became one of the paper's most prolific writers of "Q Heads," news analysis pieces. (The title comes from the *Times* stylebook name for the headline used over the articles.) Reston initiated the Q Head, and for a time he was the only person permitted to write them, because they incorporate opinion and interpretation into reporting. Then Ed Dale began writing them, about economics, and they spread gradually to other specialists. Given Shanahan's assignment to esoteric tax matters—she was said to know more about the intricacies of the tax code than most Congressmen—she frequently wrote Q Head explanations requiring subjective commentary not permissible in a straight news story.

New York noticed her work, and favorably. She received uncountable citations and congratulatory memos about the wonderful job she was doing; some came from Abe Rosenthal, others from bureau chiefs, yet others from Punch Sulzberger. "Herograms," these were called in the Washington bureau, and over the years Shanahan accumulated a sheaf of them.

Rosenthal explicitly recognized that Shanahan had talents beyond reportage. Soon after he became managing editor in 1968 he called her to New York and they went to Sardi's for dinner. The *Times's* financial section at the time was "not of *Times* quality," they both agreed, and Abe looked her square in the eye and asked, "OK, what would you do if *you* were managing editor?"

"God, Abe, I'm *not* managing editor," Shanahan replied, but she proceeded to go through the financial section, listing what she considered to be its weaknesses, including a number of writers and editors. As if confirming her judgment, Rosenthal later eased several of these persons out of their jobs. To Shanahan, the fact that he sought her advice suggested strongly he respected her ability to judge talent—a requisite for an editor.

Her first years in the bureau, Shanahan was content to work as a reporter; inevitably, she desired a more responsible position, as an editor. When a desk opening occurred she asked Tom Wicker, now the bureau chief, if she could have it. "Oh, come on, Eileen," Wicker said, "that job you have now is much better."

"Yes, but I want to be an editor," she said.

"You know why that's not going to be," Wicker said.

With feigned innocence, Shanahan asked, "Why, Tom? Why is it not going to be?" ("I wanted to force him to say it," Shanahan remembers, with glee.) Through clenched teeth, Wicker stated, "No woman will ever be an editor of *The New York Times*." (Wicker followed *Times* policy; male chauvinism has long since been leached from his bones.)

Shanahan had other problems relating to sexism issues. She had begun writing about the women's movement, in a self-assigned way, from the Washington vantage point. She could never persuade Washington editors to make this even a part-time beat. She could write about women's issues "once you get your important work done." She could do no advance planning. "I'd tell the bureau chief about a women's conference coming up in Houston in three weeks, and he'd say, 'What's coming up on your beat?' Fortunately, most women's meetings were on the weekends because like me, they had to 'do their jobs first.' "

But Shanahan credited David Jones, the national editor, with giving women's stories good play because he was sensitive to the issues involved. She thought of urging Rosenthal to make the beat a full-time one which she would cover from Washington. But she was beginning to have other troubles with Rosenthal, and she did not wish to stir new ones. Further, by continuing to do heavy tax-policy and other economics stories, "they would take me seriously in the bureau, and I would not be 'crazy Shanahan' for covering women's news."

In any event, by the early 1970's much discontent was stirring among women who worked for *The New York Times*. In New York, for instance, as Grace Glueck remembers, "Grace Lichtenstein was *kvetching* about the fact that the *Times* would not permit use of the word 'Ms.' in the paper. Several of us, including Grace, of course, got to thinking that this style rigidity was symptomatic of more basic problems." So the New York women formed a group. At this time, as Glueck said, "We had on our white gloves and party manners."

The first step by the caucus was to write a polite letter to Punch

Sulzberger (with copies to directors of the Times Company) pointing out the inequities in male-female salaries, the total absence of women in management jobs, and the "stringent patterns of our non-promotion." Not all women on the *Times* wished to have anything to do even with a mild protest. For instance, Betsy Wade, long a copy editor on the foreign desk, approached Gloria Emerson, who had been reporting from Southeast Asia. "Oh, dear," Emerson sighed, "they've let me ride my water buffalo, why should I get involved in this?" Wade, who tends to be direct, told her why, in several terse sentences; Emerson signed.

Rosenthal responded by calling the women into his office singly—he wished the psychological advantage of breaking their unity—and denouncing them as "troublemakers" who were "divisive" to the paper. Rosenthal at full temper can be an intimidating man, and here he dealt with persons whose careers he controlled with nigh-summary authority. Several women quavered; none, however, withdrew her name.

So next Punch Sulzberger agreed to meet with a women's delegation. Nan Robertson, by then doing the women's side of the White House in Washington, talked with Eileen Shanahan about attending. Since Sulzberger set the time for nine o'clock in the morning, getting to New York would be difficult. Robertson said, "Eileen, we have *got* to go up there and meet with management, to show that two stars in the most elitist bureau have something to say." As it happened, the air shuttle ran late, and the meeting was already ten minutes underway when they arrived.

"I could see Punch's face fall," Robertson said. "He has a face like mine—Danish standard—where everything is out there to see. He shows emotion, and he was thunderstruck. He did not expect us. I could see him thinking, 'This must be serious when two of the most successful women in the paper are here to complain.' "

Sulzberger listened politely; he mouthed some generalities about appointing a committee of executives to study the women's evidence. But unwittingly he displayed his ignorance of his own newspaper. Several reporters were cited as examples of talented women who were not equitably paid. One of these was Judy Klemesrud, a feature writer whose byline appeared about twice weekly in the paper. After several references to Klemesrud, Sulzberger asked, "This Judy Klem . . . uh . . . just who is this woman you keep referring to?"

Meetings with Sulzberger and lesser executives followed. Nothing happened. Grace Glueck described the publisher's attitude as "hoping, I suppose, that we would go away." Grace Lichtenstein finally suggested that the women talk to Harriet Rabb, a law professor at Columbia University. Rabb's Employment Rights Project at Columbia had filed discrimination suits against the National Broadcasting Company and other media companies. In March, 1973, Rabb lodged formal complaints against the *Times* both with the state and federal Offices of Equal Opportunity. Since these offices were jammed with hundreds of similar complaints, the *Times* case remained dormant. "We waited well beyond the statutory nine months we needed to wait before filing a court action, in the foolhardy belief that management was still negotiating seriously with us," Glueck related. Then, reluctantly, the women were ready to "take off the white gloves and sue the *Times* in federal court." (The case was formally styled *Elizabeth Boylan v. New York Times Company*, 74 Civil 4891, Southern District of New York. "Boylan" is Betsy Wade, who used her married name as one of the first of six named plaintiffs.)

The suit stung Sulzberger, Rosenthal and other persons in the *Times* hierarchy, for they felt it violated the concept that the *Times* was a "family" that could work out its own problems without involving other persons, let alone the government. Rosenthal at various times was to call the suit "blackmail," and also an "infringement of our newspaper's First Amendment rights." None of the women bothered to answer the first charge, for they had met repeatedly with management to seek resolution. One of them scoffed at the other charge: "Does the First Amendment make the *Times* immune from suit when a delivery truck knocks down a pedestrian? Need I say more?"

Attorney Rabb proved ideal for the women. She was a deceptively slow-speaking Southern woman who unwittingly lulled her adversaries. One pounce, however, and they were forever afterwards on the alert. Rabb's first chore, a laborious one, was to elicit from the *Times*, through depositions and documents, the facts the women alleged in their suit. *Times* management produced this information, albeit in laboriously slow fashion. Then came an unanticipated breakthrough.

Through the 1960's and the 1970's, salaries tended to be among the more-closely-guarded secrets of a newspaper; what one earned was one's own business, not to be shared even with a friend. The contract with the American Newspaper Guild set minimums for various job categories; merit raises, however, were at the discretion of management, and it was in this area that disparities arose. That men earned more than women was confirmed, in undisputed form, by some sleuthing by Robert Smith of the Washington bureau in a manner so simple that people stood around asking themselves, "Why the hell didn't *I* think of that?"

A sometime Guild officer, Smith obtained from the union a list of the salaries paid persons in the bureau and put it on the newsroom bulletin board. He did not list the name which went with each salary; not even the Guild could obtain that specific information. But everyone in the bureau knew their own salary, and the posting told them where they stood *viz-a-viz* other persons. So people stood around the bulletin board, and compared notes. To her astonishment, Eileen Shanahan, one of the more senior and productive members of the bureau, was sixth from the bottom of thirty-one persons. The only male earning less than she did was John Crewdson, who only recently had been promoted from news interne. Twelfth in seniority, Shanahan was nineteenth on the salary scale. She earned $33,583.68, $12,334 less than R. W. Apple, Jr., and $11,426 less than Charles Mohr, the two highest paid men in the bureau, both of whom had less experience before coming to the *Times* than did Shanahan. The five persons below Shanahan on the list were all women. The bottom person was Nancy Hicks, "who was both female and Black."

Shanahan felt these wage differences "outrageous," and after some fuming she protested to Rosenthal directly. She kept her letter polite. She noted she had been nominated for a number of prizes, and that she had received several publisher's awards. "I made a specific proposal: I should make no less than the average of the top third of the Washington bureau." She gave a copy to Clifton Daniel, now the Washington bureau chief, and he told her not to mail it for, "Abe doesn't like confrontations." But Shanahan did anyway.

"The reply from Rosenthal was vituperative, a shocking letter," Shanahan said. No, Rosenthal would not consider the pay bracket she suggested, and he wished to hear no more from her; if she had any complaints, they should be raised with her bureau chief. A few days later Daniel called Shanahan into his office and relayed a message from Rosenthal: "Do not expect any further raises beyond those provided in Newspaper Guild contracts." He quoted Rosenthal as saying, "That's enough for her."

Almost immediately bad things began happening to Shanahan. Her prolific production of the popular Q Head analytical pieces was curbed by New York editors. "All of a sudden I couldn't get a Q Head in the paper. The first few times it happens you don't think anything about it. Then you say, 'What the hell is going on?' " During a two-year period she had only one Q Head published, and this one on the business-financial page when business editor John Lee was on vacation; his substitute asked for the article. As Shanahan surmised, the fact that she was blacklisted was known to the New York editors with whom she regularly dealt—the national desk and biz-fin—but not to their subordinates. (Oddly, when attorney Harriet Rabb took Rosenthal's deposition, according to Shanahan, "One of the attacks against me was that I hadn't produced more Q Heads!")

The victims of this vindictiveness were readers who rely upon *The New York Times* to explain the complexities of tax policy. Shanahan continued to write straight news stories. But to Rosenthal, disciplining a rebellious reporter required punishment, even at the expense of the quality of his newspaper.

Pride can be stretched only so far. For Shanahan, the break came when the *Times* passed her over for a job that justice suggests should have been hers. During her time in the bureau she had cheerfully worked at number-two behind Ed Dale, who headed "the economic cluster." Dale was assigned abroad, and many persons in the bureau felt, and said publicly, that Shanahan should replace him. But the job went to Clyde Farnsworth, who was brought back from Paris. "It had to be Abe," Shanahan stated. "I realized I had to get out. I didn't want to become embittered."

By happenstance, the weekend she decided to quit, she received a phone call from an old friend, Joseph Califano, the Secretary of Health, Education and Welfare. Come work for me, Califano said, I need a good press officer. Shanahan talked with friends who knew her discontent; they were almost unanimous in urging her to go; given Rosenthal's attitude, she had no meaningful career left at the *Times*. Whether she could ever get off his blacklist she knew not, for she had seen other persons similarly shunned. To do so would require insincere contrition which she did not owe.

Nonetheless no one lightly resigns from *The New York Times*. Two editors she trusted, David Jones and Seymour Topping, urged that she stay. But the one call that might have given her pause never came—one from Abe Rosenthal.

Shanahan's talk with Califano had been on Sunday. "On that Thursday afternoon I was talking with Topping, and I mentioned that I had not heard from Abe; that if the paper really wanted me, it seemed logical that Abe would say something. I asked Topping if Abe was aware I was considering leaving."

Topping said, "I guess so, for I told him about eleven this morning what was going on."

"That's it," Shanahan said. "I just made up my mind, Top. I'm leaving." Thus ended her career as an economics writer for the *Times*; she was a victim ironically of the suit to better women's rights at the newspaper.

Shanahan's forced resignation came in 1977, and by that time attorney Harriet Rabb was far along in amassing documentary and statistical evidence of *Times* discrimination, and in a broad range of categories. Economists who analyzed *Times* payroll material concluded that men at the *Times* were paid on the average $98.67 per week more than women, or $5,160 per year. A portion of the difference ($1,425) could be attributed to differences in education, years of experience, and the division of the paper in which they worked. But as stated by one of the experts, Dr. Orley Ashenfelter, Princeton University, "The remaining $3,725 of the excess of male over female mean salaries at the *Times* cannot be attributed to any presently measured productivity-related factors."

Rabb found numerous instances where the disparities were even more unfair. One among many, according to her pleadings: "The only female assistant metropolitan editor before the commencement of this suit earned $2,435 less than her immediate male predecessor, $7,126 less than the man who succeeded her, and $6,675 to $12,511 less than the men who held the same job at the same time. Five of the men who have been assistant metropolitan editors have been given such stock." (According to Arthur Sulzberger's deposition, stock was given to persons the *Times* considered "up and coming," and whom the *Times* wanted to keep on the staff.)

The disparities continued even after the suit was filed. Marilyn Bender became editor of the Sunday Business/Financial section in 1976 at a salary of $36,000. Her immediate predecessor, a man, had earned $50,988. That the *Times* would permit such a gap during litigation seemed to the women a deliberate affront. So did another appointment. In early 1977 Al Marlens, editor of the Sunday Week in Review section, died of a heart attack. Most persons expected him to be replaced by his deputy, Betsy Wade. But Wade was the lead named litigant in the women's suit. Rosenthal's choice for replacement was Mitchell Levitas, whose performance as metropolitan editor had not been universally praised.

By the fall of 1978 Rabb had what she considered a "can't lose case," and a trial date was set. The prospect of a public trial before a media audience troubled the *Times*.

Judith Coburn wrote in *New Times*:

> As an institution, the *Times* is enormously secretive; those familiar with its corporate ways compare it to the Nixon Administration, or even the papacy in its resentment of public scrutiny. No wonder *Times* executives are worried these days; the proceedings will lay bare company files and compel testimony from its top executives. While it explores the paramount issue question of whether . . . the *Times* has discriminated against women, the case will also display how the *Times* really works on a day-to-day basis.

What was not generally known was that many women in the case were equally nervous. The reason was Abe Rosenthal. Rabb's deposition of Rosenthal stretched over three days, and they were both grueling and informative, for he signalled what *Times* management intended to do. During the depositions Rabb called Shanahan to check a fact, and Shanahan asked how the questioning was going.

"Nothing I have heard from all of you in all these months prepared me for the reality of it," Rabb told Shanahan. "He [Rosenthal] trashed everyone. It was like being in the presence of raw sewage." Rosenthal had something nasty to say veritably about every woman who worked for the *Times*. *A* had drinking problems. *B* was almost a mental case. *C* let her family life interfere with her work. *D* was an "awful writer and a worse reporter." (These initials bear no relation to the women named by Rosenthal.)

The ferocity of Rosenthal's attack, and the personal nature of his comments, disturbed many women. Some of them, such as Nan Robertson and Betsy Wade, had the self-assurance to withstand anything Rosenthal might say about them. Such was not true of all of them. As one woman active in the suit told me, "We had some people who could not take the humiliation of being attacked publicly. Look into anyone's life, and you can find a weak spot, some vulnerability. We had to decide what we really wanted—whether to embarrass the *Times* in court, or to get some sort of guarantee that policies would change." Another factor was a New York newspaper strike that began just as the case was due for trial. Without the print media, the women would be denied the bludgeon of publicity they otherwise would have wielded on the *Times*.

So the parties settled. The *Times* agreed to hire significant numbers of women at every level in every news and commercial department. During the four years following the settlement, the *Times* agreed to place women in one of every eight of the top corporate positions; and in one of four positions in the news and editorial departments. Monetarily, the *Times* got off lightly. It agreed to a back-pay award of $235,000 for the 550 women covered by the suit, in the form of annuities maturing when they reach age sixty; this came to about $472 per person cash value. (The amount ultimately paid to each woman is covered by a formula not easily described in lay English.)

To the women, the money was secondary. As Betsy Wade stated, "The important thing is that the *Times* was mandated to give women a certain percentage of the good jobs, and fair salaries. In that sense, we won."

The women's suit changed hiring practices at the *Times*. But Rosenthal and other top editors somehow still did not seem to grasp the point that women were trying to make. As Stephanie Harrington wrote in *New York* Magazine a few years after the suit was settled:

> If, on a page or in a section designed primarily for women, they run stories on rape, abortion, ERA, female politicians and public officials, or on the struggle by women for power in the labor movement, Rosenthal and Gelb feel they are demonstrating an awareness that women are interested in more than recipes for gazpacho. They just don't get the point that women, like men, expect to find hard news on hard-news pages and that treating issues of political or social significance to women in a soft-news section does not dignify the section but trivializes the issues.

As recently as 1985, according to people who worked directly under him, Rosenthal several times broke off an all-male staff meeting and

rubbed his hands and said, "OK, now let's bring in the cup cakes"—
his way of saying that women departmental editors would be heard. A
man who has been Rosenthal's friend since the 1960's says in his defense, "Abe tries, Abe really does. He knows what he should say
about women, and do for women. But let's fact it, Abe still thinks of
women as either being good secretaries, good reporters, or good
pieces of ass. There's no way Abe is ever going to consider them equal
in the newsroom. Forget it."

But in truth women *did* begin to appear in more conspicuous levels
at the *Times*. Two of the daily sections had women editors. The general counsel of the paper, Katharine Darrow, was female. Women
held two of the more demanding foreign correspondent jobs—
Barbara Crosette, based in Bangkok, whose beat extended to strife-
torn Sri Lanka; and Judith Miller, in the Middle East, where Mos-
lems frown upon women even venturing outside the home, much less
holding jobs. But she did well. (Miller had problems with Rosenthal
earlier when as a Washington reporter she lived for a while with Representative Les Aspin, a ranking member of the House Armed Services Committee. Rosenthal wisely forbade her to write about any
matter involving Aspin.) In Libya in 1986 she had sexist troubles of
another sort. During an interview, Colonel Muammar al-Quaddafi
took her to the rear of his tent and made a crude sexual overture. She
included the incident in a long story she wrote months later when
back in New York. Artie Gelb asked her, "Judy, there's a line missing
in this story."

She looked at him quizzically. "Shouldn't you note that his overture was rejected?" Miller grinned, and said, "Oh."

Yet no women headed either of the four major desks that constitute
the core of the *Times*—metropolitan, national, foreign and Washington. The only three women directors were the Sulzberger sisters.
Rosenthal continued to look at women staff members with an interest
beyond their journalistic talent. His especial favorite in 1986 was Es-
ther Fein, who that year made the jump from news assistant to reporter and was immediately assigned to cover the fortieth anniversary
of the founding of the United Nations. Fein is petite and button-
pretty, and she has the knack of making Rosenthal smile.

Rosenthal stood in the door of his office one afternoon, talking with
a correspondent visiting 43rd Street from assignment elsewhere, and
he suddenly broke off in mid-sentence, and his eyes were staring

many feet across the room. The reporter turned and realized he was staring at Fein.

"God, what a bottom!" Rosenthal said, and shook his head with a smile. Then he resumed the conversation.

Rosenthal could be nudged on feminist issues; it helped, however, if the person doing the nudging was of prominence. In December, 1984, a woman he respects very much, Jeane Kirkpatrick, at the time the U. S. ambassador to the United Nations, gave a talk to the Women's Forum in which she pointedly objected to being called "Mrs." rather than "Dr." or "Professor." As Dr. Kirkpatrick stated, "Now I think 'Mrs.' is an honorable title; certainly it's an earned title, like 'Doctor' or 'Professor.' But it's a non-differentiating, non-professional title." Why should her predecessors such as Henry Kissinger and Zbigniew Brzesinski be called "Dr." or "Professor" when the *Times* wrote her off as "Mrs."?

Someone in the audience asked Dr. Kirkpatrick whether these terms "emanated from the media or emanated from some other place, such as the White House, and the media picked them up." She responded:

> I don't know. Journalists themselves make decisions like titles; and journalists themselves make decisions about what they include in how they characterize people. What I would say about journalism is that it is—like most other power processes in our society . . . overwhelmingly male as you get near the top, the top being prestige papers like *The New York Times*, the Washington *Post* and so forth. . . . [I]n my experience none of it is ultimately disabling. What it does is make difficult jobs more difficult. . . .

Dr. Kirkpatrick's office made sure *The New York Times* received the text of these remarks, and thereafter she was "Dr." Kirkpatrick, not "Mrs." Kirkpatrick.

But other vestiges of sexism remained. A copy editor changed a sentence from "Americans are to *man* three early-warning stations" in the first edition to "Americans are to *staff* . . ." A higher editor snapped, "Let's not make the *Times* look silly." Writing of President Reagan's 1985 State of the Union address, financial columnist Leonard Silk said the President singled out for "recognition as an American hero a Black woman. Indeed, both of his heroes were women. . . ." (Read the sentence again slowly with an eye for nouns that have both masculine and feminine forms.)*

But Rosenthal for years remained adamant on a minor but symbolic point. He refused to permit the *Times* to use the word "Ms." to refer to a woman. His friend Gloria Steinem bearded him constantly on the point. At a summer dinner party in the Hamptons she pushed him so mercilessly that another woman finally said, "For god's sake, Gloria, get off the man's back." She desisted then, but she continued picking at him.

The afternoon of June 19, 1986, a notice signed by Rosenthal appeared on the bulletin board in the *Times* newsroom, stating that an Editors' Note would appear in the paper the next day:

> Beginning today, *The New York Times* will use "Ms." as an honorific in its news columns.
>
> Until now, "Ms." had not been used because of the belief that it had not passed sufficiently into the language to be accepted as common usage.
>
> The *Times* believes now "Ms." has become a part of the language, and is changing its policy.
>
> The *Times* will continue to use "Miss" or "Mrs." when it knows the marital status of a woman in the news unless she prefers "Ms."
>
> "Ms." will also be used when a woman's marital status is not known, or when a married woman wishes to use her maiden name professionally or in private life.

Word of Rosenthal's capitulation spread rapidly around Manhattan, and Gloria Steinem sent flowers from herself and the staff of *Ms.* Magazine with a glowing thank-you note. Women in the news room who normally keep their distance from Rosenthal made a point of looking into his office and smiling and waving their thanks.†

That evening Artie Gelb was talking with news editor Allan Siegal and a visitor when cultural editor William Honan stuck his head through the door and said, in a pained voice, "Artie, we've got a prob-

---

*Heroine, perhaps?

†The *Times*'s change was noted by a column-length article by Eleanor Randolph of the Washington *Post*. Randolph noted her own newspaper's stylebook states, "do not use the term Ms. except in direct quotations, in discussing the term itself or for special effect."

lem. Beverly Sills is going to be in the paper tomorrow, and she just
called and said she heard of the new 'Ms.' ruling. Artie, she hates the
term. She doesn't want to be called 'Ms.' She is content with Miss."

Honan sighed, and none of the three editors said anything for a few
seconds. All knew that Beverly Sills was a very close friend of
Rosenthal—indeed, she introduced him to Shirley Lord, whom he intended to marry.

"Bah," said Siegal. "You know what I'd like to do? I'd like to start
the world all over again, and the newspapers, too. No one would have
a title. We would all pick our own."

"Very funny, Allan, very funny," Gelb said. "But that doesn't help
with Mrs. Sills or Miss Sills or whatever the hell we are going to call
her." He read the last sentence of the policy announcement, and to
him—and to Honan—it seemed clear it dictated that as a married
woman using a professional name she must be a Ms.

"How about it?" Honan asked. "Do we go along with the lady?
Make an exception for her?"

"Hell," Gelb said, "I don't want to start fudging on the policy the
very first night, even before we put out a single issue of the *Times*.
Abe went through hell on this decision." He found a piece of paper
that contained Rosenthal's schedule for the evening, and he dialed
the telephone. The person who answered obviously had trouble understanding him but through laborious effort Gelb had him repeat
back the words, "Mr. Rosenthal call office."

Gelb put down the phone. "A dinner party, and he hasn't arrived
yet. This waiter or houseboy got the message. I think. Hell, this is
Abe's baby. Whatever he says, OK, do it."

Siegal glanced at the visitor. "Should he really be listening to all
this?" Gelb responded with a so-what shrug.

Honan was thinking about deadlines, and he started out the door
and turned and asked Gelb, "If Abe doesn't call back right away, how
long should we wait?"

Gelb said, "Given that he's executive editor of *The New York
Times*, and that she is one of his very best friends, I suggest we wait
just as long as it necessary."

The New York Times calls her Miss Sills.

Concurrent with the women's struggle for recognition, the *Times*
also groped for a means of satisfying yet another minority group, the

paper's Black employees. During the 1950's, when the civil rights movement first began to stir America, someone suggested to *Times* managing editor Turner Catledge that the time was appropriate for the paper to hire a Black reporter. Catledge, a Mississippian by birth, was not a blatant racist, but he had the attitude of many Southern men of his generation—that Blacks somehow were not fitted for professional jobs, save for rare exceptions. Still, he had persuaded his predecessor, Jimmy James, to hire the *Times*'s first Black reporter, in the late 1940's, from a labor paper. Catledge said the reporter "found it almost impossible to be objective when covering stories involving race. Once he admitted to me he'd invented some quotes for A. Philip Randolph, because he was sure he knew what Randolph meant to say, whether or not he said it." After several episodes of bad judgment "we had to let him go." Catledge also played a role in the hiring of Laymond Robinson, the first Black ever to cover politics for a major American newspaper.

Now the *Times* needed more Blacks, and Catledge talked over the problem with publisher Arthur Hays Sulzberger, who protested, "But I don't *know* any blacks!" Sulzberger thought a moment. "Oh, yes, I do, I know Ralph Bunche at the United Nations. We saw him the other evening. Let me try him." Soon Sulzberger had the distinguished Black American diplomat on the phone, and the conversation went like this, according to Catledge:

"Hello, Ralph, this is Arthur Hays Sulzberger over at *The New York Times*. Some of us were thinking that it would be good for us to have a Black reporter. I remembered that you had a daughter. Do you think she'd be interested in becoming a reporter for us?"

There was a pause. "What's that? Oh, she's going to medical school. How good." Pause. "Say, Ralph, do you know anyone else who . . . that's right, some Black youngster who might like to work for the *Times*. OK, that would be fine, give me a call if you think of anyone."

Sulzberger put down the phone and shook his head and frowned. "I think I somehow offended him." Bunche never called back.

The *Times* did find Black reporters, through more conventional channels, during the 1960's and 1970's. Nonetheless, even as the *Times* editorial page thundered against racial discrimination in the South, it did so through an all-white voice. Interest in finding a Black editorial writer seemed to increase in 1972, when Roger Wilkins, formerly an officer of the Justice Department and the Ford Foundation, joined the editorial board of the Washington *Post*. Rosenthal, who knew Wilkins socially, and often had him to the paper for an after-work drink, asked, "Why did you go there instead of here?"

"Two reasons, Abe," Wilkins replied. "One, they asked me, and two, you didn't" Wilkins shared in the *Post*'s Pulitzer for editorial excellence for Watergate. His marriage in disarray, in 1976 he quit the *Post* to move to New York to be with a new woman friend, and Punch Sulzberger, at the urging of Harrison Salisbury, arranged for him to join the paper. In 1977, as noted earlier, he was one of the four editorial writers who survived the purge that ousted John Oakes as editor of the editorial page. Wilkins looked around the paper for another job, uncertain as to what he wished. Sulzberger suggested he write an urban affairs column.

One day Wilkins encountered Rosenthal and managing editor Seymour Topping in the elevator. Rosenthal, who had always been friendly, seemed specially so this day. He played with Wilkins' tie, and grinned as if he had a big secret. Wilkins was not surprised when one of Rosenthal's secretaries called and asked that he stop by for drinks at the end of the day.

Rosenthal was still exuberant, and he talked about his plans for the paper, and how Wilkins fit into them, and that he had a major job in mind for him: editor of the News of the Week in Review section, a prestigious position. Wilkins knew the implications. "No Black person before—or to this day—had editing responsibility on *The New York Times*."

Rosenthal put a high gloss on the appointment. "You'll be one of the people helping to shape and make the paper. You'll move up. You'll be one of the principal editors of the paper."

"This is all very flattering," Wilkins said, "but I want to think about it." "Take your time," Rosenthal said. They agreed to talk again within a week.

Wilkins thought hard about the offer. Becoming an editor of *The New York Times* had intrinsic appeal. Yet he had spent much of his life in staff jobs, at the Agency for International Development, at the Justice Department, at the Ford Foundation. When he entered newspapering, at age forty, "it was because I wanted to be a writer, not a bureaucrat." He talked with many persons—Tom Wicker, Sydney Gruson, David Schneidermann, Harrison Salisbury, Charlotte Curtis, Ramsey Clark. "People kept telling me, 'That's not you, Roger.' " Only Ramsey Clark urged acceptance "because it would have meant a move-up at the paper." Word that he would refuse the offer got back to Rosenthal.

After the week lapsed Wilkins returned to Rosenthal's office. "He clearly knew what the answer was going to be. The atmosphere and his attitude were markedly different. The week before, he kept refilling my glass with martinis. Now he poured himself a glass of Tab and didn't bother to offer me anything. His face was hard and ugly. His shirt tail was out and his pants hanging off his hips. He sat and glowered at me."

Wilkins explained his decision, and why he did not want to become a bureaucrat and worry about budgets and money and administration. He preferred to write the urban affairs column that Sulzberger suggested. He mentioned some of the persons with whom he had talked.

Rosenthal picked up on one of the names. "Syd who?" he demanded.

"Why, Syd Gruson," Wilkins said.

As Wilkins recollected later, "I never saw a man get so mad so fast in my life. Rosenthal literally came alive with rage. He began prancing up and down the office. He was livid, really mad. 'All right, you won't help, I asked you to help me, you won't help. You want to be a w-r-i-t-e-r.' " (Rosenthal dragged out the word, sarcastically.) He waved towards the newsroom, a contemptuous gesture of dismissal. "I got writers coming out of my asshole," Rosenthal continued. He would not listen to Wilkins. He walked over to his desk and began going through papers, a clear signal for Wilkins to leave.

Wilkins was quick to learn the consequences of refusing the assignment. "When you turn Abe down, you cross a bridge. . . . When I went down there I was already on Abe's shitlist." What happened thereafter Wilkins attributes to racism which he feels is inherent in the *Times* and many of the editors who work there. Indeed he was mistreated. But an equally logical explanation was that the underlings with whom he dealt were simply expressing Rosenthal's displeasure, and making Wilkins' life so miserable he would leave the paper. From Rosenthal's perspective, Wilkins was offered one of the more prestigious jobs in the news department. On that basis, by what perverted torture of judgment could Rosenthal be accused of racism? In Rosenthal's estimate, he was breaking significant new ground within the *Times* for Blacks. Wilkins, however, a decade later remained firmly convinced racism was the reason for the "harassment" he now encountered.

The paper, through Sulzberger, was committed to the urban affairs column. Rosenthal could not stop this; what he could do was to make Wilkins' life uncomfortable. The agreement had been that the column would be edited by the national desk, which Wilkins considered a better choice than metropolitan, which was busier and controlled far more reporters. "Syd Schanberg was running metro at the time, and he was pretty frantic," Wilkins said. "David Jones, who had the national desk, was placid; he was no dynamite editor, but he had good news judgment."

When Wilkins moved into the newsroom he met with Rosenthal and Seymour Topping and explained why he preferred to work under the national desk. "Tough shit!" Rosenthal exclaimed, and walked away. There was other bad news. The column would be displayed as "news analysis." Unlike other regular columns controlled by the metropolitan desk, it would have no standing headline. Wilkins did not have a regular editor; his column would be edited by whoever happened to be available.

Wilkins wrote his first column and gave it to Schanberg. Three or four days passed, and the column did not appear. Wilkins went to the editor ("a humiliating thing to have to do") and asked, "Have you looked at my copy?"

The editor looked up and frowned, "I'm really busy, I'll get to it when I have a slow day."

In an early column Wilkins challenged an assertion by Senator Daniel Moynihan that affirmative action laws, if applied to New York public schools, should be likened to the anti-Jewish Nuremburg Laws of the Nazi Germany era. Editing was to be done by an editor who Wilkins asserts was "a creep all the Blacks knew was a racist," based on his previous conduct.

The editor called Wilkins to his desk to discuss the column, and the conversation got heated. "Phone calls went out to Blacks all over the paper, saying, 'The shit is on, X is dealing with Roger's copy.' " The editor challenged quotations Wilkins attributed to Moynihan. "Did he *really* say that?" he demanded. As Wilkins says, "Can you imagine the implications of me making up quotes in *The New York Times*, and attributing them not to some minor figure, but to a New York senator who is the publisher's friend and buddy?"

Finally, Wilkins lost his temper. Yes, he said, Moynihan said the things I attributed to him. "If you ever ask me anything like that again, you miserable motherfucker, I'll break your jaw."

The editing session ended. "He went around bellyaching and bitching he had been threatened with assault," Wilkins said. Rosenthal intervened. "Abe said, 'You just can't do that—you can't threaten a fellow worker.' "

Wilkins replied, "Any son of a bitch who calls me dishonest, and keeps on saying it, I'm going to deck him."

The problems continued. Schanberg made him rewrite a column about one of the borough prosecutors three times, and promised Wilkins he would run it on a particular day. Wilkins bought an early edition of the paper. No column. He called Schanberg at home, and they had a long cursing match. The next day Seymour Topping (who heard Schanberg's version first) told Wilkins he must apologize. "Ain't that the American way," Wilkins said, "fuck the nigger and apologize to the white man?" Eventually Wilkins had editorial problems with virtually every column he submitted.

To several editors who worked with Wilkins, the columnist (in one man's words) "was a royal pain in the ass." He stated, "Roger was hypersensitive. He saw racism if anyone changed a comma or corrected his grammar or asked him to amplify something for clarity." This man concedes that Rosenthal did not care for Wilkins or his column. "But to blame Roger's troubles on racism is a total distortion of what happened. Total."

When Wilkins had come to the news department he was aware that Blacks elsewhere in the paper had sued *The New York Times,* charging racial discrimination in hiring, job classification, salaries and other issues. The plaintiffs were mostly clerical and business office workers, and no Blacks in the news department supported them. "We writers were specialists," Wilkins says. "We weren't into all that stuff. We could not see ourselves in the same class as some guy or woman who took classified ads over the phone." Now Wilkins decided to involve himself in the suit, and he was joined by Black reporters Barbara Campbell and Rudy Johnson.

"The suit started taking on steam when writers got into it, and the *Times* took it more seriously," he said. "Here you had reporters challenging them, not some clerks down in the business office." Wilkins knew his *New York Times* career was ending, and he decided to exit with a flourish. He had been an assistant attorney general in the Justice Department's civil rights division, and he had handled several big cases. With these credentials, and his experience at the *Times*, he blistered the *Times* in a deposition. He called Rosenthal a "vicious racist liar," and he accused Punch Sulzberger of running a "racist paper."

A few days later he encountered Rosenthal, and he realized Rosenthal had read the deposition. "His face turned purple, and got as tight as if he had five lemons in his mouth." Another day Wilkins stood outside Rosenthal's office, going through a rack of out-of-town newspapers. Rosenthal came out and saw him. "He literally ran away." At Sardi's Rosenthal sat with James Greenfield when Wilkins walked in. "He slaps a big bill down, and leaves his drink, and grabs Jimmy and leaves the bar."

Wilkins finally stopped Rosenthal in the newsroom. "You and I disagree, but that's no reason for you to stop speaking to me. That's juvenile," he said. Rosenthal muttered something unintelligible and walked on.

Eventually, the Blacks settled their case out of court for reasons similar to those cited by the women in their case. During his deposition (which is under court seal) Rosenthal gave what Wilkins called "vicious and horrible" testimony about various Black reporters. He said of Wilkins, "He's not as good as he thinks he is," to which Wilkins replies, "Why, then, did he offer me a job?" Wilkins argued for settlement, for the *Times* "would not hesitate to destroy the reputations of all Blacks on the staff. Some of us could weather it; some could not. More importantly, it was unlikely that anybody in the press would cover a trial fully. . . . These people would be talking into the wind."

The amount of the settlement, although never disclosed, was said by Wilkins to be "substantially more" than that received by the women. The *Times* agreed to put Blacks into more responsible positions throughout the paper.

As he prepared to leave the *Times* in late 1979 Wilkins decided to try to talk to Rosenthal about the impact his personality and policies were having on the paper. He had seen a dozen talented writers leave the *Times* for various reasons. Rosenthal agreed to meet with him. "Punch sent Gruson down to make sure we didn't come to blows." Wilkins told Rosenthal, in effect, "You are making many writers unhappy. You've lost X, Y and Z. This is an inhospitable place for writers, and it is crazy for this to happen."

Rosenthal replied, "Roger, you're almost overwhelmingly intelligent but you don't understand me."

"But I've been talking about *The New York Times* . . ." Wilkins could go no further. He realized Rosenthal had so meshed his identity with that of the *Times* that he saw no difference. Wilkins shrugged and walked out of Abe Rosenthal's office for the last time.

TWENTY

"I Do Not Want to See *That* Word in Print Again"

The lead article in the Sunday travel section of *The New York Times* for April 6, 1975, contained the raciest language, direct and suggestive, ever to appear in the newspaper. Under the headline, "The All-Gay Cruise: Prejudices and Pride," freelance writer Cliff Jahr told of a week-long cruise on the deluxe French liner *Renaissance* from the Florida Everglades to the Yucatan. The headline was a tad inaccurate: some 300 of the passengers were gays, but fifteen witting straights were also aboard. Jahr described a jolly scene, with lawyers, businessmen, academicians, even a few physicians—persons of both genders—partying to soft drugs and hard rock for the week. There were "leathermen in black cowhide outfits trimmed with chains, zippers and metal studs. " There was the youthful blond architect (male) "draped in a crepe dress and a silver fox clutchcape." What happened in the staterooms Jahr left to conjecture, but with enough guidelines to provide a nudge for even the most naive reader. Many of the below-decks couplings involved lesbians, including "Lois, a

396

blond ex-showgirl from Miami" who formed a brief but torrid friendship with a young woman dean from an East Coast college.

Although Robert Stock, then the travel editor, approved the article with only minor editing changes, several old-timers on the paper blinked when first-runs of the section appeared in the *Times* newsroom late Friday evening. One veteran copy editor read the article "with interest, but with that 'oh-oh feeling' at the same time, 'cause I knew this piece had trouble written all over it, in bold lavender letters." Indeed it did. By Monday afternoon both editor Stock and Max Frankel, the Sunday editor, stood sheepishly on Punch Sulzberger's carpet. Sulzberger was livid to the extent of his abilities. How *dare* the *Times* and its reputation be sullied by such an article! Since when are *orgies* news? And especially *orgies* by a bunch . . . a bunch of. . . he had to force the words through lips curled with disgust . . . *orgies by a bunch of faggots.*

Even his mother, Sulzberger continued, had called in indignation. How am I, as her son and as publisher of our newspaper, how am I supposed to explain such an article, much less defend it? You have caused me grave embarrassment, you have offended my mother, you have put a stain on *The New York Times.* Iphigene Sulzberger was an understanding woman, Sulzberger went on, but she was also a lady, and ladies did not like reading such "garbage" anywhere—and especially on Sunday morning in her very own newspaper.

As the editor who directly approved the article, Stock knew his career rested in an uneasy sling. He babbled about "brightening the paper," and "recognizing alternative cultures," and the like, but the frown on Sulzberger's face cut him short. He murmured an apology. He had erred, and he would take a closer look at "articles likely to cause controversy" in the future.

Punch made himself plain. He wanted no more "gay glorification" articles in his newspaper; indeed, he did not even want to see *that word* in print again. That word? Yeah, gay, Sulzberger said, first forcefully to Rosenthal and some other editors, then more politely in a memorandum. Persons of that persuasion chose a lifestyle, and the *Times* would happily let them so identify themselves—as homosexuals. Such was *Times* style hereafter.

A functionary on the copy desk several days later raised a question, most politely. Even in the mid-1970's the word "homosexual" was seldom used in the community the *Times* wished to so label. Many activist groups incorporated "gay" into their formal names, and the word was bandied about in public utterances and statements. After some argument Sulzberger permitted an exception: in direct quotations, or naming an organization, "gay" was permissible. But in no other form. "Don't disappoint me again," he told one editor. "And above all, I don't want another call from my mother on this point. Understand?"

Understood, and with a blind vengeance.

That the *Times* policy was patently offensive to many of its readers can be explained, if not excused, by the fact that the paper followed the general journalistic policy of the era. By whatever name, "homosexuals" were mentioned with snickers in the nation's newsrooms. "Queer killings" received paragraphs—the middle-aged bachelor stabbed in his apartment by a youthful visitor—and the victim's sexual preference needed no further explanation than that "he was said by friends to be interested in the fine arts." For decades the *Times Index* listing for homosexual contained a single line reference, "*See Perversion, Sexual.*" The *Times* ignored the sexual preferences even of such renowned persons as Tennessee Williams and Gore Vidal (in the latter instance, *Times* book reviewers avoided him for years after his 1940's homosexual novel *The City and the Pillar*).

The *Times*'s homophobia commencing in the mid-1970's was a grave editorial error, and on several levels. As a paper devoted to "styles of life" the *Times* missed the emergence of a major sociological phenomenon in New York City. Flaunting centuries-old mores, scores of thousands of New York men and women "came out of the closet" to live openly with persons of their sex. One of Rosenthal's first projects when he became metropolitan editor had been to assign reporter Paul Hoffman to do a series on the emergence of gays. The persons directly concerned were generally pleased with the series. A gay man at the *Times*—he is in his sixties and he remains "closeted"— told me, "Hoffman's series was a 'gee-whiz' thing, like 'Look at this colony of rare butterflies we discovered over in the Jersey Meadows.' " Hoffman's series, lauded as a "landmark," remained just that; for years it was the *Times*'s only serious attempt to report on a new community.

As a large, lively sub-culture, the gay community provided ample reasons for serious coverage. In many electoral districts politicians assiduously courted the "gay vote;" although no such monolithic bloc existed, persons in the community learned to vote for persons who supported them on important issues, such as recognition of same-sex pairings for insurance policies. The gay political activism went unnoted by the *Times*, save for occasional tangential references.

From a business viewpoint, the *Times* homophobia was stupid. Statistics on the gay community are inherently fuzzy, given the preference of many persons for continuing privacy. But even a surface observer who lunched on the East Side, or walked through the Village, could not be oblivious to "gay yuppies," men and women under forty years of age, with the high-ticket dress suggestive of affluence. Sexual preference aside, such was the very audience for which the "new" *Times* was designed.

Rosenthal made his own preference clear. At page-one conferences he talked about "fags" and "queers" and "faggots." Upon learning that one of his favored clerks was homosexual, Rosenthal reacted with sincere shock: "Goddamn, he sure fooled me!" For months Rosenthal referred to this man frequently when drinking, and he would go into lengthy salacious speculation as to the exact sexual role he assumed with his lover. Rosenthal expressed dismay that his personal antenna failed: "I can spot a fag a mile away," he would say, "but _____ sure fooled me, the smarmy little bastard."

A gay woman told me of a reporter with a choice assignment outside of New York City. During a visit to his station in 1985 Rosenthal realized that the writer was gay. Soon after his return to New York, Rosenthal ordered the man brought back to 43rd Street. As he told a subordinate, "This guy has a sensitive beat, and we can't afford a Foster Winants mess." (He referred to *The Wall Street Journal* columnist convicted of giving advance market information to a broker; the proceeds benefited, in part, his gay roommate.) Yet the reporter's byline appeared frequently on major stories after his return; whether he was "penalized" for his sexuality would be unprovable. The reporter did not respond to a written inquiry, hence he is not named.

Andrew Humm, who writes frequently about gay issues and the media, feels that Rosenthal's attitude is endemic in much of the New York media. He recalls only one reporter for a daily newspaper who is openly gay, having so declared at a gay rights demonstration several years ago. "Yet I know more than a dozen persons at the *Times*, including some who byline regularly, who are gay and scared silly that an editor there will find out about it. They just don't know what the reaction would be. The *Times* is a New York institution, like the [Catholic] Archdiocese. It is conservative, and it does not go out of its way to make gays appear welcome."

Roger Wilkins, during the brief (and unhappy) period he wrote an urban affairs column for the *Times*, got on the mailing lists for several gay publications; other reporters and editors sniffed and asked, "Why are you bothering with that queer junk?" "To learn something about this city, goddamn it," Wilkins replied.

The *Times*'s treatment of gays—its ignoring of them, more accurately—is acutely illustrative of the paper's arrogance in dealing with issues with which it is not comfortable, and its ability to deny them credibility. The *Times*'s decision to exclude serious discussion of gay issues from its columns is unique only in that Sulzberger made the impulsive decision in writing as an announced and internally-publicized policy. That Sulzberger put something in writing about banning the word "gay" is a blunder that the publisher rarely makes. Again, however, the publisher only rarely receives the quasi-public spanking Iphigene administered to him the Monday after the gay-cruise article.

The *Times*'s record on gay coverage for much of the decade following the gay-cruise affair is one of unremitting silliness and callousness; gay readers of the paper can offer enough homophobic examples to fill a Sunday edition of the *Times*. David Rothenberg for several years wrote a media column for *The New York Native*, and he found frequent reason to criticize the *Times*.* As Rothenberg wrote, "The *Times* takes justifiable pride in employing experts in a multitude of subjects—Terry Robards on wine, Paul Goldberger on architecture, Jane Brody on personal health, to name only three. Small nations around the globe contain *Times* correspondents who are well-versed in even the slightest nuances of regional customs and politics. Yet, the paper's main prerequisite for covering a gay event or reviewing a gay book or play seems to be boastful ignorance—therefore, downgrading—of the subculture. . . . Inquiring reporters are woefully ignorant of the differences even between such contrasting gay organizations as the National Gay Task Force and the Gay Activists Alliance." One reason, Rothenberg says, is that gay persons on the

---

*Some of the examples cited in this section are drawn from Rothenberg's article, "Homophobia at *The New York Times*," *The New York Native*, June 1-14, 1981. As shall be seen, the *Times* took its revenge on Rothenberg four years later.

Times staff feel compelled to keep their sexual preference secret; that to declare themselves openly would dash any chances for serious career advancement. Resultantly, they must hide "their knowledge of one of the more important sociological phenomena to occur in recent years."

A striking deficiency in *Times* coverage of gay stories was the inability of key editors to recognize the stories that required no deep understanding. These stories represented a conscious decision either to ignore or trivialize news pertaining to gays:

—In November, 1980, "fag-bashers" fired a machine gun into the Ramrod, a West Street homosexual club, killing two men and wounding seven others. "VILLAGE BLOODBATH," the New York *Post* headlined; the story was front-page in the tabloids for three days; the *Times* dismissed the attack with an inside page story in the second section. One of David Rothenberg's friends was a victim, and he delivered an eulogy at a memorial service in a church on Christopher Street. Thousands of men marched with candles, through a rain, to the service; so many came there were not seats for all, so hundreds stood outside in the cold. "Our community was in a rage. The *Times* did not cover the services. The man with the machine gun was yelling 'faggots' as he shot. I wonder what the *Times* would have done had he come into a delicatessen and yelled 'kikes' and killed two people," Rothenberg said.

—The night of July 30, 1980, a crowd of turn-away size appeared for a political first in New York: a debate between U. S. Senate candidates Bess Myerson, Elizabeth Holtzman and John Lindsay on gay issues. No candidate for the office had ever accepted an invitation from the sponsoring gay groups. The *Times* ignored the debate. It had its own "gay" story the next morning, headlined on the front page of the Metro Section, headlined "Rest Room Shut to Foreclose Use By Homosexuals." This is the grubby vice squad perennial found in virtually any American daily newspaper at least once annually.

—Another "mindset" happening concerned the filming of the movie *Cruising* in the leather bar area of the Lower West Side. The movie deals with the heavy-action sadism-and-masochism fringe of the homosexual world. The world exists; its devotees are publicized in such "main stream" gay publications as the *New York Native.* Nonetheless gays picketed the filming locations, saying the movie presented a misleading picture of their community. The *Times* ran a small story quoting a bystander accusing the protesters of being "First Amendment fascists." The *Times* missed the point of the demonstration. The company had the right to make the film; the gays had an equal right to protest, and they did so by the thousands. That so many persons were outraged was not made known to *Times* readers.

—In 1978 an NFL player named Dave Kopay wrote a book, *The David Kopay Story*, that was a considerable departure from the usual sports autobiography. Throughout his career, Kopay wrote, he had been gay, and he found companionship at many unexpected places in the sports world, including pro football. Kopay's memoir was one of the first sports books on *The New York Times* bestseller list. It was also unique in that it was one of the rare books to make the list without being reviewed in either the daily or the Sunday *Times*. (Review coverage elsewhere was broad.) *Times* sports columnist Dave Anderson recognized the uniqueness of the book, and wrote about Kopay and his long-secret sexuality. The column was killed, for one of the few times in Anderson's career. A reason was suggested by a man who had a long association with the *Times* sports department, although he never formally worked for the paper: "The NFL went bonkers when Kopay came out of the closet, because he hinted that a helluva lot more players in the league were gay. Women's tennis had just taken a hard shot financially because of the publicity about Billie Jean King being sued by her former girlfriend; there was fear in women's tennis that the sponsors would be driven away by that naughty word 'lesbianism.' And now here is the NFL facing the same cookie-monster. The NFL called in its chips. So the *Times* ran a feature about the Westchester dog show rather than explore a damned good man-bites-dog story."

—For years the *Times* refused to acknowledge same-sex pairings, even of prominent persons in obituaries. Several examples, of hundreds: The theatrical lawyer Arnold Weissberger lived for years with agent Milton Goldman; actress Ethel Merman called them "the happiest couple on Broadway." When Weissberger died in 1981 the *Times* obituary did not mention Goldman. One *Times* editor argued, "Well, how do we know that the surviving person wants to be identified as a homosexual?" An invalid argument, since many surviving companions *asked* to be named in obituaries.

In February, 1983, the award-winning playwright Jane Chambers died. Her longtime publicist Francine Trevens issued a release referring to the fact that Chambers won the 1983 Los Angeles Alliance for Gay Artists Award, and that she was survived by "her life's companion, Beth Allen." The *Times*'s obituary did not refer to the Los Angeles award or to the gay themes of Chambers' work. It listed numerous blood relatives as survivors, but not Beth Allen, who had shared her life for fourteen years.

Allen "felt the omission of my name from her obituary to be hurtful both to me and to the gay community. The *Times* chose instead to recognize some family members Jane hadn't seen in twenty years." Again: when actor Harvey Fierstein won a Tony Award, he gave an impassioned speech thanking, among other persons, his lover. The *Times* did not mention this statement. And a long subsequent profile did not mention that he was gay.

Dozens of similar slights or misreporting exist in the files of such *Times* critics as Dave Rothenberg. Not all are the horror stories he makes them out to be; they can be explained as exercises of news judgment. Yet even when discounted for anger, Rothenberg's salient point remain valid: *The New York Times* consistently unreported or misreported a major community through the first decade of Abe Rosenthal's editorship.

Thus the *Times* was ill-prepared to report the first signs of the ominous AIDS epidemic when they appeared in the early 1980's. And here is where the complaints of gay activists turn away from the trivial—a slighted play, an ignored book, an unreported meeting—to the deadly serious, the lives of thousands of persons in New York and the nation.

Medical reporter Jerry Bishop wrote the first major newspaper article about AIDS for *The Wall Street Journal* in December, 1981, relying upon a report in the *New England Journal of Medicine* about a baffling disease that destroyed the body's immunological system. As fatality figures continued to mount (as recorded by the Center for Disease Control in Atlanta) Bishop wrote other articles. He sensed a major tragedy in the making, yet he could not convince superiors at the *WSJ* of the seriousness of the disease; what he wrote as a proposed front-page article for his paper ended up in the magazine *Discovery*. His own paper's skepticism, Bishop said, was "because no one else was covering it. You know, 'How come there's an epidemic going on in the *Times*'s backyard, and they're not writing about it?' "

The *Times*, in fact, had brushed against the story, but with no great detail. On March 11, 1982, the *Times* offered two definitions: acquired immunity deficiency, or AID; or "gay-related immunodeficiency," or GRID. Other stories in 1982 and 1983, chiefly on the science pages, told of increasing concern among physicians and public health specialists.

In a daring breach of *Times* prudery policies, a 1983 *Times Magazine* article mentioned as a possible cause the mixing of blood and semen during "oral-anal or anogenital contact." (Not until 1985 did "anal intercourse" appear in run-of-the-paper stories.) What the *Times* did not report was the human impact of the epidemic, and the lack of any meaningful city response. Although hundreds of New York men were dying of AIDS, the *Times* never mentioned the disease as the cause-of-death in obituaries.

Working on their own, without significant city support (or mention by the *Times*) community activists formed the Gay Men's Health Crisis (GMHC), both to care for afflicted friends and to press for research on an AIDS cure. In April, 1983, GMHC bought out Madison Square Garden for a performance by Ringling Brothers Barnum & Bailey Circus, and 18,000 persons attended. Mayor Edward Koch served as opening ringmaster, and Leonard Bernstein directed the circus band in the National Anthem. Stories about the fund-raiser appeared the next day in the Chicago *Tribune*, the Philadelphia *Inquirer*, and the Washington *Post*—but not in *The New York Times*.

The *Times* was not pressed for space that day. The front page carried an article about seven Austrian show horses burned to death in a stable blaze. Months later, Geraldo Rivera of ABC News did a segment on AIDS on the "20/20" program. He displayed a front page of *The New York Times* on camera, and he pointed to the horse story, and how the *Times* had boycotted coverage of the AIDS benefit circus. Several days later the *Times* ran two long stories on gay issues. Both began on the front page in exactly the same position given the horses earlier.

The slight stirred Rothenberg and other activists to deep anger. "Our community was responding to the major health problem of our time, and even the presence of the Mayor and Bernstein did not legitimize the event in the eyes of *The New York Times*. This did it. We had griped in silence long enough. We decided to picket, and to stage a one-day boycott." First, however, was an appeal for an audience with Punch Sulzberger, by a four-person committee composed of Rothenberg; Andrew Humm; Virginia Apuzzu; the New York State Assistant Commissioner for Consumer Affairs; and Richard Failla, a New York City judge.

Sydney Gruson, acting for Sulzberger, heard their "long laundry list" of complaints, and promised a "get back to you." But Humm leaked an account of the meeting to Page Six, the gossip page of the New York *Post*, which infuriated Gruson—and presumably Sulzberger and Rosenthal. Gruson told Rothenberg that the *Times* "felt betrayed," that he had indicated a willingness to work for a solution, only to be hit by a public complaint. "Gruson was most upset," Rothenberg said. Nevertheless Gruson did arrange a lunch meeting with Rosenthal with three of the original group (Humm, the leaker, was excluded by direction of Gruson).

Over lamb kebabs, the gay group took a positive approach. Rothenberg decided not to appear as an outspoken activist. "I went in as an old theatrical press agent. I did not lament the woes of the past, but identified stories the *Times* could cover." He suggested three stories: the creation of a "buddy system" whereby AIDS victims receive care from a designated person; a scheduled national conference of parents of gays; and political trends among gays nationally.

Rosenthal received the ideas with interest. "Mr. Rosenthal was disarmingly charming," Rothenberg said. "He admitted the *Times* blew the AIDS story, that they were a year behind on it."

But Rosenthal would not yield on the group's insistence that the *Times* use the word "gay" rather than "homosexual" in news accounts. "Give me one good reason we should use gay," Rosenthal said.

Rothenberg thought, "I've been waiting for ten years for an editor to ask that question." He grinned at Rosenthal and said, "It fits into a headline easier than 'homosexual.'"

Rosenthal laughed heartily but would not agree to the requested change.*

But he did carry through on the promised coverage. Reporter Judy Klemesrud arrived at the parents conference with an assignment slip marked "MUST" and bearing the initials "AMR." A story on the front of the Metropolitan Section publicized the "buddy system." As Rothenberg commented, "This was a major breakthrough, the first story the *Times* did that talked about AIDS in the terms of the people it was killing, rather than citing some statistics from a medical headcounter."

In another significant shift of policy not formally stated, the *Times*

---

*In 1987, after Rosenthal's retirement as executive editor, the *Times* began using "gay" as a synonym for homosexual.

began listing same-sex relationships in obituaries. The first came on December 10, 1983, for the actor David Rounds, with a reference to the Tony Award winner as being survived by a brother and "his companion, John Seidman." Five days later the obituary for Mary Renault mentioned "the writer's companion of the last 50 years, Julie Mullard."

The new policy brought applause from gay spokesmen. As one person told the *New York Native*, "The person one chooses to spend one's life with, to share one's death with, is the person loved and needed the most. The deletion of that person's name from an obituary is a double blow to the survivors. . . . I'm pleased to see that it seems the *Times* is finally in step with the times." (Yet the *Times* applied the policy inconsistently. When the writer Merle Miller died in June, 1986, the *Newsday* obituary mentioned that "survivors include his friend of twenty-two years, David W. Elliott." The *Times* obituary stated, "There are no survivors.")

But David Rothenberg, whose writings did the most to focus community attention on *Times* shortcomings, was not to be forgotten nor forgiven. At the lunch Abe Rosenthal had suggested he have follow-up meetings with Peter Millones, the metropolitan editor, and David Jones, the national editor, and also with the editorial board. These meetings were less satisfactory; Rothenberg felt Millones "most resistant and non-understanding and uncomfortable." Millones had reason for discomfort, for it was his section that had muffed coverage of local gay events, including the circus benefit. And he was to wreak hurtful revenge on Rothenberg two years later, and in a manner that revived Rothenberg's past complaints about the *Times*'s unwillingness to give gays objective and non-sexual coverage.

The sequence began when Rothenberg announced his candidacy for a City Council seat from the lower East Side in the September, 1985, Democratic primary. Rothenberg's chief qualification was his seventeen years of experience as founder and director of the Fortune Society, a self-help program for men and women (straight and gay) who had been released from prison. Given his expertise in the criminal justice system, Rothenberg felt he could make a contribution to city government. He announced not as a "gay candidate" but as a candidate who happened to be gay; to do otherwise would be yielding either to homophobia or to "self-hatred."

Rothenberg happened to announce on the same day as a Hispanic-American woman. The *Times*'s city political reporter, Frank Lynn, devoted most of his story to an analysis of the Hispanic vote; the article was illustrated with a three-column photograph of the woman and her supporters. Rothenberg's candidacy was an "also announced" two paragraph tag at the end of the story. Lynn noted Rothenberg's association with the Fortune Society but did not offer any analysis of how an openly-declared candidate might fare in Manhattan's largest gay community.

"I made a mistake," Rothenberg said later. "I sent a letter to Peter Millones saying that for the *Times* to ignore the gay fact was to ignore part of the story." Millones did not respond.

Three other *Times* stories briefly mentioned Rothenberg's candidacy, again without stating he was gay. Rothenberg was re-learning, at first hand, the futility of attempting to deal on a rational basis with a powerful institution which neither explains nor apologizes. But even with the virtual *Times* blackout of coverage of his campaign, Rothenberg and his managers felt a surge of support. Long ignored by the establishment press, the gay community relies upon word-of-mouth and its own network of publications to spread information. By the late summer of 1985 Rothenberg felt he had the chance to unseat the 16-year-incumbent, a woman whose City Council record was undistinguished.

Yet the *Times*'s attitude still rankled Rothenberg. Despairing of any response from Millones, he did something fatal to his candidacy. "This was the sort of story I knew Geoffrey Stokes would love for the *Village Voice*, so I made the mistake of mailing him a copy of my letter to Millones."

This time Millones did respond, by sending a reporter to go around Rothenberg's district with the candidate. When Rothenberg skimmed the resulting story he knew his chances for election were dead. The story brushed past his work with the Fortune Society; he was pictured solely as a "homosexual running against a nice lady." The tone of the story, with leering references to winks-and-nods being exchanged as Rothenberg campaigned at Sheridan Square, "made it sound like being in a gay bar on Saturday night." The serious nature of his campaign was ignored. The stress given his gayness apparently disturbed the conservative and elderly persons living in the upper portion of the council district. Previously, he had drawn support from all elements. The day the *Times* article appeared, Rothenberg says, "our phones stopped ringing." He lost the election by a handful of votes.

TWENTY-ONE

"Nor Do We Live by Grudges and Conspiracies"

What hurt Richard Severo most of all was the shunning, to have other people turn their backs on him, and ignore him. So he tried to make the walk from the Port Authority Bus Terminal to the *Times*—five minutes, even for a dawdler—last as long as possible. He would wander along Eighth Avenue, looking at the fruit displayed outside the Korean family markets, pausing to try to talk with a drug derelict squatting against a store front. He once wrote much about addicts, and he remained curious about life in their sub-culture. But eventually the hour to be at work would arrive, and Severo would turn east onto 43rd and walk down half a block and push through the revolving doors into the lobby and ride the elevator to the third floor.

He is a lithe man at the fifty-year mark, with broodingly intense eyes, and curls, and he walks in a slight slouch, as if intent on getting close to things around him, and understanding them. He is northern Italian by origin, son of first-generation immigrants, and he has the fairness of Tuscany, and also the moody determination.

Gus, to his credit, never let Severo down. Gus is the man who sits at the receptionist desk just inside the newsroom, grainy blow-up photographs of the various mutations of the Times Building at his back, a large oil portrait of the late publisher Orvil Dryfoos to his right. Gus has trained his ginger mustache so that each end loops up and around and back again to form a perfect O. He would grin at Severo and say, "Hey, old fellow, how they doing?" and Severo would nod and walk on into the main newsroom.

The younger reporters—the "shiney asses," someone called them, a veteran reporter who didn't like yuppies in a newsroom—were the worst, for they were the Young Men on the Make, eager for success at Abe Rosenthal's *Times*. Their eyes would look right through Severo as he passed, and neither a nod nor a flicker of an eye would mark his passage. A couple of times, to discomfort them, he would pause and try to strike up a conversation, and there would be an awkward, flustered silence, and the Young Man on the Make would murmur an inaudible blur of words and hurry away as if he had something important to do.

The older fellows were better, some of them, at least. The labor writer William Serrin always made sure he had a smile and little joke and even a tidbit of gossip to offer to Severo as he settled into his chair. Gene Maeroff, the education writer, was another, and even if he was busy he would look up from his word processor and say something encouraging. But for the most part, Severo sat totally ignored, shunned by fellow reporters of *The New York Times*.

Nor did he hear much from Peter Millones, the metropolitan editor, or his deputies. Many days he would sit at his desk an entire eight-hour shift without being called upon to write a single word. Other days, the "busy" ones, he might condense a press release into one or two paragraphs.

Richard Severo was being shunned because he did something of rare audacity for someone who worked for *The New York Times* in the 1980's. He defied an order by A. M. Rosenthal because he thought he had the right to sell a book to a publisher other than Times Books, and now he suffered. He thought back to the start of his ordeal, when someone said, "Dick, you're fucking crazy to go up against Abe, he'll slaughter your ass."

And on the bad days—there were many in the winter of 1985, when the dirty snow froze solid on the sidewalks, and the temperature did not go above freezing for weeks—Severo would agree that Abe Rosenthal truly had made his life a hell.

When Dick Severo came to the *Times* in the 1960's, from the Associated Press and CBS News, he was an immediate success in the exciting city news room run by "Abe and Artie"—the Rosenthal-Gelb combination that was revitalizing *The New York Times.* He was specially close to Gelb, who asked him to do long articles on the "realities" of the city's drug problems, something beyond statements made by the cops and the politicians at City Hall. So Severo concentrated on the addicts themselves—how they got into drugs, what they did each day to support their habit, whether the touted "rehabilitation programs" made any sense to persons caught by heroin.

Many nights Severo came home from the Bronx reeking of urine, odors absorbed by his clothing as he crouched in doorways, interviewing addicts. "This was worse than covering a war because there was no front," he says of those days. One afternoon he was in an abandoned Bronx building looking for a shooting-gallery—a room where addicts inject themselves—when a man approached him brandishing a knife. Severo did two things. First, he showed his press card and explained he was seeking information for a story, not an arrest. Then he put the card back in his pocket.

"If you stab me," he told the man, "you better kill me with the first swipe, otherwise I'm going to pick up your fucking ass and throw you down the stairs." The man walked away. Severo never mentioned the episode to Gelb or other editors; it was part of his job.

Severo and Gelb were close enough that they enjoyed exchanging practical jokes of varying subtlety. Gelb passed plans for a Brooklyn street fair to Severo as the supposed blueprint for a jailbreak and sent him out, on a cold and rainy day, to do the story. Severo saw a hoax right away. "I went home and for the next three days I listened to Brahms. I would call in occasionally and say, 'Artie, it's hard to get information from the Brooklyn House of Detention, but I'm working on it.' " When Severo wrote critical stories about the petrochemical industry's environmental record, Gelb sent him a plastic deskweight containing the Texaco corporate seal and the label, "Working to keep your trust for seventy-five years."

But Gelb's humor had its limits. He and Barbara spent several weeks in Europe when the *Times* was renovating the news room and installing computer terminals for reporters to use instead of typewriters. An executive urged reporters to use the computers frequently to become accustomed to them. So Severo wrote a bogus news dispatch with the Reuters symbol and a Cairo dateline, the first lines of which read:

> CAIRO—The National Organization of Egyptian Women today honored Arthur Gelb, deputy managing editor of *The New York Times*, as its man of the year. . . .

The award was announced by a 137-year-old matriarch who was so smitten with Gelb she wished to give the honor "personally and privately."

Severo put the printout on Gelb's desk. Sydney Schanberg, then the metropolitan editor, witnessed what followed. Gelb read the article, snatched the paper from his desk, and ran to Rosenthal's office. Rosenthal emerged in a rage, snarling, "This is nothing short of an anti-Semitic attack on Gelb's manhood." Rosenthal called a *Times* lawyer to see if whoever wrote the story could be fired.

Schanberg saw that the intended gag had misfired horribly, and he hurried to Severo. "You better apologize—Artie took it the wrong way." Severo hastily did so, reminding Gelb of past pranks. The men tacitly agreed to joke no more.

Severo also did jokes in Rosenthal's name, but discreetly. He would take a memorandum bearing Rosenthal's signature and fiddle with the copy machine until he had a blank piece of paper with both letterhead and signature. One he used to send a note to a reporter warning about a loose necktie, and saying he "must abide by the *Times* dress code." The man tightened his tie and avoided Rosenthal the next days.

By late 1970 Severo had tired of local reporting. He asked for a foreign assignment, and Rosenthal sent him to Mexico City, which meant he would cover everything from the Rio Grande to Colombia and Venezuela, plus the Carribbean minus Puerto Rico and the American Virgin Islands.

Severo arrived in Mexico City on November 11, 1971, and from the very first day he was at odds with Alan Riding, the *Times*'s $100 a month stringer. Apparently angered at not being named correspondent, Riding told Severo, "I will not be your runner boy." A few evenings later Severo entered the *Times* bureau at Reforma 122 to find a strange woman reading his files. She identified herself as Marlisle Simon, Riding's girlfriend, a stringer for a Dutch paper who also sent articles to to the Washington *Post*." Severo suggested she keep out of his files. Next she arrived at a press conference in a car owned by the *Times* bureau. Next Severo scanned the bureau's phone bill and found calls to the Washington *Post* (he had worked there earlier, he recognized the number). Severo mentioned these conflicts with Riding to Jimmy Greenfield, the foreign editor. "Work with him, Dick, he's got great charm," Greenfield said. "He may have great charm," Severo replied, "but he is in a conflict of interest with the Washington *Post*."

Severo's complaints about Riding's personal work came to a head when the stringer went to El Salvador (without notice) to cover an election and returned to Mexico City and wrote a story datelined San Salvador, the capital. This was a breach of *Times* policy against fudging of datelines, a rule intended to enforce honesty in reporting. Severo called Greenfield to complain—he had been at Greenfield frequently, by phone and by post—and this time the editor had had enough. He fired Severo, and told him to return to New York with his wife immediately.

This conversation was on February 12, 1972. Regardless of the merits of his quarrel with Riding, Severo in only three months had so alienated Greenfield that he faced loss of his job. He called Rosenthal, who had him return to New York for a talk. "My God, I wish the man would get on with his work and stop worrying about who's driving the car," Rosenthal thought. But he sided with Severo. A stringer does not work full-time for the *Times*; a correspondent does. "When you have a dispute between a stringer and a staff member, the stringer goes." So Severo returned to Mexico, and Greenfield dismissed Riding, writing "I must take this step in an effort to disengage the paper from what has become a highly awkward entanglement with the Washington *Post* and, consequently, a major source of irritation between you and our correspondent."

Back in Mexico, Severo continued complaining about what he thought unwise journalistic practices. For instance, he discovered that Reuters, the British news service, had as its stringer in Guatemala a public relations man for the foreign ministry. Severo wrote Greenfield that a man holding such a position could not report objectively, and noted that the *Times* regularly ran Reuters articles from Guatemala. Greenfield told him the situation was none of his business. Rosenthal finally wrote Severo a letter warning him against becoming a crank:

> Frankly, your messages are so frequent, so voluminous and often so passionate they simply overwhelm me and I need somebody to sift through them. . . . You are working yourself into a situation where your relationship to the paper seems to be one of constant complaint, grievance, hurt and accusation. You seem to find it difficult to believe that you are dealing with editors who are as honest, hard working and well motivated as you are.
>
> In any organization, there are always a few people who are a constant emotional and psychological drain on everybody else. They are constantly miserable and succeed in making everybody around them miserable. They constantly see plots, conspiracies and ill motivation. . . .

Severo served out the remainder of his two-year tour; he returned to New York in late 1973 to rejoin the metropolitan staff. (Greenfield immediately rehired Riding, who went on to become the *Times* chief correspondent for Latin America; he married Simon, who continued stringing for the Washington *Post*.)

That Christmas Severo fell ill. A headache lingered for a week; there was a dull, throbbing pain behind his eye, and he felt "unfocused." Just before leaving Latin America he had visited a malaria control area in El Salvador. The incubation period of sixty to ninety days had passed, so at first he feared he had malaria.

At Columbia Presbyterian Hospital, physicians diagnosed his condition as encephalogy, a swelling of the membrane around the brain. For a time "I lost my memory." He could not work for a period. His memory returned gradually. "When I came out of the illness, I had a problem in responding adequately on the telephone. I could not have normal telephone conversations. It was a halting quality about my speech, and it diminished as time went on."

He forced himself to return to work, although still "woozy" at times. Arthur Gelb permitted him to fix his own schedule. He investigated reports that a prominent milk processing plant was watering its product. He stood around outside the plant as shifts changed and persuaded workers to talk to him, and he made sure he wrote down everything the moment it was said; he still did not trust his memory. The articles won the George Polk Award for distinguished investigative reporting—a journalistic honor that ranks next to the Pulitzer. Severo drew complaints from editors that he worked too slowly, yet he notes with pride, "The *Times* never had to run a single correction on any of my stories."

In 1975 Severo became interested in the interplay between industry and the environment, and he asked Gelb if he could make the subject a full-time job.

"Are you crazy?" Gelb asked. "You are going to jeopardize your career. This is never going to be a priority for this newspaper."

Severo went ahead anyway, and he did stories that attracted wide attention. For instance, he wrote for months about the dumping of the toxic chemical PCB into the Hudson River by a General Electric plant above Albany. He did stories on Agent Orange and nuclear power. He won a continuing series of awards. And, he found the *Times* increasingly hostile to what he called "investigative scientific reporting."

Opposition peaked in 1980, when Severo wrote a four-part series about genetic screening—briefly, attempts by industry to determine whether the genes of workers made them hypersusceptible to chemicals encountered in the workplace. The issue was controversial, with union officials charging that companies used genetic screening to refuse jobs to entire classes of workers, and civil libertarians calling screening a throwback to the discredited "eugenics" schemes of the 1930's. Severo spent many weeks researching and writing the articles, and editing them kept the national desk busy for days. The stories came down hard on the Du Pont Company, which made wide use of such screening. And although Du Pont officers said nothing directly to Severo, he heard indirectly of the company's anger—and how the *Times* reacted.

The first came from William Stockton, a *Times* science editor. Stockton told Severo, in referring to the genetic screen articles, "We have to put the fire out. Art and Abe do not want you to do any more science investigative reporting." Gelb confirmed this; Severo should do no more investigative stories, for they "took too long." Severo spoke back sharply. Thereafter "Artie was very cold; he was never friendly again after that day."

Later Severo received a call from Jeff Gerth, a reporter in the

Washington bureau whom he knew only casually. Severo recon-
structs the conversation this way:

"Dick, this is Jeff Gerth in Washington. Are you all right?"

"Yeah, I'm fine. Why?"

"I just had lunch with a public relations guy from Du Pont and they
tell me they've 'settled your hash.' What are you doing now?"

They talked a bit longer and rang off. Gerth's comments convinced
Severo that Du Pont protests contributed to the *Times*'s decision to
take him off investigative stories.

But Severo was having other problems of his own creation. Arthur
Gelb, for instance, had been one of his strongest supporters at the
paper for more than a decade. Now Gelb had second thoughts.
Severo's bursts of temper were notorious in the newsroom, and when
he got particularly loud Gelb would go to him, and suggest he take a
walk and cool off. Gelb acted as confidant during a turbulent period in
Severo's personal life, when he temporarily separated from his wife.
According to Gelb, Sydney Schanberg, the metropolitan editor,
finally told him he had had enough of Severo; that he was too disrupt-
ive and argumentative, regardless of his merits as a reporter.
(Schanberg was to testify later at an arbitration hearing that he had no
complaints about Severo's work.) Regardless of the reason, Severo
was told he was being reassigned to the science department, the major responsibility of which was producing the Science Times section
each Tuesday.

Severo had troubles with Stockton, the Science Times editor, veritably from the start. Stockton felt that Severo's articles had an "accu-
satory" tone, that he seemed determined to find a villain in every situation. This did not fit the Science Times concept. Nor did Science
Times have the personnel to permit Severo to spend weeks on a
single assignment. To Stockton, Severo was petulant, a complainer
who did not take editing well and who saw conspiracy behind the
slightest criticism.

Stockton eventually broke virtually all his contacts with Severo,
even though they worked in a small office suite. And when Holcomb
Noble joined Science Times as deputy editor, Gelb leaped from his
chair in excitement and said, "That's it, Hoc, you be the Richard
Severo rehabilitation editor!"

Indeed Science Times was a strange working ground for a street
reporter such as Dick Severo, whatever his personality. Another edi-

tor, Richard Flaste, liked to enhance "titles" of staff reporters. Harold Schmeck was "our chief biological correspondent," and David Sobel the "chief behavioral writer." The *Times's* propensity for over-editing came into full blossom at Science Times. Severo did a short article—a funny piece—about a professor who published *Maledicta*, a lively but scholarly journal about swearing. Flaste wanted to turn the item into a major study of why people cuss—"the good reasons as to why people use offensive or hostile language, among them the relation between the parts of the brain known as the cortex and the hypothalmus." Severo's little feature caused Flaste acute agony:

> I anguished over it. I can remember . . . quite clearly walking into the deli across the street from the *Times*, buying my coffee, wondering whether, even though I felt this was a story that somehow I didn't trust, I shouldn't publish it, because . . . I didn't want to leave myself vulnerable by publishing a weak story on the cover of Science Times.

That Severo was not compatible with the Science Times operation should have been obvious to all persons involved by late 1981. Stockton, Flaste and Hoc Noble had their own ideas as to how science should be covered. Severo clearly wished to do hard investigative articles; such was not the meat of Science Times, and especially in the years when the paper was turning away from critical coverage. Severo began building a record of his perceived mistreatment; he put story suggestions into writing, and he kept copies of any communiques that came to him. Sensible management cried out for better handling of Severo. Whatever his quirks and prickly personality, Severo had demonstrated he could produce quality work. Yet Gelb left him in Science Times, with editors obviously unhappy with him. "I would hire Lucifer if he got on page one every day," Richard Flaste was to say much later. But he could not accommodate Severo. The result was a series of misjudgments, bad decisions and outright poor management that self-compounded for weeks, to the detriment of both the *Times* and Severo.

In the fall of 1981, Shay McConnell, a public relations woman for the University of Pennsylvania hospital and medical school, came to the *Times* and suggested a variety of stories to Stockton and Flaste. PR people make these rounds hopeful of getting favorable stories about their institutions. Almost in passing she mentioned a young Philadelphia woman afflicted with neurofibromotosis—Elephant

Man's disease, an ailment in which huge tumors distort human features in grotesque proportion. A hospital surgeon was to attempt an operation to give the woman normal features. "That's the story we want," Stockton told McConnell. Both the surgeon and the woman— Lisa H., she came to be known, to protect her privacy—agreed. Stockton and Flaste looked around Science Times for a reporter to do the story. As Stockton said, they decided on Severo. "Almost in unison, we said, 'He can't screw this one up.' And that's how he got the assignment."

Severo spent several days with Lisa H., gaining her confidence through a shared interest in music. She was frightened, both about the operation and about someone writing about her. Her physical appearance meant she had been shunned all her life. To Severo, his most important work was convincing Lisa H. to permit him to write about her life.* She agreed, and Severo wrote two articles, one on how she lived with the affliction, the other an account of the corrective surgery. Readers responded with an avalanche of mail, both to the hospital and to the *Times*.

By coincidence, Severo had been talking with International Creative Management, the talent agency, about doing a novel. Over lunch he mentioned to Peter Stamelman of ICM the Lisa H. story (the articles had yet to appear) and Stamelman suggested he write the story in a book or a television play or both. Severo decided to go for a book. He knew the Times Company had had book subsidaries over the years—Arno Press, Quadrangle, now Times Books. But his impression was that the company "published compilations of things, home improvement books, cook books, things like that. In my own mind I did not really associate them with this kind of narrative that I was contemplating getting into." But Severo took no chances. He telephoned Arthur Gelb and told him of the Lisa H. story, and of his hope of doing a book. He asked "what the company rules were for my doing such a project. . . ." Severo mentioned movie and TV possibilities. "I told him that I wanted to share it with him."

Gelb replied, "Abe and I are sick and tired of reporters who abuse their position on the paper and make a lot of money and give nothing to the paper."

Severo protested he was offering the *Times* a share of any earnings.

---

*Severo's establishing empathy with Lisa H. is a moving section of his book, *Lisa H.*, published by Harper & Row in 1985.

"It grew out of a *Times* assignment. . . . And I thought it entirely appropriate that I offer to share in the proceeds . . . with the *Times*," he
told Gelb. Several times he stressed that he wished to follow company policy. Gelb referred Severo to Sam Summerlin, who he said
was "in charge of putting books and films together in packages."

Severo and Summerlin had known one another for years; both had
worked for the Associated Press, and their careers overlapped again
in Latin America. Now Summerlin had an office next to Science
Times. Summerlin told Severo that on a book, "Times Books should
be included in the first round of any auction." If only a television play
materialized, "I should be prepared to make a token payment to the
Times so that they would not feel as though I were taking advantage of
them." Summerlin did tell Severo, "Abe was a little crazy about people who do things outside the company and don't give the paper anything." Severo reported this conversation to Gelb.

Severo visited Lisa H. several times, and he told her about the
book. She was to receive 25 percent of the net proceeds. Severo intended to focus on the shunning to which she had been subjected. "I
couldn't believe that people would treat anybody that way."

What Severo could not realize was that the *Times* had decided to
bring order to a long-ambiguous policy on the property rights to material developed by reporters working for the newspaper. The
Sulzbergers historically were protective of their rights; the information gathered by persons working for the *Times* belonged to the
Times.

When Thomas J. Hamilton, head of the UN Bureau, asked permission in the late 1940's to make broadcasts of a General Assembly session, then-publisher Arthur Hays Sulzberger sniffed that the *Times*
was not a "Christmas tree from which roaming Santas might pluck
packages at their will." Permission denied. But during the many
years when the *Times* had no book outlets, writers took books where
they wished. In the 1970's, however, the New York Times Company
created Times Books with the intent of making it a major trade house,
rather than a reprint/anthology operation.

The first correspondent to be brought to heel was Fox Butterfield,
who in 1978 was dispatched to Peking as the paper's first resident reporter in more than twenty years. Butterfield recognized the value of
his observations of the People's Republic of China, previously off-

limits to most Western journalists. When he left San Francisco he had two book offers—$125,000 from Times Books; $247,500 from Summit Books.

Butterfield's choice was obvious until a telephone call awakened him in a Hong Kong hotel. Seymour Topping, the *Times* foreign editor, told Butterfield he was free to accept the Summit Books offer. But if he did so, the *Times* was not sending him on to Peking. The *Times* had invested years of effort in obtaining his visa and thousands of dollars on his Chinese lessons. His presence in Peking would not be possible otherwise. If Butterfield took the Summit contract, fine; but then he must get to Peking on his own. Butterfield did not spend many minutes deciding he would write for Times Books.

But should a newsman surrender all proprietary rights to his impressions in exchange for a paycheck? And should not his employer be willing to at least match the price put on a book in the open market? The *Times*'s attitude was that the Butterfield book did not exist without the work the *Times* had done to obtain his visa. To the *Times* this investment offset the difference between the Summit and Times Books advances. Although Butterfield had the discretion not to complain publicly, he told many friends that the net result was an initial out-of-pocket loss of $122,500. (The book earned more than the $247,500 Summit offered.) Nor did rival publishers care for the *Times* attitude, for they saw it as a means of signing books at forced bargain-basement rates.

The policy was inconsistent, for many prominent *Times* reporters continued writing books for other publishers. Walter Sullivan, the science writer, published regularly through McGraw-Hill. Tom Wicker, the columnist and former Washington bureau chief, had a longtime relationship with Viking. There were many others. Punch Sulzberger tried to restate the policy in a memorandum to staff members concerning books: "When a book grows out of a *Times* assignment, we must get first chance to see whether the *Times* is interested in publishing it; and if its bid is competitive, we would hope that the *Times* gets the book."

The ambiguities are obvious. What did Sulzberger consider a "competitive bid"? Surely Butterfield did not think the $125,000 offered by Times Books for his China book was "competitive" with the $247,500 bid by Summit. Did "first chance" mean no submissions other than to Times Books; and if so, how did an author obtain a "competitive" bid? And the words "we would hope" lacked the authority of Sulzberger stating, "we insist" or "you must."

That Sam Summerlin told Severo only that "Times Books should be included in the first round of any auction" showed that members of *Times* management themselves were uncertain as to policy. Several days later Summerlin repeated this condition to Jed Mattes of ICM, Severo's agent; Mattes subsequently confirmed his understanding of the procedure in a letter to Summerlin. No reply was received, so he and Severo felt confident to proceed with an auction of the book.

On January 20, 1982, Mattes made a multiple submission of Severo's outline to a score of publishers, asking for bids. This is a common practice for a book in which interest has been expressed by more than one house; it is tantamount to an auction. Jonathan Segal, the head of Times Books, called Severo a few days later and they had an affable chat. Segal intended to bid; he said nothing to indicate that Times Book should have had an exclusive offer on the book.

On January 28 Severo's morning mail contained a note from the University of Pennsylvania medical school stating he had been nominated for a Pulitzer Prize. The *Times* had nominated Severo three previous years; nothing had been said about submitting the Lisa H. stories; so the outside interest pleased him. But after lunch his euphoria was dashed. Richard Flaste, a deputy science editor, relayed an order from Abe Rosenthal. The auction must be stopped. Flaste quoted Rosenthal as saying the story was "not mine to sell outside of Times Books, that he had to go to Times Books, that it grew out of a *Times* assignment, and he wanted the auction stopped."

"My God," Severo told Flaste, "do you know what I've done to try to find out what company policy is?"

Flaste replied that "everybody knows what company policy is, and I think you should capitulate to them or there will be trouble."

Severo called Mattes, who was alarmed. "Of course," Mattes said, "you can stop the auction, but that would be at great damage to you, because there would be a credibility problem. . . . You have tied up all these people at publishing houses and you will not look very good if you now say you're terminating the auction. . . ."

Stunned, Severo walked around the science department. He paused at the desk of Jane Brody, the medical writer. The dust jacket of her new book was on her cork board. The publisher was W. W.

Norton & Company. He asked Brody, "Did the *Times* give you any sort of problem in regard to the book?" Only a minor one, she said. The dust jacket identified her as a *New York Times* writer, and Norton wished to put the affiliation in the same type font used on the *Times* masthead. The *Times* refused, so Norton used ordinary Roman type.

Severo called other people in the building who had written books. Viking had published Sydney Schanberg's account of Cambodia. Schanberg said there had been a "suggestion" he go to Times Books. He refused, for he was to divide the proceeds with the Cambodian who had been his assistant and escaped a Khmer Rouge death camp. The veteran science writer Walter Sullivan told of his "long relationship" with McGraw-Hill. None of his books had been offered to Times Books, and he felt stopping the auction was "ridiculous." Two other science department writers said the same.

Severo eventually was to go through *Books in Print* and ascertain that 57 *Times* staff writers had published 268 titles the preceding decade, 232 of them through houses not connected with the New York Times Company. Russell Baker had published five books, "collections of columns from *The New York Times*," with outside publishers. The economics writer Leonard Silk had done seven books drawing on material originally written for the *Times*; none was published by Times houses.

Over a long weekend Severo decided that Rosenthal did not know the facts. Oddly, no *Times* editor or executive had bothered even at this point to show Severo the policy memorandum circulated by Sulzberger after the flap over Butterfield's China book. Severo wrote a three-and-one-half page memorandum to Rosenthal, telling the genesis of his book and stressing he had followed *Times* procedures as stated to him by Gelb. He asked a personal meeting.

Severo's memorandum clearly reflected the puzzlement of a man who thought he had done the right thing, only to be slapped down. But Rosenthal did not see fit to listen to any explanation. He cut Severo down with a curt memorandum:

> It seems to me that what was happened, Dick, is that an assignment conceived by the *Times*, assigned by the *Times*, reported by the *Times* on *Times* time and money, and a story that is still ongoing suddenly was being auctioned off and the *Times* finds itself in a position of bidding for what strikes me as pretty much its own property.

I really am not making any judgments as to how it happened, and I assume there was decent intent all around. It simply strikes me as an extremely strange situation.

But I do not wish to become involved any further because, obviously, I have a great many other things to do. . . .

Rosenthal concluded by telling Severo take the matter to Sydney Gruson, since it involved company policy rather than news room policy.

Gruson was sympathetic; he heard Severo's account, and he said, "All right, we fucked up. I am convinced that you acted in good faith. Now, what can we do to keep you out of trouble?" Gruson hoped that Rosenthal and Gelb "would not put [you] on night rewrite because of this matter." But he agreed with Severo that the auction should proceed.

Jonathan Segal of Times Books called several times the next days, first to report he would be bidding on the book, then again to make a statement that chilled Severo. "I want to disassociate myself from what the *Times* is doing to you," he told Severo.

"What is the *Times* doing to me?" Severo asked. "I don't understand what this is all about. I don't get it."

"It's most unfortunate," Segal said. He repeated, "I want to disassociate myself from it." He would say nothing more, but now Severo realized that he truly was in "trouble" as Gruson had suggested.

Severo decided that if Times Books came within several thousand dollars of any other offer, he would accept. But Harper & Row mooted the question by bidding $50,000; Segal stopped at $37,500 because, as he told Severo, he felt the subject was too squeamish for a mass-market book. So Harper agreed to publish a book that came to be called *Lisa H.*

Most nervous about his future, Severo had a lawyer friend, Robert Tannenbaum, a former New York prosecutor now practicing in California, talk with Gelb and Barbara Dill, a *Times* lawyer. By Tannenbaum's account, Dill told him that although Severo probably would not be fired, his "career will probably be in jeopardy and damaged" if he did not sign with Times Books. Twice she said this, in what Tannenbaum considered "a nasty tone of voice."

Both Tannenbaum and Severo considered Dill's statements a threat, and they hurriedly conferred with two officers of the New York Newspaper Guild, Joan Cook, the *Times* unit chairman, and

Barry Lipton, the president. Keep a written record of anything punitive done to you, Cook counselled. "Keep your powder dry. This might all blow over," Cook said.

By happenstance, Severo's decision to take *Lisa H.* to Harper coincided with a change of editorship of Science Times. Stockton moved on to another job, to be replaced by Richard Flaste, who had worked at the *Times* for almost two decades. He had spent his entire professional life under Rosenthal and Gelb, and he knew what they wanted with the *Times*. Flaste held many positions enroute to his editorship. He worked on the city desk, he wrote news for WQXR, the *Times*'s radio station, he wrote columns entitled "Parents/Children" and "Child's World," which he described as a "consumer column for children." He moved to Science Times when the section was created in 1979 with a sense of mission. "I used to think of it as sort of establishing the nation of Israel," Flaste said. But clearly heavy investigative reporting of the sort that Severo had done was not Flaste's forte.

Severo considered Flaste a friend. Indeed, when in Mexico, he tried to help Flaste and his wife adopt a child from Latin America. When Arthur Gelb "suggested" that Severo be taken into Science Times, Flaste was supportive, although he did remember a Gelb warning: "Arthur said . . . that Dick was crazy, but that you needed crazy people in your department. . . ." Otherwise "all you have is a lot of sane, sober types, you're going to have a sane, sober report, and that's not what we want."

Now it fell to Flaste to deal with a reporter who had gone against the wishes of the top editors of *The New York Times*, men who would control his own career. According to Severo, Flaste told him in February, 1982—a few weeks after the *Lisa H.* contract was signed— "You have called their bluff, maybe you will get away with it, maybe you won't. We'll see."

But Flaste's attitude soon changed, according to Severo. Under Stockton, Severo submitted story ideas via memorandum. This is the common practice at the *Times*. An editor can read a written proposal at his leisure. Putting an idea on paper requires a writer to focus his thinking, and to capsulize the story. Severo did this time and again; Flaste did not respond. Severo asked for a meeting; again, no response. Flaste's attitude "became very cold." Science Times is structured; an editor must approve a story idea before the reporter proceeds. Flaste's inattention meant that Severo effectively was sidelined; from February through mid-May, 1982, he published only a few routine items. His diary entries tell his frustration. On April 30 he wrote: "No stories in Science Times; no comment on story suggestions; Flaste refused to talk during entire month." Severo concluded that Flaste was executing an implied, unspoken directive from Rosenthal and Gelb that he be punished. Flaste needed no formal order (and he was to deny that any was given) but the end result of his inattention meant that Severo sat in idleness for months.

What must I do? Severo asked his newsroom friends. He received a common answer: "You're on Abe's shit list and nobody can help you until you get off it. So many people are on Abe's shitlist he can't remember them all. Wait a couple of months and go to Art [Gelb] and apologize for something you didn't do, and you'll be off it." Severo refused; he would make no hollow apology.

Flaste, however, saw Severo as a problem reporter who bridled at editorial suggestions, and who worked at too slow a pace for Science Times. Severo wanted a story to have a hero and a villain. He single-sourced. He protected persons who had helped him on past stories. Severo would not take orders. Flaste and Stockton learned that the Center for Disease Control in Atlanta had a new study on toxic shock syndrome, the deadly female ailment related to use of Tampons. Severo knew the researcher involved, but he refused to ask for the study, saying he had an "arrangement" that precluded him from making such a request. Flaste concluded Servero was "embarrassed to show that he was under control of editors and wasn't just a free operator." The *Times* fell behind on the toxic shock syndrome story, and never caught up. Some disputes seemed petty. Severo refused to telephone a scientist at one o'clock in the morning European time to ask where the man attended high school—something Flaste thought necessary for a profile.

Troubles continued after the Lisa H. Story. Severo wished to treat the university surgeon and public relations lady to dinner to thank them for their cooperation. Flaste thought this unncessary because "I don't think we thank people in that way." But he approved and suggested a medium-priced Italian restaurant, Giordano's. Severo got a better—and much more expensive—recommendation from critic Mimi Sheraton, the Four Seasons. Flaste was upset when he learned that Severo took along a woman friend from the *Times* as an extra guest, for a bill of more than $260.

Flaste's reaction was to stop talking with Severo, even to exchange a casual greeting when he came into the small office housing the Science Times staff. Severo submitted story ideas, dozens of them, and Flaste would not respond. In other memos Severo asked that Flaste talk over the ideas with him in person; even though they sat only a few feet apart, Flaste did not answer. What guidance Severo did receive—and it was not much—came from Flaste's deputy, Hoc Noble.

The shunning lasted two months, through April. Then Flaste asked Severo into a small conference room. Severo, with deliberate motions, picked up a tape recorder; he followed Flaste and placed the recorder on a small telephone table. Flaste stared at it in disbelief; he is intending to *tape* this conversation, he thought. Then Severo wordlessly slipped the recorder into his pocket. Flaste told him thereafter he would be covering anthropology. Happy for the direct assignment, Severo accepted. When he left Flaste went to Hoc Noble and said, "The son of a bitch wanted to tape me!"

Yet after this conference Flaste resumed the silent treatment. Severo would come into the office and say, "Good morning, Dick," and the editor would look the other way, or continue working. Severo sent Flaste numerous memos telling what he was doing; no response. He went to a small town in Illinois that in his words, "had been taken over by archaeologists for a dig;" he told Flaste in advance, in writing, the story would focus on the interplay between the scientists and the townspeople. No response. He wrote 1,500 words which were trimmed to 900 and run in the national pages, not Science Times. Flaste complained the article "did not have enough science."

So Severo fretted in inactivity, doing rewrites of odd press releases but little substantive work. In 1981 he had nineteen byline stories in Science Times, a respectable output considering the amount of time required to research each article. The next year, through October, 1982, he had only four.

The most petty act came when the Newspaper Guild announced its annual Page One Awards. These awards carry much respect within New York journalism, and the *Times* always found space for an article on the winners. In 1982 Severo won a Page One Award for his Lisa H. articles. For the first time ever *The New York Times* did not carry a report. (In 1983 and subsequent years—when Severo was *not* a winner—the *Times* resumed coverage.)

In October Severo wrote another long memo to Flaste asking about his proposed stories. They met, with Hoc Noble present, and wrangled over many things. This was a Friday. When Severo came to work the following Monday he found a curt message from Flaste: "After our conversation on Friday, I came to the conclusion that it really would be better if you were to begin working in another department. I spoke to Jim Greenfield and he assured me he would follow up on the issue promptly."

Flaste did not bother to speak to Severo personally, although he stole a look at him across the room. Severo sat with his head on his hand; when he returned Flaste's glance "he looked hurt, and he said nothing." Neither did Flaste; he had made his decision, and "I didn't wish to be dissuaded."

Flaste has insisted that the controversy over the Lisa H. book had nothing to do with his decision to have Severo transferred from his department; further, that neither Rosenthal nor Gelb directed him to withhold assignments from Severo and ignore him.

That no direct order was needed was in itself the damning feature of the entire episode.

Severo talked with James Greenfield, who said he must either write sports or return to the metropolitan desk, where he had begun his *Times* career in 1968. Severo protested. "I don't want to go back to doing things I had done twenty-five years earlier." Greenfield said he understood; nonetheless, "you have to do it."

So Severo found himself doing the scut work of a novice journalist. He was to spend eighteen miserable months on the metropolitan desk, during which time he wrote twenty-four stories, many of them one- and two-paragraph rewrites of press releases. On a "busy" day he might do a six-paragraph obituary. During his long-ago years as a city reporter he had done heavy investigative stories; now he found himself covering a Christmas/Chanukah party at a lower East Side settlement house for children.

Give us 250 to 300 words, a night assignments editor said when Severo returned. Forget it, Severo said, I can do it in less. He did so, and metropolitan editor Peter Millones called his work a "snide piece of shit." It did not run.

Only once did an editor ask Severo to do a story of consequence; the result was a shouting match. After the chemical plant disaster in Bhopal, India, in early 1985, assistant metro editor James Glieck assigned Severo to do a story about risks of such a tragedy in the New

York metropolitan area. Given the high visibility of chemical plants in the area, Severo did not wish to write about the obvious. He looked for a specific instance where a spill had occurred. In *Times* files he found a two-paragraph item about a chemical accident in upstate New York two months earlier which caused the evacuation of a nearby school. Severo spoke to more than thirty-five persons to document what went wrong; a New York legislator told him he would push for more state inspectors. But over several days he could not obtain a statement from the company, so he did not submit the story. To write in January about an event that occurred in November and put in the stock line "no company spokesman was available for comment" offended his journalistic senses. He wrote Glieck a memo saying he wished to await comment.

Glieck took offense. He came down the newsroom aisle towards Severo's desk in a rage. "I never told you that you *could* write that story without a comment from the company," he said. Severo stood up. "There is nobody in this building who can talk to me like that," Severo said. Glieck crumpled Severo's memo in his fist and threw it to his feet and walked away. The story never ran. Severo's already meager work load lessened even further; the next six weeks he was to receive a single "assignment," the rewrite of a 300-word B'nai B'rith press release.

To officers of the New York Newspaper Guild, whose jurisdiction includes some 1800 editorial and news employees of the *Times*, Severo's transfer and mistreatment seemed clearly punitive. At the urging of unit chairman Joan Cook, a rewrite woman who had never been in Rosenthal's favor, Severo kept a running diary of his work, and what he considered hostile incidents. In 1983, following contractual procedures, the guild filed a grievance asking that Severo be put back in his old job on Science Times, and that harassment cease. The *Times* refused. So the guild took the next contractual step and asked for a hearing before an arbitrator.

The hearings commenced in February, 1984, and dragged for more than four years, producing a transcript in excess of 10,000 pages—and public relations problems of nightmare proportion for *The New York Times*. Severo's case was direct: The *Times* punished him for taking the Lisa H. book outside the *Times*, first by making his existence so miserable in Science Times that he could not work; and then transferring him to insulting cub reporter's work. The *Times*'s position was that Severo had long been a crank and a malcontent, albeit one who did occasional good work, but that his behavior became so bizarre he could not function. The book dispute had absolutely nothing to do with his treatment and transfer.

Many persons at the *Times* agreed that Severo was a classic pain in the ass, one who griped so loud, and often, that people dared not greet him with the conversational banality, "What's new, Dick?" unless they were prepared for arms-waving billingsgate about his cause of the moment.

The *Times*'s position in the arbitration hearings was that Severo's transfer was done in the normal course of business; that assignment to the metropolitan desk should not be considered a demotion; that he had not met the standards demanded of a writer for Science Times. To Rosenthal and Gelb, the paramount issue was the right of the *Times* to transfer reporters to suit the paper's needs.

Gelb posed a hypothetical situation. Suppose the *Times* assigned a reporter to Paris, and after three years or so decided to send her elsewhere, and she refused. Did the reporter have a *right* to continue working in Paris? To underscore the *Times*'s position, attorney John Stanton announced at the start of the hearing that regardless of how arbitrator James V. Altieri ruled, the paper did not intend to put Severo back in Science Times; any ruling to that effect would be taken all the way to the U.S. Supreme Court if necessary. For a court to dictate a reporter's assignment violated the *Times*'s First Amendment rights.

The *Times*'s legal burden required proving that the Lisa H. book did not cause Severo's transfer. This meant discrediting everything he had done in a *Times* career of almost twenty years, and depicting him as a malcontent whose quirks outweighed his value as a newsman. So Severo's superiors testified about long-ago newsroom quarrels over stories, and for endless days Severo sat in a conference room and heard his entire life demeaned.

Philip Tobin, Severo's attorney, is a labor specialist who, imbued by Jesuit schooling, pursues the truth with tenacity. He is a small man, quiet in private, but easy to anger when he feels he or a client is being shoved. When time came for Rosenthal's testimony, *Times* lawyer Jack Stanton promised he would appear voluntarily. He did not, so a day was wasted.

Angered, Tobin called his office for a process server. "Find me a guy who wears $20 suits and picks his nose all the time," he said. Rather than embarrass Rosenthal by having the subpoena served at the Times Building, the server called Rosenthal's limousine company and asked where he would be going the following day. The first pickup would be at 9:30 A.M. outside Rosenthal's apartment at Central Park West and West 86th Street.

But the company also alerted Rosenthal that a process server was prowling for him, for he did not appear at 9:30 A.M. The server patiently waited, trying to ignore a wet April snow. At eleven o'clock Ann Rosenthal laboriously made her way to the car, and a few minutes later Rosenthal furtively peeped from the doorway. Seeing no one, he dashed for the limo, brief case flapping from his arm. The server raced him and got to the door just before Rosenthal slammed it and hurled the papers inside. Stanton was to complain later that the server "said some indelicate things that could be heard by Mrs. Rosenthal."

Combative, sarcastic, quick to retreat behind a protective memory when he did not wish to address a point, Rosenthal sparred with Tobin for three days, and the men disliked one another intensely before the bout ended. The hearings were closed to the press but the New York Newspaper Guild made daily transcripts available to reporters, and Rosenthal felt the first stings of adverse publicity.

Two professional publicists, Mary Jane Curley and James Delihas, volunteered their services and sent out mailings to "Friends of Severo," somewhat presumptuously titled in that it included Punch's mother, Iphigene Sulzberger. Severo wrote periodical reports in the form of guild bulletins, and he needled Rosenthal by referring to him as "Abraham M. Rosenthal," which he knew he detested. Rosenthal complained at one point that "this has become a propaganda case, orchestrated by Mr. Severo and others."

Rosenthal took hot exception to the headline over a story in *Editor & Publisher*, the newspaper trade magazine, and he called editor John Consoli to complain.

"The headline, the headline. It's wrong," Rosenthal said. "It says 'Controversy at *New York Times*.' "

"What's wrong with it?" Consoli asked. He thought the headline accurately and fairly described the situation that was tearing the *Times* apart and hurting staff morale.

"There's no 'controversy' at *The New York Times*," Rosenthal said. "There's a difference of opinion."

Consoli disagreed; *E&P* did not run the demanded "correction."

During his testimony Rosenthal talked at length about why he objected to a reporter undertaking a book while he "was still working on the story," as he insisted was the case with Severo and *Lisa H*. Several years earlier reporter Myron Farber wrote about a doctor accused of murdering patients. A judge demanded he produce his notes. Farber refused and went to jail in New Jersey for several days. Unbeknownst to Rosenthal, Farber had signed a book contract with Doubleday. ". . . [T]he book company, not being as terribly interested in . . . First Amendment cases as was *The New York Times*, promptly handed it all over to the judges," Rosenthal said.

When Rosenthal accused Severo of writing adversarial stories, Tobin demanded examples. "I am not going to review the clips," he said. "I have other things to do." Rosenthal disputed claims that Severo's transfer was punitive. "We are not an organization that talks about discipline or punishment, nor do we live by grudges and conspiracies." And Rosenthal made absolutely clear who ran *The New York Times*.

Tobin asked, "Have you ever had one of your employees who is under you as an editor tell you that 'I suppose one of us has got to go'?"

"Not since I became executive editor."

"If someone did that to you today, what would you do to him?" Tobin asked.

"I think he would be crazy," Abe Rosenthal replied.

In the *Times* newsroom people watched the Severo case unfold with an eerie detachment, as if something awful was happening that they could not deter. The consensus accepted Severo's contention that he was being punished. Rosenthal's reputation for vicious retaliation discouraged anything more than cursory support for Severo. Yet some significant people had sobering second thoughts about A. M. Rosenthal.

One of these persons was Nan Robertson, who loved Rosenthal for several acts of past kindness. She and her husband Stan Levey, the former *Times* labor reporter, who later worked for Scripps-Howard, had remained friendly with Rosenthal. In June, 1970, they were vacationing in Turkey when Levey suffered a massive heart attack.

Abe sent cables to the Istanbul hospital almost daily. "I could feel Abe throbbing at the other end [of the cable wire]. I was aware of his grief, his strength, his support, his love. Abe has a lot of soul." Levey was flown to an American military hospital in Germany, and he had a further attack that destroyed half his heart. Abe sent a cable which Nan taped to the bed where Levey could read it: "Ann and I send love every hour on the hour and every moment in between."

When Levey recovered enough to be flown to the United States, Rosenthal had Bob Phelps of the Washington bureau meet the plane with an ambulance and ride with him to the hospital. The next day Rosenthal flew to Washington and took Robertson to lunch at Provençal and cried with her. "You are a tough and brave person and you will not let Stan die," he said. He offered material help as well. "The *Times* would give me the money without interest—$10,000 this week, $20,000 the next. If I wanted to pay it back, I could; if I couldn't, they did not care." Rosenthal went to Levey's bedside, where his friend was a wizened, dying old man. They embraced, and Rosenthal told Robertson later, "I went back to the hotel and sat and sobbed for three hours." Levey died in 1971 during open heart surgery.

Now commenced a rough time for Robertson. To break her depression, Rosenthal arranged for an assignment to the Paris bureau. She had drinking problems. The depression put her into Payne-Whitney for a bit. Then yet another tragedy. Vacationing in Illinois, she was struck down by toxic shock syndrome. As she described the horror for *The New York Times Magazine*, "I lay dying, my fingers and legs darkening with gangrene, I was in shock, had no pulse, and my blood pressure was lethally low." She fought, and she clung to life. Doctors had to amputate the end joints of her fingers. "For Chrissake," Rosenthal told her doctor, "tell Nan we don't love her for her typewriter; tell her we love her for her mind."

She went through months of painful surgery and rehabilitation, Rosenthal coaxing and cajoling her along. With her reconstructed fingers she wrote a long article about her ordeal for the *Times* magazine. Rosenthal nominated her for the Pulitzer Prize for the work in 1983, and she won.

This background is cited at length to document that Nan Robertson was emotionally and professionally indebted to A. M. Rosenthal. Hence what she did in the summer of 1984 is specially telling.

She sat at her desk one July afternoon and someone handed her a guild bulletin about the Severo hearing. *Times* lawyer Jack Stanton was demanding that Severo produce "all date books, calendars, diaries, notebooks and other similar materials maintained by Severo, or by someone else on his behalf, for the period January 1, 1980, to the present date." He also demanded Severo's original notes on the Lisa H. story. As justification he noted Severo had referred to diaries and other papers to refresh his memory on dates and details.

Horror tumbled through Nan Robertson's mind as she read the *Times*'s demands. "Holy shit!" she thought. "They have really gone too far." She thought of Myron Farber and Earl Caldwell, *Times* reporters who had gone to jail to protect the very confidentiality the paper now demanded that Severo violate. "This is not *Abe's* newspaper. It belongs to all of us. I devoted thirty years of my life to this great newspaper, and I love it."

People stood in clusters around the newsroom, quietly talking about what should be done. Someone suggested a petition. "No, a letter to the publisher, that's the route," Robertson said. "We've got to do this right, and in a method that will be effective."

Robertson after dinner got out her internal *Times* phone book—one which lists office and home phones of *Times* people wherever they are assigned—and began calling. She looked for the "right signers," people "extremely impressive and persuasive." Why a letter? "If we do a petition, it's going to leak, and Abe will be furious. I thought it best to work with a small group, and go quietly to the publisher." She also wished to avoid further public embarrassment of *her* newspaper.

She realized the consequences of what she was doing. "I knew it would mean an irrevocable rupture in our long friendship, but I could not live with myself unless I took some action and stood up for something I felt strongly about. I wanted it to come from an elite group. I wanted it to be a committee of reporters so successful, so distinguished, and whose loyalty was unsullied, that the publisher would take it seriously. There was not a loser, a sorehead, a complainer in the group." Ultimately seventeen persons signed, including five Pulitzer Prize winners: Robertson, Russell Baker, Anthony Lewis, Paul Goldberger and Sydney Schanberg. The letter was succinct:

Dear Punch:

    A number of us have felt growing concern about the harm being caused to the paper in the Severo case. We write to you as members of the *Times* family. Foremost in our minds is our fear that the First

Amendment principle that the *Times* has always stood for is being compromised. We would greatly appreciate the opportunity to meet with you as soon as possible—and Abe Rosenthal and others, if you think it appropriate—to discuss this and other aspects of the case that trouble us. We make this request in strictest confidence.

Sulzberger refused to meet the petitioners, but their letter apparently had an impact. Within a very few days the *Times* backed away from its request that Severo produce his diaries and other papers, and in a most defensive fashion. As Sulzberger wrote in a memorandum to the news department staff, "The *Times* has and had no intention of asking Mr. Severo to reveal any confidential documents and our lawyers have been instructed to withdraw any requests to the Guild lawyers that might be construed as such." But the *Times* capitulation in withdrawing with demands was eloquent in itself.

Accompanying the Sulzberger memorandum to the staff was a lengthy legal opinion by Floyd Abrams, the esteemed First Amendment lawyer, a partner of Stanton in Cahill & Gordon. Abrams had successfully represented the *Times* in the Pentagon Papers case, and in succeeding years he was in the courts frequently on First Amendment issues, both for the *Times* and other media. And, ironically, some of these cases involved *Times* reporters opposing demands for their notes. Through artful argument Abrams attempted to draw a distinction between these cases and what the *Times* demanded of its own reporter. Abrams noted that Severo used documents to refresh his memory during testimony. "As a result, requests were made to Mr. Severo . . . to see the documents he referred to and others like them. Charges that the request imperiled First Amendment rights is not only a distortion but in my mind grossly and unfairly maligns a newspaper which has consistently led the defense of First Amendment rights of reporters." Abrams' "opinion" slid around the fact that Stanton's demand was so broad that it effectively ordered Severo to turn over all his files for inspection.

Even Rosenthal was appalled by Stanton's request. "A stupid thing," he said of it months later. Rosenthal realized the damage had been done—that the *Times* had lost any claim to moral high ground in the case. Now, in addition to bullying its own reporter, it was on the questionable side of a First Amendment issue. Comment elsewhere in the press was uniformly hostile to the *Times* and its position.

Oddly neither Sulzberger nor Rosenthal used the embarrassment as a justification for abandoning the distasteful proceeding. Rosenthal's response was to shun or denigrate the staff persons who had appealed to Sulzberger to end the suit. Nan Robertson, the instigator, found herself cut out of Rosenthal's life. Previously he would drop by her desk several times a week for a pleasant chat. Now he would muster a cool "hello" if he encountered Robertson in the elevator or a corridor, but the informal little visits ended. Artie Gelb followed Rosenthal's suit.

Robertson was at first hurt, for she felt that by organizing the letter to Sulzberger she was trying to prevent further harm to the *Times*, an institution both she and Rosenthal had loved. But as his curt snubs continued over the months she grew amused. She contrived excuses to get near them in the newsroom, and say sprightly, "Hi, Abe," or "Hi, Artie." As she remembered with a smile, "They would look at their shoes and walk away." She eventually abandoned even this byplay. "I feel it's up to him; he snubbed me, he cut me off. If he wants me back, as a friend; he must come to me."

Other persons who signed the letter to Sulzberger had unexpected experiences. Leslie Bennett, a lively reporter in the cultural department who specialized in show business personality features, found herself detailed to write a "calendar column" for Friday's Weekend Section—a clerical chore that wasted several days weekly of her demonstrated talent. Two other signers, Tom Wicker and Charlotte Curtis, had been listed in the masthead on the editorial page as "associate editors," befitting their former ranks on the newspaper (Wicker as Washington bureau chief, Curtis as women's editor) and current tasks as columnists. They were curtly told by Sulzberger they were being dropped from the masthead. When Wicker asked why, Sulzberger said something lame about "we need the titles for future promotions."

Wicker grinned; he knew better. More than a year lapsed before promotions caused the *Times* to appoint another associate editor.

As a recent Pulitzer winner Nan Robertson was beyond direct retaliation; Rosenthal could break their personal relationship, but he could do little to her professionally. In the year after she signed the letter, she received two bylines in the *Times*. She did not care; she had given what she could to *her* paper. As she stated, "Abe changed over the years, increment by increment. Memory makes me sad. But I won't be a sycophant, and I will not be a friend with what Abe Rosenthal has become."

As the arbitration hearings dragged into their second year, Severo tired of his tenuous existence at the *Times*, and he took a leave of absence for six months, to write a book on how America treats its war veterans, and to teach a course at Vassar College, just across the Hudson River from his home in Newburgh. Vassar paid him $9,000 a year for his part-time work; he rented his late parents' home; he took interest off his savings. With scrimping, he survived. After the first six months leave ended, he asked that it be extended. Lawyer Phil Tobin feared city desk editors—"Abe's Dobermans"—would goad Severo into an incident that would justify firing him for cause—e.g., punching somebody in the nose. Severo has a temper and a tongue, and Tobin did not want to lose the protracted case on the technicality of an office fist fight.

The arbitrator, Joseph Altieri, an attorney in his late sixties, did little to move the case along. He scheduled hearings infrequently; to Severo he seemed overly accommodating to the *Times* when its lawyers asked for continuances; he did not appear to keep testimony in his head from hour to hour. A further complication was the illness of Phil Tobin, who was hospitalized midcourse during the hearings for treatment of cancer.

Finally, at Altieri's suggestion, Severo met privately with Artie Gelb at his apartment to see if any compromise could be struck.

Come back to the *Times*, Gelb told Severo; we'll walk into the newsroom, and I'll have my hand over your shoulder. This will tell everybody that you are a good reporter and that you will be receiving the best assignments available.

"Put it in writing, Artie," Severo said.

No, no, Gelb protested, Rich, you must *trust* me.

Severo shook his head again. "No thanks, Artie, put it in writing."

Gelb refused. The meeting ended.

In the late spring of 1988 the proceedings approached their fifth year, with no resolution in sight. Lawyers for Severo and the New York Times company each filed lengthy motions, with both sides avowing they would appeal, to federal district court should arbitrator Altieri rule against them. The transcript of testimony swelled past 10,000 pages; there were hundreds of pages of motions and other findings.

Near the end of Rosenthal's testimony, attorney Tobin asked about his temperament.

Q.   [By Tobin] Would you say that you're difficult to deal with, Mr. Rosenthal?

A.   No.

Q.   Would you say that you were when you were a reporter?

A.   No, I was very easy to deal with. In fact, I had a reputation for it.

Q.   Would you say you were pleasant to work with as an editor?

A.   Depends on the person. I think I am. I am sure many people do not.

TWENTY-TWO

"Will I Still Have It This Afternoon?"

In 1984 Rosenthal made the decision that had long been so inevitable. He would leave Ann Rosenthal, and he would see if he could find happiness with another woman. This hurt, deeply. He was not a religious man, yet, "I meant it when I said I would never leave her."

But when he left, it would not be for a particular woman. That his conscience would not bear. So first he must end the long but deteriorated affair with Katharine Balfour. Doing so meant the functional equivalent of two divorces at the same time, a staggering psychic challenge for any man, and especially for one of the emotionalism of Abe Rosenthal.

To steel himself for the break with Balfour he began seeing a psychiatrist, Dr. Peter Neubauer, who had offices on East 70th Street near Fifth Avenue. Each day the limousine would pick up Rosenthal at his apartment on Central Park West and drive across town, and he would go into Neubauer's office for an hour, and talk. He cried a lot the first months—tears of guilt about leaving Ann, now old and fat and sick, but nonetheless the woman who bore him three sons, and endured the hardships of New Delhi and Poland. There were tears of shame that the marriage had failed, and that he had shared so many years with another woman whom he now realized he did not love.

Was his entire life a failure as well? He knew he was largely un-loved at his own newspaper, and a subject of jokes among journalists elsewhere, who eagerly collected and traded "Abe stories" like kids do baseball cards. He had reached the pinnacle, only to find himself an unhappy man who faced the prospect of spending the rest of his life alone. Oh, he had the sycophants at the office—the "newspaper fool" Artie Gelb, among others—but their pseudo-friendship would vanish along with his power. And he knew enough about the hypocrisies of New York society to realize the deadening effect the words "the former" have upon one's appeal to hostesses.

So the psychiatrist Neubauer worked through Rosenthal's prob-lems and fears, which were many. By happenstance Neubauer knew Katharine Balfour slightly, for her divorced husband was also a psy-chiatrist, and they attended several parties together. Neubauer is a striking man with stylish blonde hair, and although in his seventies he prefers much younger women as dinner partners, for he finds their laughter rejuvenating. The first months of the consultations, Rosenthal let slip enough comments for Balfour—who knows shrink jargon and techniques—to realize that he was building towards a break in their relationship. Balfour thought back to the immediate past and remembered some episodes that in retrospect did not portend a happy future.

The previous summer, Rosenthal had gone to the People's Repub-lic of China. Although Ann went along for part of the trip, he man-aged to send Balfour loving postcards daily. "When I get back," he promised, "we'll take some time off. I want to write a *Times Magazine* piece. Let's go out to the Island." Balfour called a theatrical friend who had two houses in Amagansett and who agreed to lend them one for a long weekend. People like to do favors for the executive editor of *The New York Times*.

Rosenthal appeared happy as they drove out through Long Island. He talked about what he had seen on his trip, and his magazine piece, and what he should title it. "It's not as if I'm an old China hand," he said.

"Well, then, call it 'Memories of a New China Hand,' " Balfour suggested.

Rosenthal whooped with laughter. "Hey, that's damned good," he said. "I'm going to use that." They settled into the cottage, and Rosenthal found a place for his typewriter, and the first day went smoothly.

Then Balfour did something that annoyed Rosenthal beyond reason. She had half a cantaloupe for breakfast and put the remainder back into the refrigerator, thinking that she or Abe would eat it later. This upset Rosenthal. He did not like half-eaten fruit left around like that. Did she not have any goddamned brains? That was a dumb thing to do.

Late that afternoon, when Rosenthal was finishing his work, someone telephoned to invite them to a party which Henry Kissinger would be attending. Balfour reacted excitedly; she had been cooped up in the cottage all day while Rosenthal worked, and she liked the prospect of meeting Kissinger.

Rosenthal shook his head. "I can't take you to that party," he said, "be realistic. All sorts of important people are going to be there." He repeated the cruelest of words again. "I can't take you."

The comment stunned Balfour, who burst into tears. Surely their relationship was public enough now that Rosenthal should feel free to escort her anywhere he wished. Balfour realized, with a jolt that literally took the breath from her, that she would never be Mrs. A. M. Rosenthal.

As the months passed Balfour sensed Rosenthal drawing deliberately away from her. This she blamed on Neubauer, for one of his counselling strategems was that patients should rid themselves of unpleasant associations—a job, a spouse, an unwanted lover. Balfour's friends in the psychiatric community told her Neubauer's operating slogan was, "Do what makes you feel good." And to Rosenthal this obviously meant getting rid of Balfour.

At a restaurant one evening she casually draped her coat over a chair, and did not notice that part of it slipped to the floor. Rosenthal berated her noisily for "being sloppy." A waiter brought white wine, rather than the red she ordered. When she asked for a replacement, Rosenthal scolded her for "being fussy" and said, "You embarrass me." They dined on a terrace one evening, and the wind tousled her hair. "You look awful," Rosenthal said.

Now Rosenthal disappeared. He stopped telephoning her, and he would not accept or return her calls. Katharine Balfour retreated to the privacy of her apartment and started crying, and she continued to do so for months.

So Rosenthal took his things from Central Park West—a few clothes, some books, pictures of the sons, a couple of plants—and rented a small apartment elsewhere. He told this author emphatically, "I did not leave her for someone else. I wanted to be sure and careful about that. I made sure she [he did not say the words Katharine Balfour] was gone earlier. Only then could I leave Ann.

"I went through some periods when I would break into tears walking down the street, or just sitting in my office, and especially at night, when I would be by myself, all alone. I was worse off, my friends now tell me, than I realized."

Some of these friends had him over for dinner, to break his loneliness, and he cried again, this time as he talked about the Bhopal chemical disaster, which killed several thousands of the Indians he had loved so dearly. A dinner partner made a startling discovery. "Abe literally did not know how to go to the grocery store, or to find a laundry to do his shirts. He had had these things done for him for so long he was helpless and lost." She felt it odd that a man of such sophistication should be so ignorant about the logistics of everyday life, then she thought, "Hell, that's what Ann Rosenthal has been doing for Abe all these years." With that thought her sympathy for Rosenthal's plight lessened. But over coffee she gave him a crash course on Gristede's and Chinese laundries, and how to find a cleaning lady.

He sought, and he found, other women, many of them, and immediately. A story came out of the *Times* concerning what he supposedly said at a front page meeting. "I've left Ann, and I want to let everyone know it. I don't want you to find this out on Page Six," meaning the New York *Post* gossip column.

He had a brief but intense liaison with a woman who worked at the paper, at a desk only a few quick steps from his office, and sometimes he would take a position just feet from her, and watch her as she worked. She marked their fifteenth day together by sending him fifteen red roses.

But he made clear, to her and to the other women, that a permanent relationship had no appeal to him. He told one friend, a man no longer on the paper, "One of the big regrets of my life was that I never had the chance to have enough women. That is going to change."

It did.

But despite the freedom to roam as he wish, to awaken in the morning in the bed of a new woman who found him funny and exciting (and powerful), these were the worst of times. He realized that Punch Sulzberger would not waive the mandatory retirement age of sixty-five and continue him as executive editor. Punch began saying as much to other publishers around the country when they asked why he endured the embarrassment Rosenthal had brought to the *Times* through the Severo episode and other nastiness.

So Rosenthal realized that soon he would gather his things and move up to the tenth floor, where the *Times* keeps its columnists, and be listed on the floor-directory along with Russell Baker and Tom Wicker. He would have freedom to travel at *Times* expense (one blessing) and he would be a "consultant" to the news department. He realized the hollowness of the latter, for the last thing the new executive editor wanted wandering around his newsroom was Abe Rosenthal.

Money was no longer a worry. By 1986 Rosenthal was earning, in salary and executive bonuses, more than $600,000 a year. The *Times* had been generous with stock options, and Rosenthal's portfolio was valued at in excess of $3 million. A good chunk of this amount—plus the Central Park West penthouse, itself worth almost a million dollars—ultimately passed to Ann Rosenthal as part of the divorce settlement. But the bottom line was that Rosenthal no longer had to work; he could be the comfortable "elder statesman," and puff on his pipe and deal in opinions rather than news.

He realized, too, that although Sulzberger would ask his thoughts on the choice of a successor, his recommendation would not necessarily be followed. This hurt, for he had shaped a *Times* of his liking, and he did not wish it spoiled by another man.

But for that matter, would Sulzberger do the choosing? The publisher was sixty-one years old, and not particularly interested in his job. The Times Company was in splendid financial condition, and its 1986 revenues would reach a record $1.3 billion with net income of

$116 million. Sulzberger had taken a job his family thought he could not handle, and he both saved *and* transformed the *Times*. Soon he could be content to give the publishership to a new generation, and retire to his beloved machine shop behind his home in Connecticut.

Punch that year sat next to a woman at dinner who mentioned she'd like to work for the *Times*. Oh? What position? "Assistant to the publisher," she said.

"Too bad you don't want to be publisher," he said. "You could have my job first thing tomorrow morning." The tone of his voice was such that the comment did not come off as a joke.

During a conversation with a visitor in early 1986 Sulzberger talked vaguely about the succession. What input would son Pinch Sulzberger have in choosing the new executive editor? the visitor asked. Punch Sulzberger grinned.

"You mean when he's sitting here?" indicating his own chair. Yes.

Punch Sulzberger grinned again. "That assumes he *will* be sitting here," he said. "There are a lot of other relatives around the building, you know."

He would say nothing further; when Punch Sulzberger decides to fall silent, further conversation is akin to playing ping-pong with a dead ball. But he had passed the subtle suggestion that sister Ruth Sulzberger Holmberg's son Steven Golden—like Pinch, then wending his way through various Times Company divisions as an executive trainee—should not be dismissed as a future publisher.*

As many as half a dozen men—everyone seemed to have his own list—nervously awaited the news of who would be annointed for Abe's job as executive editor of *The New York Times*. Media watchers shuffled endlessly, futilely, witlessly, watching for the omen that would reveal the successor.

Although only three years Abe's junior, Arthur Gelb surely wanted

---

*By 1987 Pinch had moved up to the position of assistant publisher, working directly under his father. He earned $137,712 and a bonus of $58,100, a total of $195,812. Steve Golden directed the Forest Products Group, earning $100,167 in salary and a bonus of $30,450, a total of $130,617. Two other family members held executive positions. Michael Golden, another of Mrs. Holmberg's sons, and a brother of Steve, was senior vice president of the New York Times Company's single-copy magazine distribution subsidiary, with a salary of $75,000 and a bonus of $10,803. Daniel Cohen, son of Judith Sulzberger, was group manager, area development, in the advertising department of *The New York Times*, with a salary of $55,400 and a bonus of $26,925. All these men also received income from *Times* stock they owned directly or indirectly through various family trusts.

the job, or at least a significant portion of it, for he felt he deserved nothing less after so many years at the paper. He talked with Jimmy Greenfield and other friends about the administrative mechanics of bifurcating the executive editorship, with one person responsible for hard news, and the other for "soft" sections such as culture, the book review and the magazine. This second person, with commensurate title, should be someone versed in culture and soft news. Someone such as Artie Gelb.

John Lee surely thought he had the qualifications. He had worked in Asia, edited the business-financial section, then moved to the news desk and taken a heavy role in production of the daily paper. For technical professionalism he surpassed perhaps everyone. He had no flash—but no serious enemies in the newsroom either.

Bill Kovach surely could not be ignored, for he had managed to run an honest Washington bureau under the strictures imposed by Rosenthal. Two things were said about Kovach around the tables where reporters gathered for after-work drinks. He "kept his virginity" during the Rosenthal era—that is, he had not compromised himself by becoming either a sycophant or one of "Abe's Dobermans." And if the election was decided by popular vote of the news staff, he would win hands-down. He lacked foreign experience, yet that had not hurt Turner Catledge's performance as executive editor almost two decades before. Kovach had another hole card. Two, in fact. Pinch Sulzberger liked him. So did Steve Golden's mother Ruth Sulzberger Holmberg, a fellow Tennessean (via her editorship of the Nashville paper owned by the Times Company).

John Vinocur surely *behaved* as if he were a contender, and of the field his politics certainly were most closely in tune with those of Abe Rosenthal. He was given a major test of managerial fire during the summer of 1986 when he worked with Artie Gelb on a major overhaul of the metropolitan section, which he edited. But Vinocur, a vigorous, muscular man, had trouble getting along with staff members, and a couple of times people in the city room thought he intended to use his fists to win an argument. One reporter said in not-so-mock horror: "That's all we need—someone with Abe Rosenthal's temper and John Vinocur's physique."

Max Frankel, although once rejected for executive editor, surely wanted another chance. He would be the interim editor, serving only two years while Punch arranged for the inauguration of a new publisher—either young Pinch or Steve Golden—who would then pick *his* executive editor. Frankel had been comfortably distant from the turmoil of the third floor—the news department—during the grimmest years of Rosenthal's reign, and he was untainted by office politics. Yet could he shift from the editorial page back to news? And could he produce a paper with the conservative ideological thrust obviously desired by Punch Sulzberger? (Reed Irvine, the combative head of Accuracy in Media, pointedly reminded Punch during a visit on July 16, 1986, that Frankel let thirteen days lapse before getting around to running an editorial over the Sandinista closure of the opposition newspaper *La Prensa*. That's very interesting, Sulzberger replied.)

Several times Sulzberger asked Abe, "Who do *you* think we should pick? Who's the best man to take your place?" Rosenthal would give no answers; you're the boss, he told Punch, it's up to you. Sulzberger eventually decided Rosenthal was engaged in gamesmanship: that by not pushing any particular person as his successor, Sulzberger would throw up his hands and say, "OK, Abe, you win, you're executive editor as long as you want the job." But this game Sulzberger would not play. In the spring and summer of 1986 he began canvassing persons within the paper as to who would be the best choice as executive editor. Several directors of the New York Times Company—particularly his sisters and William Scranton, the former Pennsylvania governor and former UN delegate—emphatically opposed any waiver of the *Times*'s retirement age to benefit Rosenthal. The man, they said, has caused too many problems; when he reaches sixty-five, he should be out of here. Punch did not argue, for he now felt the same.

But lacking any specific signal from Punch, no one at the *Times* really knew what to expect, other than continued speculation. One short-lived rumor had the popular Gene Roberts being brought back from the Philadelphia *Inquirer* to replace Rosenthal, the theory being that he had not been tainted by the turmoil of recent years. Sulzberger never gave this idea serious thought—"wishful thinking," one man called it—but Rosenthal did, and a friend summarized his attitude towards Roberts *redux*: "Abe would ring the Times Building with army tanks to keep Roberts from coming back here."

So the succession questions dragged, and more than one of the contenders thought about where they might go, to what other papers, should they be passed over. For they had invested too much mental anguish working under Rosenthal to be satisfied with any reward save total success.

Rosenthal gradually shook himself out of his grief in 1985 and entered a new period characterized by outright weirdness. For a brief period he prowled New York at night with Jerzy Kosinski in the writer's van. Kosinski is a man of eclectic tastes, and he knows the odd corners of New York grime that escaped Rosenthal's awareness despite his years as the top newspaperman in the city. Kosinski liked places family newspapers overlook. So they would set out in the van after midnight, Abe clad in blue jeans and a jacket, trying to emulate Kosinski's rumpled casualness, but never quite succeeding.

They sneaked into a basement in the Bronx with several score men, mostly Hispanics, and watched brutal and bloody cockfights. Abe felt queasy after a couple of chickens perished and they left. Nor did he like the glimpse into the S&M bar off the West Side docks. He described to a friend one bizarre sexual activity he witnessed and shook his head and said, "I wouldn't have thought that was anatomically possible." This was one discovery he did *not* pass along to the metropolitan desk as a story idea.

Eventually Kosinski moved away, to live and work on a new book in New Haven, and Rosenthal sought out other companions. One of them was Katherine Balfour.

He surprised her with a telephone call on Valentine's Day, 1985, and the suggestion that she join him for dinner. She had an invitation to a cocktail party in Greenwich Village, but at an early hour, and she would be happy to meet him at a nearby restaurant, just off Bleecker.

He was nervous and he did not wish to talk much about what he had been doing the absent months. He seemed to relax as they fell into the easy chatter that had long made them friends and companions as well as lovers. For several deliriously happy minutes Katharine Balfour thought, "He still loves me. He has come back to me."

Then she said something that she later realized, with horror, was the worst possible thing she could have uttered.

"Abe, darling," she said, "I've been reliving some very good memories of us. I was sorting through some drawers in the living room this afternoon after you called, and I found those photographs we took in Italy. Do you remember that one of you riding in the gondola in Venice? You looked so happy and handsome that day, and I loved you very much."

She raised her eyes and glanced across the table, and she saw Rosenthal's face twist into the oh-so-familiar scowl, the black one, the one that signalled true rage, not just pique.

"I do not want to talk about the fucking past," he said. "All that shit is history. If you don't have the sense to talk about the future, shut the fuck up. All that happened in the past, let that go."

When they left the restaurant he put her into a cab. No, he did not want to come to her place for a drink. He had some other things to do. Balfour glanced out the rear window as it drove north. Rosenthal stomped angrily around the curb, as if his waving arms might physically seize a passing cab. He never called her again.

In June, son Andy came to New York on leave from his job as Moscow correspondent for the Associated Press. For the first time since leaving Ann, Abe went to the Central Park West apartment for a party. He was worried, for Andy had not liked it when he left his mother, and they had had some bitter words.

Ann was worried as well, for she had taken the initiative in asking him to the party, and she speculated with several friends as to whether he would actually appear. She was keeping a list which she intended to use if they ever reconciled. It contained names of the persons who continued to call her after the separation, and acted nice towards her. These were the people who would be the future friends of the reunited Rosenthals. The rest of the people in the world would not be invited.

Abe was both formal and friendly towards Ann. He did not talk much. He mixed and he listened. Gene Rosenfeld, who had been his good friend at the United Nations and then in New Delhi, tried to make small talk about the news, and he got nowhere. So he finally asked, "So how *are* you, Abe?" an invitation to talk with an old friend about his personal status.

"Oh, I'm doing fine, I'm doing fine," Rosenthal said. Rosenfeld knew him well enough to sense the hurt, and so he left him alone.

Later Rosenthal wandered out onto the terrace to visit his beloved plants, some of which stood man-high. Gene Rosenfeld watched through the glass door as Rosenthal stroked the leaves of some of them, and murmured softly, as if he were talking to them.

"That hurt," Rosenfeld said. "You could see that the man missed his garden, if nothing else."

The singer Beverly Sills made the introduction. She had known and loved Rosenthal as a friend for years, and she hated to see him lonely, flitting from one empty-headed woman to another. Eventually, she worried, Abe is going to be hurt, and hurt badly.

The woman Sills found was Shirley Lord, a British-born journalist and writer Sills had known around New York for years. Lord was what people politely call "fortyish" that year, a full-figured blonde who wore her long hair uncurled and tossed back beyond her face. She was pretty, and she could talk about any conceivable subject. Lord went to Fleet Street, London's newspaper row, at age seventeen and she eventually worked as women's editor for each of the three major evening dailies. She married, briefly, a young electrical engineer, James Hussy, by whom she had a son. On assignment to write an article "How to be a Millionaire" she encountered carpet tycoon Cyril Lord, a feisty man of five feet and a few inches who hawked his rugs in loud television ads. Marriage followed, and the new Mrs. Lord became a gushed-over feature of the Fleet Street tabloid pages. The Lords had a son of their own, and in the late 1960's they moved to the Bahamas. Shirley commissioned a prominent builder, David Anderson, to design and build them a house. In due course, she split from Lord and in 1974 married Anderson aboard the developer William Levit's yacht off Monte Carlo.

Now to New York, where Shirley and her new husband bought an apartment on Central Park South and a weekend house in Bellport, a fashionable Long Island enclave. She and New York society liked one another, and for a decade she and Anderson were a fixture of charity balls and the also-present items in the New York *Post*. In 1974 Anderson dropped dead of a heart attack. Although a moderately wealthy woman, Shirley went to work, in a manner that blended her worlds of fashion and society. She worked at *Harper's Bazaar* as a senior editor, and then became a corporate vice president of Colgate's Helena Rubenstein division, and a syndicated writer on beauty and fitness. When Rosenthal met her she was with *Vogue* magazine as "Director of Special Projects, Beauty and Fitness."

Shirley Lord was also a novelist, and soon after meeting Rosenthal she published *One of My Very Best Friends*. The *Times* review rightly called it "steamy . . . novel of sex and success." Lord drew upon her insider's knowledge of journalism and the cosmetics industry to craft a page-turning tale of betrayal and revenge. And sex: ". . . [E]ven a eunuch would have been stirred up by the sight of Nell one spring day in a pretty white blouse which in some way had emphasized her amazingly large nipples. . . . He'd been so full of longing to run his tongue around each pink areola, to roll each exquisite plump point between his fingers." (Lord is sexually ecumenical; a lesbian seduction scene is even more graphically written.)

Rosenthal was smitten with the lady from the very beginning, and she began to host parties featuring him at her duplex apartment on Central Park South. She had been around the New York social world long enough to know the places he should go, and the people he should meet, and those persons recognized at a glance that Abe Rosenthal was enraptured with the exciting new woman in his life.

Reporters at *W* called her "that great marzipan creation" and in February, 1988, *New York* Magazine described her as a "busty chick." But all agreed that her presence had planted a permanent smile on the face of A. M. Rosenthal.

No more guilt. His seventeen years with Balfour had been furtive ones, when he felt constrained at taking a mistress to parties where people frowned upon flagrant extra-marital affairs. The last of his years with Ann she had been so physically handicapped—and unattractive—that he simply did not like to take her places, for he could hear (he thought) people saying, "So *that* is Abe Rosenthal's wife." No more guilt—just the joy of the company of a beautiful and striking woman who made him feel loved and important.

Some of Abe's old-line friends did not take to Shirley Lord as readily as he did. One woman had them to the house for dinner, out of curiosity, and she was appalled. "A barracuda," she said, "a female barracuda. Poor little Abe. He doesn't have the slightest idea of what's happening to him."

This woman said that Rosenthal would be welcome to return—but not with Shirley Lord.

On an October weekend in 1985, the communications tycoon John Kluge invited 120 guests to the unveiling of his new 4,000-acre estate, Albemarle House, a stone's throw from Monticello, Thomas Jefferson's old home. The New York *Post*'s society columnist Suzy:

". . . a magnificent landscape of verdant rolling hills and five silvery-man-made lakes . . .

". . . ravishing creamy yellow satin curtains and a superb carpet and glowing antiques in the drawing room, a dining room fit for a king . . .

". . . great inverted topiary baskets overflowing with lilies and assorted roses, each weighing twenty-five pounds . . .

". . . a dinner of lobster thermidor, rack of lamb and fresh raspberries with *crème fraîche* . . ."

The guest list ranged from Mrs. Douglas MacArthur to Helen Gurley Brown, David Frost, Armand Hammer, and "Shirley Lord with Abe Rosenthal."

Katharine Balfour's daughter Mary, after graduating from college, had joined the *Times* as a graphic designer. Artie Gelb gave her special attenion. They sometimes ate at the same restaurant, around the corner from the *Times*, and when she walked in Gelb would greet her with a hug.

Once Rosenthal broke with Balfour, Mary ate at the same restaurant a few times. Gelb did too, and he ignored her. She found a new place for lunch.

Rosenthal gave her special attention in the past, at the risk of making her "the boss's pet." He would stop by her desk and ask her how her work was going.

Now he ignored her in the newsroom, even when they walked by one another. Her face broke out in ugly splotches; she could not stand rejection by the man who for seventeen years had treated her as a daughter. She quit the *Times* and took a job at a magazine in Connecticut, which meant leaving her Manhattan apartment at 5:30 A.M. to catch a train.

Katharine Balfour mentioned this in one of the few brief phone talks she had with Rosenthal after Mary quit. So what, he said, lots of girls ride the train to work.

There were times, as his final year dragged on, when Rosenthal showed symptoms of boredom with the paper. He spent long weekends with Shirley Lord, and editors who worked the desk on Saturday nights often enjoyed the rare treat of having their entire shift pass without receiving a single telephone call from Rosenthal. Sometimes, on Monday mornings, his limousine would bring him directly to 43d street from the Hamptons or elsewhere, and he would bound into the office wearing a sport coat and a pastel shirt (and a hint of a tan) rather than the severe blue suits he had preferred in the past.

And when circumstances tugged at him, he could be the "old Abe," the smartest newspaperman in New York. A casual oversight of Rosenthal in action shows the wellspring of his talent. He is curious. He asks himself the sort of questions that might occur to the average reader. He wants the *Times* to be written for readers, not for other newspapermen. (The difference is subtle but far too many editors and writers never recognize it.)

On the afternoon of April 2, 1986, Rosenthal sat at a long conference table in his outer office and faced twenty men and two women sub editors, seated along the table and at chairs against the wall. (Punch Sulzberger would come into the conference at mid-course and take the chair behind Rosenthal's desk and listen for half an hour and not say a word. At the *Times* the news is the editor's province, not the publisher's.) This is the meeting at which Rosenthal and others begin putting the next day's editions into final form, particularly the "display pages" at the front of each of the four sections. The procedure is for each department—metropolitan, national, Washington, foreign, cultural, business and sports—to "offer" the stories in progress, hoping one might land on the front page. Each editor gives a two- or three-sentence precis of the story, then Rosenthal goes into action.

He has the ability to spot a hole in a story, the unanswered question. His questions, once stated, sound obvious, yet no one had thought of them previously. The major story that day was an explosion of a terrorist bomb on a TWA flight bound from Rome to Athens, killing four persons. John Darton, the deputy foreign editor who outlined the story, mentioned that the bomb was taken aboard in hand baggage that cleared airport security.

"I don't expect you to know the answer right now," Rosenthal asked Darton. "But hand baggage. What do you see in the X-ray machine when it goes through security? This gives us a chance to show what can be detected." The next day's paper carried a story by science writer Malcolm Browne with the answers to Rosenthal's question.

Yet another story dealt with Vice President George Bush's appeal to Middle East countries to juggle oil production to halt the plunge of prices. Rosenthal frowned, and he banged the table with his fist and interrupted the presentation. "Let's look at it this way," he said. "You pick up *The New York Times* and somebody from our government is going off to persuade Saudi Arabia to produce less oil so we can pay more for it. We write like this is normal. It knocks my socks off, and we write it *as if this is normal.*" (A Donald Duck soundtrack came on during the last words.) He continued, shaking his head. "It is a whacko story. I know it is true, which makes a more interesting story." The next day's paper carried a story by Robert D. Hershey, Jr., explaining the complexities of what the Reagan Administration was trying to do about oil prices.

Rosenthal picked at story after story; seventeen times he had probing questions which editors promised to answer in the final version of the article. Such conferences are famed for ugly Rosenthal performances, the days when he "decides to bang somebody around a little bit, kick them in the nuts just for fun," as a frequent editor-target put it. Today, however, perhaps mindful of my presence as a monitor, he had only one mild criticism, on a story about supposed U. S.-Egyptian planning to topple Colonel Muammar al-Quaddafi of Libya. Howell Raines of the Washington bureau said the article "confirms the Washington *Post* story" published that morning. "I don't think we have been leading the pack on this," Rosenthal said snippishly.

As the meeting broke up, Rosenthal paused for a few private words with news editor Allan Siegal about a story that might require changes later that evening. He insured that Siegal had the phone number of the home where he would be attending a dinner party. As he explained a few minutes later, "My idea of editing a newspaper is to get it right the night before publication, and not sit around the next day and have a post mortem. I want it perfect before it's published, not the next morning."

Of the cascade of bad publicity that gushed over Abe Rosenthal during the mid-1980's, the article that stung him perhaps the most ran in the *Village Voice* under the byline of Peter Hamill. This was soon after the firing of Sydney Schanberg, and the cover illustration cast Rosenthal as a combat tank whose cannon blasted at unseen adversaries. The article was rough, but no more so than any of a dozen concerning Abe published in the *Voice* the past year by Nat Hentoff. But the circumstances infuriated Rosenthal.

Hamill called (this is Rosenthal's account) and said the *Voice* had asked him to do a piece on the *Times,* and he said he would do so only if Rosenthal would grant him an interview. Rosenthal was talking to few journalists these months.

"No," Rosenthal said, "the *Voice* has never been fair to either me or the *Times.* This is no reflection on you, but I'm not going to waste my time on a paper that won't give me fair treatment. I don't ask for favorable treatment, only fair treatment."

"Well," Hamill said, "in that case, since you won't talk to me, I won't do the piece."

The article appeared anyway. Several references suggested Hamill and Rosenthal were old chums. Nonsense, not true; Rosenthal wouldn't recognize the guy on the street. He had met him only on the two occasions that Hamill approached the *Times* about writing a column. Both times he was rejected.

Several months later Rosenthal attended a stag party for his friend Peter Maas. Rosenthal did not catch the name of a man to whom he was introduced, and he asked someone, "Who is that guy?" Pete Hamill, he was told.

Rosenthal turned and strode across the room and stood in front of Hamill. "Excuse me," he said. "I understand you are Pete Hamill."

Yes, Hamill said, puzzled.

"Well, I just want you to know, if I had recognized you, I would have never shaken your hand." He turned and walked away.

One interview I postponed until the very end was with Katharine Balfour. Any contact with her, I realized, would immediately shut off my tenuous access to Abe Rosenthal. But over the months I had heard many stories about her situation, mostly sad ones. And most of them came from women who had been Balfour's "friend" when she dated Rosenthal. Now these women, for professional and other reasons, shunned her; they preferred to remain socially active with Rosenthal. But they would cluck with sympathy about "poor Katharine" and "what a mess her life is in" and "how she still carries the torch for Abe, bless her heart."

I telephoned Balfour at 1:15 P.M. on Monday, May 26, 1986. Things did not start on a promising note.

Balfour had the affected voice of the professional actress. She drops many "my dears" and "my darlings" into her patter. Yes, she knew of me, and what I was doing. "My darling, I *cannot* say a word about him, he's too frightening." She said the last word with a verbal shudder, as if she really meant it, and I think she did.

She spent almost an hour telling me she did not want to talk about Rosenthal, and in fact that she *could* not, that the memories were too painful. She began asking me questions about Abe. Was he happy? Did he seem healthy? What, if anything, had he said about her? What did other persons say of her? of them? of (a shudder again) *that woman*? Finally, she promised me fifteen minutes, and she told me of a cafe around the corner from her East Side apartment, and we set a time.

I'll make a reservation, I said.

Panic. No, no, she said, not under *your* name. What if *he* would find out? What if he knew I was talking to *you*? I agreed to make the reservation under an alias I used decades ago during time as a novice spook for military counterintelligence.

She arrived sharp upon the appointed time of one P.M. on Monday, June 2, 1986. Knowing her desire for privacy, I had taken a booth on the upper level of the cafe, away from the window. No, she did not wish to sit there. "That booth is where we used to sit," she said, referring to Rosenthal. So we moved up a tier.

Balfour is a woman of striking appearance—a casual swirl of brownish-red hair, tall (five feet seven she told me later), slim, erect; yet at close view she is tired, especially in the eyes and the hands. But her face can change in an instant. When she speaks of sad things she is wan, pathetic; when she reverts to a happy subject, it is as if her face has been given an injection of air, for she becomes full-cheeked and buoyant. A good mood strips perhaps fifteen years off her face.

The promised fifteen minutes turned into an hour, then two hours, then much longer, and the conversations were to continue, off and on, by phone chiefly but sometimes in person, for far more than a year. Balfour discovered I wrote at night; eventually, if the telephone rang at midnight or thereafter, I would answer it, "Hello, Katharine," without hesitation. And then she would talk, about the life she had had with Abe Rosenthal for more than twenty years, and the emptiness of the life she has alone, now that he is with another woman.

Eventually I came to recognize that Balfour spoke from two levels:

First, she had been cast out of a life she had shared with another person, even though she sacrificed her career for him. And, secondly, and perhaps most important, she had been left in a professional and personal lurch. "If you go with someone for any period of time," Balfour told me, "you assume some devotion, some caring about what happens to them. Now he goes about town in his limousine, and I'm standing in the rain, waiting for a bus."

Her accounts of Rosenthal became more detailed, more personal each time we spoke. Many times I chastised her, "You are sounding like a broken record, Katharine, stop talking about your misfortunes and get on with your life." Some subjects I did not wish to pursue— for instance, her account of Rosenthal's liking for unusual erotic devices sold in the leading specialty shops of West 42d Street (these he abandoned in Balfour's closet; they remained there long after he left her life).

But one recurring statement chilled me. She knew Rosenthal intended to wed Shirley Lord. When the story would finally appear in the paper, she said, she intended to kill herself. "I say this truthfully," she said. "The day he marries is the day I kill myself."

Don't be stupid, I said; if he is as unfeeling as you claim, he won't even notice.

"What should I do?" she asked.

"Write a book; do it in novel form, but write a book."

A long pause. "Damn him," she said, "that is exactly what I will do."

It was inescapable that Katharine Balfour should see them together at a party. She had wondered how she would react, for she had read on Page Six of the *Post* of their frenetic social life, and that Abe had moved into Shirley's apartment on Central Park South. She even knew when they left for work in the morning, via limousine.

This evening she braced herself when she saw the familiar squat figure, and heard the familiar high-pitched voice. Oh, Abe, she thought, do something about your hair, it's falling everywhere. She looked at Shirley Lord, and she sniffed.

Rosenthal walked right past Katharine Balfour, and did not even glance at her. She left the party and rode the Lexington Avenue subway home. She did not care to wait and see Rosenthal and Lord ride away in their limo.

Ann Rosenthal, meantime, clung to hopes her Abe would return home. She found herself no longer invited to the parties she had enjoyed as the wife of the executive editor of *The New York Times*. New York "friendships," she realized, are ephemeral. Nonetheless, she continued to answer her telephone, "This is Mrs. A. M. Rosenthal speaking."

But the call she really desired never came—one from Abe, saying he wished to live with her again.

Once a year the Boys' Club, the luncheon group that includes Rosenthal, John Chancellor, William Buckley, and some others, has a formal dinner that includes the wives. Late into a crisp winter night, Rosenthal walked out onto a terrace with Pat (Mrs. William) Buckley, and they stood silently and looked out at the city lights. Rosenthal sighed and he waved his hand out at the horizon. "See that city—that city belongs to me. This is *my* city."

Back inside, over brandy, he talked with another woman. When he shaves each morning, he said, the face he sees reflected back at him is the man who runs *The New York Times*.

"Then I'll say to myself, will I still have it [the *Times*] this afternoon?"

Epilogue

In the autumn of 1986 Punch Sulzberger decided the time for change had come. Abe Rosenthal had accepted, psychologically, the fact that he would not be permitted to remain as executive editor past the retirement age for news department employees. Love-struck with Shirley Lord, his mood mellowed; seldom did the third-floor newsroom echo with his shouts and curses. Punch made "retirement" to a column sound attractive.

Rosenthal had always been a compulsive traveler—the sort of reporter who would make an arduous trip by truck to the Khyber Pass just for the satisfaction of filing a bylined story from there. Part of the early-retirement bait Sulzberger extended was unlimited travel. Go where you wish, as you wish, just do us a couple of columns a week for the Op-Ed Page.

So in September and October the shuffling began. Given Rosenthal's deliberate inaction in training a successor as executive editor, Sulzberger really had no choice. Max Frankel, with a third of a century at the paper, had the most rounded background, from city reporter to foreign correspondent and Washington bureau chief, Sun-

456

day editor, and for a decade editor of the editorial page. Sulzberger spent some years forgiving Frankel for his abrupt resignation letter in the early 1960's, when he almost left the *Times* to join Max Ascoli's *Reporter* Magazine. But proximity bred respect.

This was obvious one morning in March, 1986, when Sulzberger came into Sydney Gruson's office on the executive floor of the Times Building and after a cursory word to a visitor, said, "Max just got the news about Toby, and it's the worst thing imaginable."*

"Tumor?" Gruson asked, and he winced as he said the word.

"Yeah, tumor. And on the brain. They don't know the prognosis yet, but Max will be down after a while." In obvious shock and distress Sulzberger said a few inane things about what one should do for a colleague who has just learned that his wife might be terminally ill.

The next hour Sulzberger was in and out of Gruson's office three, four, even more times. He made small talk, he seemed intent to keeping his mind—and the conversation—away from the plight of Toby Frankel.

And then Frankel appeared in the doorway, a chubby, aging man with grief lines on his face. Gruson saw him first, and he raised his Irish face as if silently asking, "What can you tell us?" Frankel spread wide his hands; he did not know, he did not trust himself to speak. Sulzberger realized then that Frankel was behind him, and he turned and arose and without a word put his arm around his shoulder and walked him from the room.

Gruson stared silently at his desk a few moments, and then he said, "Oh, shit, can't life be awful to decent people?" and then he stared some more.

The visitor did not bother to reply. But the compassion and the empathy Sulzberger displayed with the clasp of his arm around Max Frankel's shoulders answered, in his mind, the question of Abe Rosenthal's successor.†

Sulzberger made the change of command effective as of November 1, 1986, in a story at the bottom of Sunday's front page. (Word leaked out of the *Times* the preceding Friday, so ironically the *Times* was "scooped" on its own announcement by the *Daily News*, the Wash-

---

*His reference was to Frankel's wife, the former Tobia Brown, a sometime teacher, editor and writer who was then pursuing law courses at Columbia University.

†Tobia Brown Frankel was to die of the brain tumor March 16, 1987, at New York Hospital, aged 52.

ington *Post*, and the Associated Press, among other media.) What Rosenthal thought of Frankel's promotion he kept to himself. (Katharine Balfour remembered numerous Rosenthal tirades about "that damned Frankel" in past years, especially in the Watergate period, when the Washington *Post* dominated the story.) Rosenthal's consolation prize, such as it was, concerned his sometime chum Arthur Gelb, who was promoted to managing editor, a good end to a loyal career.

Almost to the end Gelb hoped he would become executive editor. Whatever faint chance he had he muffed during the Chernobyl nuclear disaster.

Several days after the accident Gelb sent a cable to *Times* European correspondents asking what effect nuclear contamination would have on caviar supplies from the Soviet Union and neighboring countries. This thoughtless query confirmed Sulzberger's lingering suspicion that Gelb had a narrow vision, whatever his talents elsewhere at the newspaper. There were other ripples up and down the masthead, with the new-succession attention turned now to, "Who will replace Artie Gelb after three years, when he retires?"

It was at media tycoon John Kluge's penthouse apartment that Rosenthal and Lord wed in June, 1987. Beverly Sills and Barbara Walters, fittingly, served Lord as bridesmaids. The guest list included such luminaries as Donald Trump, Henry Kissinger, Gloria Steinem, Senator Patrick Moynihan, and Mayor Ed Koch. The newlyweds moved into a $1.7 million apartment on East 61st Street—a big one, with 3,500 square feet. (Rosenthal characteristically got into an ugly squabble with the previous owner over who would get a shower curtain, and who owned the cable television box. *Spy* magazine, which recorded these tiffs, made plain that even marriage and retirement had not soothed Rosenthal's combative personality.)

Now Abe Rosenthal became an almost full-time socialite. If he put any intellectual effort into his Op-Ed Page column, no evidence was discernible in the product. In one early effort, on street people and their woes, he babbled maudlinly about his guilt in walking around people he saw slumped in the city's streets. Harking back to the Genovese case, his first big "New York story" as metropolitan editor, he called himself the "39th Witness." In sixteen paragraphs he used "I," "my," or "myself" 36 times.

Rosenthal's new—and apparently coveted—life as a parlor lion was chronicled in depth in *New York Magazine* February 8, 1988, in the gushing prose of Jeanie Kasindorf. "The newest darling of New York's New Society," wrote Kasindorf, and she quoted Aileen "Suzy" Mehle as calling the retired editor "that sweetheart Abe." She quoted the columnist Cindy Adams as putting him on the same plane—for the season, at least—with Blaine Trump, wife of building mogul Donald. (*Spy* magazine unkindly reported that several barbs were plucked from Kasindorf's copy by *New York* editor Ed Kosner, an old Rosenthal chum. All parties offended entered the customary denials.)

The never-friendly *Spy* also described Shirley Lord as "the bosomy dirty book writer" while noting that "Employees of *The New York Times*, once abjectly terrified of Rosenthal's erratic temper, rarely even think of that silly little man anymore."

Don't bet on it.

In the meantime, while *Present Tense* described the Max Frankel reign as "*Glasnost* at the *Times*," columnist Abe Rosenthal, although busy with his memoir for Times Books (at a reported advance of $200,000) also became an acquisitions editor for G.P. Putnam, one of the promotional houses that dominate book publishing. In this role, he would be reporting to a woman, Phyllis Grann.

His signing on with Putnam was reported in the *Times* on January 11, 1988, in a three-paragraph item headed "Rosenthal Appointed Editor at G. P. Putnam." Rosenthal did not like the way the affiliation was announced, for four days later the *Times* ran an "Editors' Note," which stated in its entirety:

> A brief article on Monday reported that A. M. Rosenthal, columnist and former executive editor of *The New York Times*, would serve as an editor at large for G. P. Putnam, book publishers.
>
> Mr. Rosenthal was in Pakistan when his new arrangement was disclosed. On his return, he concluded that the announced title was creating confusion about his role. He and Putnam have agreed on the title editorial consultant. Working part time, Mr. Rosenthal will suggest ideas for non-fiction books and authors to Putnam and will suggest book topics to authors.
>
> Mr. Rosenthal retired from the *Times* on Jan. 1 and continues to write his twice-weekly column under contract with the paper. Before his retirement, he informed the *Times* of his plan to be a consultant for Putnam, and the newspaper gave its approval.

In his column, the insecurities of childhood visibly tugged at Rosenthal. In his crippled youth he'd set his ambition no higher than a career in the postal service. He went on to great things including a seat on a pedestal of power undreamed of in his youth. At 65, he entered a new phrase of that career: columnist. Rosenthal's first column appeared January 6, 1987, under the standing head "On My Head." He also wrote the headline which ran across the top of the page: "Please Read This Column."

The pathos of Abe Rosenthal may be summarized in these sad words. The little boy on the center of the stage shouting for attention.

He'd enjoyed power equalled by few persons in American journalism. He'd made and destroyed careers. He'd affected the course of his country's history and of the world. But beneath it all the deep doubts remained. To the very end it was obvious that Abe Rosenthal wasn't sure that he deserved it, or that it would continue.

Sources and Acknowledgments

The core of this book comes from more than 300 interviews between December, 1984, and July, 1986, chiefly with persons who were current or former employees of *The New York Times*, plus others who in one fashion or another had significant contact either with the *Times* or with A. M. Rosenthal. That each of them cannot be cited by name and position is a pity, and chiefly one of Rosenthal's making. As stated in the Prologue, Rosenthal did not wish this book to be written, and he so stated. Given the climate around the *Times* in 1985, when I began serious interviewing, Rosenthal's frown posed a serious obstacle, for persons at the paper knew his vindictive nature. Just a year or so earlier, for instance, Rosenthal convinced himself that a Washington bureau reporter named Ben Franklin leaked news of pending staff changes to *USA Today*. The offense, even if it could be proved (and it was not) was trivial, for within hours the changes were of public record. Nonetheless, Rosenthal made a non-person of Franklin, barring his byline from the paper, stripping him of a company car (although his territory included the Middle Atlantic States, vast stretches of

461

which are inacccessible by public carriers) and generally making his life miserable.

Franklin's purgatory lasted for months, and no one wished to risk repeating it. Hence I found myself doing cloak-and-dagger interviews with *Times* reporters and editors at odd locations in Manhattan and New Jersey and (in one instance) in a Staten Island diner. Rosenthal's *Times* was such that few persons who worked for him wished to be suspected of cooperating in a book he did not wish written.

A second group of persons was also nervous about interviews. These are people whose livelihoods depend upon remaining in the good graces of the *Times*—writers, theater and political figures, a gamut of interests, none willing to risk the disfavor of Rosenthal and his chum, Arthur Gelb. The recurring phrase I heard was, "Look, I write books, and these guys control *The New York Times Book Review*. If I spend four years writing a book, and they happen to be pissed at me. . . ." Many of these persons thus spoke off the record. Several of them had risked their physical lives to win Pulitzer Prizes for Abe Rosenthal's *Times*; yet they did not care to risk their professional lives by offending him.

People who did speak on the record are identified in the text of the book; the others made their decisions to speak anonymously for what they considered to be good reason, and they are not named within. For more than a year Rosenthal himself turned away my repeated requests for interviews. After I informed him, in early 1986, that I had interviewed more than 200 other persons, curiosity apparently got the best of him, and he began talking with me. Our four interviews spanned upwards of twenty hours, most of them productive; further, Rosenthal permitted me to sit in on a "front page meeting" at which the next day's paper was being planned. Rosenthal had his own agenda. He had a six-figure contract with Times Books to write a memoir, and he clearly did not want to waste his memories on another person's book. But what he did share with me was helpful.

Another obstacle was *The New York Times* itself, in the corporate sense. At first blush this might seem surprising, for publisher Punch Sulzberger regularly receives plaques from press lodges and the like praising his support of the First Amendment. Further, Sulzberger's editorial page preaches regularly for "openness" in government, business and elsewhere. But hypocrisy is one of many failings of the

American press. Early in my work I approached Leonard Harris, who does corporate public relations for the New York Times Company, and told him who I was, and what I was doing. Harris amiably told me he intended to do nothing to make life easier for me, and to his credit he kept his word. Hence this book did not benefit from the insights of such key persons as Walter Mattson, the president of the New York Times Company, and his chief assistants.

Only after more than a year of prodding did Punch Sulzberger agree to an interview monitored by Leonard Harris. After a very few minutes he made plain he intended to be so unresponsive to questions as to be unintelligible. (Oddly, a few weeks later Sulzberger wandered into an interview I was having with Sydney Gruson, his assistant. He joined the conversation, and he told me many things I had asked about earlier with no success. But on this occasion he spoke without the protective presence of his public relations man Harris.) Circumstances gave me the semblance of a last laugh in one area. Harris promised to, but did not, put me on the mailing list for the quarterly statements the *Times* mails to shareholders and the Securities and Exchange Commission. These are public documents. Supplying them to me would have cost the *Times* pennies. So, to get on the mailing list, in the autumn of 1985 I bought, for my Keogh retirement plan, 200 shares of *Times* stock for a total price of $9,269.32. Thereafter the postman brought me the desired financial statements each quarter, and the *Times* stock rose, and then split, two-for-one. As of this writing in March, 1988, my investment has increased in value to $15,950, a gain of $6,680.68. Although the profit is appreciated, I would be happier had the *Times* taken the First Amendment as seriously in practice as it does on the editorial page and in Sulzberger's speeches.

For guiding me through the Turner Catledge Papers, I am grateful to Anne S. Wells of the Mitchell Memorial Library, Mississippi State University. D. Clayton and Erlene James made my stay in Mississippi pleasant. Chris Rosenfeld, of Washington, D. C., kindly loaned me her bound copies of *The News Circle*, publication of the American Women's Club of Delhi, for the years Rosenthal was stationed in India. Martha Keehn, of Forest Hills, New York, shared with me the lengthy letters she wrote to her family describing life in India those same years. Logistical and psychic support during my months in New York came from Tom Mechling and Frank and Su Madison Sherry. Barbara McConaghy typed several versions of a long manuscript, and well.

Among the eleven or so lineal feet of books I read about the *Times* (many written by persons from the paper) the following proved of particular value:

Turner Catledge, *My Life and The Times*, Harper & Row, 1971; Sidney Zion, *Read All About It*, Summit Books, 1982; Meyer Berger, *The Story of the New York Times, 1851–1951*, Simon & Schuster, 1951; Harrison E. Salisbury, *Without Fear or Favor*, Times Books, 1980; Gay Talese, *The Kingdom and the Power*, Anchor Books edition, 1978 (originally published by New American Library 1969); Chris Argyris, *Behind the Front Page*, Jossey-Bass Publishers, 1974; Gloria Emerson, *Winners & Losers*, Random House, 1976; Tom Goldstein, *The News at Any Cost*; Simon & Schuster, 1985; Seymour Freidin and George Bailey, *The Experts*, Macmillan Company, 1968; Herman H. Dinsmore, *All the News That Fits*, Arlington House, 1969; Raymond Bonner, *Weakness and Deceit*, Times Books, 1984; Myron Farber, *Someone Is Lying*, Doubleday, 1982; Reed Irvine, *Media Mischief and Misdeeds*, Regnery Gateway, 1984; and James L. Tyson, *Target America*, Regnery Gateway, 1981.

Finally, and most importantly. Robert Sherrill, an old journalistic chum, took uncountable hours from his own work to read an earlier, more troubled version of this manuscript, and then proceeded to write a 15-page memo which is a masterpiece in telling someone how to salvage a book. Sherrill's confidence spilled over to me, and it was largely through his inspiration that I stayed the course. "Thanks" really isn't enough of an encompassing word, Sherrill, but you get what I mean.

—JOSEPH C. GOULDEN
Washington, D. C.
March, 1988

HOLDINGS OF THE NEW YORK TIMES COMPANY

Daily Newspapers

The New York Times
Sarasota Herald-Tribune (Fla.)
The Press Democrat (Santa Rosa, Calif.)
The Ledger (Lakeland, Fla.)
Gainesville Sun (Fla.)
Santa Barbara News-Press (Calif.)
Spartanburg Herald-Journal (S.C.)
Wilmington Morning Star (N. C.)
Ocala Star-Banner (Fla.)
Times Tri-Cities Daily (Florence, Ala.)
The Tuscaloosa News (Ala.)
The Gadsden Times (Ala.)
Houma Daily Courier (La.)
Leesburg/Commercial (Fla.)

The Times-News (Henderson, N.C.)
Daily World (Opelousas, La.)
The Dispatch (Lexington, N. C.)
Lenoir News-Topic (N. C.)
The Comet (Thibodaux, La.)
Palatka Daily News (Fla.)
The Messenger (Madisonville, Ky.)
The Daily Corinthian (Corinth, Ms.)
Lake City Reporter (Fla.)
Daily News (Middleboro, Ky.)
Harlan Daily Enterprise (Ky.)
State Gazette (Dyersburg, Tenn.)

Weekly and Semi-Weekly Newspapers

York County Coast Star (Kennebunk, Maine)
Sebring News (Fla.)
Marco Island Eagle (Fla.)
The News-Leader (Fernandina Beach, Fl.)
Claiborne Progress (New Tazewell, Tenn.)
The Banner-Independent (Booneville, Ms.)
Avon Park Sun (Fla.)

Magazines

Family Circle
Golf Digest
Golf World
Tennis
Cruising World

Broadcasting/Cable TV

WREG-TV, Memphis, Tenn. (CBS affiliate)
WNEP-TV, Wilkes-Barre/Scranton, Pa. (ABC affiliate)
WQAD-TV, Moline, Ill. (ABC affiliate)
WHNT-TV, Huntsville, Ala. (CBS affiliate)
KFSM-TV, Fort Smith, Ark. (CBS affiliate)
WQXR AM and FM radio, New York City
NYT Cable TV, 56 franchises, all within 25 miles of NYT Cable TV's
  headquarters in Cherry Hill, N. J., outside of Philadelphia.

Syndication Sales

New York Times Syndication Sales Corporation, operator of The New York Times Service, which transmits selected material from each day's paper to some 500 newspaper, news agency and magazine subscribers.

Special Features, which sells written material, features and photographs not derived from *The New York Times*.

NYT Pictures, which sells photographs from *The New York Times*.

Associated Companies

Gaspesia Pulp and Paper Company, Ltd., 49 percent interest

Spruce Falls Power and Paper Company, Limited, 49.5 percent interest.

Donohue Malbaie, Inc., 35 percent interest.

Madison Paper Industries, a partnership between Northern SC Paper Corporation, of which the Times Company is an 80 percent owner, and Myllkoski Oy, a Finnish paper company

The International Herald Tribune, S. A., which publishes the *International Herald Tribune*, edited in Paris and published simultaneously in Paris, London, Zurich, Hong Kong, Singapore, The Hague, Marseille and Miami; one-third owner with The Washington *Post* Company and the IHT Corporation, a subsidiary of Whitney Communications Corporation.

Index

471

About the Author

Joseph C. Goulden is the author of 15 nonfiction books. These include *The Superlawyers*, which was on *The New York Times* bestseller list for more than 20 weeks, and *The Best Years*, a main selection of Book-of-the-Month Club. Although on diverse subjects, most of Goulden's books have dealt with the acquisition and use of power: on the military (*Korea: The Untold Story of the War* and *Truth Is The First Casualty*, on the Gulf of Tonkin incident); on the intelligence community (*The Death Merchant*, on rogue spook Edwin P. Wilson); on foundation philanthropy (*The Money Givers*); on the corporate world (*Monopoly*, a pioneering book on abuses of AT&T); on labor (biographies of George Meany and Jerry Wurf); and on the law (*The Benchwarmers* and *The Million Dollar Lawyers*).

Goulden's previous book on publishing was *The Curtis Caper*, about the rise and fall of *The Saturday Evening Post* and the Curtis empire.

Goulden spent ten years as a newspaperman before becoming a fulltime writer in 1968. His last reporting job was as Washington bureau chief of *The Philadelphia Inquirer*. During those years he played baseball with Fidel Castro (he struck out, swinging, on a three-two slider); skinnydipped with President Lyndon Johnson in the White House pool; and wrote prize-winning stories about official corruption in Philadelphia and elsewhere.

Goulden's avocations include cooking chili, stock car auto racing, and H. L. Mencken (he is a founding member of the H. L. Mencken Society and edited an anthology of HLM'S 1948 articles entitled *Mencken's Last Campaign*). He is reputed to be the only citizen extant who simultaneously subscribes to the *New York Review of Books*, *Stock Car Racing Magazine*, and *Soldier of Fortune*.

Goulden lives in Washington with his wife, Leslie C. Smith, an attorney. His sons are Trey and Jim Craig.